Media and Religion | Medien und Religion

edited by | herausgegeben von

PD Dr. Anna-Katharina Höpflinger
Ludwig-Maximilians-Universität München

Prof. Dr. Stefanie Knauss
Villanova University, USA

PD Dr. Marie-Therese Mäder
Ludwig-Maximilians-Universität München

Prof. Dr. Daria Pezzoli-Olgiati
Ludwig-Maximilians-Universität München

Volume 5 | Band 5

Marie-Therese Mäder

Mormon Lifestyles

Communicating Religion and Ethics in Documentary Media

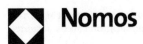

© Coverpicture: Marie-Therese Mäder, Salt Lake City/UT, US 2015

The prepress was supported by the Swiss National Science Foundation (SNSF).

SCHWEIZERISCHER NATIONALFONDS
ZUR FÖRDERUNG DER WISSENSCHAFTLICHEN FORSCHUNG

The Deutsche Nationalbibliothek lists this publication in the
Deutsche Nationalbibliografie; detailed bibliographic data
are available on the Internet at http://dnb.d-nb.de

ISBN   978-3-8487-5241-6 (Print)
       978-3-8452-9421-6 (ePDF)

British Library Cataloguing-in-Publication Data
A catalogue record for this book is available from the British Library.

ISBN   978-3-8487-5241-6 (Print)
       978-3-8452-9421-6 (ePDF)

Library of Congress Cataloging-in-Publication Data
Mäder, Marie-Therese
Mormon Lifestyles
Communicating Religion and Ethics in Documentary Media
Marie-Therese Mäder
385 pp.
Includes bibliographic references.

ISBN   978-3-8487-5241-6 (Print)
       978-3-8452-9421-6 (ePDF)

Onlineversion
Nomos eLibrary

1st Edition 2020
© Nomos Verlagsgesellschaft, Baden-Baden, Germany 2020. Overall responsibility
for manufacturing (printing and production) lies with Nomos Verlagsgesellschaft mbH
& Co. KG.

This work is subject to copyright. All rights reserved. No part of this publication may be
reproduced or transmitted in any form or by any means, electronic or mechanical,
including photocopying, recording, or any information storage or retrieval system,
without prior permission in writing from the publishers. Under § 54 of the German
Copyright Law where copies are made for other than private use a fee is payable to
"Verwertungsgesellschaft Wort", Munich.

No responsibility for loss caused to any individual or organization acting on or
refraining from action as a result of the material in this publication can be accepted
by Nomos or the author.

Table of Contents

Opening Credits		11
Part I:	The Field of Documentary and Religion	13
1.	Framing the Question	15
1.1.	Religious lifestyles in the media	17
1.2.	Documentary media and religion – and a Mormon case study	19
1.3.	Hermeneutic horizon of the researcher	21
1.4.	Structure of this book	27
2.	Spaces of Communication: Theoretical and Methodological Framework	31
2.1.	The field of media and religion – an overview of approaches	32
2.2.	Documentary media and religion	36
	The Semio-pragmatics of documentary media	39
	Documentary reading mode of "real life"	41
	Mediated religion in society and culture	44
	Reading modes of religion	46
2.3.	Religion in spaces of communication	48
	Space of production	51
	Space of representation	52
	Space of distribution and circulation	54
	Space of consumption	55
	Spaces of communication in the LDS Church's media library	56
2.4.	Researching audio-visual representation of religious communities	63
	Approaching spaces of communication	63
	Applied methods for the research	67
	Documentary sources of the study	73

Table of Contents

3.	Shifting Perceptions of Mormons and Mormonism	81
3.1.	Mormons in the media	83
3.2.	Telling the story of Mormonism	88
	From religious movement to institutionalized Mormonism	89
	Mormonism as a new religious tradition	94
3.3.	Mormon theology, ethics and worldview	99
3.4.	Mormonism as a new world faith	101
3.5.	The universal but different ethnic culture of Mormonism	105
	Mormon history is American history	109
3.6.	A sociological approach to *The Mormon Quest for Glory*	113
3.7.	The multifaceted and scholarly reconstructed world of Mormonism	116

Part II:	Interactions between the Communication Spaces of Documentary Media and Religion	117
4.	The (Ex-) Mormon Image Campaigns	119
4.1.	Two sides of an image campaign	120
4.2.	*I'm a Mormon* campaign	121
	Space of production and distribution of a global campaign	122
	The limits of diversity in the space of representation	124
	The space of representation in *I'm a Mormon, Parisian, and Mother of 7*	126
	Controlling the reading modes in the space of consumption	130
4.3.	*I Am an Ex Mormon* initiative (US 2010–15)	135
	Space of production as a private initiative	136
	A close look at Ex-Mormons in the space of representation	139
	The space of representation in *My Name is Heather and I'm an Ex Mormon*	141
	Online comments in the space of consumption	145
	Eliciting sympathy in the reading modes	152
4.4.	Spaces of communication in competition	153

5.	The Private is Public in Reality Shows about Religion	159
5.1.	Image cultivation	160
	RTV as documentary media	160
	RTV between private and public	162
	Religion in the public sphere of the media	164
	RTV as interface between the private and public sphere of religion	165
5.2.	Entertainingly instructing the audience in *The District*	167
	Communication strategies of *The District 1* and *The District 2*	171
	Success stories	174
	Proselytizing in private	174
	Baptism in public	179
	Reading modes of proselytizing in private to be baptized in public	182
5.3.	Instructively entertaining the audience in *Sister Wives*	183
	Here are the Browns	184
	Binary gender roles in *Sister Wives*' four spaces of communication	187
	Polygamist Family Brown and the Apostolic United Brethren (AUB)	189
	Reading modes of the private and public in the wedding sequence	195
	The gendered and mediated religious worldview of *Sister Wives*	200
5.4.	Religion linking the private and the public sphere	202
6.	Researching Spaces of Production and Consumption of Latter-day Saints Media	205
6.1.	A semio-pragmatic analysis combined with an audience study	206
	Audience responses to religion in *Meet the Mormons*	207
	Framing the semio-pragmatic audience study	208
	Extracting the represented values, opinions, and attitudes towards Mormons	209
	Audiences perception of a Mormon world view	219
6.2.	Qualitative interviews with LDS Church media professionals	221
	Preparation of the interviews	224
	Evaluation of the interviews	227
	Media professionals and their religious worldview	243
6.3.	Persuasion through documentary media	244

Table of Contents

Part III:	The Ethical Space of Documentaries and Religion	247
7.	Sensationalized Mormons	249
8.	The Ethics of Entertainment and the Transmission of Information within Spaces of Communication	257
8.1.	Values, norms, and moral judgements	257
8.2.	Responsibility and power relations	259
8.3.	Ethical spaces of documentaries	262
8.4.	Loyalties and hermeneutic horizons of the social actors	266
9.	The Spectrum of Mormon Documentaries	271
9.1.	Mormons and the race debate	271
9.2.	Who are the Mormons?	280
9.3.	The LDS Church and Mormon truth, historical and global	292
9.4.	Participants' loyalties and their impact	307
10.	Telling about Mormons	309
10.1.	Getting close to Mormons	309
10.2.	Revealing abuses in the FLDS Church	324
10.3.	The LDS Church as supervising shadow	332
10.4.	Telling about strange and perverted Mormon practices	342
11.	Religion as Sensation and Infotainment	345

Part IV: Approaching Religion and Ethics in the Communication
    Spaces of Documentary Media   349

12. Concluding Thoughts   351
12.1. The interface of documentary media and religion   352
12.2. Spaces of communication under scrutiny   352
12.3. The ethical space of documentaries about religion   355
12.4. Reading modes of Mormonism in the
      spaces of communication   357
12.5. Religion through the lens of documentary media   360

Bibliography   363

Film Index   383

Opening Credits

The seven years of research for this book benefited from the support of a remarkable number of people, to whom I wish to express my appreciation. I am profoundly grateful for:

My habilitation committee at the Ludwig-Maximilians-Universität in Munich/DE, composed of Daria Pezzoli-Olgiati (chair), Ulrich Schwab, Robert Yelle and the external evaluator Mia Lövheim. In committing to this duty, they donated a very valuable and finite commodity – their personal time.

The research group Media and Religion, a vital network of not only inestimable learning but also steadfast friendships. Natalie Fritz, Anna-Katharina Höpflinger, Stefanie Knauss, Michael Ulrich, and Paola von Wyss-Giacosa provided substantial support as I was writing. The publication process has been accompanied by the patient and capable Beate Bernstein from the publication house NOMOS and the incredibly gifted editor and linguistic adviser Rona Johnston.

Two scholarships, a Marie Heim-Vögtlin grant from the Swiss National Science Foundation (SNSF), which also co-funded this publication, and a grant from the Bayerische Gleichstellungsförderung of the Ludwig-Maximilians-Universität. This financial support was vital, and the academic acknowledgement these scholarships represented was highly motivating.

The research for this project was an opportunity for me to spend time at a number universities and departments, where I was welcomed by several academic hosts: Charles Musser at Yale University in New Haven/US (Film Studies Program), Jürgen Mohn at the Universität Basel/CH (Science of Religion), Heather Hendershot and Edward Schiappa at the Massachusetts Institute of Technology in Cambridge/US (Comparative Media Studies), David Holland at Harvard University in Cambridge/US (Divinity School), and Daria Pezzoli-Olgiati at the Ludwig-Maximilians-Universität in Munich/DE (Evangelisch-Theologische Fakultät). The opportunity to collaborate with María Teresa Soto Sanfiel (Departament de Comunicació, Audiovisual i Publicitat, Universitat Autònoma de Barcelona) was academically invigorating and also produced a prized friendship.

My family showed great patience and understanding as hour after hour was given over to this research, even seven days a week. My three children, David, Zoë and Levin, had good reason to ask what exactly I was working on, a question that gave me useful pause for thought. My family accompanied me in different constellations on two research stays in the United States. And above all, this adventure was only possible because of the support of my beloved husband, Markus Hofmann, who cares for our family in so many ways and to whom I wish to express my deepest gratefulness.

Part I: The Field of Documentary and Religion

1. Framing the Question

Read the newspaper or listen to radio or watch television – reporting on religion seems to be everywhere. So, for example, we are now accustomed to wide-ranging debates on radical Islam, while the Pope's travels around the globe are regularly described – two instances from a seemingly endless choice.[1] Reporting on religion is often accompanied by images. Two kneeling and praying Asian women are shown at the memorial to the attack in Barcelona on August 18, 2017, when a car was driven into a crowd, killing thirteen people and injuring many others (Fig. 1). Flowers and candles – the red candles usually used in cemeteries – were left in honor of the victims. The commentary below the image, published one month after the Barcelona terrorist attack, explains that it is wrong to think that all religion is backward; we must remember that our free world is a product of the Enlightenment and also of Christianity.[2] Yet this claim is dubious, and its defense of religion, in this case Christianity, problematic.

First of all, the commentary immediately makes the two women Christian, yet they could belong to any religious tradition or grouping. In the article and via the image, readers are given information about religion, namely that Enlightenment is connected to Christianity and results in free will. The newspaper has adopted the role of an authority, as a source of religious knowledge.

Secondly, in European countries knowledge about religion, specifically of religious traditions and of Christianity in particular, is decreasing, a phenomenon that has been described as "religious analphabetism."[3] The implications for the role of the media are noteworthy. Scholars of religion Kim Knott, Elizabeth Poole, and Teemu Taira have argued, "At a time

---

1 Süddeutsche de GmbH Germany Munich, "Papst Franziskus als Friedensmahner," Süddeutsche.de, accessed October 19, 2017, http://www.sueddeutsche.de/news/panorama/kirche-papst-franziskus-als-friedensmahner-dpa.urn-newsml-dpa-com-20090101-170910-99-991119.
2 Michael Rüegg, "Warum wir in Europa Religion brauchen," NZZ am Sonntag, accessed October 19, 2017, https://nzzas.nzz.ch/meinungen/warum-wir-in-europa-die-religion-dringend-brauchen-ld.1314055.
3 Monique C. H. van Dijk-Groeneboer, "Religious Education in the Secularised Netherlands," *International Studies in Catholic Education* 9, no. 1 (January 2, 2017): 17.

Part I: The Field of Documentary and Religion

Fig. 1 Two women praying for the victims in Barcelona (Image: Sergio Perez/ Reuters).

when the numbers of people who participate regularly in religious practices and have access to religious knowledge is declining, the media's role as an information provider, even educator, is potentially important."[4] Drawing from their comparative investigation of the representation of religion in British media in the 1980s and the late 2000s, they have concluded that "[m]ore and more, people depend on the media – newspapers, radio, television, and increasingly the Internet – for education, information and news about religion."[5] The combination of these two phenomena – decreasing awareness of religious traditions and increased media reporting of religion – hands to media a prominent role in defining broad public understandings of religion.

How, then, does the media frame its communication about religion? As the photography and commentary related to the terror incident in Barcelona make evident, the media's approach is not neutral. Its informa-

---

[4] Kim Knott, Elizabeth Poole, and Teemu Taira, *Media Portrayals of Religion and the Secular Sacred: Representation and Change* (Burlington: Ashgate, 2013), Kindle Locations 4708-4709.

[5] Knott, Poole, and Taira, *Media Portrayals of Religion and the Secular Sacred* , Kindle Locations 4688.

tion strategy is to be compelling, credible, and appealing, and its approach follows certain conventions to attract consumers. Because their reports and commentary about religion have a factual base, when responding to a specific event or accounting for specific circumstances they define what religion is and how religion is performed. The media is concerned to ensure that its consumers believe that it is conveying a reality, not an invention. To that end, it adopts a documentary mode of representation, communicating to consumers that what is seen, written, and spoken really happened. Religion is not overtly theorized; the media professional's hermeneutics is not explicitly addressed. To uncover the medial conceptualization of religion, we must read between the lines.

And our follow-up question must be: What is, then, the media construction of religion? These questions provide the impetus for this book, which examines media's spaces of communication, namely spaces of production, circulation and distribution, representation, and consumption.

1.1. Religious lifestyles in the media

Addressing media portrayals of religion, I use the term "religious lifestyles". The term draws from Max Weber's highly influential *The Protestant Ethic and the Spirit of Capitalism* and from other approaches that similarly consider lifestyle a helpful category.[6] It is noteworthy that the English translation of the German term "Lebensstil", used extensively and consistently in Weber's text, is never literal, so never "lifestyle" or "style of life". "Lebensstil" is rendered variously as "way of life",[7] "uniformity of life",[8] "type of life"[9] and in other forms. One occasion on which Weber employs "Lebensstil" is his explanation of how the Puritans' asceticism and under-

---

6 Laurie Ouellette, *Lifestyle TV*, Routledge Television Guidebooks (New York et al.: Routledge, 2016), 55; Lynn Schofield Clark, "Introduction: Identity, Belonging, and Religious Lifestyle Branding (Fashion Bibles, Bhangra Parties, and Muslim Pop),"in *Religion, Media, and the Marketplace* (Piscatawa/NJ: Rutgers University Press, 2007), 1–36; Barbara Hölscher, *Lebensstile durch Werbung?: zur Soziologie der Life-Style-Werbung* (Opladen: Westdeutscher Verlag, 1998), 16; Benjamin D. Zablocki and Rosabeth Moss Kanter, "The Differentiation of Life-Styles," *Annual Review of Sociology* 2, no. 1 (1976): 269.
7 Max Weber and Anthony Giddens, *The Protestant Ethic and the Spirit of Capitalism*, trans. Talcott Parsons (London, New York: Routledge, 2001), 111.
8 Max Weber, *The Protestant Ethic and the Spirit of Capitalism* (London: Routledge, 2005), 72.
9 Weber, 115.

standing of work contributed to the development of capitalism: "Wir suchen uns nun noch speziell die Punkte zu verdeutlichen, in welchen die puritanische Auffassung des Berufs und die Forderung asketischer Lebensführung d i r e k t die Entwicklung des kapitalistischen Lebensstils beeinflussen musste."[10] Conduct ("Lebensführung") and lifestyle ("Lebensstil") are two different but closely related terms in this paragraph. The first is used with reference to daily routine; the second embraces the more generalizing concept of how life is shaped within a broader worldview. Even though it may seek conformity, "lifestyle" leaves more space for individual variety.

In the approach taken in this study, religious lifestyles are understood as located in that tension between conformity and individual preference. Additionally, the religious lifestyles encountered here take account of the interaction of media and religion. The media report on and inform about religious topics, and in so doing they shape religion's representation within the media space. The media are also part of the wider public space, where they influence how religion is reconstructed, diffused, and understood. These communication processes are constitutive of religious lifestyles.

Lifestyles, and how they are presented by the media, are understood to be determined by a lack of social value coherence, a state described by Benjamin D. Zablocki and Rosabeth Moss Kanter as when "members of a society cease to agree on the value of the currency of the markets in commodities and prestige or at least come to recognize other independent sources of value."[11] Religious traditions, their practices and often conservative worldviews have been one conventional source of shared values. A religious lifestyle, however, is a product of an independent source of value more individual and less fully defined by traditional institutions. As Jörg Stolz has shown for Switzerland, religion has become just one choice amongst many, and its value is no longer distinct from that of other activities. Religion has become something to do during leisure time. An individual might choose between going to the cinema, the gym, or a religious service. In Stolz' analysis, a majority of people see such activities or practices as

---

10 Max Weber, *Max Weber, Schriften, 1894–1922*, ed. Dirk Käsler, Kröners Taschenausgabe (Stuttgart: Kröner, 2002), 211; Weber and Giddens, *The Protestant Ethic and the Spirit of Capitalism*, 111. "Let us now try to clarify the points in which the Puritan idea of the calling and the premium it placed upon ascetic conduct was bound directly to influence the development of a capitalistic way of life."
11 Zablocki and Moss Kanter, "The Differentiation of Life-Styles," 281.

equivalents.¹² But the person who makes that decision needs to be able to defend their choice, which is more than just a simple option but bears inherent meaning. That meaning is encompassed by a lifestyle that provides *value coherence* and is expressed in practices that might concern dress, food, social interactions, or sexual relations.

Another angle to the interaction of media and religious lifestyle concerns the portrayal of religion. The depiction of religious worldviews follows representation conventions like those of other realms of media depiction, for sports or politics, for example. These realms are not simply in competition, but might also intersect, for example in audio-visual parameters like camera, light, and sound. When viewed in terms of media conventions, religion is then just another cultural practice like any other human activity, be it vegetarianism or sports. According to media representations, there is very little difference between practicing religion or practicing sport. Adapting everything to the same standards of entertainment and information results in a levelling and conformity of values. If values converge, values start to blur, like a bland meal where everything tastes similar. According to Zablocki and Moss Kanter, such equalizing of values has the result that "individuals will seek other means of attaining value coherence."¹³ The media has a role to play in establishing such value coherence, deploying strategies that shape and express popular and global lifestyles. Social-religious actors, media institutions, and consumers participate collectively in this process of producing, representing, and consuming religion. Zablocki and Moss Kanter propose that "To the extent that a person's position in the markets for wealth and prestige will leave some degree of freedom of choice, differentiation of life-style results."¹⁴ Religion is evidently captured in the media landscape as an element of lifestyle, as an entertaining and informal mode of value coherence.

1.2. Documentary media and religion – and a Mormon case study

As the title suggests, at the heart of this investigation is the construction of religion in documentary audio-visual media. The analysis is rooted in ex-

---

12 Jörg Stolz et al., *Religion und Spiritualität in der Ich-Gesellschaft: vier Gestalten des (Un-)Glaubens*, vol. 16, Beiträge zur Pastoralsoziologie (Zürich: Theologischer Verlag Zürich, 2014), 57.
13 Zablocki and Moss Kanter, "The Differentiation of Life-Styles," 283.
14 Zablocki and Moss Kanter, 293.

tensive research into Mormons in the media, which acts as a case study. Five core issues are decisive:

(1) The effects of documentary media on how religion is perceived: How do documentary media, in this instance commercials, television reporting, television series, reality shows, and documentary films influence representations, public perception, and opinions about Mormonism, particularly in light of a documentary's need to be able to convince its audiences that it depicts "real life" that is not in fact real but mediated.[15] The study recognizes that circulation and distribution for this media category are largely via television and the Internet.

(2) The effect of media on religious communities and traditions: How do Mormon organizations adapt to the logic of documentary media? This question is examined in light of the construction of religion in the media, which can be termed mediatization.

(3) The interaction between economics, religion, and access to media: How does Mormonism – the economically powerful Church of Jesus Christ of Latter-day Saints (LDS) as well as other Mormon groupings – adapt to and profit from the logic of the documentary, particularly in light of LDS Church's interests in mission and conversion? The LDS Church, the largest group of Mormons, headquartered in Salt Lake City, Utah, has more than 16 million members, more than nine million of whom live outside the United States.[16]

This critical analysis is accompanied by theoretical and methodological reflections that explore two additional issues. The goal is to develop an approach to the interaction of documentary media and religion within the study of religion:

(4) The scholarly conception of religion, and the need for its reevaluation: What theoretical framework is most effective for an investigation of religion as seen through the documentary lens? This study understands religion as a cultural phenomenon that interacts with other cultural fields. In media studies, it can be useful to embrace religion through communication theory, a perspective that allows media and religion to be understood as interactive systems where religious meaning is formed by media practices.

---

15 Patricia Aufderheide, *Documentary Film: A Very Short Introduction*, Very Short Introductions (New York: Oxford University Press, 2007), 2.
16 "LDS Statistics and Church Facts | Total Church Membership," www.mormonnewsroom.org, accessed January 29, 2019, http://www.mormonnewsroom.org/facts-and-statistics.

(5) Methodological approaches to representation and self-representation of a religious community: how can a diversity of sources and data most effectively be systematized and analyzed? The book focuses on specific media fields, acknowledging the fund of symbols and codes that can be used to address, process, and transmit ideas about religion and concepts of religion.

These five main concerns are examined in the context of a transdisciplinary approach to religion and media that I have refined over the last 7 years. The path taken by such research is winding, and may include dead ends, but the view is always rewarding. The setting is scholarly, but also personal. Readers will find it helpful to be aware of the hermeneutic horizons that have accompanied and influenced this book.

1.3. Hermeneutic horizon of the researcher

My focus on documentary media emerged from the significant time I had invested in the in-depth study of religion and fiction film, which generated awareness of the neglect of relations between documentary media and religion. To extend and intensify my scholarly engagement with documentary media, I took up a postdoctoral opportunity with Charles Musser at the Film Studies program at Yale University. Before arriving in New Haven I followed a friend's suggestion that I plan a visit to Broadway to see the most acclaimed musical of the year 2011, *The Book of Mormon* (script, lyrics, and music by Trey Parker, Matt Stone, and Robert Lopez). I did indeed find the musical highly entertaining, although at the back of my mind I wondered why the audience was so intrigued by Mormons and Mormonism.

At Yale I was to produce my own documentary film, a very effective hands-on approach to understanding the concept and its realization. It was 2012 and the presidential campaign was in full swing, with debates on television and at the university. I recognized that Republican candidate Mitt Romney's Mormon affiliation attracted much media interest. The worshiping communities to which other candidates belonged were also part of the election rhetoric – Barack Obama's affiliations with the Black Church and two vice-presidential candidates' membership of the Roman Catholic Church. In my 30-minute long documentary *The Politics of Religion* (CH/US 2013), I conducted conversations with leaders within each of these three religious communities, including Mormon bishop Steve Weber, and attended their congregations' worship. My first personal contact with the

Mormons left me with a sense not only of their friendliness and readiness to talk but also of their political engagement. I came to realize that not all the Mormons I met supported "their" candidate.

As a scholar of the study of media and religion, I wanted to understand more about this community and launched an intensive exploration of Mormon studies, a young and diverse scholarly field in which Mormons themselves are very productive, especially in engaging their history. Their drive to communicate is also given voice in the rich production of their own media, be it for educational, missionary, political, or public affairs purposes. Mormon media productions are distinctively elaborate and also professional in terms of both quality and wages. Yet while Mormon theologians have no specific academic home, Mormon historians are often part of an official and well-financed church history department, staffed by professionally trained historians.[17]

While living in the United States, I learned more of the Mormon groups than are distinct from the LDS Church. While it was impossible for me to develop personal connections with these groups, not least as some of them exist in a precarious legal situation because they are polygamist, I did encounter them intensively in the media – in documentaries, TV reporting, and the reality show *Sister Wives* (US, TLC, 2010–2020, 14 seasons) produced by TLC (The Learning Channel). TLC established a German arm in 2014, since when the Mormon reality show has also been accessible in German-speaking European countries. The more I explored Mormonism, the more apparent became the vital role played by audio-visual documentary media for Mormon communities. Here one encounters both portrayals of Mormons and Mormonism whose vantage point may be either internal or external to the religious community.

Finally, in 2015, having made contact with the LDS Church to explain my research goals, I visited the capital of Mormonism in Salt Lake City.[18] (During this period I spent a year as a visiting scholar at MIT [Massachusetts Institute of Technology] and at Harvard Divinity School).[19] In Salt Lake City I was able to interview media professionals from the LDS Church, to talk to people from the Public Affairs and Missionary Depart-

---

17 "Church History Library," accessed June 19, 2019, https://history.churchofjesuschrist.org/section/library?lang=eng.
18 I would like to thank Colleen McDannell who generously hosted me when I undertook my research in Salt Lake City, UT.
19 I wish to thank my hosts Edward Schappa and Heather Hendershot, of MIT's Comparative Media Studies, and David Holland, of the North American Colloquium at Harvard Divinity School, for their support.

ments, to visit the film studios that are closely related to the church (their outdoor setting is a mid-19th century Mormon settlement), to experience a VIP tour through the temple district with Swiss missionary Sister Myrtha and Elder Weston R. Innes, to visit the missionary education center in Provo, and to be given a private tour at Brigham Young University in Provo.

Throughout my stay in Salt Lake City I was accompanied by the helpful and friendly Karlie Brand Guymon from the Public Affairs Department (Fig. 2). Guymon scheduled and drove me to the interviews, accompanied me on the tour, and showed me Salt Lake City and parts of Utah. I was able to talk about religious worldviews with Guymon and also with other Mormons on many other occasions.

I identified myself as having been raised Roman Catholic and as married with three children. The Latter-day Saints respected my background but still referred from time to time to the advantages of being a member of the church. The director of the Missionary Department, Stephen B. Allen, ended our conversation with the announcement: "Now I'm proselytizing," and then presented, half seriously and half joking, the advantage of the ritual of sealing in producing a marriage and family for eternity. "It's possible to stay with your family forever,"[20] Allen encouraged me. I am really not sure if this is a desirable perspective. The Christian concept of "till death do us apart" certainly disposes of some advantages too. The members of the LDS community whom I met in Salt Lake City seemed to perceive me partly as Roman Catholic, partly as a Swiss mother, partly as a guest academic at MIT, and probably just a little bit as a scholar engaged in the study of religion.

Another field trip brought me to Frankfurt/M., Germany, where I had conversations and interviews with media professionals from the Public Affairs Department of the German LDS Church. The experience in Germany was quite different from my encounters in Utah, for although again very polite, the LDS were more reluctant and less generous with their schedule. They were also somewhat reserved. Perhaps their presence in Germany and Frankfurt, where the European administration for the LDS Church in Europe is located, feels less firmly rooted. Their attitude was also more defensive.[21]

In January 2016 I travelled back to Utah to visit the Provo City Temple before its dedication with Karlie Brand Guymon and my daughter Zoë. Karlie advised us "to dress in Sunday clothes as if going to a service"

---

20 See interview with SA1, Salt Lake City/UT, June 22, 2015.
21 See interview with SA7 and SA8, Frankfurt/M., August 19, 2015.

Part I: The Field of Documentary and Religion

Fig. 2 At Temple Square North Visitors' Center, from left to right: nn, Marie-Therese Mäder, Sister Myrtha, Karlie Brand Guymon (Image: Marie-Therese Mäder, Salt Lake City/UT, US 2015).

(Fig. 3), which brought to mind the VIP tour of the temple district I had been given in June 2015, when I had been the only woman wearing trousers and a brightly colored shirt with a checked pattern. On being shown the group picture taken during the tour in front of the famous statue of Jesus, a friend commented that my clothes reveal me to be a non-Mormon (Fig. 2).

The tickets for the temple visit had to be bought in advance and they sold out quickly, evidence of the immense interest in the renovated Mor-

1. Framing the Question

Fig. 3 Zoë Hofmann, Karlie Brand Guymon, Marie-Therese Mäder dressed in their Sunday best for their visit to Provo City Center Temple (Image: Marie-Therese Mäder, Provo/UT, US 2016).

mon temple. When we arrived, many families – most were Mormon and often had small children – waited in front of the entrance to the temple, with the women in skirts and all well dressed, as if "attending a church service." The parents were showing their children the temple to generate anticipation of the time when, aged 12, they will be allowed to enter the consecrated building (Fig. 4).

That step also requires a recommendation – based on an interview at which the applicant is asked if they keep the commandments – from the appropriate bishop and from the president of the stake. Baptism is also essential. The visit to the temple was not unlike a quick stroll through an over-crowded historic home, with many impressively quiet children. No

Part I: The Field of Documentary and Religion

Fig. 4 A Mormon family in front of the LDS temple in Provo, UT (Image: Marie-Therese Mäder, Provo/UT, US 2016).

lingering was possible as the line of those still waiting would grow quickly, and the rooms could only be accessed in single file. Temple workers purposefully invited the visitors to keep moving. While more of the building can be seen on the temple website than I was able to take in on my tour,[22] the visit to this temple before its dedication was fully immersive and enlightening for a scholar of Mormonism.

In hermeneutic terms, then, this research has been approached with a perspective drawn from the methods of the social science, media studies, and ethnographic studies. The field work in Salt Lake City, Provo, and Frankfurt was indispensable in generating a comprehensive view of documentary Mormon media spaces. Meeting Latter-day Saints and the opportunity to conduct rich conversations made me more sensitive to how documentary media and religion interact in the case study.

---

22 "Tabernacle to Temple: Provo's Legacy of Worship," accessed October 20, 2017, https://history.lds.org/exhibit/historic-sites/utah/provo/provo-city-center-temple?lang=eng.

1.4. Structure of this book

This book contains three parts. Part I, "Opening the Field of Documentary Media and Religion", consists of three chapters (chapters 1–3). The *first chapter*, "Framing the Question", introduces the research questions, which address the interface of documentary media and religion, its effect on the perception of religion, and how religious and non-religious agents interact with documentary media. At this point the hermeneutic horizons of the researcher are laid out, including academic background and field-work experience. The *second chapter*, "Spaces of Communication: Theoretical and Methodological Framework", locates the research in the field of media and religion and expands upon the theoretical framing of the interface of documentary media and religion. There the heuristic concept of semio-pragmatics is introduced as a research tool and linked with the understanding of religion with which this study operates. The four communication spaces of production, representation, distribution/circulation, and consumption are presented and illustrated by sources used for this project. The multidimensional concept of "crystallization" is also explained. It defends the idea that the outcome of research is "inevitably situated, partial, constructed, multiple, and embodied."[23] That recognition endorses the use of a diversity of theories and methods in qualitative research and the presentation of the results in various forms. The methods drawn from social science, ethnographic studies, media hermeneutics, and film analysis that are applied in this study are discussed in detail. These methods are systematized in the spaces of communication of documentary media and partly elucidated with examples from the study. Finally, the types of documentary source on which the study is based are introduced: advertisements, documentaries, corporate videos, television reporting, series and reality television shows. *Chapter three*, "Shifting Perceptions of Mormons and Mormonism", considers existing approaches to Mormonism. We consider their methodological exploration of the religious community, the sources they have employed and the perspective from which the community is constructed. The chapter also provides necessary information about the historical and contemporary context of the community. The literature explored here is focused on Latter-day Saints, members of the biggest Mormon church with its headquarter in Salt Lake City/UT, but until 1890, when the

---

23 Laura L. Ellingson, *Engaging Crystallization in Qualitative Research: An Introduction* (Los Angeles: SAGE, 2009), 13.

community split over the issue of polygamy, all Mormon groups had a common history.²⁴

Part II "Interactions between the Communication Spaces of Documentary Media and Religion" (chapters 4–6) explores the four spaces of communication in light of a variety of sources and methods. *Chapter four*, "The (Ex-) Mormon Image Campaigns", puts video series from two different production spaces in conversation. The media strategies found in *I'm a Mormon*, an advertising series launched – and produced – by the LDS Church between 2010 and 2016, are interrogated. Additionally, the chapter looks at the *I Am an Ex Mormon* video series, produced by former LDS members in response to the LDS campaign. The conclusion of the chapter compares the reading modes generated by the series' different communication spaces. *Chapter five*, "The Private is Public in Reality Shows about Religion", looks in detail at the interface between religion and reality television shows and explores how it blurs the boundaries between the private and public spheres of religion. The chapter focusses on two reality shows: *The District* (US 2006/2012), produced by the LDS Church, instructs missionaries for the field. *Sister Wives* (US 2010–2020), produced by the US TV network TLC, entertains its audience with depictions and discussions of the life of a polygamist Mormon family. The chapter aims to show how the public and the private interact and considers how the shows address their audiences with different reading modes. *Chapter six*, "Researching Spaces of Production and Consumption of Latter-day Saints Media", applies qualitative and quantitative methods to the spaces of consumption and production. It explores how the semio-pragmatic approach can be combined with an audience study. The audience study considers the effectiveness of the communication of religion through documentaries and also highlights cultural differences in the space of consumption, as it was conducted in Switzerland (Zürich) and Spain (Barcelona). The second part of the chapter considers how media professionals who are members of the LDS Church understand their own work in light of their religious affiliation. The results of the two approaches and their methodological implications and limitations are brought together and analyzed.

---

24 The case Reynolds versus United Stated (1878) is an important turning point in the legal question of polygamy. The court decided unanimously that marriage is a "sacred obligation" but regulated by law. People therefore cannot avoid a law because of their religious convictions. "Reynolds v. United States, 98 U.S. 145 (1878)," Justia Law, accessed May 31, 2019, https://supreme.justia.com/cases/federal/us/98/145/.

Part III "The Ethical Space of Documentaries and Religion" focusses on film's ethical principles, moral reasonings, responsibilities, and power relations (chapters 7–11). *Chapter 7*, "Sensationalized Mormons", introduces the central questions of part III. *Chapter 8*, "The Ethics of Entertainment and the Transmission of Information within Spaces of Communication", establishes the theoretical framework within which ethical questions are located and systematizes them in the communication spaces of documentaries, where the role of values, norms, and ethical judgements are discussed. Responsibility and power relations are given particular attention, as they are especially relevant for the ethical space of documentary media. *Chapter 9*, "The Spectrum of Mormon Documentaries", and *chapter 10*, "Telling about Mormons", consider the ethical space of ten documentaries in light of the following categories: the hermeneutic horizons of social actors in the spaces of production, representation, and consumption, the social actors' loyalties, the camera gaze, and the production context. *Chapter 9* discusses documentaries by filmmakers affiliated with Mormonism, mostly as members of the LDS Church. *Chapter 10* examines documentaries that are produced by private or public television channels or independent filmmakers. *Chapter 11*, "Religion as Sensation and Infotainment", provides concluding thoughts for this section on how religion is defined in the ethical space of documentary media.

The conclusion, Part IV (*chapter 12*), "Approaching Religion in the Communication Spaces of Documentary Media", assesses the outcome of this study by reconsidering the interface of documentary media and religion in light of a semio-pragmatic approach; asks how the different reading modes reconstruct Mormonism; and looks again at the concept of religion as engaged in this study.

2. Spaces of Communication: Theoretical and Methodological Framework

The approach to Mormonism adopted in this study is located in the field of media and religion. Mormons form the case study, while the media specific to the project is identified as "documentary media", a term that we will explore below. The relationship between documentary media and religion is key on a systematic level and determines the theoretical and methodological parameters. It likewise shapes the study's approach to religion.

This chapter addresses a number of fundamental questions . How is the interface between documentary media and religion constituted? How is the term "documentary" defined and used? How is religion construed? And finally, how might documentary media allow us to research a religious group? The questions sketch an approach to religion that places center stage the media and their spaces of production, representation, consumption, distribution and circulation. The following deliberations are to be understood as working tools, to be employed and refined in the course of this inter- and transdisciplinary endeavor, as we scrutinize a diversity of documentary sources and their particular contexts.

The chapter starts with a short introduction to the field of media and religion. Next, the semio-pragmatics of documentary media are outlined, along with a discussion of how religion is conceived. The model of spaces of communication is then introduced, and discussed in relation to The Church of Jesus Christ of Latter-day Saints' (LDS Church) media library.[25] Finally, the methodological approach is explained with specific reference to the sources available for this study.

---

25 "LDS Media Library – Art, Videos, Pictures, and Audio Downloads," accessed September 28, 2017, https://www.lds.org/media-library?lang=eng&_r=1.

Part I: The Field of Documentary and Religion

2.1. The field of media and religion – an overview of approaches

In the last two decades "media and religion" has become established as an innovative and multifaceted field of research.[26] According to Stewart Hoover, whose own field is media studies, this research has taken two directions in particular: (1) examination of the ways in which religious groups and traditions use the media in the practice of their religion and (2) investigation of the engagement of the media with religion.[27] Audio-visual media makes up a subgroup, with its diverse forms – the "electronic church," feature films, television, or the Internet, for example – as subjects of research. Documentary media are frequently at the same time audio-visual media. Even though the literature that is mentioned in the following does not address audio-visual sources alone, they play a key role in the field of media and religion.

The interface of audio-visual media and religion can be divided up according to the lens through which the topic is viewed. For research on the use of media by religious communities three aspects are significant: (1) the producer and the production context, (2) the media itself, and (3) the consumer, aka the recipient. A focus on production will frequently deal with institutional and economic issues, for example the links between market and media within popular religion,[28] religious media as lifestyle,[29] or the

---

26 Mia Lövheim, "Introduction: Gender – a Blind Spot in Media, Religion and Culture?," in *Media, Religion and Gender: Key Issues and New Challenges*, ed. Mia Lövheim, Media, Religion and Culture (London: Routledge, 2013), 1–15; David Morgan, "Religion and Media: A Critical Review of Recent Developments," *Critical Research on Religion* 1, no. 3 (November 15, 2013): 347–56; Daniel A. Stout, *Media and Religion: Foundations of an Emerging Field* (New York: Routledge, 2012); Daria Pezzoli-Olgiati, "Eine illustrierte Annäherung an das Verhältnis von Medien und Religion," in *Religiöse Blicke – Blicke auf das Religiöse: Visualität und Religion*, ed. Bärbel Beinhauer-Köhler, Daria Pezzoli-Olgiati, and Joachim Valentin (Zürich: TVZ, 2010), 245–266.
27 Stewart M. Hoover, "Media and Religion," in *Encyclopedia of Religion*, ed. Lindsay Jones (Detroit: Macmillan Reference USA, 2005); Alf G. Linderman, "Approaches to the Study of Religion in the Media," in *Rethinking Media, Religion, and Culture*, ed. Stewart M. Hoover (Thousand Oaks, CA: Sage Publications, 1997), 305–315.
28 Hubert Knoblauch, *Populäre Religion: auf dem Weg in eine spirituelle Gesellschaft* (Frankfurt/M.: Campus-Verlag, 2009); Hubert Knoblauch, "Populäre Religion. Markt, Medien Und Die Popularisierung Der Religion," *Zeitschrift Für Religionswissenschaft* 8, no. 2 (2000): 143–162.
29 Lynn Schofield Clark, *Religion, Media, and the Marketplace* (Piscataway/NJ: Rutgers University Press, 2007), 1–36.

2. Spaces of Communication: Theoretical and Methodological Framework

marketing of religion in the media.[30] Investigation of media representations, or texts, might consider their symbolic-mythical dimension.[31] In addition, studies on representation have subjected media texts to qualitative or quantitative analysis.[32] With a focus on explicitly religious themes, religious significance becomes an analytical category in its own right. Emphasizing the communication process and its aesthetic qualities likewise brings a focus on the medium and its religious representations.[33] When the central concern is with consumers and recipients, that accentuation has highlighted, inter alia, the ritual aspects of the media or the social practices of recipients.[34] Behind the concept of media consumption as ritual is the idea that groups and individuals adopt the modes of interpretation transmitted in the media and that these modes are subsequently transferred by the recipients into other social spheres. One topic that has been addressed in this context is how the media portrays issues of identity, belonging, and

---

30 Mara Einstein, *Brands of Faith: Marketing Religion in a Commercial Age*, Religion, Media, and Culture Series (London: Routledge, 2008).
31 Jörg Rüpke, "Religion medial," in *Religion und Medien: vom Kultbild zum Internetritual*, ed. Jamal Malik, vol. 4, Vorlesungen des Interdisziplinären Forums Religion der Universität Erfurt (Münster: Aschendorff, 2007), 19–28.
32 Andreas Hepp and Veronika Krönert, *Medien, Event, Religion: die Mediatisierung des Religiösen*, Medien – Kultur – Kommunikation (Wiesbaden: VS Verlag für Sozialwissenschaften, 2009); Oliver Krüger, "Exkurs: Die Präsenz von Religionen im deutschen Fernsehen," in *Religionen im Fernsehen: Analysen und Perspektiven*, ed. Constanze Jecker, Kommunikationswissenschaft (Konstanz: UVK, 2011), 161–184; Constanze Jecker, *Religionen im Fernsehen: Analysen und Perspektiven*, Kommunikationswissenschaft (Konstanz: UVK, 2011).
33 Daria Pezzoli-Olgiati, "Religion und Visualität," in *Religionswissenschaft*, ed. Michael Stausberg (Berlin, Boston: de Gruyter, 2012), 343–364; Pezzoli-Olgiati, "Eine illustrierte Annäherung an das Verhältnis von Medien und Religion"; Heather Hendershot, *What's Fair on the Air?: Cold War Right-Wing Broadcasting and the Public Interest* (University of Chicago Press, 2011); Heather Hendershot, *Shaking the World for Jesus: Media and Conservative Evangelical Culture* (Chicago: University of Chicago Press, 2004).
34 David Morgan, "Religion, Media, Culture: The Shape of the Field," in *Key Words in Religion, Media, and Culture*, ed. David Morgan (New York: Routledge, 2008), 1–19; David Morgan, *The Sacred Gaze: Religious Visual Culture in Theory and Practice* (Berkeley: University of California Press, 2005); Stewart M. Hoover, "Media and Religion"; Stewart M. Hoover, "The Culturalist Turn in Scholarship on Media and Religion," *Journal of Media and Religion* 1, no. 1 (February 1, 2002): 25–36; Wayne Luther Thompson, "Religion and the Media," in *Encyclopedia of International Media and Communications*, ed. Donald H. Johnston (New York: Elsevier, 2003), 81–90.

human existence.³⁵ These three categories are certainly useful, but they are also not as clearly defined as these descriptions might suggest, for in practice media representation, reception aesthetics, and media production, as well as their institutionalization, are not only linked, but also influence one another, bolstering the interface of media and religion.³⁶

The interface of film³⁷ and religion forms a subcategory of the broader topic of audio-visual media and religion. At first blush, film media and documentary media would appear to overlap, with both media forms conveying at least 24 images per second to provide the impression of motion, which is technically the case. But distinctions do exist, mirrored in scholarly activities in the field of film and religion, where researchers have primarily focused on the fictional feature film, and the experience of viewing has largely been addressed within the context of the cinema.

Five principal directions in scholarly approaches to the relationship between film and religion can usefully be identified.³⁸ First, since its earliest days, film has been used to convey theological narratives – we think, for

---

35 Stewart M. Hoover, *Religion in the Media Age*, Religion, Media and Culture (London: Routledge, 2006).
36 Oliver Krüger, *Die mediale Religion: Probleme und Perspektiven der religionswissenschaftlichen und wissenssoziologischen Medienforschung*, vol. 1, Religion und Medien (Bielefeld: Transcript, 2012); Stewart M. Hoover, "Media and the Imagination of Religion in Contemporary Global Culture," *European Journal of Cultural Studies* 14, no. 6 (2011): 610–25; Hubert Mohr, "Auf der Suche nach der Religionsmedienwissenschaft oder: Wie die audiovisuellen Medien unser heutiges Bild von Religion verändern," in *Aspekte der Religionswissenschaft*, ed. Richard Faber (Würzburg: Königshausen & Neumann, 2009), 159–182.
37 I am using the term „film" for audio-visual sources instead of movie because film encompasses a broader spectrum of media sources. Furthermore, it refers to the academic discipline "film studies" that is a relevant field for the current approach.
38 Some important approaches and overviews to the field of film and religion are mentioned here: Natalie Fritz, "Von Rabenvätern und Übermüttern: das religionshistorische Motiv der heiligen Familie im Spannungsfeld zwischen Religion, Kunst und Film" (Marburg, Schüren, 2018), 17–44; Marie-Therese Mäder, *Die Reise als Suche nach Orientierung: eine Annäherung an das Verhältnis zwischen Film und Religion* (Marburg: Schüren, 2012); Marie-Therese Mäder, "A Cultural Studies Approach to Film and Religion, Context and Film Analysis of YES (Potter, GB / USA 2004)," in *Approaches to the Visual in Religion*, ed. Daria Pezzoli-Olgiati and Christopher Rowland, vol. 10, Research in Contemporary Religion (Göttingen: Vandenhoeck und Ruprecht, 2011), 101–118; Marie-Therese Mäder, "Film und Religion: ein multidisziplinäres Forschungsfeld," in *Religiöse Blicke - Blicke auf das Religiöse: Visualität und Religion*, ed. Bärbel Beinhauer-Köhler, Daria Pezzoli-Olgiati, and Joachim Valentin (Zürich: TVZ, 2010), 325–348; Marie-Therese Mäder, "Film und Religion am Beispiel von EXISTENZ (David Cronenberg,

example, of narratives drawn from the Hebrew Bible or New Testament or films that deal with fundamental questions of human existence. Theological approaches were then constitutive of early scholarly engagement with film and religion, and their presence is therefore extensive and varied. We find films examined in light of, for example, theological aesthetics[39] and fundamental theological questions.[40]

Secondly, film and religion have been conceived as functional equivalents in everyday life. The functionality of feature films can be compared with the functionality of religion, in both instances at the narrative level. This direction highlights film and religion as competitors and film as a form of religion that tackles the contingencies of life and makes sense out of them.[41] Thirdly, film can represent religious phenomena within a specific cultural context. When that cultural context is key, various strategies are employed in reading the film in relation to its production and reception.[42] Fourthly, film and religion can be seen as communication systems, and as communication systems that interact in manifold ways.[43]

USA 1998)," in *Outer Space: Reisen in Gegenwelten*, ed. Charles Martig and Daria Pezzoli-Olgiati, vol. 13 (Marburg: Schüren, 2009), 256–282; Colleen McDannell, *Catholics in the Movies* (New York: Oxford University Press, 2008).

39 Charles Martig, *Kino der Irritation: Lars von Triers theologische und ästhetische Herausforderung* (Marburg: Schüren, 2008); Lothar Warneke, *Transzendenz im populären Film*, vol. 59, Beiträge zur Film- und Fernsehwissenschaft (Berlin: Vistas, 2001); Paul Schrader, *Transcendental Style in Film: Ozu, Bresson, Dreyer* (New York, N.Y: Da Capo Press, 1972).

40 Gerhard Larcher, *Zeit, Geschichte und Gedächtnis: Theo Angelopoulos im Gespräch mit der Theologie*, vol. Band 5 (Marburg: Schüren, 2003); Stefan Orth, Joachim Valentin, and Reinhold Zwick, *Göttliche Komödien: religiöse Dimensionen des Komischen im Kino* (Köln: KIM, 2001).

41 Margaret R. Miles, *Seeing and Believing: Religion and Values in the Movies* (Boston, Massachusetts: Beacon Press, 1996); John Lyden, *Film as Religion: Myths, Morals, and Rituals* (New York: New York University Press, 2003); Matthias J. Fritsch, Martin Lindwedel, and Thomas Schärtl, *Wo nie zuvor ein Mensch gewesen ist: Science-Fiction-Filme: angewandte Philosophie und Theologie* (Regensburg: Pustet, 2003).

42 Melanie Jane Wright, *Religion and Film: An Introduction* (London: Tauris, 2006); S. Brent Plate, *Representing Religion in World Cinema: Filmmaking, Mythmaking, Culture Making* (New York: Palgrave Macmillan, 2003); Nadine Christina Böhm, "Sakrales Sehen: Strategien der Sakralisierung im Kino der Jahrtausendwende" (Bielefeld, Transcript, 2009).

43 Daria Pezzoli-Olgiati, "Film und Religion: Blick auf Kommunikationssysteme und ihre vielfältigen Wechselwirkungen," in *Religious turns – turning religions: veränderte kulturelle Diskurse – neue religiöse Wissensformen*, ed. Andreas Nehring and Regina Ammicht Quinn (Stuttgart: Kohlhammer, 2008), 46–66; Daria Pezzoli-Ol-

These first four characteristics of the interface of film and religion are as valid for documentaries as they are for fiction films, with no distinction needing to be drawn between these two audio-visual forms. The fifth, and final, dimension to the relationship between film and religion provides an opportunity to characterize the relation between documentary media and religion more specifically. We now leave behind fiction film, and focus on documentary media.

2.2. Documentary media and religion

Film and religion can be understood as interacting cultural moments.[44] Stuart Hall first described a "circuit of culture" in his textbook *Representation: Cultural Representations and Signifying Practices*, published in 1997[45] and returned to the concept in the introduction to the revised edition of 2013 (fig. 5).[46]

For Hall, the term culture encompasses a way of life, a system of values and practices. Central to moments in culture is the sharing of meaning and a focus on practice. Persons, objects, and events never carry fixed meaning. Hall suggests that

> the question of meaning arises in relation to *all* the different moments or practices in our "cultural circuit" – in the construction of identity and the marking of difference, in production and consumption, as well as in the regulation of social conduct.[47]

---

giati, "Vom Ende der Welt zur hoffnungsvollen Vision: Apokalypse im Film," in *Handbuch Theologie und populärer Film*, ed. Thomas Bohrmann (Paderborn: Schöningh, 2007), 255–275; Brent S. Plate, "Filmmaking and World Making. Re-Creating Time and Space in Myth and Film," in *Teaching Religion and Film*, ed. Gregory J. Watkins, Teaching Religious Studies Series (Oxford: Oxford University Press, 2008), 219–232; S. Brent Plate, *Religion and Film: Cinema and the Re-Creation of the World*, vol. 43, Short Cuts (London: Wallflower, 2008).

44 Mäder, *Die Reise als Suche nach Orientierung*.
45 Stuart Hall, *Representation: Cultural Representation and Signifying Practices*, Culture, Media and Identities (London: SAGE in association with The Open University, 1997), 1.
46 Stuart Hall, "Introduction," in *Representation: Cultural Representation and Signifying Practices*, ed. Stuart Hall, Jessica Evans, and Sean Nixon, 2nd ed. (Los Angeles, CA: SAGE, 2013), xvii.
47 Hall, xx.

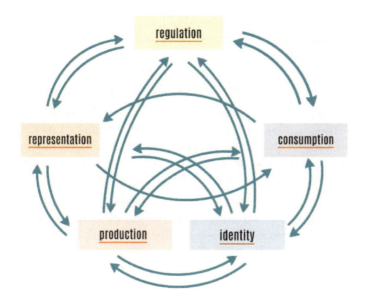

Fig. 5 Circuit of Culture (Paul du Gay and Stuart Hall).

In order to be able to make meaning in language, representation, or practices, people must possess shared codes. For example, sounds, clothing, images, or verbal expressions generate and communicate meaning. They represent human concepts, ideas, and emotions that are decoded, interpreted, and read. As communication is not a one-sided transmission but rather a dialogue, meaning is an unstable and alterable process. Also, different circuits of meaning can exist within a single culture, and they may intersect.

Difference and (associated) power relations are integral to cultural communication.[48] People communicate with a diversity of cultural practices – for example, the style of clothes and the manner in which they are worn, language expressions, visual representations of people in social media, the celebration of cooking, food prohibitions, or the consumption of specific products. These communicative interactions have in common that they are fundamentally defined by difference and power relations expressed in reg-

---

48 Natalie Fritz et al., *Sichtbare Religion: eine Einführung in die Religionswissenschaft*, De Gruyter Studium (Berlin: De Gruyter, 2018), 120–128.

ulations. For example, dress policies are implemented in secular as well as religious places. In some sacred spaces, shoulders and upper legs must not be bared or shoes be worn. Dress codes are often communicated for weddings. Designer dresses might distinguish the rich from the poor. Such practices differentiate people one from another, and demonstrate how difference functions as a defining aspect of culture. Hall has suggested that

> We should perhaps learn to think of meaning less in terms of "accuracy" and "truth" and more in terms of effective exchange – a process of translation, which facilitates cultural communication while always recognizing the persistence of difference and power between different "speakers" within the same cultural circuit.[49]

This quote highlights that difference and power relations are established in the "same cultural circuit", within its distinct moments; those relations can therefore be revealed through analysis of cultural communication.

And so we reach the fifth dimension of the relationship between film and religion: representation. Cultural representation has three forms. The material world, individuals and their experiences, and events belong to the first; mental concepts, the imagined, and ideas are associated with the second;[50] signs representing these concepts belong to the third realm, with such signs consisting of codes that are shaped by social conventions.[51] It is in terms of representation that we find a marked distinction between the fiction film and the documentary.

The audience for a film will likely believe they know whether they are watching a fictional film or a documentary film, even though the genres use the same techniques and can draw on the same aesthetics. But *how* do they know that they are watching a documentary instead of a fiction film, or vice versa? How do they perceive that difference? And how *do* documentaries differ from fiction films? We turn now to explore these questions.

---

49 Hall, "Introduction," xxvi.
50 Daria Pezzoli-Olgiati, "Religion in Cultural Imaginary. Setting the Scene," in *Religion in Cultural Imaginary: Explorations in Visual Und Material Practices*, ed. Daria Pezzoli-Olgiati, vol. 13, Religion – Wirtschaft – Politik (Zürich, Baden-Baden: Pano Verlag Nomos, 2015), 9–38.
51 Anna-Katharina Höpflinger, *Religiöse Codes in der Populärkultur. Kleidung der Blackmetal-Szene* (Baden Baden: Nomos Verlag, 2020), 13–25.

2. Spaces of Communication: Theoretical and Methodological Framework

The Semio-pragmatics of documentary media

An opposition of documentaries and fiction films, with the former conveying reality and the latter conveying an invented world, is hard to maintain. In place of the contrasting categories of fiction and documentary film, semio-pragmatics construct a heuristic approach, one that allows for a "documentary reading mode." The concept of "documentary media" then – derived from the documentary reading mode as used here – assumes the semio-pragmatic model, in which, according to Roger Odin, two paradigms – semiotics and pragmatics – are connected:

> It seems that both paradigms had been present all the time, present in the mind of the theorists, but also in everybody's mind: at the same time confidence in a text and in its autonomous existence, and the insight that the meaning of a text changes in accord with its context.[52]

The semio-pragmatic approach places audio-visual media in the tension between film and the communication spaces within which media function.[53] Rather than adopt the binary categories "fiction" and "non-fiction," we are encouraged through semio-pragmatics to construct a theoretical approach that is based on the variety of situations in which media communication takes place. These situations are then termed "reading modes."[54] Reading modes are generated and steered both by internal reading instructions, clues within the media itself, and also by information provided by the medium's context, which we can understand as external instructions. Internal reading instructions, also called peritexts,[55] comprise everything that is displayed in the film, including the information in the opening credits, the body of the film, and the closing credits.

---

52 Roger Odin, *Les Espaces de communication: Introduction à la sémio-pragmatique* (Grenoble: Presses universitaires de Grenoble, 2011), 15. French original version reads: "Tout se passe comme si les deux paradigmes étaient toujours là, en même temps, présent dans l'esprit des théoriciens, mais aussi dans l'esprit de tout un chacun: à la fois, la croyance au texte et à son existence autonome, et la reconnaissance que le sens d'un texte change avec le contexte." Translation mine.
53 Frank Kessler, "Historische Pragmatik," *montage a/v, Zeitschrift für Theorie und Geschichte audiovisueller Kommunikation* 11, no. 2 (2002): 106.
54 For an extended discussion of Roger Odin's concept of communication spaces see Warren Buckland, *The Cognitive Semiotics of Film* (Cambridge: Cambridge University Press, 2000), 77–108.
55 Gérard Genette and Marie Maclean, "Introduction to the Paratext," *New Literary History* 22, no. 2 (1991): 263.

Part I: The Field of Documentary and Religion

External reading instructions, or epitexts,⁵⁶ are drawn from the context for a source's production, representation, and reception. They are less limited than the internal reading instructions, which are mostly fixed as soon as the film is finished. External reading instructions are constructed by, for example, the cultural context of the audience member, which will be different in each reception process. Depending on their cultural and social background as well as their mental and emotional disposition, they might interpret a film differently, although not completely arbitrarily.⁵⁷ If the audience doesn't feel a comedy is funny, then the film may not have achieved its explicit goal, although tastes in humor vary, which is why different kinds of comedy are produced.

In addition, the institutional context often provides reliable and precise information that functions as reading instructions. A semio-pragmatic approach therefore pays attention to the institutional context within which the audio-visual sources are produced, distributed, and consumed. A film viewed on television in a family home is received differently from a film viewed by a church community or as part of a news program. An advertisement on a cinema listing or information available on an Internet site will shape how a film is read. Watching a show on a smart phone or tablet is not the same as watching a film in a cinema, surrounded by other spectators. Colleagues talking about a show they have seen might provide external information. The immediate responses of your neighbor in the cinema might influence your reception experience.

Production circumstances generate additional external reading instructions. Amateur productions will likely differ from generously financed, professionally created documentary productions, which is of particular relevance in the case of the (re)presentation of religious groups. Financing can play a central role, making possible lavish audio-visual representations that will be read very differently from home-movie style films. At the same time, connections can be made between individual films that we know were created within a single production framework.

---

56 Genette and Maclean, 264.
57 Stuart Hall discerns in his paper „Encoding and Decoding" three different positions in the media communication process. These are the dominant-hegemonic position, the negotiated code and the oppositional code. All of the three codes are based on the idea that the media producers intend a specific message that might be read in different reading modes. See Stuart Hall, "Encoding/Decoding," in *Documentary Research*, ed. John Scott, vol. 1, 4 vols., Sage Benchmarks in Social Research Methods (London: SAGE, 2006), 233–246.

2. Spaces of Communication: Theoretical and Methodological Framework

A semio-pragmatic approach locates the cultural practice of meaning-making between the media representation and its spectators. Meaning is not inscribed by the media before consumption. Meaning is generated within the tension of the two parameters formed by the media representation and the spectator. Each is situated within a specific context that affects the reading mode, and thus they generate varied reading modes. A semio-pragmatic approach therefore tries to anticipate possible "readings" of a specific film in a specific social and cultural space.

> Such a contextual framing is neither social nor cognitive but rather pragmatic in nature: It works by constructing the fullness of hypotheses that are in a first step corroborated phenomenologically (as spectators, we can all undertake such "readings"), and subsequently can be reassessed sociologically and/or cognitively.[58]

One such contextual framing allows a "documentary reading mode". The expression "documentary mode" contains a reference to what Odin has termed the "real enunciator."[59] An essential element of the documentary mode concerns the credibility and authenticity of the social actors on screen.

Documentary reading mode of "real life"

In documentary material, the impression is given that those who are portrayed are expressing their own opinions, imparting their own experiences, and providing their own insights about life; they are not, or so it appears, following a script as for a feature film. The documentary mode conveys a reality on which all those involved seem to draw in order to determine how the film looks and how that information is conveyed. Interviews are a concrete example of internal reading instructions that identify a real enun-

---

58 Roger Odin, "Wirkungsbedingungen des Dokumentarfilms. Zur Semio-Pragmatik am Beispiel 'Notre planète la terre' (1947)," in *Perspektiven des Dokumentarfilms*, ed. Manfred Hattendorf, vol. 7, Diskurs Film (München: Diskurs-Film-Verlag Schaudig & Ledig, 1995), 96. The German version reads: "Dieser kontextuelle Rahmen ist pragmatischer und nicht soziologischer oder kognitiver Natur: Er funktioniert als Gesamtheit von Hypothesen, die in einem ersten Schritt auf phänomenologische Weise bestätigt werden können (wir alle können als Zuschauer diese 'Lektüren' vornehmen), um anschließend eventuell soziologisch und/oder kognitivistisch überprüft zu warden." Translation mine.
59 Odin, *Les espaces de communication*, 53–58, 289–291.

ciator. A viewer might ask, can I believe this expert? or what authority do you have to make such statements? They seek out a "real" enunciator who can be interrogated for information about topics, past events, persons, and the truth.

For Odin, the moral mode is closely connected to the documentary mode. This moral mode produces value by asking, who are you to tell me the truth? What is your authority to affirm what you affirm?[60] The producer and the social actors on screen need to appear credible to the audience within the communication process. If either or both lack such credibility, then the whole film fails. The audience does not need to share the opinions presented, but they do least need to believe that the opinions expressed are authentic. In a nutshell: films fall into the genre of documentary if they are received as showing real people in credible situations. For Patricia Aufderheide a documentary is "a movie about real life." She continues,

> And that is precisely the problem; documentaries are about real life; they are not real life. They are not even windows onto real life. They are portraits of real life, using real life as their raw material, constructed by artists and technicians who make myriad decisions about what story to tell to whom, and for what purpose.[61]

This definition has two crucial aspects. First, the narrative in a documentary conveys stories "about real life." The preposition *about* is central in the understanding of what documentaries are. The same proposition is also encountered in Bill Nichols' three-step definition:
1. Documentaries are about reality; they're about something that actually happened.
2. Documentaries are about real people
3. Documentaries tell stories about what really happened.[62]

Compared to Nichols understanding of "about" Aufderheide's implies that documentaries do not necessarily tell or show the truth, but that documentary narrations are shaped *as* real. And according to both Aufderheide and Nichols, documentaries build their world out of the factual world. A director might influence or even change the factual world through filming, but

---

60 Odin, 56.
61 Aufderheide, *Documentary Film*, 2.
62 Bill Nichols, *Introduction to Documentary*, 2nd ed. (Bloomington: Indiana University Press, 2010), 6–14.

the goal remains for the film to show images from the actual world to which the audience belongs.

The definition of documentary media would suggest that the individuals who appear within the film are not hired actors and that no screenwriter has crafted the lives, family relations, friends, work places, homes, and hobbies that are portrayed. But we can be in no doubt that the presence of a camera and film team crucially influences the situation of the social actors who appear before that camera. Choices have been made, often within a script, before shooting begins, and they continue to be made as the shooting takes place, and subsequently. For example, who is to be deemed representative of a religious community? What should be included in the portrayal, and what left out? Which moments in the life of a religious social actor are to be depicted? And then, how should the audio-visual depiction look? Which camera angles will be used, and when? How close should the camera be? What questions will be posed to the participants? What do the producers and filmmakers want to hear from the social actors, and what do they not want to hear? Documentary film makers often have a narrative in mind, and their decision-making in light of that narrative continues during the postproduction process. Which takes will be used and in which order will they be edited? What kind of music would be in accord with the desired effect? Such questions, and the decisions that follow, determine the documentary-media staging and representation of people and objects that live or exist in the everyday world.

Aufderheide embraces the complex relationship between documentary film and reality as follows: "The genre of documentary always has two crucial elements that are in tension: representation, and reality. Their makers manipulate and distort reality like all filmmakers, but they still make a claim for making a truthful representation of reality."[63] If this claim is made in a religious context, whether that religious context be associated with the social actors, setting and the stories told in front of the camera or with the audience, its inherent truthfulness becomes more ambivalent.

Understanding the interface of documentary media and religion requires each aspect be examined for how it shapes and is shaped by the other. How, then, should we approach this interactive process involving religion and documentary media theoretically? We now turn to find a framing for this reciprocity.

---

63 Aufderheide, *Documentary Film*, 9/10.

Part I: The Field of Documentary and Religion

Mediated religion in society and culture

Two useful concepts, *mediation* and *mediatization*[64], address how the media influences religion.[65] These concepts embrace the communication of religion through an independent institution – namely, the media – that shapes religion in turn. Stig Hjarvard has argued, "Through the process of mediatisation, religion is increasingly being subsumed under the logic of the media, both in terms of institutional regulation, symbolic content and individual practices."[66] This perspective highlights (a) how communication processes are defined by social and cultural practices[67] and (b) how communication processes change in the short and long term.[68] For "mediation" and "mediatization" must be recognized as distinct phenomena, according to Hjarvard:

> Mediation describes the concrete act of communication by means of a medium in a specific social context. By contrast, mediatisation refers to a more long-term process, whereby social and cultural institutions and modes of interaction are changed as a consequence of the growth of the media's influence.[69]

Hjarvard further distinguishes three vehicles for the mediatization of religion: religious media, journalism on religion, and banal religion.[70] All

---

64 The term "mediatisation" is sometimes also spelled and synonymously used as "mediatization".
65 Stig Hjarvard, "Three Forms of Mediatized Religion. Changing the Public Face of Religion," in *Mediatization and Religion: Nordic Perspectives* (Göteborg: Nordicom, 2012), 21–44.
66 Stig Hjarvard, "The Mediatization of Religion: A Theory of the Media as Agents of Religious Change," *Northern Lights: Film & Media Studies Yearbook* 6, no. 1 (2008): 11.
67 Hubert Knoblauch, "Benedict in Berlin: The Mediatization of Religion," in *Mediatized Worlds: Culture and Society in a Media Age*, ed. Andreas Hepp and Friedrich Krotz (London: Palgrave Macmillan UK, 2014), 143–58; Stewart M. Hoover, "Media and the Imagination of Religion in Contemporary Global Culture"; Friedrich Krotz, ed., "Medienkommunikation als Modifikation von Kommunikation, Typen von Kommunikation und der Bedeutungswandel mediatisierter Kommunikation," in *Mediatisierung: Fallstudien zum Wandel von Kommunikation* (Wiesbaden: VS Verlag für Sozialwissenschaften, 2007), 85–116.
68 Stig Hjarvard, "The Mediatisation of Religion: Theorising Religion, Media and Social Change," *Culture and Religion*, 2011, 124.
69 Hjarvard, 124.
70 Hjarvard, "Three Forms of Mediatized Religion. Changing the Public Face of Religion," 26–39.

2. Spaces of Communication: Theoretical and Methodological Framework

three are related to documentary media, for example in the broadcasting of religious services, news, moderated debates, or entertainment. Only banal religion, probably the vaguest category of the three, includes narrative fiction. Hjarvard describes banal religion as "a bricolage of decontextualized elements from a variety of sources, including institutionalized religious texts, iconography and liturgy, brought into new contexts and serving purposes other than those of religious institutions."[71] Maybe the interface of media and religion is strongly coined by bricolage elements of religion and the category might seem somehow blurred.

The mediatization of religion changes its public face and is closely connected not only with secularization but also with other social and cultural processes like globalization, commercialization, and individualization.[72] As used here, "secularization" is not to be understood as the disappearance of religion, but as a transformation process influenced by the social process of mediatization among others.[73] To gain a hold on this process, Hjarvard has investigated how mediatized forms of religion challenge the Protestant church in Nordic countries. His conclusions draw on the three forms of mediatized religion. First, religious media allow multiple and individual voices and representations. Secondly, journalism on religion conveys a criticism of religious institutions that fail to adapt to the secular values of democracy. Thirdly, the "bricolage" of banal religion functions as a source of cultural knowledge about religion. In the current study, these three forms are used with reference to documentary media and are taken as factual, as opposed fictional.

The mediatization concept continues a historic tradition that has seen the media transform religion, generating new forms of religious communication. Additionally, in this exploration of the mediatization of religion, we will scrutinize how the documentary style influences, shapes, and transforms the public face of religion. On that score, the study looks in detail at religion's cultural moments, and specifically at practices and diverse forms

---

71 Hjarvard, 36.
72 Hjarvard, 22.
73 José Casanova, "Eurozentristischer Säkularismus und die Herausforderung der Globalisierung," in *Politik, Religion, Markt: die Rückkehr der Religion als Anfrage an den politisch-philosophischen Diskurs der Moderne*, ed. Wilhelm Guggenberger, Dietmar Regensberger, and Kristina Stöckl, vol. 4 (Innsbruck: Innsbruck University Press, 2009), 19–40; Charles Taylor, "Why We Need a Radical Redefinition of Secularism," in *The Power of Religion in the Public Sphere*, ed. Eduardo Mendieta and Jonathan Vanantwerpen (Columbia University Press, 2011), 43–59.

Part I: The Field of Documentary and Religion

of documentary representation, which will be sketched at the end of this section.

Reading modes of religion

We have been using the complex term "religion" in this discussion and need now to elaborate on the concept for which it stands. "Religion" as understood in this study is rooted in communication theory,[74] where religion can be understood as a specific system of communication.[75] Religious communication will often address human contingence, the idea that everything in life might be different.[76] It allows to transfer the transcendental into an immanent realm. The approach adopted here allows us to see this transformation happen within media practices. We must bear in mind, however, that what is deemed to belong to the transcendental realm differs according to cultural context.[77]

Detlef Pollack and Gergely Rosta choose to combine functional and substantive definitions of religion, an approach that is useful for the current

---

[74] Kerstin Radde-Antweiler, "Religion as Communicative Figurations – Analyzing Religion in Times of Deep Mediatizations," in *Mediatized Religion in Asia: Studies on Digital Media and Religion*, ed. Kerstin Radde-Antweiler and Xenia Zeiler, Routledge Research in Digital Media and Culture in Asia (New York: Routledge, 2019), 11–24; Volkhard Krech, "Religion als Kommunikation," in *Religionswissenschaft*, ed. Michael Stausberg (Berlin: De Gruyter, 2012), 49–64; Edmund Arens, "Religion as Communication," in *The Social Psychology of Communication*, ed. Derek Hook, Bradley Franks, and Martin W. Bauer (London: Palgrave Macmillan UK, 2011), 249–65; Jürgen Mohn, "Die Religion im Diskurs und die Diskurse der Religion(en). Überlegungen zu Religionsdiskurstheorien und zur religionsaisthetischen Grundlegung des Diskursfeldes Religion," in *Religion – Wirtschaft – Politik: Forschungszugänge zu einem aktuellen transdisziplinären Feld*, ed. Antonius Liedhegener, Andreas Tunger-Zanetti, and Stephan Wirz, 1st ed. (Baden-Baden: Nomos, 2011), 84–111; Pezzoli-Olgiati, "Eine illustrierte Annäherung an das Verhältnis von Medien und Religion. ".

[75] Fritz Stolz, "Religiöse Symbole in religionswissenschaftlicher Rekonstruktion," in *Religion und Rekonstruktion: ausgewählte Aufsätze*, ed. Daria Pezzoli-Olgiati (Göttingen: Vandenhoeck & Ruprecht, 2004), 67–70; Robert A. Yelle, *Semiotics of Religion: Signs of the Sacred in History*, Bloomsbury Advances in Semiotics (London: Bloomsbury, 2012), 2.

[76] Detlef Pollack and Gergely Rosta, *Religion in der Moderne: ein internationaler Vergleich*, Schriftenreihe "Religion und Moderne" (Frankfurt/M.: Campus-Verlag, 2015), 63; Krech, "Religion als Kommunikation," 58.

[77] Pollack and Rosta, *Religion in der Moderne*, 66; Martin Riesebrodt, *Cultus und Heilsversprechen: eine Theorie der Religionen* (München: Beck, 2007), 113.

study with its examination of how people communicate about religion through different media.⁷⁸ Representations carry meaning, even if that meaning is situational and has a specific function. People communicate content and want to achieve something by doing so. This approach also connects religion to its religious agents, as Pollack and Rosta propose: "For religious actors, communication with what they hold to be transcendental, by means of rituals, prayers, scriptures, images, dances, sermons, songs of praise, experiences or discoveries, is central to their religion."⁷⁹ The meaning of religious practices is defined in the tension between social actors, media practices, and the vast fundus of religious symbols and expressions.⁸⁰ This study therefore approaches not only media but also religion from a semio-pragmatic perspective, with religious meaning-making understood to be constructed through the interaction of the media and social actors.

Different institutional contexts generate different meaning for religious communication and influence its production, distribution, circulation, and consumption. With reference to Odin, Warren Buckland has described this institutional basis and the resulting modes of comprehension:

> Each institution consists of several modes – for example, the institution of commercial cinema comprises the spectacle, fictional, and dynamic modes, whereas the institution of non-professional cinema includes the home movie, aesthetic, and artistic modes. Institutions determine the mode in which a particular film is to be comprehended. For Odin, an institution is "a bundle of determinations which govern the production of meaning in selecting, hierarchising, and structuring the modes of production of meaning which are put to work."⁸¹

---

78 Pollack and Rosta, *Religion in der Moderne*, 48–72.
79 Pollack and Rosta, 72. Translation mine: "Die über Rituale, Gebete, Schriften, Bilder, Tänze, Predigten, Lobgesänge, Erlebnisse oder Erfahrungen ermöglichte Kommunikation mit dem als transzendent Vorgestellten steht für die religiösen Akteure im Zentrum ihrer Religion."
80 Robert Yelle uses the term "semiotic recognition" (12–17) to describe the religious discourse as an act of communication and how it "contributes to the transmission of its message" (13). See Yelle, *Semiotics of Religion*, 13. His approach is useful to understand how transformations of language characterize religious processes like secularism.
81 Buckland, *The Cognitive Semiotics of Film*, 98.

The question is, then, which reading mode comes into play when religion is communicated? This question guides this research and its analysis of its sources.

Drawing on the theoretical considerations we have just encountered, this study considers, from a semio-pragmatic perspective, media practice as developed for a targeted audience. Its analysis understands religion as a cultural phenomenon that interacts and intersects with diverse other cultural fields, such as the media.[82] It seeks to understand communication related to religion by focusing on religion in documentary media, aided by consideration of production, representation, distribution, circulation, and consumption. In every space, we find religious and non-religious agents with active roles, as makers and consumers. Additionally, the medium has its own fund of religious symbols and codes that can be used to address, process, and transmit ideas about religion and the content of religion. In this understanding of religion, communication is placed center stage, linking diverse activities by diverse social actors. The interface of religion and the media is thus examined in light of these points of reference for readings of religion.

The semio-pragmatic approach to religion and documentary media demands its own methodology. Spaces of communication for documentary media and religion include production, representation, circulation, distribution, and consumption, to which we have made reference, but which now require more detailed discussion.

2.3. Religion in spaces of communication

The interface between documentary media and religion can be explored through a semio-pragmatic approach that interrogates sources to see how they function within specific contexts, those of production, representation, distribution/circulation and consumption. These contexts are understood as *spaces of communication*, which systematize the levels at which documentary media and religion interact. Analysis that considers communication spaces will focus primarily on reading modes in the material under consideration. Roger Odin's definition discerns three elements of the "world" generated through film:

---

82 Linda Woodhead, "Five Concepts of Religion," *International Review of Sociology* 21, no. 1 (March 1, 2011): 123–127.

2. Spaces of Communication: Theoretical and Methodological Framework

> By film's communication space, I mean a space where communication actors share the experience of constructing a film: building a world which the viewer is invited to enter, a world within which various events occur (usually structured by narrative), and whose rhythm the spectator is encouraged to share (I call this the "phasing" process).[83]

The active agents identified by Odin are not just the actors who appear in front of the camera. The production process, or "the experience of constructing a film," creates a world the viewer can become part of. The film itself is the "world within which various events occur" and the reception process is "the world [...] whose rhythm the spectator is encouraged to share." When the actors who participate in all the film's communication spaces, from production to consumption, agree upon a single "axis of relevance," then, according to Odin, the communication space works successfully. This "axis of relevance" describes the situation when producers and audience share a common understanding of what is screened, or according to Odin, "share the same rhythm." This situation is an ideal that all too often is absence, as Stuart Hall highlighted in his renowned encoding-decoding model.[84] Odin also provides another definition of communication spaces:

> Within my semio-pragmatic approach, a communication space is a space through which the harness of constraints directs the transmitter and receiver – the actants of the communicational process – to produce meaning along the same axis of relevance.[85]

This definition again describes an ideal situation, in which the consumer (receiver) decodes the message such that it reads just as the production (transmitter) intended when it was transmitted. But such is not always the case. Our tendency to identify that variation, rather than successful transmission, may be problematic. Why, we might ask, would any company invest in an image film or advertisement if audio-visual communication is so ambivalent? Any company with a pre-determined aim wants to see its investment in media production achieve that aim, and reap rewards. Reli-

---

83 Roger Odin, "Spectator, Film and the Mobile Phone," in *Audiences: Defining and Researching Screen Entertainment Reception*, ed. Ian Christie (Amsterdam: Amsterdam University Press, 2012), 156.
84 Hall, "Encoding/Decoding."
85 Roger Odin, "The Home Movie and Space of Communication," in *Amateur Filmmaking: The Home Movie, the Archive, the Web*, ed. Laura Rascaroli, Gwenda Young, and Barry Monahan (Bloomsbury Publishing USA, 2014), 15.

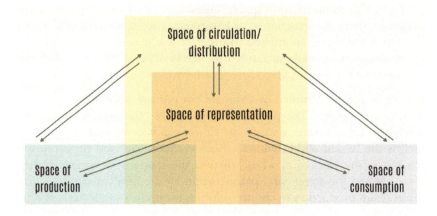

Fig. 6 Model spaces of communication (Marie-Therese Mäder in reference to Roger Odin).

gious communities are no different. Their investment in media productions – in a film with educational purpose, for example – needs to prove profitable, or otherwise will be judged a failed investment.

Spaces of communication in relation to religion have specific qualities to which we shall now turn our attention. We will learn of these four spaces by considering their general characteristics and also their interactions, which are usefully illustrated by the types of documentary media encountered in this study.

As figure 6 depicts, the four spaces of communication overlap but also diverge.[86] The space of production interacts with the spaces of representation, distribution, and circulation. The space of media consumption in turn interacts with the spaces of representation, distribution, and circulation. The spaces of representation and distribution/circulation both influence the spaces of production and consumption. The model proposes, however, that the spaces of production and consumption do not intersect, which is intriguing in a communication model. It supports the argument that media communication is not a one-way process where meaning is generated by the sender and unambiguously decoded by the recipients. Odin

---

86 Marie-Therese Mäder, "Documentary Media and Religious Communities," *Journal for Religion, Film and Media (JRFM)* 1, no. 1 (2015): 32.

calls this model a non-communicative communication model.[87] But where do we position religion in these spaces and their interactions?

Space of production

The production space is defined by the agents that produce the audio-visual sources. These agents might, or might not, be part of a religious institution. They can be affiliated with a religious institution while the production company for which they work is not. The religious agendas behind each production can vary, and the interests behind each production are therefore highly significant. Religious institutions, religious actors, governments or political parties finance films for certain purposes. Who has financed a production can provide an indication of the role religion plays in the material, and how religion is not only represented but also understood by the makers. The space of production will naturally affect the space of representation. Financial resources and religious affiliations will shape the narration. The space of production also influences where a source will circulate. Religious institutions as producers can use their distribution and circulation networks – television channels, public affairs or media departments, for example – to sell and broadcast their products. But producers are not dependent on their own networks, for they can also use publicly accessible platforms such as Vimeo, YouTube or their own websites. Where a production is to circulate shapes the production. For example, whether the audience will pay or access the material freely will shape the business model and the nature of the product. If the goal is to make a case to the audience about a cause or a product, such as a religious community and its values, the product may be given to the audience without charge, much like an advertisement. As soon as the source provides additional benefit, perhaps in the form of entertainment, the audience may be more willing to pay for its access. These economic factors also shape the production space.

---

87 "L'intérêt de mettre au point de départ de la reflection un modèle de non-communication est évident." See Odin, *Les espaces de communication*, 19.

Part I: The Field of Documentary and Religion

Space of representation

For religion, the space of representation is the most frequently discussed space, whether in reviews, by the audience, in scholarly discourse, or within religious institutions. Religious agents or individuals representing a religious institution will have a specific perspective on religion within the space of representation, where religion can be represented visually and aurally and can be addressed directly and referenced in the narrative. Aural and visual representation is more likely to be explicit in religious narratives and portrayals of religious communities. Religious references such as symbols and signs, both aural and visual, may be part of the narration, but not necessarily at the center of the story world, playing instead what we might term a "supporting role." The church bell rings as diegetic sound, symbolizing the beginning of a new day – a symbol that is religious but also understood in a broad context. When that church bell is heard to ring in a television report on noise pollution, then the sound of the bell is a religious topic, not simply a reference point.

In the space of representation, religion can be examined analytically and hermeneutically, with consideration given to filmic parameters such as camera, sound, and light and to their interaction. The question is then how the cinematic style shapes religious symbols, references, characters, or narratives and how they interact with the non-religious parameters. Light per se is not religious, but if the light represents a halo, it has become a religious sign. Clothing is not religious in its own right unless it references a religious tradition and practice, like a monk's cowl. The interaction of the cinematic parameters can be described as "homogenization," a term employed by Odin, as all the visible and audible signs, symbols, and references combine into the narration. Each parameter is merged with all the other parameters.[88] The model in figure 7 shows how the relationship between the parameters and the relationship between the audience and the film are shaped. The two levels of film and the audience are synchronized in the reception process – the ideal situation in which the spectators are able to follow and make sense of the narration.

The model suggests that any kind of representation can influence, shape, and foster religious stereotypes, be it a Muslim woman wearing a headscarf or Moses as a white-bearded old man. Religious representations can support, pass on, question, and even transform traditions. They can inform

---

88 Mäder, *Die Reise als Suche nach Orientierung*, 35; Roger Odin, *De la fiction* (Bruxelles: De Boeck, 2000), 35–52.

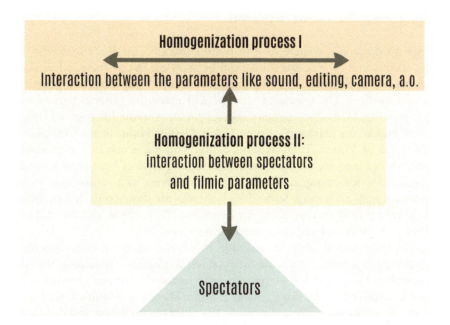

Fig. 7 Model of homogenization between filmic parameters and between the spectators and the film.

about and communicate religion to a varied target audience comprising religious and/or non-religious spectators from diverse cultural backgrounds.

Different representation styles, genres, and subgenres demand different aesthetics, which influences the production space. A reality show is not funded and organized as is a short documentary or commercial. A historical documentary with scenes of re-enactment may well be costlier than a TV report that must be available quickly. And specific forms of narration favor specific forms of distribution. An ethnographic documentary might be shown at a festival for visual anthropology, whereas a reality show will likely be distributed through streaming services or television channels. The representation style defines the subgenre, with the space of distribution and circulation implied to a certain degree. Additionally, however, the space of distribution and circulation can shape a film's narration.

Part I: The Field of Documentary and Religion

Space of distribution and circulation

Our third space, the space of distribution and circulation, defines where, for whom, and by whom a source can be accessed. In this space, television channels and distribution companies, for example, buy films and provide access to them. The television channel will make the material part of its programing. Many documentary sources circulate on the Internet, whether with paid access (Amazon's Prime Video, Netflix, Hulu) or for free, as on YouTube or Vimeo. These services define who has access to the product and who cannot stream the material. Streaming services have geographical restrictions, for example, which means that access to a source may vary from country to country. Some documentaries are shown only at film festivals, others only in cinema or on television. They might also be sold as DVDs or can be ordered electronically to stream.

The institutional aspect is crucial in this space because it influences the reception experience. A documentary about a religious community that is transmitted as part of the programing of a national television channel will not be received in the same way as is a film shown at a visitor center belonging to that religious community. The space of circulation and distribution also shapes the space of production. The required length of the documentary will influence its style and production. And the distribution network might determine the production's financial requirements. Thus, production volume will be affected by the level of financing a network receives. For streaming networks Netflix and Amazon, circulation and production spaces can collapse, because both services are also producers. If a production is independent of any distribution network, as is often the case with religious institutions that are not officially represented by the state, the producers may need to acquire financial partners at the start. Officially represented religious institutions – for example, the state churches in some European countries – might benefit from access to circulation provided by a public television network, as is the case in Switzerland. The Roman Catholic, Protestant and Christ-Catholic churches in Switzerland are given transmission time and technical support to broadcast on Sundays.

Media professionals working for a production may also be part of a distribution network. Networks of religious communities often cooperate with media professionals who are members of those communities to ensure the audio-visual style and content are in accord with the ethical standards of the community. Control of the production space is often fostered by close connections between production and circulation. Educational religious films provide a good example of how the distribution and circula-

2. Spaces of Communication: Theoretical and Methodological Framework

tion space can govern the production space. If a church needs audio-visual sources for instruction, the production will be framed by the nature of the target audience and the context in which the material will circulate and be received. The space of media consumption then coincides with the space of distribution and circulation. Where a documentary is shown defines who has access to the source, as we noted. Home movies such as wedding recordings, for example, are shared in private settings, by friends, family, and wedding guests; they may be shared on streaming platforms. Also, a film may not have only one form of circulation: a single film might be consumed on the Internet, or in social media accessed via a laptop, smart phone, or tablet, or at the cinema, or as a television program, or on DVD, and on either the big screen or a small display.

Space of consumption

The space of media consumption is defined by the audience and their reception experience. It includes the effect and function of audio-visual sources. Most sources are produced with a certain audience or, at least, a predetermined effect and function in mind, be it education or entertainment. In this way consumption influences the space of representation. Audiences also expect films and shows of a certain type, following fashions of representation in the media market.

For example, the subgenre of the reality show became prominent in the late 1990s with the production *Big Brother,* which was not the first reality show but was particularly influential; *Big Brother* was followed by many other reality shows that adopted its format, with people exposed to a challenging situation.[89] In *Big Brother*, a group of people live together in a container, with cameras observing them for 24 hours a day. The inhabitants of the container are exposed to different tasks and the audience votes on who must leave, namely those who, in their eyes, are least deserving of staying; the last person remaining is the winner and receives the prize money.

The commercial media business is based on supply and demand like any other market. Audiences demand specific representations according to genre, with expectations of how characters should dress, talk, and behave. A religious-motivated production has to be aware of such needs, and adapt its message accordingly. Additionally, the audience might favor specific

---

89 Anita Biressi and Heather Nunn, *Reality TV: Realism and Revelation* (Wallflower Press, 2012), 9–15.

spaces of circulation: the popularity of streaming has bolstered companies that stream films. Religious productions are indeed available on such platforms.

The construction of public discourse through the distribution of films, above all for films that occupy multiple distribution channels, can only be controlled to a limited extent by their producers. Documentary media are not distributed only via television and cinema, where distribution takes place within a strictly regulated and institutional framework, but are often also accessible via the Internet. In general, the Internet is crucial to the distribution and circulation of audio-visual sources about religion, connecting the spaces of distribution and circulation with the space of consumption. A film that appears in a single context, on YouTube for example, engages one form of public discourse. When a film with ties to a religious community appears on the church webpage it has a distinct and controlled context, but these particular external reading instructions vanish when the film is accessed via a different site.

We can explore the interaction of spaces of communication on the Internet in a religious context through the example of the LDS Church webpage.[90]

Spaces of communication in the LDS Church's media library

Reconstruction of the historical Mormon community has been a concern of LDS Church media production in movies, on television, and, as a later arrival, on the Internet. Portrayals of the LDS Church and its members deemed inappropriate by its leadership can then be countered by self-representation. In his work on the Mormon university in Jerusalem, Blair G. Van Dyke has written of the elaboration of such communication strategies as a primary goal of the Public Affairs Department of the LDS Church: "The LDS must be self-defining in the media. The LDS Church has learned in Jerusalem and elsewhere the damage caused by allowing disingenuous opponents to define Mormonism in the media."[91] Van Dyke's expression

---

90 The LDS Church's communication strategy is discussed in part II and III.
91 Blair G. Van Dyke, "The Mormon University on the Mount of Olives: A Case Study in LDS Public Relations," *Journal of Media and Religion* 12, no. 4 (October 1, 2013): 194. Van Dyke examines anti-missionary organization's use of the media to block the construction of the Jerusalem Center for Near Eastern Studies on the Mount of Olives in the mid-1980s.

"self-defining in the media" is used with reference to the process whereby Latter-day Saints represent themselves, largely by means of depictions of other Mormons, their theology, and their history, through media production sponsored by LDS Church agents or institutions. The attitude toward the church recounted by these productions is mostly positive and respectful, for Mormon media makers are evidently most concerned to construct and then distribute within the public sphere representations of their institution and agents that are affirming.

The LDS Church promotes their audio-visual media through their media library website.[92] The selection of material is vast and covers mostly short films of diverse genres and sub-genres, with the resources available including fiction, documentaries, advertisements, educational material, and conference proceedings, as well as films addressing a specific social group, such as children, women, leaders, or missionaries. The recordings are grouped and displayed according to key terms or topics, with each grouping often containing a series of short films between one and four minutes in length. The short films and movies can easily be downloaded for use in the classroom or to be sent to a third party.

Audio-visual material that draws on the Gospel and Book of Mormon, documentary media with re-enacted scenes from the believer's perspective, provides an example of just how elaborate and professional is the LDS Church use of film as a media to promote its worldview. The material in the media library is sorted into categories such as "Church History," "Auxiliary Training," "Easter," or "General Conference," to name just few of the forty-one possibilities, and under keywords such as "Mothers," "Religious Freedom," and "Temples."

The Gospel films are numerous and, under the heading "Bible Videos", they are arranged in two ways. Listed as "Life of Jesus Videos Chronologically", they follow the life of Christ, with sections entitled "Birth," "Ministry," "Final Days," "After Resurrection," and "Other"; they can also be accessed by scriptural topic or event. The Gospel is filmed in 100 episodes, with each episode a short film with actors that can be watched on the webpage. The site is set up also to allow accesses to the Bible shorts available on DVD and via an app for smartphone and tablet.[93] The LDS Church's production of its own Gospel films allows it to provide material that

---

92 "Social Media Index Page – LDS Media Library," accessed June 14, 2019, https://www.churchofjesuschrist.org/media-library/social?lang=eng.

93 "Bible Videos – The Life of Jesus Christ – Watch Scenes from the Bible," accessed June 14, 2019, https://www.churchofjesuschrist.org/bible-videos?lang=eng&_r=1.

abides by its strict ideas about the representation of sexuality, language, and violence. The many audio-visual Gospel adaptions that do not respect these restrictions are not permitted viewing for LDS Church members. Over three years the LDS Church produced the short Gospel episodes in an ancient Israel that had been elaborately constructed in the desert of Provo in Goshen in the state of Utah.

In this example, by and large all those involved in the production and its consumption belong to the same institution, although everybody can watch the short films online without payment. The clips are also available on YouTube and iTunes for free and can be downloaded and shared very easily, as they are offered in different formats. When accessed on the LDS Church website, the Bible videos reference the scripture and a task (Fig. 8): "Ponder what the savior means to all humanity –and to you personally. And then share the good news."[94]

While the Bible-based videos are stylistically very homogenous – they employ the same actors in consistent settings – the videos for *The Book of Mormon*, listed just below the Bible category, are of various genres and styles. The first category is introductory, with several talks or sermons, mostly by LDS Church leaders, that reference *The Book of Mormon*. In the chapter entitled "Jacob–Mosiah" the script is provided by experts who chronologically and historically reconstruct the story of *The Book of Mormon*; the sections entitled "Alma-Helaman" and "Nephi-Moroni" are composed similarly. The section entitled "Book of Mormon stories (animated)" consists of 58 animated short films of between 1:30 and 3 minutes in length that tell the story of *The Book of Mormon* in the style of a graphic novel, with commentary in a male or female voice. The term "animated" is used to describe a format in which, on the whole, the background moves while the characters and objects in the foreground remain still. For example, in a clip from chapter 8 (fig. 9), the sea seems to churn and lighting flashes, but the figures are motionless. The voice-over is spoken by a warm and light female voice that reminds one of a kindergarten teacher reading a picture book for children. The target audience may well be young children of preschool or kindergarten age.

---

94 "He Is Risen," accessed June 15, 2019, https://churchofjesuschrist.org/media-library/video/2011-10-025-he-is-risen.

2. Spaces of Communication: Theoretical and Methodological Framework

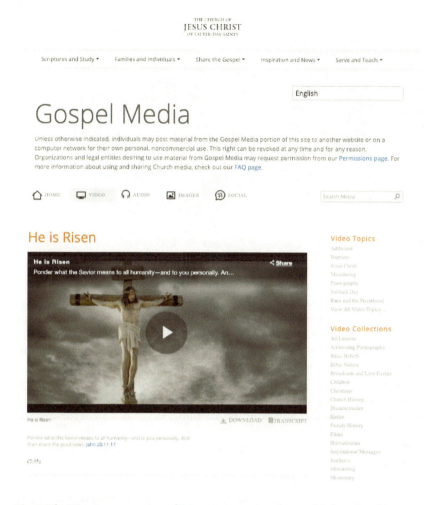

Fig. 8 The King James version of John 20:11-17 is referenced below the video with a task and the request to share "the good news."

Part I: The Field of Documentary and Religion

Fig. 9 Screenshot from "Chapter 8: Crossing the Sea.[95]

The last section in the media library, entitled "Book of Mormon Presentation," contains educational films that discuss religious experiences and revelations in short narrations. For example, in "Becoming Children of Christ," two young women learn about "what it means to put off the natural man and become children of Christ."[96]

The variety in the genres and styles of *The Book of Mormon* material suggests it may be intended for an audience different from the audience for the material in the Bible category, an audience composed of diverse age groups. The character of the audio-visual material in this section, which covers talks, sermons, and educational films, suggests a pedagogical purpose.

The LDS Church offers its members advice on the use of social media and the Internet and is also very clear in setting up standards for online resources in general.[97] Its interest in appropriate media practice and in preventing harassment through social media and cyber bullying is evident in a video clip produced by the LDS Church that can be found on the mor-

---

95 "Chapter 8: Crossing the Sea," accessed June 15, 2019, https://www.churchofjesuschrist.org/media-library/video/2010-12-08-chapter-8-crossing-the-sea.
96 "Becoming Children of Christ," accessed June 15, 2019, https://www.churchofjesuschrist.org/media-library/video/2007-01-0003-becoming-children-of-christ.
97 "Share Goodness," accessed June 14, 2019, https://www.churchofjesuschrist.org/church/share/goodness?lang=eng; "Social Media Index Page – LDS Media Library"; "Use of Online Resources in Church Callings," accessed June 14, 2019, https://www.churchofjesuschrist.org/pages/online-resources-for-church-callings?lang=eng.

monchannel.org site. The Mormon Channel website lists the video "Bullying – Stop it"[98] as one of the most-seen videos of 2014.[99] This short film tells the story of a girl who is bullied by classmates via social media. One boy steps up, first approaching the girl to show her his empathy and then stopping the other boys from continuing their attacks on the girl. At the beginning of the short film, Dieter P. Uchtendorf, LDS Church president and second counselor in the First Presidency, speaks in a voice-over about "the destructive spirit of contention, resentment, and revenge." By June 16, 2019, this video had had 12,370,764 views on YouTube, and had attracted 17,335 comments and 229,827 likes and 6,408 dislikes.

Even this short discussion of the LDS Church's use of the media, which draws on examples of videos that engage the Bible and *The Book of Mormon*, indicates the extent of LDS Church involvement in the media, from production to consumption, as it seeks to control output on every level. Audio-visual media are not the only means used by the LDS Church to represent itself and spread its message for missionary purposes and to sustain the loyalty of its members, but particularly with the added contribution of the Internet, such media have become well-trod, if challenging, terrain for the LDS Church as it seeks to craft its image in accord with its worldview.

This example also shows how in the case of religion, and specifically in the case of a religious institution, communication spaces interact. In each of the spaces, individuals are active agents – as media professionals, producers, social actors, and audience, for example – who perform their functions in light of their belief system. Heidi Campbell has identified a similar process employed by the Catholic Church: "The negotiation and adoption of new technologies requires the religious group to create public and private discourses that validate their technology choices in light of established community boundaries, values, and identities."[100] In the instance examined here, that "new technology" is the Internet, which functions as a distribution network and an instrument of circulation. Its use requires a con-

---

98 Mormon Channel, *Bullying - Stop It*, accessed September 28, 2017, https://www.youtube.com/watch?v=FYVvE4tr2BI.
99 "Mormon Channel's Top 10 YouTube Videos of 2014," accessed September 28, 2017, https://www.mormonchannel.org/blog/post/mormon-channels-top-10-youtube-videos-of-2014.
100 Heidi Campbell, "How Religious Communities Negotiate New Media Religiously," in *Digital Religion, Social Media, and Culture: Perspectives, Practices, and Futures*, ed. Pauline Hope Cheong, Digital Formations (New York: Peter Lang, 2012), 86.

Part I: The Field of Documentary and Religion

trol mechanism that allows the public face of the LDS Church to be shaped according to an established institutional framework. The online image must be consistent with the offline institution. To that end, the LDS Church has published guidelines, encountered above, that address the appropriate use of social media and the Internet for material related to the LDS Church, and also by individuals as they engage the Internet more broadly.[101] As the titles suggest – "Use of Online Resources in Church Callings" and "Gospel Media" – these guidelines are intended for LDS Church members, and they seek to establish a media consumption culture that conforms to the LDS Church's "boundaries, values and identities," as itemized by Campbell.

Thus, the Internet is a vital component of the interface of documentary media and religion, not least because as a virtual space of distribution and circulation it enables easy access to numerous audio-visual sources. With religious groupings or traditions interacting virtually with members and non-members,[102] the Internet becomes a place of social activity for social actors that influences their religious practices.[103]

The Internet is a challenge not only for religious institutions and social actors but also for those undertaking research. On one hand, as analysis of Internet use expands, it has developed useful ways of approaching the categorization of the often vast amount of material available. [104] On the other

---

101 "Use of Online Resources in Church Callings."
102 Campbell, "How Religious Communities Negotiate New Media Religiously"; Mark D. John, "Voting 'Present': Religious Organizational Groups on Facebook," in *Digital Religion, Social Media, and Culture: Perspectives, Practices, and Futures*, ed. Pauline Hope Cheong, Digital Formations (New York/NY: Peter Lang, 2012), 151–168; Robert Glenn Howard, *Digital Jesus: The Making of a New Christian Fundamentalist Community on the Internet* (New York: New York University Press, 2011); Erica Baffelli, Ian Reader, and Birgit Staemmler, eds., *Japanese Religions on the Internet: Innovation, Representation, and Authority*, vol. 2, Routledge Studies in Religion, Media, and Culture (New York: Routledge, 2011).
103 Stewart M. Hoover, "Concluding Thought: Imagining the Religious in and through the Digital," in *Digital Religion: Understanding Religious Practice in New Media Worlds*, ed. Heidi Campbell (Abingdon: Routledge, 2013), 266–268; Knut Lundby, "Theoretical Framework for Approaching Religion and New Media," in *Digital Religion: Understanding Religious Practice in New Media Worlds*, ed. Heidi Campbell (Abingdon: Routledge, 2013), 225–237.
104 Heidi Campbell, *When Religion Meets New Media*, Media, Religion and Culture Series (Abingdon: Routledge, 2010); Heidi Campbell, *Exploring Religious Community Online: We Are One in the Network*, vol. 24, Digital Formations (New York: P. Lang, 2005).

hand, we must consider the extent to which researchers should locate themselves within the Internet presence through their commentary. Mark D. John has demanded in the paper "Ethical decision-making and Internet research" that the engagement of the researcher be exclusively passive, a call that this project follows.[105]

2.4. Researching audio-visual representation of religious communities

The spaces of communication of documentary media and religion that we have encountered fulfil different functions. First, and we have seen, they enable the systematization of the audio-visual sources, their contexts, preconditions, and potential interactions, on a theoretical level. They then allow us to situate a research question in a specific space or between spaces. Secondly, they shape methodology, determining that different spaces and interactions be scrutinized. Each space and the interaction between the spaces is then analyzed using a particular methodological approach. Research question and method are thus synchronized. And lastly, but significantly, the sources on which a study is based can be identified, characterized, and accumulated in light of the different spaces of communication.

That methodological framing for the current project will now be outlined and, finally, the corpus of material will be introduced.

Approaching spaces of communication

As we saw in the introduction to our discussion of spaces of communication these four spaces both overlap and diverge. Their differences require appropriate methods of examination. This study's methodological approach therefore draws from discussion of mixed-method approaches[106] and triangulation.[107] Specifically, it adopts a multimethod research design.

---

[105] Norwegian National Ethics Committees, "Ethical Guidelines for Internet Research," December 2014, https://www.etikkom.no/globalassets/documents/english-publications/ethical-guidelines-for-internet-research.pdf.

[106] Norman K. Denzin, "Triangulation 2.0," *Journal of Mixed Methods Research* 6, no. 2 (2012): 80–88; Norman K. Denzin, "Moments, Mixed Methods, and Paradigm Dialogs," *Qualitative Inquiry* 16, no. 6 (2010): 419–27.

[107] Christel Hopf, "Qualitative Interviews – ein Überblick," in *Qualitative Sozialforschung: eine Einführung*, ed. Uwe Flick, Ernst von Kardorff, and Ines Steinke, Rororo (Reinbek bei Hamburg: Rowohlt Taschenbuch Verlag, 2016), 519/5206;

Part I: The Field of Documentary and Religion

Both mixed-method and triangulation approaches have been much debated within the social sciences and are generally employed when quantitative and qualitative data are gathered within a single project by different researchers, at different places, times and with different social actors.[108] Such an approach aims to complement and condense the data sampling in order to prevent one-sided and biased results. Triangulation can take place on a theoretical level, by working with different theories, and at the methodological level, by applying different methods. Applications of triangulation have expanded over time such that now it designates not only quantitative and qualitative approaches but also hermeneutic methods that combine with these approaches. Sociologist Uwe Flick has provided a useful summary:

> Triangulation comprises the capturing of different perspectives on an object of research or, more generally, in responding to research questions. These perspectives can take concrete form in the application of varied methods and/or in the selection of varied theoretical approaches, with the two aspects then to be connected or combined. Additionally, triangulation refers to the combination of different types of data, in each case in light of a theoretical perspective adopted, in turn, in light of the data.[109]

The sociologist Norman K. Denzin has described the advantage of using multiple methods as "an attempt to secure an in depth-understanding of the phenomenon in question."[110] No single method, neither qualitative nor quantitative, fully covers any object of research, he notes:

> Objective reality can never be captured. We only know a thing through its representation. The combination of multiple methodologi-

---

Uwe Flick, *Triangulation. Eine Einführung*, Qualitative Sozialforschung (Wiesbaden: VS Verlag, 2011), 13–26.
108 Hopf, "Qualitative Interviews – ein Überblick," 519.
109 Flick, *Triangulation*, 12. Translation by the author. German original version: „Triangulation beinhaltet die Einnahme unterschiedlicher Perspektiven auf einen untersuchten Gegenstand oder allgemeiner: bei der Beantwortung von Forschungsfragen. Diese Perspektiven können sich in unterschiedlichen Methoden, die angewandt werden, und/oder unterschiedlichen gewählten theoretischen Zugängen konkretisieren, wobei beides wiederum miteinander in Zusammenhang steht bzw. verknüpft werden sollte. Weiterhin bezieht sie sich auf die Kombination unterschiedlicher Datensorten jeweils vor dem Hintergrund der auf die Daten jeweils eingenommenen theoretischen Perspektiven."
110 Denzin, "Triangulation 2.0," 82.

cal practices empirical materials, perspectives, and observers in a single study is best understood as a strategy that adds rigor, breadth complexity, richness, and depth to any inquiry.[111]

Triangulation involves an attempt to draw near truth through a diversity of approaches, which is exactly what Laura L. Ellingson, a communication scholar trained in women's and gender studies, rejects: "Whereas triangulation seeks a more definitive truth, crystallization problematizes the multiple truth it presents."[112] The post-modern concept of crystallization nuances the idea that a multitude of methods of analysis and genres of representation can be combined to form a coherent interpretation of any kind of phenomenon, and it eschews the incompatibility of different methods.[113] Even though Ellingson's concept is focused on qualitative methods, it also covers hermeneutic approaches. Ellingson describes five components of crystallization.[114] (1) Any qualitative approach, she argues, should generate a deeper account, or, in reference to Clifford Geertz, a "thick description". (2) She understands the concept as an intrinsically multimethod approach, with varied qualitative approaches standing in a continuum, in opposition to dualistic approaches, be they quantitative or qualitative. That continuum embraces qualitative methods – from the positivistic that claims objective truth to the interpretative – as inclusive and not contradictory. (3) She notes that crystallization allows for variety in the way in which findings are presented. The examination of a religious community through the lens of the media undertaken in this study uses textual interpretation of the sources and stills from audio-visual sources in its argument, and quotes from interviews with media professionals, and statistical data of a quantitative audience study. (4) The researcher's position within their endeavor is reflected. An explicit hermeneutic position is key for the

---

111 Denzin, 82.
112 Ellingson, *Engaging Crystallization in Qualitative Research*. Ellingson defines crystallization as follows (2009: 4): "Crystallization combines multiple forms of analysis and multiple genres of representation into a coherent text or series of related texts, building a rich and openly partial account of a phenomenon that problematizes its own construction, highlights researchers' vulnerabilities and positionality, makes claims about socially constructed meanings, and reveals the indeterminacy of knowledge claims even as it makes them."
113 Charles Teddlie and Abbas Tashakkori, "Overview of Contemporary Issues in Mixed Methods Research," in *SAGE Handbook of Mixed Methods in Social & Behavioral Research*, ed. Abbas Tashakkori, 2nd ed. (Thousand Oaks, CA: SAGE, 2010), 1–44.
114 Ellingson, *Engaging Crystallization in Qualitative Research*, 9–12.

examination of a religious community. Sources, methods, theories, and questions are all deliberate choices made by the scholar while undertaking research, choices that must be explained explicitly. Furthermore, and in particular in the study of religion, the relation between researcher and subject needs to be clarified (see chapter 1.3). (5) The idea of a single, discoverable, and eternal truth is rejected in favor of an understanding of knowledge that is "inevitably situated, partial, constructed, multiple, and embodied."[115]

A diversity of theories, methods, sources, and ways to present results allows a plurality of perspectives and counters hegemonic and biased positions. In this sense crystallization is not only a methodological program but also a political and ethical understanding of scholarship and research. The results of such research are complex, diverse, and possibly contradictory, for they are not submitted to uniformity and singular paradigms in method and theory. The term "interpretation" is key for this approach, because it is consistent with the idea that there cannot be a single fixed reconstruction of any object of research.

Dutch filmmaker and cultural theorist Mieke Bal describes the multiplex character of interpretation in her method of cultural analysis by discerning four principles.[116] (1) Objects, theories, methods, and their interpreters interact within the analytical process, with the object, in particular, playing an active role. (2) Interpretation is based on dialogue, both between the object and the researcher and between researchers. (3) There is no meaning without interpretation or without interpretive activity, from which we can conclude that objects have no predefined meaning and that meaning is not to be found in the work itself. (4) Analysis, a performative

---

115 Ellingson, 12.
116 Mieke Bal, "Working with Concepts," *European Journal of English Studies* 13, no. 1 (April 1, 2009): 13–23; Mieke Bal, "Visual Essentialism and the Object of Visual Culture," *Journal of Visual Culture* 2, no. 1 (April 1, 2003): 24/25; Sigrid Schade and Silke Wenk, *Studien zur visuellen Kultur: Einführung in ein transdisziplinäres Forschungsfeld*, vol. 8, Studien zur visuellen Kultur (Bielefeld: Transcript, 2011), 65–68. On Mieke Bal's webpage there is also a video in which the theorist explains the five aspects of cultural analysis slightly differently from how they are discussed here. See "Home – Www.Miekebal.Org," accessed June 16, 2019, http://www.miekebal.org/. For the fifth aspect she proposes that the object has always the last word in the sense that must be closely evaluated again and again. Furthermore, Bal emphasizes that cultural analysis always takes place in the present: "The historical past matters to the extent as it matters in the present." This inevitably includes later readings of an art work as part of each new interpretation.

2. Spaces of Communication: Theoretical and Methodological Framework

practice, is always accompanied by a learning process on the part of the recipient. Researchers are also consumers, with a store of interpretation that builds through perception and contemplation and is constantly growing. Reflecting crystallization at the micro-level of the research itself, the four levels form fundamental analytical-hermeneutic considerations for the current study and are inherent in the approaches it adopts.

The concept of crystallization also works well with the theoretical definition and methodological strategy provided by spaces of communication. Crystallization explains how a religious community can be engaged through the media according to theory, method, sources, and data sets and how the results can be presented.

Applied methods for the research

The current study combines methods from social science, ethnographic studies, media hermeneutics, and film analysis. The methods will now be discussed in the context of spaces of communication, as encountered earlier in this chapter and the methods will be elucidated with reference to the data and sources and elaborated upon. This discussion will provide an overview of the methods applied in light of theoretical premises and sources.

Let us start with the space of production. Qualitative, semi-structured interviews with eight media professionals who belong to or are close to the LDS Church were conducted during field work in Salt Lake City/US in June 2015 and in Frankfurt/DE in August 2015. During the intense one-hour conversations, a narrative-biographical approach and a guided interview style were combined. The conversations provide insight into the media self-representation strategies of a religious community. The interviews had been coded with reference to grounded theory[117] and evaluated by working with sociological hermeneutics of knowledge.[118] In a second step

---

117 Jörg Strübing, "Grounded Theory und Theoretical Sampling," in *Handbuch Methoden der empirischen Sozialforschung*, ed. Nina Baur and Jörg Blasius (Wiesbaden: Springer Verlag, 2014), 457–72; Andreas Boehm, "Grounded Theory - wie aus Texten Modelle und Theorien gemacht werden," ed. Andreas Boehm, Andreas Mengel, and Thomas Muhr, Schriften zur Informationswissenschaft 14 (Konstanz: UVK Univ.-Verl. Konstanz, 1994), 121–40.
118 Jo Reichertz, "Objektive Hermeneutik und hermeneutische Wissenssoziologie," in *Qualitative Forschung: ein Handbuch*, ed. Uwe Flick, Ernst von Kardorff, and

Part I: The Field of Documentary and Religion

the interviews are compared, and parallels as well as oppositions are discussed.

The space of production is frequently closely related to the space of distribution and circulation, they can therefore be analyzed using the same methods and sources. Therefore, the elaboration of the production, distribution, and circulation spaces often refers to the same "documents" providing information about the nature and purposes of the media.[119] "Documents" are understood as standardized artefacts in different formats, material such as press kits, websites, archive resources, press interviews with the media professionals and literature.[120] Analysis of the documents is undertaken by exploring the production, representation, distribution/circulation, and media communication spaces of their information. That analysis asks who produced the document, what is represented and how, where and how is it circulated, and for whom it is intended.

In the space of representation, documentary sources by and/or about Mormons are scrutinized and critically analyzed[121] in a semio-pragmatic approach that takes the sources' communications spaces and their reading modes into account. Further analysis based on cognitive assumptions scrutinizes the film's style by analyzing parameters such as camera, light, editing, and sound.[122] Along with the sources' style, plot and story are highlighted. The "plot" is the part of the film that is visible and audible, which includes all the sequences, each scene and shot. The "story" is more than

---

Ines Steinke (Reinbek: Rowohlt Taschenbuch Verlag, 2015), 514–524; Hopf, "Qualitative Interviews – ein Überblick," 436–449; Ronald Kurt and Regine Herbrik, "Sozialwissenschaftliche Hermeneutik und hermeneutische Wissenssoziologie," in *Handbuch Methoden der empirischen Sozialforschung*, ed. Nina Baur and Jörg Blasius (Wiesbaden: Springer Verlag, 2014), 473–91.

119 Uwe Flick, "Zur Verwendung von Dokumenten," in *Qualitative Sozialforschung: eine Einführung*, Rororo (Reinbek bei Hamburg: Rowohlt Taschenbuch Verlag, 2016), 312–326.

120 Stephan Wolff, "Dokumenten- und Aktenanalyse," in *Qualitative Forschung: ein Handbuch*, ed. Uwe Flick, Ernst von Kardorff, and Ines Steinke, Rororo (Reinbek: Rowohlt Taschenbuch Verlag, 2015), 503.

121 Rainer Winter and Sebastian Nestler, "'Doing Cinema': Filmanalyse als Kulturanalyse in der Tradition der Culltural Studies," in *Film – Kino – Zuschauer, Filmrezeption = Film - cinema – spectator, film reception*, ed. Irmbert Schenk (Marburg: Schüren, 2010), 99–115; David Bordwell and Kristin Marie Thompson, *Film Art: An Introduction*, 10th ed. (New York: McGraw-Hill, 2013); Louis D. Giannetti, *Understanding Movies*, 13th ed. (Boston: Pearson, 2014).

122 Bordwell and Thompson, *Film Art*; Louis D. Giannetti, *Understanding Movies*; Edward Branigan, *Narrative Comprehension and Film*, Sightlines (London: Routledge, 1992).

the plot. It encompasses the whole narrative world, or diegesis, that is constructed by the spectators from the plot, including inferences and premises. David Bordwell's conceives "plot" in a narrative film as

> all the events that are directly presented to us, including their causal relations, chronological order, duration, frequency, and spatial locations; opposed to story, which is the viewer's imaginary construction of all the events in the narrative.[123]

Documentary sources have a narrative quality like that of fiction films. Several story lines may be drawn from the same plot. In most cases there is no wrong or right understanding, for different readings can be made of a single source. This project applies an approach that allows for varied readings of religion from diverse points of view. It takes into account that religious and non-religious recipients may read differently, and that their readings may be shaped by their belonging or not-belonging to the community portrayed by the source. The principal question must be: what kind of meaning does the source have for whom? Denzin talks about subversive readings of documentaries (he does not refer to Halls' encoding and decoding model but the parallels are compelling). Many films present a version of truth by suppressing contradiction and by constructing consistency. Such constructed consistency happens when arguments form a chain of cause and effect that leads to a "truth."[124] For example, social actors in the *I'm a Mormon* series generally appear very happy and seem more successful than average in what they do. At the end of each video they say their name and then the phrase: "… and I'm a Mormon." This statement, standing at the end of the video, suggests that the social actor's success and happiness are a product of their membership of the LDS Church.[125] Readings can, however, vary: LDS members might feel affirmed, taking that they belong to the right church; former Mormons might however be offended, aware that their experiences in the LDS Church were less upbeat.

A subversive reading locates the values behind such arguments and detects the narrative's worldview. In the context of religion, reading film in this way can generate an understanding of how a religious community

---

[123] Bordwell and Thompson, *Film Art*, 503.
[124] Norman K. Denzin, "Reading Film – Filme und Videos als sozialwissenschaftliches Erfahrungsmaterial," in *Qualitative Forschung: ein Handbuch*, ed. Uwe Flick, Ernst von Kardorff, and Ines Steinke, Rororo (Reinbek: Rowohlt Taschenbuch Verlag, 2015), 424/425.
[125] For a more detailed analysis of the series see chapter 4, part II.

wants to represent a topic and its members, values or practices, or how it wants to be perceived by members and non-member. Or a subversive reading might establish how non-members want to represent a religious community in light of their particular political, social, or cultural agenda. Denzin notes, "Subversive readings look at how the film idealises specific key moments like family, work, religion and love,"[126] drawing attention to how this approach can expand the film-analysis through critical evaluation of the cultural values and norms that are depicted. Such issues must be addressed in an evaluation of religion in documentary media, and they pick up on the features of documentary media noted, as we have seen, by Odin. To resume the *moral mode* addresses the authority and credibility of a documentary source: the audience might ask, why should I believe what is presented here? It looks critically at the argument or communications strategy presented and considers for which audience the narrative is credible and for which it is not.

In addition to applying a semio-pragmatic approach in the space of representation, this study considers the space of consumption by examining online comments about the material. Comments are found on YouTube, in blogs, on webpages, and in reviews, for example. Joseph Reagale has described the "comment" as follows:

> As I use the term, comment is a genre of communication. [...] Although comment is reactive, it is not always responsive or substantively engaging. [...] Comment is short—often as simple as the click of a button, sometimes measured in characters, but rarely more than a handful of paragraphs. And it is asynchronous, meaning that it can be made within seconds, hours, or even days of its provocation. Putting aside future transformations, comment is already present: comment has a long history [...], and it is pervasive. Our world is permeated by comment, and we are the source of its judgment and the object of its scrutiny.[127]

This characterization highlights dual character of this form of social interaction: members of an online community can make judgements but they can also themselves become an object of scrutiny. Their judgments express

---

126 Denzin, "Reading Film - Filme und Videos als sozialwissenschaftliches Erfahrungsmaterial," 425. Translation by the author.
127 Joseph M. Reagle, *Reading the Comments: Likers, Haters, and Manipulators at the Bottom of the Web*, First MIT Press paperback edition (Cambridge, MA: The MIT Press, 2016), 2015.

2. Spaces of Communication: Theoretical and Methodological Framework

opinions that might range from appreciation to excoriation, depending on personal preferences. Comments in a religious context can be very emotional. They also show how variously the source material can be received. In their comments, some commentators may judge a religion or the religious actors very harshly, while members of the relevant church express sympathy and identify with the institution. Comments can be used to bond with other commentators with a shared worldview or to distance the commentator from an institution. Overall, as a specific form of communication, comments can help clarify how a documentary source works and can allow the researcher to determine the triggers for audiences found within in the source.

Let us look at one example of comment on a religious topic, drawn from postings in the online forum for the reality show *Sister Wives* (US, 2010–2020), broadcast by the US television channel TLC.[128] The show depicts a polygamous Mormon family in the United States with one husband and four wives; the number of children in the family grows over the course of the 14 seasons from 13 to 18 plus 2 grandchildren. Since 2014 the reality show has also been aired in German-speaking countries, with the title *Alle meine Frauen*. The channel TLC is geared to a female audience.[129]

Those who participate in the online forum are mainly women. The German TLC webpage asks the audience if they could imagine a life as a polygamist. While the discussion is initially guided by that question, it expands into a critical discussion of the lifestyle of the Brown family, from the viewers' perspective. The most frequent topic of discussion is Kody Brown, the husband. The online comments are mixed in their feelings about and attitudes toward the family. Generally, the comments reflect an ambivalence about polygamy, but opinions on the family itself are mostly positive, of the type we see in figure 10.

> Hats off to them!! We can definitely learn something from Kody and his wives. This polygamist family works so well because of these five great people brought together by fate. This family still has values and morals. Unfortunately, most people no longer understand what this means. In times when everybody only thinks of themselves, and nobody is willing to back down for a greater common purpose. Nowa-

---

128 See for detailed discussion of the reality show *Sister Wives* chapter 5, part II.
129 Brenda R. Weber, "Trash Talk: Gender as an Analytic on Reality Television," in *Reality Gendervision: Sexuality & Gender on Transatlantic Reality Television*, ed. Brenda R. Weber (Durham and London: Duke University Press, 2014), 2/3.

days respectful and loving relationships with each other are more likely to be the exception. They [the Browns] cannot multiply enough. [130]

Jenni Fischer
chapeau !!
Von Kody und seinen Frauen kann man sich ein paar Scheibchen abschneiden.
Das diese polygame Familie so großartig funktioniert, liegt an den fünf großartigen Menschen, die das Schicksal hier zusammengeführt hat.
In dieser Familie gibt es noch Werte und eine Moral.
Das können die meißten Menschen leider nicht mehr nachvollziehen.
In einer Zeit, in der jeder nur noch an sich denkt, und niemand sich zurücknehmen würde, für ein gemeinsames großes Ziel.
Heutzutage sind respektvoller, liebevoller Umgang miteinander, schon eher die Ausnahme.
Die können sich gar nicht genug vermehren.
Like · Reply · Jul 19, 2015 4:37pm

Fig. 10 Screenshot of a comment in the online forum of Sister Wives on the German TLC webpage.

Jenni Fischer praises the adults' relationships with the words. "This family still has values and morals." As in many other comments, the focus here is not the sexual relationships but the interpersonal relationships. Fischer's comment suggests a very tolerant attitude toward the polygamous and religiously oriented lifestyle depicted in the show.[131] She uses the platform to present herself as open-minded, eschewing judgement based on a different worldview. At the same time, she engages in a public discourse about moral standards. Her comments come across as both appreciative and defensive. Fischer evidently likes to express her affection for the show and for the polygamous family it depicts. Reagle terms such positive experiences in a small online community "intimate serendipity."[132] People like to bond with others, to share their enthusiasm, with crass dissenting commentary unwelcome; such interventions can wreck the atmosphere of a chat and bring it to an end.

Online comments are just one window into the space of consumption, but they are particularly revealing for this study. We can also establish how documentary media is received via quantitative audience studies. This project thus also considers how audiences from two cultural backgrounds, Spanish and Swiss, perceive the values, opinions, and attitudes related to

---

130 Translation mine. The online forum isn't active anymore and has been deleted.
131 A detailed discussion of the reality show *Sister Wives* follows in chapter 5.
132 Joseph M. Reagle, *Reading the Comments*, 11.

religion in documentary media and thus how effective such communication strategies can be.[133] A quantitative study was conducted with as its subject the documentary *Meet the Mormons* (Blair Treu, US 2014), produced by the LDS Church, an image[134] or advocacy film[135] about LDS Church members intended to promote the institution.

Documentary sources of the study

Most of the audio-visual sources examined in this study are from the last 15 years and therefore can be deemed "current"; this cohesion also opens the door to comparisons. This period saw a strikingly high number of audio-visual productions with Mormons as their subject or stemming from the context of the LDS Church. One reason for this boom was the establishment of a satellite TV station by Brigham Young University (BYUtv) in 2000; by 2019 its programing was reaching 53 million households.[136] Advances in technology that guarantee distribution have also encouraged intensified production of audio-visual material.[137] Particularly later in this period, the Internet, with its speedier transmission of data, availability and easy access, has also provided a vital means of distribution of documentary sources. Additionally, in the 2012 U.S. Presidential election a Mormon, Mitt Romney, was the nominee of the Republic Party, making Mormonism a much-discussed topic in the media.[138] And last but not least, and especially relevant for this project, broadcast series and shows set in a Mormon context brought Mormonism public attention.

---

133 The audience study is presented in chapter 6.1, part II.
134 A corporate video portrays a product, an institution, or a company in in the context of advertising.
135 Aufderheide, *Documentary Film*, 77–90.
136 "What We Do," BYUtv Giving, accessed March 25, 2019, http://www.support-byutv.org/what-we-do.
137 Sherry Pack Baker, "Mormonism," in *Encyclopedia of Religion, Communication, and Media*, ed. Daniel A. Stout, Routledge Encyclopedias of Religion and Society (New York: Routledge, 2006), 264–266.
138 The documentary *Mitt* (Greg Whiteley, US 2016) portrays former governor of Massachusetts Mitt Romney. Romney twice entered the race to become president of the United States: in 2008, when he failed to secure the Republican Party nomination, and in 2012, when he was defeated by Barack Obama. The film is produced by and can be streamed through Netflix.

The sources are classified according to their spaces of communication. This approach allows distinctive categories to be identified: material from within the LDS Church forms one large category, while material that cannot be attributed to a single religious entity forms a separate category. The "series," a typical format for television, DVDs, and the Internet, is found in both categories; since around 2000 series have been a prominent form of television production and extremely successful as an audio-visual format. Many such series, as well as television reporting, documentary films, and advertisements, can be consumed via the Internet, providing them with a potentially global audience.

The sources are described according to their axis of relevance, a term used to refer, as we have seen, to the relationship between the spaces. When filmmaker, producer and director, and consumer agree upon the source's meaning a single axis of relevance is generated, with the same meaning created in the encoding and decoding processes. That understanding is based on an ideal relationship between spaces and can be applied heuristically, as a way to identify and describe the sources.

The study works with four documentary media types: advertisements, documentaries and corporate videos, television reporting, series and shows. Each type deals differently with religion. Alongside their distinct characteristics within their spaces of communication, their distinct goals also distinguish them one from the other. The source descriptions that follow function as a typology that classifies and presents the documentary media employed in this project's case study. While there are exceptions and incompatibilities within each section, this typology can provide a useful overview of the corpus as long as we remain alert to a potentially reduced complexity and variety. Detailed examination is found in the chapters that follow, where most of the examples mentioned here will be expanded upon.

Our first type of documentary media about religion is advertisements. Advertisements want to sell religion – the goal is to acquire members, raise money, or make values or an image desirable. The *I'm a Mormon* (LDS Church, US 2010–16) series of advertisements – 184 videos produced by the missionary department of the LDS Church – is one such source.[139] The counter-series *I Am an Ex Mormon*, with 44 episodes (2010–16), is an audio-visual response to the LDS Church advertisements and included in the analysis. The producers of the advertisements have economic or ideo-

---

139 The number of videos may vary because the LDS Church deletes outdated videos and also uploads new ones

logical goals. The advertisements must be persuasive and spread a positive message; they have a short format, at two to six minutes long, with testimonials at the center of the narration. The advertisements also circulate in the Internet, on YouTube, and on other platforms and are embedded in the webpages of the institution or group that executes the production process. They address three groupings: Mormons, non-Mormons, and Ex-Mormons. Within these three groupings there are also sub-groups to be reached, for example, men, women, and specific nationalities and ethnicities.

The second type of media is documentaries or corporate video that seek to inform or convince their audiences. They are single productions, often with a single responsible author or director. Some documentaries are supported by public funding, others by private, perhaps religious, institutions. The backers of such documentaries are not always explicitly named. Some documentaries are produced by religious actors and institutions; others claim an outsider's perspective on religion. The production context can range from arthouse film to corporate video, and their purpose can be as varied as are the production contexts. Some documentaries adopt an unfavorable approach to religion while others promote religion. There are both short- and long-format documentaries, running between 20 and 90 minutes. Documentaries are shown variously at festivals, in cinemas, and in religious institutions, perhaps in a visitor center. Most can be bought as DVDs and watched on streaming services. They may seek to persuade and/or to entertain their audience.

The documentaries included in this study can be identified as explicitly promoting Mormonism, as adopting a more distanced approach, and as critical of Mormon communities, institutions, and agents. Documentaries that cast Mormons in a critical light include *Inside Polygamy: Life In Bountiful* (Olivia Ahneman, US 2009), *Tabloid* (Errol Morris, US 2010), *8: The Mormon Proposition* (Reed Cowan, Steven Greenstreet, US 2010). One of the documentaries that, by contrast, promotes or defends Mormons is *Nobody Knows. The Untold Story of Black Mormons* (Darius A. Gray, Margaret B. Young, US 2008), which, as the title suggests, reconstructs the history of black Mormons in the United States, from their explicit exclusion to their admission to the official ministries of the LDS Church. *American Mormon in Europe* (Daryn Tufts, Jed Knudsen, US 2006) and *American Mormon* (Daryn Tufts, Jed Knudsen, US 2005) blend comedy and documentary with revealing interviews in which the directors ask passers-by what they know about Mormonism and show how limited the interviewees' information is. Both films display a humorous side to Mormons in order to promote the LDS Church. *Meet the Mormons* (Blair Treu, US 2014), a corporate video produced by the LDS Church that we have already encountered, portrays the lives of outstanding Mormons around the globe and presents an international, multicultural, and upbeat image of the Church.

Television reporting is another type of documentary source. As the term indicates, these sources are produced in formats made for television and will be advertised as television production. They follow the rules of journalism in gathering, assessing, and presenting information, and they may have a sensational edge. Some adopt the format of so-called "infotainment" by combining information and entertainment. The various collaborations that make up the production context can be complex. Private or public networks affiliated with religious institutions might produce such television reporting, and religious actors working for networks might be involved in the production process; in some productions that focus on religion, however, no religious experts or institutions are involved. The journalistic style might seem to claim the standpoint of an objective outsider, and talking heads and expert interviews can be used to foster credibility and claim relevancy. The editing and music score often dramatize the story. TV reportings include material like from the German-language television networks Pro Sieben, ZDF, DokuTV, and ARTE, with titles that include *Der Kampf ums Weisse Haus* (ARTE, 2012), *Dawn Porter unter Polygamisten* (ZDF neo, GB 2007), *Die größten Mormonenmythen* (ProSieben, 2014), and *Polygamie in Gottes Namen – Willkommen bei den Polygamisten* (DokuTV, 2013).

TV reportings are also produced by English-language networks and originated in the United States like *Secrets of Mormon Cult, Breaking Polygamy* (ABC, US 2012) and *Life After Polygamy: The Daughters & Wives of a Polygamist Cult Reclaim Their Hometown* (HBO, US 2016), or in Canada (*Inside Bountiful, Polygamy Investigation* (GlobalNEWS, CN 2012) or in the United Kingdom (*The Culture Show – The Mormons Are Here* (BBC, GB 2013). The listings of such titles highlight the frequency with which TV material addresses polygamy. Polygamy is far from prevalent amongst Mormons in the United States or in Europe yet attracts attention as in these reportings, a presence that part III about the ethical space of documentaries will discuss.

The fourth and final type of audio-visual material comprises *series* and *shows* about religion, terms used to refer to their fictional and documentary character respectively. Each series or show is made up of individual episodes. Shows and series differ fundamentally in their nature. *Big Love* (US 2006–11, HBO) is a *fictional television series* with documentary elements and is set in the milieu of the Fundamental Latter-day Saints (FLDS). The history show *History of the Saints* (US 2010–present) is produced by Glenn Rawson, Dennis Lyman, and Bryant Bush, all members of the LDS Church. The show covers early Mormon history of the 19th century, for 1805–1835 and 1844–1877.[140] Two *reality shows* are discussed in detail in the current study. *The District* (LDS Church, US 2007–2013), comprising eight episodes, is produced from within the LDS Church and is shown at the Church's visitor center. It depicts the everyday life of eight missionaries as they encounter and proselytize potential members of the LDS Church. *Sister Wives* (US 2010–20, TLC, 14 seasons), which we have already encountered, depicts a polygamous Mormon family with one husband, four wives, 18 children, and two grandchildren, first in Utah, later in Las Vegas, Nevada, and finally in Flagstaff, Arizona. This last show garnered high ratings and has been discussed on shows such as *Good Morning America* and the *Ellen Degeneres Show*, on which the adult participants have appeared.

The intention behind these series and shows is varied. The main goal of the fiction series *Big Love* is to entertain, with religion used as a rich and colorful context. The history show *History of the Saints* is an upbeat and uncritical explanation of Mormon history. The LDS Church reality show *The District* has an educational intent directed at future missionaries and also informs its audience about the work of LDS Church missionaries, perhaps as a way of countering prejudice. The TLC reality show *Sister Wives* is also intended as entertainment, but the social actors involved use their public presence to defend their lifestyle. In this last instance, religion and its practices are sensationalized. By definition, reality shows depict people going about their everyday lives over the course of several episodes or even several seasons. Anita Biressi has proposed, "The highly visible presence of ordinary people in 'unscripted' situations are both the watermark of reality TV and arguably an explanation of its success with audiences."[141] Social actors in reality shows may be paid as are professional actors hired for fictional series. In the case of *Sister Wives* the contract with TLC became an important source of income for the large Brown family.[142]

---

140 "History of the Saints – Television Documentary Series," accessed June 15, 2019, https://historyofthesaints.org/.
141 Biressi and Nunn, *Reality TV*, 2012, 2.
142 Derek A. Jorgenson, "Media and Polygamy: A Critical Analysis of Sister Wives," *Communication Studies* 65, no. 1 (January 2014): 24–38.

The production style is similar for both reality shows and series. Private companies and networks, religious and non-religious, invest in the production. By contrast, in the representation space the differences between the series and the shows are more obvious. *Big Love*, a fictional series, uses footage from television reports about the legal case of Warren Jeffs, the leader of the FLDS community, who was convicted of the sexual abuse of a 12-year-old girl. The so-called found footage is a bridge to the world of the audience, generating credibility and actuality. Inclusion of the FLDS news story allows the fictional characters in *Big Love* to participate in the current debate about polygamous families and their legal standing. To bolster its authority, *History of the Saints* also uses found footage whenever possible, and additionally interviews with descendants of Mormon pioneers and with historians as experts. It also includes visual and textual historical sources. Some scenes are even re-enacted with costumed professional actors. By contrast a reality show presents itself as unstaged, with its social actors located in their everyday lives, as in the case of the missionaries and the potential members they would like to see baptized.

Distribution and circulation also differ. The fictional series *Big Love* has been sold and distributed internationally, and can be accessed dubbed into languages such as German, Dutch, Finnish, Portuguese; it has also been banned in some countries, in Malaysia for example, because of the sex scenes.[143] It has been nominated for awards, including Golden Globes and Emmys, in categories such as Best Actor and Best Television Series – Drama. By contrast, the history show is presented almost exclusively in a religious context, for example on BYUtv (operated and funded by Brigham Young University) or at church-sponsored events. Complete seasons are available on DVD, and single episodes can be bought and streamed via the producer's website.[144] The distribution network for *The District* is similar but is explicitly supported by the LDS Church, with the show advertised and presented at the theater at the visitors' center in Salt Lake City (fig. 11).

The show can be watched on streaming platforms like YouTube and Vimeo and has been uploaded to the LDS media library. The space of distribution is revealing of the backing the project has received: whereas *History of the Saints* is sold as a private initiative, albeit with the permission of

---

143 *Parents Guide*, accessed October 13, 2017, http://www.imdb.com/title/tt0421030/parentalguide.

144 "History of the Saints | Product Categories Downloads," accessed October 13, 2017, http://historyofthesaints.org/product-category/history_of_the_saints_products/downloads/.

Fig. 11 The theater at the LDS visitor's center in Salt Lake City/UT presents the reality show The District (Image: Marie-Therese Mäder, 2015).

the LDS Church leaders, *The District* is officially and strongly supported by the LDS Church and can be downloaded for free. And finally, *Sister Wives* is entirely privately produced. The success of the TLC network, which specializes in reality shows, is evident in their ability to distribute their products exclusively through their webpage. When the show was first broadcast and was receiving wide media attention, the public affairs department of the LDS published a short statement noting that the church has not permitted polygamy since 1890 and that the faith of the family depicted in the series has nothing in common with the LDS Church's values. That statement is now no longer available online. Ignoring events that are inappropriate from the perspective of the LDS Church is common practice for the public affairs department.[145] But the relationship between the social actors

---

145 Interview with head of LDS Church public affairs Michael Otterson, June 22, 2015.

in *Sister Wives* and the LDS Church has been raised in tabloids and other news forums, some of them close to the LDS Church.[146]

This overview of the sources on which this project draws within their spaces of communication highlights the differences between similar types of documentary media. In the chapters that follow, a selection of the source material will be discussed according to distinct themes that highlight and elaborate the relationship between documentary media and religion in greater detail.

But first we turn to scholarly considerations of Mormonism. The following chapter looks at scholarly interpretations of Mormonism to demonstrate how the image of a religious community can vary according to the hermeneutic approach applied. That analysis will also provide insight into this relatively young religious tradition.

---

146 "Daughter of Famous Polygamist Family Denied Baptism," *LDS Daily* (blog), October 14, 2015, http://www.ldsdaily.com/world/daughter-of-famous-polygamist-family-denied-baptism/.

3. Shifting Perceptions of Mormons and Mormonism

Analyzing a religious community means looking at institutions, people, and practices in a specific perspective. The approach adopted for this project seeks to construct Mormonism in light of the presence of Mormons in the media. Other approaches to religious communities are, of course, also possible. The researcher constructs their subject by selecting a theoretical stance and a methodological framework. This chapter will provide an overview of diverse scholarly approaches to Mormonism, focusing on how the Mormon tradition is scrutinized, what knowledge is generated, and which aspects of Mormonism are highlighted. In addition the chapter provides the contextual frame of Mormonism for the study.

Rooted in a relatively young tradition, Mormons have been recording their history since the early days of their community. David J. Whittacker, associate professor of history at Brigham Young University, has noted that "From their beginnings, Mormons have been a record-keeping people", and proposes that "Such a documentary record must lie at the heart of any effort in Mormon studies."[147] The history of The Church of Jesus Christ of Latter-day Saints (LDS Church) has proved a rich seam for scholars with connections with the LDS. The library associated with the department of LDS Church history at Brigham Young University contains an impressive corpus of printed material about the Mormons, a historical archive, and handwritten sources of significant LDS leaders, including the letters of Brigham Young, the LDS Church president who succeeded the founder of the movement, Joseph Smith. Young influenced the Mormons' settling in Utah, particular their organization, infrastructure, politics, and economy, and he introduced officially endorsed polygamy.[148] For Whittacker, "Mormon involvement in the western American experience was one reason their history could not be ignored by American historians,"[149] but he notes that the LDS Church History School, an official LDS institution, has

---

147 David J. Whittaker, "Mormon Studies as an Academic Discipline," in *Oxford Handbook of Mormonism*, ed. Terryl L. Givens and Philip L. Barlow (New York: Oxford University Press, 2015), 92.
148 "Church History Library." Accessed April 1, 2017. "The Mission of Brigham Young University | Mission & Aims," accessed March 30, 2017, http://aims.byu.edu/.
149 Whittaker, "Mormon Studies as an Academic Discipline," 96.

Part I: The Field of Documentary and Religion

adopted a particular approach to Mormon history and that Mormons are often uncomfortable with methodologies used in religious studies that draw from sociology or cultural studies and run counter to the established Mormon model of the LDS Church History School.

A brief outline of the narrative of Mormon history will provide a helpful jumping-off point for the discussion in this chapter.[150] In 1830 Joseph Smith founded The Church of Jesus Christ in Palmyra in the state of New York. A vision is said to have guided him to golden plates, buried in the earth, on which the text of *The Book of Mormon* had been written in "reformed Egyptian" letters. Smith translated the text into English, and it became the principal scriptural foundation for the religious movement known as Mormons, which grew steadily. Persecution and discrimination forced them out of Palmyra and other locations as they searched for a safe place to settle. The migration from east to west across the North American continent continued until the "Pioneer Company" of Latter-day Saints finally arrived in Utah, and in 1849 a provisional State named Deseret was established in the Salt Lake Valley.[151] Joseph Smith had been killed, in 1844, in a violent raid and had been succeeded as president of the LDS by Brigham Young. The LDS Church settled permanently in Utah, and Salt Lake City became the new place of "gathering to Zion" for Mormons. 1852 the doctrine of plural marriage was announced publicly. In 1890, under pressure from Congress, LDS president Wilford Woodruff issued the "Manifesto", which stated that the LDS Church would no longer practice polygamy. Polygamist families now lived in secret, with some leaving for Mexico or other locations. Some members split away from the LDS to found their own church, in which plural marriage was encouraged, as is still the case today. In 1896 Utah became the 45th state. Since 1978 men of all colors and races have been able to be admitted to the priesthood, the result of a revelation of president Spencer W. Kimball. According to the LDS webpage there are more than 16 million LDS members worldwide, of whom more than 9.5 million live outside the United States. More than

---

150 Klaus J. Hansen, "Mormonism," in *Encyclopedia of Religion*, ed. Lindsay Jones, 2nd ed., vol. 9 (Detroit: Macmillan Reference USA, 2005), 6192–95; Jan Shipps, *Mormonism: The Story of a New Religious Tradition* (Urbana, Chicago: University of Illinois Press, 1987), 151–168. Shipps' chronology of 19th century Mormonism is a very helpful overview table.
151 Shipps, *Mormonism*, 162.

65,000 missionaries currently serve.[152] The LDS Church is the biggest of all the Mormon churches that claim Joseph Smith as their founder. Beside *The Book of Mormon* and other Mormon texts, Mormons also refer to the Old and the New Testament as their scripture.

3.1. Mormons in the media

Since 1898, an impressive body of literature about Mormons and the media has been published. Sherry Baker and Daniel Stout, scholars of communication active in the United States, identified five stages in the academic study of Mormons and the media:[153] 1890–1910, the so-called the bibliographic era; 1911–1950, the era of print history; 1951–1960, the years of press relations and cultural acceptance, 1961–1990, the era of interdisciplinary studies; and 1991–2000, the age of audience analysis.[154] These five categories of research overlap in part with media history more generally, in that, for example, print media was the major means of communication up until the 1950s, when television became widely popular and affordable for the average American household. Unsurprisingly, then, television was central to interdisciplinary studies. The "Mormons in the Media" bibliography contains, perhaps somewhat remarkably, 51 master's theses, mostly written at the universities of Utah and Brigham Young, with more than two-thirds (35) from the latter institution. Brigham Young University is located in Provo, in the state of Utah, and, as its name suggests, has close ties to the LDS Church, by which it was "founded, supported, and guided."[155] The numerous master's theses are indicative of the extent of LDS involvement in research in the field of Mormons and the media. Brigham Young University has been publishing the quarterly journal *BYU Studies* since 1959. On the journal's webpage, the editors explain the publication's purpose:

---

152 "Statistics and Church Facts | Total Church Membership," newsroom.churchofjesuschrist.org, accessed June 16, 2019, http://newsroom.churchofjesuschrist.org/facts-and-statistics.
153 Sherry Baker and Daniel Stout, "Mormons and the Media, 1898–2003: A Selected, Annotated, and Indexed Bibliography (with Suggestions for Future Research)," *All Faculty Publications*, January 1, 2003, http://scholarsarchive.byu.edu/facpub/1045.
154 Sherry Baker and Daniel Stout, "Mormons and the Media, 1898–2003," 127–129.
155 "The Mission of Brigham Young University | Mission & Aims," accessed March 30, 2017, http://aims.byu.edu/.

> BYU Studies is dedicated to publishing scholarly religious literature in the form of books, journals, and dissertations that is qualified, significant, and inspiring. We want to share these publications to help promote faith, continued learning, and further interest in our LDS history with those in the world who have a positive interest in this work.[156]

"Promoting faith [...] and further interest in our LDS history" – here are expressed core values evident in the content of the journal, which covers a broad spectrum of research into the LDS Church and its history, including the Church's interactions with the media.

In 2007 Sherry Baker compiled a "Mormon Media History Timeline, 1827-2007"[157] that displays how intensively and extensively the LDS Church has included media in its mission, education, and information practices. In the abstract accompanying Baker's timeline, she notes that while Mormon studies are now a recognized academic field, Mormon media studies have remained relatively neglected. Her timeline, accessible online,[158] starts in 1827, with the golden *Book of Mormon* plates that Mormons believe Joseph Smith excavated from the soil of the hills of Manchester, in New York State. Baker embraces "media" as a broad term that encompasses, for example, temple consecrations and LDS Church festivals, as well as meetings such as the annual General Conference, which can now be streamed online and is translated simultaneously into 55 languages. Such media practices help determine the LDS Church's public presence. Further means of communication are also cited, such as the introduction of the missionary and welfare programs, the family home evening, when traditionally each Mormon family gathers at home to read *The Book of Mormon* together, and key events for the globally renowned Mormon *Tabernacle Choir*.[159] *Music and Spoken Word*, which features the Mormon *Tabernacle Choir*, is the longest-running continually broadcast radio program in the

---

156 "Mission, Purpose, and History of BYU Studies. BYU Studies." Accessed March 31, 2017. https://byustudies.byu.edu/mission.
157 Baker, Sherry, "Mormon Media History Timeline, 1827–2007 | BYU Studies." Accessed March 31, 2017. https://byustudies.byu.edu/content/mormon-media-history-timeline-1827-2007.
158 Baker, Sherry, "Mormon Media History Timeline, 1827–2007 | BYU Studies," accessed March 31, 2017, https://byustudies.byu.edu/content/mormon-media-history-timeline-1827-2007. 3–7.
159 Baker, Sherry, "Mormon Media History Timeline, 1827–2007 | BYU Studies." Accessed March 31, 2017. https://byustudies.byu.edu/content/mormon-media-history-timeline-1827-2007.

United States, heard since 1929. The choir has performed at the inauguration of various US presidents, mainly Republicans, since 1965.

Baker's timeline of communication technology includes innovations like the printing press, radio, telegraph, television, satellite broadcasting, and the Internet, which are combined with events and statistics from the history of the LDS Church General Conferences, political events, membership landmarks, and relevant episodes from American history, such as the US-Mexican war of 1846–1848, when a Mormon battalion was assembled to fight for the United States.[160] Mormon media productions are also listed, with newspapers, books, radio and television stations, specific shows, public-relations activities, films, and websites. A specific perspective on the interaction of Mormons and the media is made possible by the combination of three media sectors within the timeline: (1) the adoption of new communication technologies, (2) the introduction of LDS Church media production and (3) the creation of church-owned media companies. The focus is on the LDS as an institution and its media production, with less mention made of media and the history of communication technology. The timeline indicates a methodological approach to research into the history of the LDS Church carried out by professionals who represent the LDS Church and Mormonism, with the few individuals cited almost all LDS Church presidents.

The timeline provides a helpful guide to US-American Mormon media history in the context of the LDS Church by drawing from media history. The chronological listing has marked overlap with this project in that in both instances the history of a religious tradition is scrutinized through the lens of the media. The data provided by the timeline lacks, however, contextualization or interpretation, for the timeline is intended to provide only a historical scaffolding for investigation of Mormon engagement in the media. The approach is characteristically similar to other Mormon studies of Mormon tradition. Sherry Baker is a Mormon and her media studies approach combines, as Mormon historian Whittacker suggested, with a distinctly Mormon approach to Mormon history.[161]

---

160 The battalion never had to fight because when they arrived in San Diego the war was already over. But the Mormons stayed and worked for the community as volunteers. A memorial "The Mormon Battalion" in the old town of San Diego mounted by the LDS Church remembers the presence of the Mormon soldiers.

161 Whittaker, "Mormon Studies as an Academic Discipline."

John Ben Haws' *The Mormon Image in American Mind, Fifty Years of Public Perception* (2013) a different but also distinctly Mormon view, too deals specifically with representations of Mormons in the media. His diachronic approach starts in 1968, when George W. Romney was the Republican candidate for the White House, and ends in 2012, when Mitt Romney ran for president of the United States as the Republican candidate. The author is assistant professor of LDS Church history and doctrine at Brigham Young University. Haws recognizes that people's perceptions are difficult to read, but he takes up the challenge by looking at a huge number of articles from the press and radio and television programs to analyze how Mormons and Mormonism are perceived by a broader public. Between the late 1960s and 2008 a remarkable shift from appraisal to criticism took place. Haws' evaluation of the public image of the LDS Mormons is deflating, and probably also realistic when one remembers the ambivalent perceptions of Mormon theology: "If Mormon culture and lifestyle had achieved acceptability in American society, Mormon religious beliefs, which are not so easily depicted or explained, were still clearly suspect."[162]

The most recent discussion of Mormons in the media is found in *Latter-day Screens. Gender, Sexuality & Mediated Mormonism*, by the gender and media scholar Brenda R. Weber, which draws on the manifold representations of Mormons to consider discourses of gender and sexuality.[163] Raised in an area of the United States in which Mormonism is prominent, the non-Mormon author has had numerous encounters with Mormons and Mormonism. Her exploration of Mormonism is principally concerned not with Mormons themselves but with their mediated narratives. Weber explains, "It is [...] mediated Mormonism as both an idea (meme) and a way of thinking (analytic) that beats the heart of my inquiry."[164] The book considers in detail the material, both (audio-)visual and literary, of mediated Mormonism. It adopts an analytical approach to gender and sexuality but also has a moral dimension, engaging issues of justice and equality. Its definition of relevant media is expansive: the material discussed includes books, RTV shows, advertisements on billboards and webpages, documentaries, fictional TV shows, musicals, and blogs.

---

162 John Ben Haws, *The Mormon Image in the American Mind: Fifty Years of Public Perception* (Oxford University Press, 2013), 234.
163 Brenda R. Weber, *Latter-Day Screens: Gender, Sexuality, and Mediated Mormonism* (Durham: Duke University Press, 2019).
164 Weber, 15.

3. Shifting Perceptions of Mormons and Mormonism

Weber states that mediated Mormonism and the related public conversation open up "channels for progressivism, by which I mean a pluralized, diverse, and polylogic regard toward meaning and identity."[165] This claim may seem surprising, but, the author explains, the church's criticism and rejection of feminist and intellectual positions and of homosexuality have led to its suppression of a group of educated and politically active individuals who are willing to speak out and have allies in the media sphere, which has resulted in lively media productions on precisely such topics.

The six chapters that follow the prologue consider the material, both (audio-)visual and literary, of mediated Mormonism. The first chapter discusses the figure of the missionary, which functions as both meme and analytic, as a projection of whiteness, masculinity, and sex;[166] it also addresses the concept of spiritual neoliberalism, fostered deliberately by the media. Mediated Mormonism constantly promotes management of the self and the community through surveillance that is expressed as caring.[167] The idea underlying this logic is that good choices bring good things and bad choices bring bad things, with everyone thus the architect of their own fortune in the open market.

Weber introduces the term "Mormon glow" in chapter two, used to refer to a specific personal appearance with racial and gendered implications. "Mormonism as a visual spectacle," she writes, "indicates that as a meme, it marks something extraordinary."[168] The Mormon glow combines a phenotype with media spectacle, signifying a racialized habitus that refers to "spiritual purity, whiteness, boundless energy, and limitless success."[169]

Chapters three and four focus on conflicting mediated versions of polygamy. The first version concerns progressive polygamy stories, as found in TV shows. The second version concerns "narratives of victimization and rescue",[170] and here Weber looks, for example, at the criminal activities and excesses of the self-proclaimed prophet of the FLDS group, Warren Jeffs. Weber explores how the media provide an opportunity for suppressed women to make their traumatic stories public, but she also highlights how media representations communicate polygamy as an open

---

165 Weber, 19.
166 Weber, 52.
167 Weber, 57.
168 Weber, 94.
169 Weber, 115.
170 Weber, 163.

secret and connect the story of Joseph Smith with the activities of Warren Jeffs, an association that will likely not amuse the LDS church.

Chapters five and six address Mormon feminist housewives and gay Mormons respectively. Deconstructing the term "toxic femininity," Weber notes how the imperative of Mormon women defined by male desire and male demands is fostered by the media. Additionally, the text addresses the tensions surrounding queer practices and Mormonism as represented in the media. The F/LDS controls non-normative intimacy, which covers not just homosexual relationships but also polygamy and premarital sex. The required self-regulation in Mormonism, which is combined with the stance that Mormons can feel forbidden desire but must not act on it, feeds a media landscape full of Mormon sex stories, as the author notes.

The combination of theory, historical and social context, and media analysis drives the argument forward effectively and demonstrates convincingly how the media can be read as a meme and a way of thinking, With its informative and enriching contextualization of its sources, *Latter-day Screens. Gender, Sexuality & Mediated Mormonism* provides an effective critical reading of Mormon media sources while also functioning as an innovative approach to Mormonism.

Mormon theology remains a topic favored in the media, where it receives both critical and uncritical appraisal and has inspired both fictional and documentary productions. Approaches that engage the period from the late 20th century up to the present day remain the exception within Mormon studies, where the early history of the church and its community are far more likely to be encountered, as we shall see.

3.2. Telling the story of Mormonism

Several published works have been focused on Mormons, with all of them concerned with the LDS, the largest grouping. These books might use the term "Mormon" or "Mormonism" in their title, a term that splitter groups also claim, but the focus of their discussion is usually the LDS. Yet all Mormons, be they from the dominant LDS Church, the Community of Christ (formerly known as the Reorganized Church of Jesus Christ of Latter-day Saints, RLDS), The Apostolic United Brethren (AUB), the Fundamental Latter-day Saints (FLDS), the Council of Friends, or any other Mormon splitter group, share an early history that starts with Joseph Smith's epiphany with the angel Moroni, which showed him the golden plates in the hills of Nauvoo from which he translated *The Book of Mormon*. Their narratives diverge only at the point when they split from what would prove to be mainstream Mormonism.[171]

The publications adopt various strategies in engaging Mormonism, as is evident when we compare how they represent, analyze, and describe the Mormons, their history, theology, practices, politics, culture, community, and social life. To discern the publication just by the binary categories of "written by a Mormon" or "written by a non-Mormon" seems too narrow[172]. Rather contextualization and evaluation of these approaches demonstrates how different pictures of a single group can be generated according to how religion is described, which sources are selected, the author's hermeneutic horizons, the theory tested, and the methods applied. This discussion of relevant academic books about Mormonism pursues three objectives: (1) to establish how a religious tradition is reconstructed in scholarly work, (2) to expand knowledge of Mormonism that eschews a homogeneous image of its manifold histories, and (3) to flesh out definitions, concepts, and debates in Mormon studies that are crucial for this project.

From religious movement to institutionalized Mormonism

That this discussion will start with Thomas Francis O'Dea's (1915–1974) monograph *The Mormons* (1957) is almost a given.[173] O'Dea's study is still considered authoritative and is frequently cited. Although now almost six decades old, remarkably his conclusions seem still apposite, despite the changing times. O'Dea, who was Roman Catholic, was a scholar of the sociology of religion; he received his doctorate from Harvard and taught at the University of Utah from 1959 to 1964. A number of comparisons of Catholicism and Mormonism appear in his study.

---

171 One important moment in Mormon history was the end of the practice of polygamy in 1890. Many families didn't follow the new policy and founded a new congregation. See O. Kendall White and Daryl White, "Polygamy and Mormon Identity," *Journal of American Culture* 28, no. 2 (June 2005): 165–77; Richard S. Van Wagoner, *Mormon Polygamy: A History* (Salt Lake City, Utah: Signature Books, 1986), 177–218; J. Gordon Melton, *Melton's Encyclopedia of American Religions*, 8th ed. (Detroit: Gale, Cengage Learning, 2009), 646–651.
172 Hansen, "Mormonism," 6195.
173 Thomas Francis O'Dea, *The Mormons*, 8th ed. (Chicago: University of Chicago Press, 1975).

O'Dea was raised in Massachusetts and lived for six months in a rural Mormon village. Trained as a sociologist, in the preface to his work he places himself within the text: "Whatever astigmatism this book may reveal it cannot be attributed to a lack of first hand acquaintance, for I have tried to supplement the necessary library research with as much living experience as possible."[174] And he explicitly describes his interpretative approach as non-Mormon:

> This book is a study of the Mormons by a non-Mormon. It is an attempt to say what Mormonism is as a religious movement and to explore what conditions and events, what kind of human decisions and efforts, have made it that. Moreover it sets forth the religious world view of the Mormons, showing what Mormons believe and how they see the world, as well as the relationship of this world view to the conditions of life under which Mormonism originated and developed. Finally, it tries to point up particular problems and dilemmas that have attended the Mormon development.[175]

Mormon history is crucial to his work. O'Dea discussed Mormon self-understanding in the 1950s, so contemporaneous with the work, noting how their history defined the challenges Mormons faced in adapting to social change. He looked, for example, at the Mormon experience of strong community, from the first days in New York State to settling in Utah in the mid 19th century. And he reflected on the consequences of statehood, and on the impact of secular modernity in the mid 20th century.

The author further interprets the LDS Church and its politics by looking at social influences and the behavior that has stemmed from the Church's worldview. The Mormons are powerfully guided by their idea of an ideal community, in which the strong support the weak and income beyond basic needs – in earlier times mostly in material form – is consigned to the church. In the context of the Mormon journey from New York State, through several intermediate stations, and then finally to Utah (as Zion), and in light of the early settlement that then took shape, a strategy of extensive communal co-operation was very successful. But after Utah became a state and was admitted to the Union, O'Dea proposed, the Mor-

---

174 O'Dea, viii.
175 O'Dea, vii.

mons became more conservative in outlook, "peculiar"[176] instead of innovative. The building of Zion was postponed. O'Dea comments on that shift, "Accommodation and withdrawal from social experimentation were part of the general trend toward conservatism that seemed to characterize Mormon leadership."[177] Co-operative endeavors in the Mormon community continued only in education and recreation. Caring for its own poor remained a concern of the LDS Church, which established its welfare plan in 1936, and poverty was reduced to a minimum.

From the beginning the LDS Church had placed great emphasis upon education.[178] The Church's seminary program, described as a "worldwide, four-year religious educational program for youth ages 14 through 18,"[179] serves to accommodate, teach, and accompany young Mormons educated outside Utah, so not in strongly Mormon contexts. The lavish investment in such education might be later returned in tithing "although this is not, of course, the motivation of the church", O'Dea stressed;[180] this strategy was designed in response to the threat of apostasy seemingly inherent in a Mormon's encounter with secular education.

For O'Dea the LDS Church's struggles to adapt to secular society were of central import. The chapter "Sources of Strain and Conflict"[181] focuses on the LDS Church's problematic relationship with learning and independent thought. O'Dea contended that the LDS Church was failing to meet the needs of the young Mormon intellectuals who questioned theological concepts as a result of reading the scriptures and adapting them to their present, challenging standard literal readings and a doctrine based on divine revelation:

> As this theology is literal and fundamentalist, the liberal can choose only between submission and personal disquietude or apostasy and

---

176 J. Spencer Fluhman, *A Peculiar People: Anti-Mormonism and the Making of Religion in Nineteenth-Century America* (Chapel Hill: University of North Carolina Press, 2012); Mark T. Decker and Michael Austin, *Peculiar Portrayals: Mormons on the Page, Stage and Screen* (Utah State University Press, 2010). Mormons call themselves peculiar in order to mark the difference between them and the others. This demarcation line also alludes how Jews historically had been called.
177 O'Dea, *The Mormons*, 216.
178 O'Dea, 224–227.
179 "LDS Seminary is a Global, Four-Year Religious Educational Program for Youth," www.mormonnewsroom.org, April 12, 2013, http://www.mormonnewsroom.org/topic/seminary.
180 O'Dea, *The Mormons*, 228.
181 O'Dea, 222–257.

suffering the guilt of deserting the tradition in which he has been reared and to which he feels great attachment.[182]

The LDS Church leaders sought to fight apostasy by its intellectuals with fundamentalist theology; a liberal theology would destroy the theological foundations of their legitimation. O'Dea proposed that one solution to this dilemma was that beyond the essential articles of doctrine, non-literal interpretation might be permitted.[183]

Mormon intellectuals can find themselves in a difficult situation: the tradition to which they are connected has traditionally been led by layman, who are often authoritarian, with no traditional theological education. They lack the academic education in theology and philosophy that might help guide the LDS Church through the challenges of modern secular thought. O'Dea was clear this was a problem: "In term of theology, the LDS Church is not only governed by laymen but also by amateurs."[184] The principle of seniority augmented the problem, for then as today the most powerful positions within the LDS Church were usually occupied by older and more conservative men. Today too, although LDS Church leaders may well be professionals in some field, they are not trained in philosophy and theology. For example, the former LDS Church president (2008–2018), Thomas S. Monson (1927–2018), studied business management at the University of Utah and his successor Russel M. Nelson (*1924) was a heart surgeon. Overall, this chapter in O'Dea's work provides a refreshing look at Mormonism of the 20th century, noting references to history, community life, worldview, and theology made as the Mormons tackled the challenges of settling in Utah.

The concept of the ideal society has continued as a factor in Mormon self-conception, and as a motivation. O'Dea argued that Mormon history had done much to shape the contemporary economic and social attitudes of the LDS Church and its members. In its early days Mormons held to the United Order, a system of communalism founded on the Law of Consecration. Each family was to contribute the surplus of its production to the community, keeping only what it needed. Members would thus support those who had less and at the same time build up the LDS Church's own resources. The law was not enacted for later LDS communities – although it was and is still applied by some splinter groups, like the FLDS – but in

---

182 O'Dea, 234.
183 O'Dea, 234.
184 O'Dea, 230.

the LDS, O'Dea suggested, it was still understood as the ideal of communal life, to be achieved eventually.[185] In 1841 tithing was adopted and continues to be practiced as the substitute for co-operative economic activity.

O'Dea proposed that economic achievements during settlement were founded in Mormon ideals of community. He highlighted the example of the irrigation of Utah as evidence of how a strong sense of community had made productive farming possible – mining was avoided on ideological grounds[186] – even in a difficult environment.[187] The Mormons developed co-operative techniques that allowed them to control the water supply for Salt Lake City and the villages of the Great Basin.[188] In the villages, groups worked together to construct and maintain the irrigation system. The use of water was restricted to those who invested in the system and was allocated according to need. The efficient irrigation of Utah led to the establishment of permanent co-operative institutions. Today these irrigation companies often continue to maintain and control the water supply in Utah. While mutual concern remained a reality in the LDS Church, this ideal of co-operative social groupings came to end, O'Dea proposed, when Utah gained statehood in 1896.

> Working together, often under central direction, group loyalty, self-sufficiency and independence, aid to the needy and mutual help – these remained constant features of Mormon activities and ideals. After 1890 the tendency to experiment with social forms, familial or economic, was curtailed. In-time, co-operative institutions declined.[189]

The approach O'Dea adopted in his book has two principal themes: (1) the LDS Church's history, from the launching of a religious movement to its institutionalization and (2) the building of community, and that community's responses to economic, social, cultural, and political forces that shaped Mormonism up until the 1950s. He leaves his reader with an understanding of the tensions within the movement in his own time, so in the 1950s. His focus on economy, theology, and politics constructs a consistent and comprehensible narrative of the LDS Church within the

---

185 O'Dea, 196.
186 The early Mormon society was based on farming, an idea of a public welfare and communality. Mining didn't fall in this category.
187 O'Dea, *The Mormons*, 198.
188 O'Dea, 201.
189 O'Dea, 215.

Part I: The Field of Documentary and Religion

American context; Mormonism was not yet a global phenomenon when O'Dea was writing his book.

Mormonism as a new religious tradition

The second book that had a huge impact on Mormon studies is Jan Shipps' *Mormonism: The Story of a New Religious Tradition*.[190] Shipps drew on historical sources to suggests that Mormonism be defined as an innovation, "the new religious tradition" of her subtitle:

> Latter-day Saints of every stripe are heirs of a radical restoration. Their forebears entered into a new age in much the same way that the Saints of early Christianity entered into a new age. In so doing the Latter-day Saints started over, not to reform the institutions of Christendom but to participate in a transformation which in its totality has now made Mormonism into a distinct, discrete, internally consistent religious tradition.[191]

Shipps bases her claim on the radicality of Mormon religion:

> It is important to note the difference between radical restoration movements, which make possible new beginnings in all the dimensions of religion – mythological, doctrinal, ritual, social, and experiential – and restoration movements, which, through processes of reformation, reinterpretation, and reintegration, revitalize religious traditions.[192]

Mormon scholars have tended to adopt Shipp's definition of Mormonism as a new religious tradition, but her definition of Mormonism as not Christian has attracted fierce criticism by Mormons and the leaders of the LDS church.[193] In contrast Mormon scholar Terryl L. Givens doesn't really understand the problem if Mormons are not perceived as Christians:

> [S]ince Mormons tend to endorse the view of Jan Shipps, who has written that Mormons have the same relationship to Christianity that

---

190 Shipps, *Mormonism*.
191 Shipps, 85.
192 Shipps, 91.
193 The Church of Jesus Christ of Latter Day Saints, "Are Mormons Christian?," accessed November 12, 2017, /topics/christians; Stephen E. Robinson, *Are Mormons Christians?* (Deseret Book, 2010).

early Christians had to Judaism. And this without seeming to realize that, at some point, early Christians stopped being offended when they were no longer considered Jewish.[194]

Shipps (*1929) introduces herself in her work as a non-Mormon and a Methodist.[195] She lived in Utah, an experience recounted in her second book, *Sojourner in the Promised Land: Forty Years among the Mormons*,[196] a collection of essays.[197] She lays claims to an insider perspective that every Mormon can share:

> A disadvantage of this manner of proceeding is its tendency to make my argument appear somewhat apologetic at times – an irony since I am not a Mormon – but that disadvantage is far out weighted by the effective means this stylistic strategy provided for reconstructing the picture of early Mormonism as perceived from the inside, a reconstruction that is crucial to the illumination of parallel patterns of development in early Christianity and Mormonism.[198]

An academic historian, Shipps is professor emeritus of history and religious studies at Indiana University-Purdue University Indianapolis. Focused on historic texts, the book provides an insightful look at how Mormonism has adapted and been transformed over time. Shipps' comparative approach is less concerned with the contemporary LDS Church than with its history and historical context. The argument is not limited, however, to the history of Mormonism in America, for it includes deliberations about the theory and methods that have allowed her to define Mormonism as a religious tradition. Shipps aimed to distinguish between the text source and her act of interpretation, for which she recognizes the implications of her not being a Mormon. She states that the present study is hermeneutic as well as historic: "It is filled with historical data, but because Mormon history itself is treated as text and subjected to interpretive analysis, it is as hermeneutic as it is historical."[199]

---

194 Terryl L. Givens, *People of Paradox: A History of Mormon Culture* (Oxford University Press, 2007), 58.
195 Shipps, *Mormonism*, xviii.
196 Jan Shipps, *Sojourner in the Promised Land: Forty Years among the Mormons* (Urbana: University of Illinois Press, 2000).
197 Shipps.
198 Shipps, *Mormonism*, xvii.
199 Shipps, x.

Mormonism, according to Shipps, has a tripartite foundation comprising prophetic figure, scripture, and experience – specifically, Joseph Smith, *The Book of Mormon*, and the corporate life of the early saints.[200] The transformations of Mormonism through time are typical of the experiences of religious traditions as they are established and become defined. Shipps explains her characterization of religious tradition as follows:

> Because the word religion is so general that it is difficult to use in a definite or precise sense, religious tradition will here be used as the umbrella category that will cover (I) all the corporate bodies and (II) individuals unattached to corporate bodies in whose systems of belief a particular story is central.[201]

The comparison of Christianity and Mormonism is key to the book's argument. For Shipps "the Mormon story is merely an idiosyncratic interpretation of the Christian story."[202] Her central contention is that Mormons have reshaped the vision of the Old and New Testaments just as the early Christian community consolidated and reshaped Israel's history. Shipps notes differences between the Mormon scriptures and the Old and New Testaments:

> As opposed to the Christian canon, which includes four narrative accounts proclaiming and interpreting the life of Jesus, plus an additional narrative covering the early years of Christianity, the only narrative description of early Latter-day Saint history is a personal account of the prophet's life in the years before the organization of the church. Smith's revelations are, in a manner of speaking, primary source materials for Mormon history, but they do not tell the Mormon story in chronological or any other systematic fashion.[203]

Mormon history is therefore an open canon. Shipps is well versed in Christian history and its scriptures; which enables the comparison with Mormon history and scriptures. Her analysis of how and by whom Mormon history has been researched and written, and thus how it has been defined, is instructive and illuminating. The Correlation Committee of the LDS Church scrutinizes historical material and compares it with existing authorized interpretation. Shipps comments,

---

200 Shipps, xiii.
201 Shipps, 46.
202 Shipps, 47.
203 Shipps, 88.

For the most part, this body works so quietly and efficiently that the effectiveness with which the LDS Church continues to control its own history is truly surprising, given the size and energy of the scholarly body, whose members pursue the study of LDS history outside of and independent from connections with either the LDS or RLDS churches.[204]

The circumstances surrounding the history written by Lucy Mack Smith, Joseph Smith's mother, is a case in point, and was particularly significant as Mack Smith's work is the only source for Smith's early life. Shipps reconstructs the struggle over the publications of that manuscript when some leading members of the LDS Church, including Brigham Young, Joseph Smith's successor as leader, did not agree with the content. In light of invasive revisions, Shipps deems the final published manuscript in 1853[205] to be "marginally authentic."[206] This example shows how LDS Church leaders have always wanted to be in charge of their past, a particular concern of the second LDS president Brigham Young, who was president for three decades, until his death in 1877. The LDS Church has remained involved in crafting its own history, and it also controls how Mormon history is researched, written, and published.

Further comparisons between Christianity and Mormonism are drawn in Shipps' argument. She proposes that like early Christianity, Mormonism is a *radical* restoration movement that believes there is a single truth, with which believers enter collectively into a new world. Shipps analyses such movements by scrutinizing how the faithful transform restoration claims into objective facts and principles. She identifies the radicality of such restoration in its totality, in its encompassing, as we have seen, the mythological, doctrinal, ritual, social, and experiential. In its comprehensiveness Mormonism differs, she suggests, from other restoration movements of the 19th century. When, at the end of 19th century, Mormons as corporate body were included in the Union, new boundaries needed to be defined.[207] From then on, Mormons lived as "peculiar" people in a sacred time and space, distancing themselves from the rest of society. Previously, polygamy had been a way to enter into the kingdom. With

---

204 Shipps, 89.
205 The title of the manuscript was Joseph Smith, the Prophet: Biographical Sketches of Joseph Smith, the Prophet, and His Progenitors for Many Generations, by Lucy Smith, Mother of the Prophet (Shipps, 100).
206 Shipps, *Mormonism*, 95.
207 Shipps, 67–86.

Part I: The Field of Documentary and Religion

that means of being present in sacred time and space now outlawed, other rituals were introduced in order to be able to enter into sacredness in the ordinary – the baptism of the dead carried out in profane time, for example.[208]

Shipps then looks at Mormonism at the beginning of the 20th century. She explains, for example, the function and aim of the original General Conference,[209] how it changed over time as the community grew, and how electronic devices have supported its transmission. And as already mentioned, she raises the critical and delicate question of whether Mormons are Christians. This issue remains contentious, ferociously debated in particular by Mormons and evangelical Christians. Shipps recognizes that Mormons perceive themselves as Christians.[210] Her own decided opinion is a product of her argument that Mormonism is a radical restoration movement and therefore a new religious tradition. In the conclusion to her work, she states that because of their specific radical restoration history, Mormons cannot be deemed Christians. But, she proposes, Mormonism can be understood as a form of "corporate Christianity."

> If the key concepts of saving knowledge of Jesus Christ and the importance of temple ordinances are kept in mind as the address is considered, it becomes very clear that Mormonism is a form of corporate Christianity. While it perceives of itself as Christian, Mormonism differs from traditional Christianity in much the same fashion that traditional Christianity, in its ultimate emphasis on the individual, came to differ from Judaism.[211]

The term "corporate Christianity" is vaguely defined, perhaps in an attempt to bring a moderation to the discussion. According to Shipps, the difference between Mormonism and Christianity is the equivalent of the distinction between Judaism and Christianity. In four points she summa-

---

208 Baptisms of the death are conducted in the temple in the room with the font with Salomon's twelve oxen that is found in every Mormon temple on the ground floor. LDS members baptize as proxies death members of the family to include them into the eternal family. The ritual provides a reassuring effect to the performers.
209 At the General Conference, held semi-annually (April, October) in Salt Lake City, members of the LDS Church gather to hear the president, the counsellors and other LDS Church leaders speak on faith issues and church organisation. The two-day event is broadcast on TV and radio in over 90 languages. The conference center seats 21'000 participants.
210 Shipps, *Mormonism*, 148.
211 Shipps, 148.

rizes concisely why Mormonism must be considered a new religious tradition:[212]
1. The goal of Mormonism is eternal progression towards godhood.
2. Salvation depends on knowing Christ.
3. True knowledge is knowledge deemed legitimate by the LDS Church.
4. The unit of exaltation is the family.

Those four points also make evident why she believes Mormons cannot be considered Christians. Godhood in eternity, legitimation by the LDS institution, and the exaltation of the family unit are not part of a Christian worldview. The only intersection with Christianity is in deeming acceptance of Christ as necessary for salvation, but even there a sharp distinction is evident, for Mormons believe they will become Christ-like Gods in their eternal afterlife.

Shipps' theoretical and methodological approach is situated in the comparative history of religion, focusing on a comparison of early Christianity and early Mormonism. Her sources are mainly historical texts. Much emphasis is placed on the differences between *The Book of Mormon* and the Old and New Testament and on the historical contexts of early Mormonism and early Christianity. Shipps' aim is to claim persuasively that Mormonism cannot be deemed Christian; it is, she proposes, a new religious tradition.

3.3. Mormon theology, ethics and worldview

Comparative elements in Mormonism and Christianity often play a role in guides to Mormonism. In his *Introduction to Mormonism* (2003), Douglas James Davies (*1947) places particular emphasis on Mormon theology, ethics, and worldview, explaining Mormon rituals in the context of doctrine.[213]

Davies is professor of the study of religion in the department of theology and religion at the University of Durham, with a particular interest in death studies. In the introduction, this author, too, highlights that he is a non-Mormon: "it is important for the reader to know that the author is

---

212 Shipps, 149.
213 Douglas James Davies, *An Introduction to Mormonism* (Cambridge: Cambridge University Press, 2003).

not and never has been a member of The Church of Jesus Christ of Latter-day Saints or any other restoration movement."[214]

Davies' introductory work is less a historic account of Mormonism and more a systematic study highlighting and analyzing elements that are constitutive of Mormonism, with a focus on rituals and doctrine. Where Shipps comparison is historical, Douglas considers the characteristics of each movement's scriptures, proposing:

> If there is no division within *The Book of Mormon* analogous to the Bible's Old and New Testaments, it is because the Bible is not a Christological document from beginning to end, even though some Christians do interpret what they call the Old Testament to make it appear so. *The Book of Mormon*, by contrast, is much more of a unity and is Christologically driven; indeed it can be read as an example of narrative theology with Christ present from beginning to end.[215]

Davies focuses on the LDS Church's sacred texts, epics, and revelations as primary sources for Mormon theology, with its concept of God and humankind, but he also includes works by other authors that are widely acknowledged by Mormon leaders. He looks in particular at "the crucial temple rituals of endowments, marriage and baptism for the dead, through which human beings may achieve their divine potential." His approach seeks, he suggests, "neither to prove nor to disprove the truthfulness of the religious claims of that faith but rather to describe them in ways that non-Mormons can understand."[216]

History and practice are revealing for Davies, for, he notes, "[b]elief affects ritual and ritual affects belief."[217] As he looks at the relationship between theology and history, Davies suggests that Mormonism has not (yet) developed a theology like that of many other Christian denominations, largely because Mormon theological practice is founded in past revelation and in the words of the living prophet in the present, "both of which constrain the exploratory tendencies of theologians in other churches. What Mormonism has come to possess is a relatively large group of historians who are sometimes thought to substitute for theologians, but that is only partially true."[218] It may indeed be only partially the case, but any substitu-

---

214 Davies, 7.
215 Davies, 59.
216 Davies, I.
217 Davies, 5.
218 Davies, 2.

tion of historians for theologians is noteworthy. A similar claim was made by Shipps when she wrote of the powerful LDS Church historians who control the Church's past.[219] While intersections of theology and history are to be expected, other faiths have a dependence on theology – for the exegesis of religious texts in the context of a belief system – that is absent for the Mormons. Davies sees LDS doctrine and the connected forms of ritual falling into two styles of religiosity: Protestant millenarian Mormonism and symbolic temple Mormonism. [220]

With a concise approach, Davies explains the Mormon religious worldview and, in particular, Mormon theology in such detail that his work is unique within the genre of introductory studies of Mormonism. His approach to Mormon beliefs as prophetic imaginations within specific social circumstances might not appeal to Mormons. He summarizes Mormon theology in light of the elements of vision, plan, and church, noting that "Through specific rites performed in temples married Saints are provided with the means of conquering death and pursuing an eternal existence in which they, themselves become Gods."[221] Marrying, having children, and following strictly the Mormon commandments will result in the individual becoming a God in the afterlife, surrounded by their sacred family. The husband is the leader of the family in heaven too, and his wife becomes a Goddess. Mormon theology, Davies proposes, is a cosmology that tackles the concept of God, the relation between God and human beings, and the reason for human existence.

Davies brings a systematization to Mormon theology that other scholars have found too great a challenge. Doctrinal analysis and comparison based on texts is very enlightening and, as this study reveals, can be engaged by a non-Mormon. But how can a non-Mormon analyze ritual that they have not seen? Davies circumvents this potential obstacle elegantly by concentrating on the theological meaning of rituals. In so doing, he provides much insight into Mormon theology.

3.4. Mormonism as a new world faith

The monograph *The Rise of Mormonism* (2005) by Rodney Stark (*1934), with an introduction by Reid L Neilson, followed close on the heels of

---

219 Shipps, *Mormonism*, 89.
220 Davies, *An Introduction to Mormonism*, 6.
221 Davies, 4.

Davies' work.[222] Stark is a US-American sociologist of religion with a Lutheran background and hence non-Mormon. Neilson considers Stark's earlier article "The Rise of a New World Faith",[223] published in 1984, with its projections of LDS membership numbers. Stark had considered the whole span from 1830 to 1980, and established the rate of increase in each decade; by the 1980 that figure was somewhere in the 30 percent to 50 percent range.[224] In his study Stark then projected numbers up to 2100. If the growth rate is maintained, Mormons will form one of the six biggest religious communities worldwide, with a projected 601,781,268 members at the highest und 108,004,354 members as the lowest estimate (the two figures are the product of statistical probabilities).

The earlier article had concentrated on the projection itself; in the later book Stark draws on those numbers to ask why Mormons are flourishing more than other religious communities. A sociological approach allows rational choice theory to be applied and the results discussed in detail in the context of conversion.[225] Stark also takes a comparative approach, in particular in considering the idea of family in the religious traditions of Islam, Christianity, and Judaism.[226]

As a whole Stark's work tackles the question of why LDS Church growth is outpacing other American religions at home and abroad. Stark argues that people dispose of a religious capital, which they guard carefully, and asks about the circumstances under which they are drawn to invest that capital in Mormonism. He describes the reasons for Mormon success as follows:

> Latter-day Saints often retain cultural continuity with the conventional faiths of the societies in which they seek converts; their doctrines are non empirical; they maintain a medium level of tension with their surrounding environment; they have legitimate leaders with adequate authority to be effective; they generate a highly motivated, volunteer religious labour force, including many willing to proselytize; they maintain a level of fertility sufficient to offset member mortality; they compete against weak, local, conventional religious organizations within a relatively unregulated religious economy; they sustain strong internal

---

222 Rodney Stark, *The Rise of Mormonism*, ed. Reid Larkin Neilson (New York: Columbia University Press, 2005).
223 5/18/2020 12:08:00 PM
224 Stark, 22.
225 Shipps, *Mormonism*, 57.
226 Stark, *The Rise of Mormonism*, 46–53.

attachments while remaining an open social network, able to maintain and form ties to outsiders; they maintain sufficient tension with their environment; they remain sufficiently strict; and they socialize their young sufficiently well as to minimize both defection and the appeal of reduced strictness. How could they not succeed?[227]

This discussion is taken further. Stark notes that Mormonism has more converts than cradle Mormons,[228] and using Mormons as a case study, he formulates 14 rational choice premises that result in conversion.[229] Thus, for example, if missionaries make contact with an individual on the street then the probability that the individual will convert is small; conversion is far more likely, happening in one third of cases, when the individual is engaged in a private space generated by friends or other family members.[230]

Stark traces the success of Mormonism to its reliance on revelation and formulates twelve theses for when revelation, broadly framed, happens.[231] Revelation describes the state in which individuals know what God asks from them. That experience requires a culture than holds to a communicative relationship with God, a culture that Stark suggests is found in the United States. Additionally, reception of God's message is eased by having contact with a "role-model, with someone who has had such communications."[232] The most fruitful place for revelatory activity is the family unit. Family has been key to Mormonism since its beginnings, with families providing a network of faith. Members' commitment is evident in the extensive tithing the LDS Church encourages – on that score Mormons are the most financially giving religious community per capita in the United States, with 48 percent of the membership contributing more than $2000 in 2004, a figure reached by only 2 percent of Catholics, 3 percent of liberal Protestants, and 14 percent of conservative Protestants.[233]

For Stark the success of the LDS runs counter to the secularization thesis:

> By now it must be evident to all but the most devoted ideologues that the thunderous religious activities taking place around the world are

---

227 Stark, 137.
228 Stark, 136.
229 Stark, 63–70.
230 Stark, 81/82.
231 Stark, 35–56.
232 Stark, 35.
233 Stark, 92.

not dying spasms but are the lusty choruses of revival and the uproar caused by the outbreak of new faiths.[234]

New religious movements arise as traditional religions lose members, suggesting that the secularization thesis is not so much wrong as only partially right. Modernization has given religious groups new strategies of circulation in the market place. Stark sees religious institutions increasingly integrated such that the distinction between LDS Church and society disappears, an argument that bears comparison with the suggestion in the introduction to this study that religion as expressed through the media has become something of a lifestyle because the coherence of traditional values is missing. When the choice is between sports activities, socializing with friends, and attending LDS Church, then religion has become a leisure-time activity.[235] Mormons have prospered even within a modern and secularized society. Indeed for Stark, "The more *secularized* the society, the *greater the success of new religions* – of cult movements that represent an *unconventional religious tradition*."[236] Stark describes Mormonism as a cult, a description that the Mormons have sought to eliminate through public-affairs initiatives, the costly image campaign *I'm a Mormon* from 2010, billboards, and many television commercials.[237]

In his chapter entitled "The Rise of a New World Faith"[238] Stark notes that religious theory has often been designed to explain why religions decline, but a case study of the Mormons requires we consider why a religious group has grown so significantly. To that end he has analyzed both quantitative data and qualitative materials from diverse sources. Stark's sociological approach to Mormonism provides an original and insightful point of access to a religious community that is hard to pin down theologically. Having projected his statistical data to identify future trends, he addresses issues of revelation, conversion, religious capital, rational choice, and the success of a religious community. Despite the detail, the discussion still contains a degree of speculation, in particular in the case of the debate over rational choice, a debate certainly worth having, but one that provides a one-sided view of human rationality. Overall, however, this sociographic approach proves innovative and rich, and particularly rewarding when applied to an unusually successful religious community.

---

234 Stark, 98.
235 See chapter 1.1, part I in the current book.
236 Stark, *The Rise of Mormonism*, 101.
237 See chapter 4, part II in the current book.
238 Stark, *The Rise of Mormonism*, 139–146.

3.5. The universal but different ethnic culture of Mormonism

In his 2007 monograph *People of Paradox: A History of Mormon Culture*, Terryl L. Givens asks: What is unique in Mormon cultural expression, and how do Mormon history and theology influence Mormon artistic production?[239] These questions carry two presumptions, that Mormons are associated with a unique artistic production and that this production is influenced by their history and theology. Givens (*1957) is professor of English, literature and religion at the University of Richmond with a particular interest in literary theory, British and European romanticism, Mormon studies, and intellectual history. He is the co-editor of the *Oxford Handbook of Mormonism*[240] and a practicing Mormon. The purpose of the study is described as

> to plumb in tentative fashion the range of Mormonism's intellectual and artistic productions, to see if one can find there the contours of consistent themes and preoccupations, a unity between theological foundations and history, on the one hand, and cultural production, on the other.[241]

For Givens there are four Mormon paradoxes.[242] The first concerns the authority of the prophets that is in tension with the idea that each member has the right to receive revelations. The second paradox is located between secure spiritual knowledge about the deity on one side and the eternal quest for saving knowledge and the burden of an endlessly sought perfection on the other. The third paradox describes Mormon life in sacred time, and is evident "in the recurrent invasion of the banal into the realm of the holy and the infusion of the sacred into the realm of the quotidian."[243] And finally the author looks at the paradox of the intertwining of exile and integration within Mormonism and a gospel viewed as both American and universal.[244] Givens' study is in two parts, covering the beginnings of Mormon history until 1890 in the first, and from 1890 until present in the second. The year 1890 is often seen as a tipping point in Mormon history, as the year when polygamy was abandoned and the LDS Church adopted the

---

239 Givens, *People of Paradox*.
240 Terryl Givens, *The Oxford Handbook of Mormonism* (New York: Oxford University Press, 2015).
241 Givens, *People of Paradox*, vii–viii.
242 Givens, xiv–xvi.
243 Givens, xv.
244 Givens, xv.

Part I: The Field of Documentary and Religion

goal of attaining statehood for Utah. For Givens, Mormonism is an essentially American religion because American and Mormon culture and history are "imperceptibly fused."[245]

A member of the LDS, Givens hopes that Mormon artists and intellectuals will facilitate the transition of Mormonism into a truly international faith.[246] These first three chapters are somewhat introductory in character, seeming in effect to explain essential elements of Mormonism for non-Mormons, noting, for example, that Mormons are aware of the tension that arises from being excluded from being defined as Christian and at the same time wanting to be different.

The study examines many Mormon sources of cultural production. Mormons invested in education, including languages and natural science, from their earliest days, fostering the education of women, men, and children. Givens also addresses Mormon architecture, suggesting that in the early years of Mormonism whole cities were built to represent Zion, but that once Utah had achieved statehood, Mormons started to build Zion in their homes and reduced their sacred buildings to temples rather than entire communities.[247] A shift is also identified in music and dance, which had been very much enjoyed until all efforts became focused on the *Tabernacle Choir*, the internationally renowned Mormon flagship. Here the author compares the Mormons to the Puritans in drawing a line between themselves and others by promoting or prohibiting practices disallowed or welcomed in other cultures.

Givens looks also at the significance of theatrical performance. Mormons, he suggests, always look for a positive message in theatre and music whereby a contented present and joyful eternity are represented and defended.[248] Outdoor spectacles have been and remain very popular. Popular pageants have an evangelizing potential, and "as the country's largest and oldest outdoor drama is America's nearest equivalent to Germany's passion play at Oberammergau."[249] The comparison with the German passion play with its first performance in 1634 highlights the success of the Mormon pageant and implicitly relates Mormon pageants to the Christian tradition. Mormonism has a specific literature. Givens stresses Mormons' biblical lit-

---

245 Givens, 61.
246 Givens, xvi.
247 Givens, 115.
248 Givens, 144–156.
249 Givens, 267. The *Hill Cumorah* pageant is one among several successful Mormon productions. Since 1937 it takes place annually in Palmyra/NY and tells the story of Joseph Smith and The Book of Mormon.

3. Shifting Perceptions of Mormons and Mormonism

eracy, with the English of the King James translation of the Bible deemed holy language.[250] He also highlights that via the Relief Society and its magazine, female authors took firm root in the Mormon literary tradition. Painting was not part of the early movement, but from the late 19th century Mormon painters turned in particular to depicting Mormon history.

Broadcast media are also a focus for Givens, whose emphasis is principally on the achievements and positive effects of Mormon media production. In the chapter "'Cinema as Sacrament': Theater and Film"[251] the content of successful Mormon movies is discussed. In producing their own films, Mormons are able to ensure that the depiction is in keeping with the moral standards upheld by the LDS Church, which may well not be the case when the same narrative is filmed by others. Independent filmmaking enables an alternative to Hollywood productions deemed too explicit in their portrayal of sex, drugs, and alcohol and in their use of crude language. Two genres are highlighted as cultural markers: comedy and missionary films. *The Best Two Years* (Scott S. Anderson, US 2003) is one such comedy, and it also has traits of missionary films such as *God's Army* (Richard Dutcher, US 2000). Mormon comedies, Givens notes, are intended for a Mormon audience:

> Like insiders to a private joke, Mormons can comfortably laugh at a genre that, by its focus on culturally distinctive eccentricities, promotes Mormon cohesion and reifies and confirms Mormon self-definition, even as it exploits a cultural grammar that is inherently exclusionary.[252]

The boundary-making capacities inherent in movies are also utilized in other forms of cultural production through which Mormons distinguish themselves from others. Givens refers to the LDS produced *Homefront* series, which comprises short films used as a public relations tool. *Homefront* was produced from 1972 to 2009 and received several awards.[253] The series upholds classical family values: thus, for example, it encourages parents to spend time with their children. Givens notes the effectiveness of the medium:

---

250 Givens, 157–178.
251 Givens, 265–284.
252 Givens, 273–274.
253 The series won three Emmys and 18 Clios. Clios are the top award of the advertising industry.

> As the most-lauded public service campaign in history, the series solidified the LDS church's reputation as family-centred, while revealing the power of film to present a Mormon message effectively and non-threateningly to a mass audience.[254]

Building on the success of *Homefront*, the LDS Church has produced many short films on social-ethical topics that are available online through their media library webpage.[255]

As Givens explores the specifics of the culture of Mormons, a "people of paradox" as he calls them, he shapes them as peculiar people. The argument goes: we are peculiar but our artistic and intellectual expressions are universal (beautiful), proving the universal truth of Mormonism. Or in Givens' own words, Mormonism's artistic expression inheres "perhaps salvational universalism." [256] He calls for the development of a Mormon aesthetic theory, noting that "Mormon belief in human preexistence provides just one possible avenue to the elaboration of a specifically Mormon theory of the beautiful, reminiscent of Platonic forms, eternal absolutes that hover at the far boundaries of recollection."[257] Having outlined the Mormon aesthetic, highlighting its beauty and universality, he can conclude, "Reliance upon such spiritual anthropologies nudges Mormon aesthetics in the direction of what is universally human rather than culturally particular."[258]

With *People of Paradox* Givens provides a revealing window on the tension between exclusivity and universality, between peculiarity and an all-embracing truth. The aesthetic theory he develops is not entirely consistent and can be read as apologetic[259] or overly enthusiastic. But his work is certainly a mine of information on Mormon artistic productions.

---

254 Givens, *People of Paradox*, 272–273.
255 "LDS Videos - Largest Collection of Official Mormon Videos Online," accessed May 5, 2020, https://www.churchofjesuschrist.org/media-library/video?lang=eng.
256 Givens, *People of Paradox*, 340.
257 Givens, 341.
258 Givens, 341.
259 According to Daniel L. Peterson an insider of a religious tradition has to be apologetic. He divides into positive and negative apologetics. The first defends inconsistencies and the second highlights them. "Indeed, knowing of the existence of competing doctrines that contradict their own teachings, representatives of a religious community might proceed to a positive apologetics, seeking to demonstrate that one or more of their claims are, in fact, very believable, or even, perhaps, superior to rival views." See Peterson, Daniel C. "'Let a Hundred Flowers Blossom': Some Observations on Mormon Studies." Mormon Studies Review, no. 1 (June 2014): 80–88.

Mormon history is American history

In *The Mormon People: The Making of an American Faith* (2012), Mormon scholar Matthew Bowman highlights the essential US-Americanness of the LDS Church. That claim is evident from the start: in the preface Bowman states: "If God indeed selected frontier America in the early nineteenth century for the restoration of his church, he could hardly have chosen better. Many scholars have called Mormonism the quintessential American faith."[260]

Bowman proposes that Mormon history is American history, that Mormons are Americans. His work provides a narrative of Mormonism that begins in 1830 and reaches up to 2011, focusing on Mormons and their struggle to be fully American. Again a potential tension marks the tale the author wants to tell, as he acknowledges: "While the story of the Americanization of a radical movement, it is also the story of the preservation of a dream and the still-beating heart of Joseph Smith's vision of Zion."[261] The timing of the work is salient, associated with Mitt Romney's efforts to take the presidency as the Republican nominee in the upcoming election; unconsciously and indirectly, however, the author may provide a partial explanation of why Romney fell short.

Bowman has a doctoral degree from Georgetown University and since 2015 has been associate professor of history at Henderson State University. His work, he makes explicit, cites only from primary sources. These sources include Mormon scriptures and historical Mormon texts. A thorough and annotated bibliography appears at the end of the book, along with appendixes that provide a useful overview of the LDS hierarchy and the four Mormon scriptures – the *Bible*, *The Book of Mormon*, the *Doctrine and Covenants*, and the *Pearls of Great Price*. Appendix 3 contains a "Cast of Characters", with short biographies of the LDS Church presidents and other notable Mormons.[262] "The Family. A Proclamation to the World" is also reprinted, a significant statement provided by President Gordon Hinckley at the General Relief Society Meeting held in Salt Lake City in 1995. The "Proclamation" sets out the official Mormon position on family and marriage, declaring that "marriage between man and a woman is ordained of

---

260 Matthew Bowman, *The Mormon People: The Making of an American Faith* (New York: Random House, 2012), xv.
261 Bowman, 253.
262 Bowman, 263–284.

God and that the family is central to the creator's plan for the eternity of His children" and that the purpose of marriage is procreation.[263]

Following his chronological narrative of Mormon history, the author looks at critical topics and turning points such as polygamy, uniformity, conversion, the exclusion of African Americans from the priesthood, homosexuality, Mormon theology, and writing the history of the LDS Church. While the discussion has a certain defensiveness, tending, for example, to highlight the positive, it is undoubtedly illuminating. In discussing plural marriage, for example, Bowman describes the responsibilities that fell on husbands, and notes that there was a strong economic impetus for the practice. His analysis seeks to explain why plural marriage was important and how it fitted within the Mormon worldview.[264] But the tone remains apologetic in its appeal to an early 21st century readership: "Perhaps the most striking effect plural marriage had on Mormon society was the creation of powerful, strongly bound female society."[265] Women living in plural marriages had the economic security and emotional space to become involved in public activities, he suggests, citing the example of the Relief Society founded by women.

Bowman also seeks to justify the often criticized Mormon practice of baptism of the dead, using the abolition of polygamy as an explanation. With the loss of polygamy, he argues, another spiritual dimension needed to be added to marriage. Reconceptualization saw the introduction of the "celestial" marriage, the idea of marriage for all eternity. With this shift Mormons could uphold American family patterns as passionately as they had polygamy. The plurality of the family came from the ritual of sealing for eternity, dead (family) members included.

The LDS Church's success in the 1950s was based, Bowman suggests, on uniformity. During these years the LDS Church organization started to synchronize and standardize representations of the LDS Church and its members, introducing, for example, white shirts for the Aaronic priesthood holders, missionary training and programs, strongly centralized institutional authority termed "correlation", and Sunday school programs, publications, and teaching manuals. Bowman proposes that "Correlated materials are designed not to promote theological reflection but to produce Mormons dedicated to living the tenets of their faith."[266] The church-

---

263 Bowman, 283.
264 Bowman, 128–131.
265 Bowman, 135.
266 Bowman, 197.

going experience became standardized across the Mormon world, and while theological innovation was met with suspicion, behavior deemed correct became increasingly normalized.[267] The success of the strategy of correlation was reflected in LDS Church growth, including outside the United States. The change, Bowman suggests, was to the inherent historic nature of Mormonism: "Standardization and simplification sounded the final death knell of the charismatic spirituality of nineteenth-century Mormonism."[268]

Bowman pays particular attention to the exclusion of African Americans from the office of the priesthood and from temple worship. In the late 19th century the number of African Americans in Utah was low, and Bowman suggests that the law of Cain, with its one-drop rule, was more symbolic than applied.[269] That comment can seem apologetic: in essence a group of people were excluded because of their race. Bowman also describes the struggles of Spence W. Kimball, president from 1973 to 1985, to revoke the lineage of Cain and with it the restrictions for Mormons of African descent.

The Mormon LDS Church and its leaders continue to eschew theological writing in favor of homiletics and devotional works:

> After the public disputes over evolution in the 1930s and after correlation (a preemptive strike against potential doctrinal schism) the leaders of the church have decided to leave theological dispute alone. They conceive of their task largely in terms of ministry and pastoral work, consonant with modern Mormons' conception of their faith as a way of life and a system of ethical behavior rather than a theological argument.[270]

According to Bowman, it is therefore difficult to describe theologically what Mormons are. He nevertheless gives it a try: Mormons have to affirm their believe in Jesus Christ, in Joseph Smith's mission to restore Christ's church, and in the authority of the priesthood of the church.

Bowman also tackles Mormon history writing. He recognizes that the LDS Church has defended the idea that there can be no accurate, objective history of the LDS "without consideration of the spiritual powers that at-

---

267 Bowman, 191.
268 Bowman, 197.
269 Bowman, 176.
270 Bowman, 229.

tend this work."²⁷¹ For most Mormons God has guided the growth of the LDS Church, and an academic history of the LDS Church, which will fail to acknowledge the spiritual at work, is therefore inadequate. In 2009 the LDS opened a large history library in Salt Lake City, with a substantial department of LDS Church history, a museum, exhibitions, and special collections. The Internet has also been used to provide access to many historical resources. Fifteenth president of the LDS Church Gordon B. Hinckley (1910–2008) had a pronounced media sensibility, and is identified by Bowman as the architect of a subtle (media) revolution for the LDS Church.

Bowman's original afterword was revised for a subsequent edition to include something of an apology for failing to distance himself in his writing from the reports of Joseph Smith's supernatural experience, and for failing to interrogate the experience with a historian's rigor. He identifies the challenges of his narrative style: "Writing about one's own religion is always a tricky proposition, and it becomes even more so when one's faith happens to be Mormonism, as it is mine."²⁷² He criticizes television productions such as *Big Love* (HBO, US 2006–11, 5 seasons) and Jon Krakauer's non-fiction book *Under the Banner of Heaven*²⁷³ for their extreme simplification of Mormonism, and regrets that for so many Americans, all their knowledge of Mormonism comes solely from such portrayals. Mormonism, he argues, has never been monolithic. The picture such sources broadcast is one-dimensional in its suggestion that Mormons are simply obedient to the instructions of a fanatical religious culture. Mormonism, he suggests,

> presses norms as any prophetic religion must. From a faith with such a powerful sense of identity, such a vivid and compelling story of origin, such a profound hold on the spiritual life of its followers, anything less would be disappointing.²⁷⁴

In response to the often-posed question about the relationship of Mormonism and Christianity, Bowman proposes that the two faiths are complementary religions in the sense that the former is built upon the latter. He makes reference to Mitt Romney and compares the fears of Mormons with fears that have beset Jews and Christians. For Bowman the LDS is a

---

271 Bowman, 243.
272 Bowman, 222.
273 Jon Krakauer, *Under the Banner of Heaven: A Story of Violent Faith* (New York: Anchor Books, 2003).
274 Matthew Bowman, *The Mormon People: The Making of an American Faith* (New York: Random House, 2012), xxi.

faith tradition with its own history, and his evaluation of Mormonism is generally positive, with an overlay of defensiveness. Bowman dedicated his monograph to Richard Bushman, a renowned Mormon scholar whose works on Mormonism included an impressive biography of Joseph Smith.[275]

3.6. A sociological approach to The Mormon Quest for Glory

Melvin Hammarberg, a social scientist who self-identifies as "not a believer",[276] began his study of the LDS in the early 1970s. His book *The Mormon Quest for Glory: The Religious World of the Latter-Day Saints* is the product of over thirty years of research. The author is associate professor emeritus of anthropology at the University of Pennsylvania. The purpose of this extensive ethnographic survey based on field study is "to provide a qualitative picture of the church in the contemporary present."[277] Hammarberg's desire to understand the culture of the LDS Church has led him into "describing and analyzing aspects and features of the LDS Church's history, rituals, social organization, kinship structures, gender roles, basis for authority, artistic traditions, use of media, recruitment of new members and other component parts that comprise this culture."[278]

The author's social scientific method draws on interviews, surveys, and observations, which are united with selective analysis of educational material, religious narratives, and historic contexts. The sources range widely to include visual material such as film and video produced by the Mormons as a vehicle for presenting their beliefs; a quantitative questionnaire distributed in the Crystal Heights neighborhood of Salt Lake City, whose resi-

---

[275] Richard Lyman Bushman, *Joseph Smith: Rough Stone Rolling*, Reprint (New York: Vintage, 2007). See also Claudia L. Bushman and Richard L. Bushman, *Building the Kingdom: A History of Mormons in America* (New York: Oxford University Press, 2001). Bushman and Bushman is not included in this discussion because the present monographs focus on the present or at least draw a bow until recent times. But of course Bushman's work is important and a valuable source specifically according to early Mormon history.

[276] Melvyn Hammarberg, *The Mormon Quest for Glory: The Religious World of the Latter-Day Saints* (New York: Oxford University Press, 2013), 3.

[277] Hammarberg, 13. The following the discussion relies on my review of Hammarbergs monograph published in the journal *Religion*. See Marie-Therese Mäder, "The Mormon Quest for Glory: The Religious World of the Latter-Day Saints by Melvyn Hammarberg," *Religion* 45, no. 1 (January 2, 2015): 128–31.

[278] Hammarberg, *The Mormon Quest for Glory*, 2.

Part I: The Field of Documentary and Religion

dents are both Mormons and non-Mormons; the LDS magazines *New Era*, *Friend*, and *Liahona*, which are all published quarterly; and *Church News*, a weekly supplement to the newspaper *Deseret News*.

Hammarberg examines the Mormon life, which the LDS Church structures and organizes in the everyday for its members. The topics are addressed descriptively and include baptism of the dead, family, sexuality, marriage, and divorce. Hammarberg also considers issues of gender and sexual orientation. The Mormon life plan is conceived such that each individual passes through a number of levels during their lifetime. Pre-earth life is succeeded by the finite life on earth, which is succeeded by an afterlife, termed "the spirit world." The Last Judgment and Resurrection that will follow characterize the hereafter.

Hammarberg systematically reconstructs the Mormon life plan, emphasizing the focus on education. Starting with early education, for children between 18 months and 4 years, he shows how personalized the lessons at this age already are. For children aged between 4 and 8 years, lessons focus on worthiness and obedience as essential conditions for the return to the "heavenly home". For those aged between 8 and 11 the program introduces canonical texts, the Old and the New Testament, and *The Book of Mormon*. At this stage interactions in class become important, with strong connections to be established between peers. At the next stage boys and girls are separated: the young men are prepared for the Aaronic and Melchizedec priesthood and also for their leadership role as husbands; the young women are instructed in how to be mothers and wives. The pedagogy is elaborated and adapted to the needs of each age group. Thus, for example, homosexuality is discussed with teenagers. According to Hammarberg,

> The church's opposition to homosexuality causes considerable anxiety within many families and undercuts the church's most fundamental doctrine that all human beings are sons and daughters of heavenly parents, who love and nurture them in the hope of a return to their eternal home.[279]

The statement makes unsparingly evident how difficult LDS policy can be for homosexual members.

Hammarberg's academic background as an anthropologist provides a fruitful and differentiated view of Mormonism and colors the whole study. A good example for his approach is found in the description of the rituals

---

279 Hammarberg, 166.

performed in the temple. He explains that the rituals have two functions: some are performed for the living, and some for the dead, with the former a rite of passage and the latter a rite of intensification. In both cases, confirmation is central. The endowment, a ritual regularly performed in the temple, is foundational to the Mormon worldview, which has salvation and, finally, exaltation constantly to the fore:

> In this plan all spirits who chose mortal experience may, by their own effort and good works, and in faith and dependence upon Christ's atonement, pass through the veil of birth into a mortal life, and again at the death return through the veil to their spirit home in the kingdom of god, and there, if worthy, achieve a place in glory before heavenly Father as a god among gods.[280]

Hammarberg also sheds light on Mormon missionary work. His detailed description shows how closely guided and well-structured the training is. It teaches missionaries how to hold an effective and agile conversation and how to follow the detailed process that guides people through the ritual of baptism.

The author mentions two apparently oppositional extremes in relation to LDS efficiency and organizational capacity. He described the disciplinary counsels as "emotionally potent identity-defining and boundary-maintaining instruments of social control."[281] Their duty is to supervise the behavior of the LDS Church members, and in the process, Hammarberg proposes, generate feelings of guilt, fear, anxiety, shame, sorrow, or remorse. At the same time the LDS Church's dense network of social welfare programs provides compassionate humanitarian and educational services, reaching out to provide assistance even to non-members. *The Mormon Quest for Glory* strikes a successful balance between closeness, which enables the author to engage his subject, and distance, which allows the author to analyze the material he has gathered, always with respect for its subject.[282]

---

280 Hammarberg, 186.
281 Hammarberg, 269.
282 Mäder, "The Mormon Quest for Glory," 131.

Part I: The Field of Documentary and Religion

3.7. *The multifaceted and scholarly reconstructed world of Mormonism*

The works selected here for discussion have been chosen to show the diversity and detail that can be found in the field of Mormon studies. These summaries revealed how the author's context, analytical approach, and personal background can all shape the subject of study. Mormon Daniel C. Peterson, professor of Islamic studies and Arabic at Brigham Young University and currently chair of the Interpreter Foundation, which publishes *Interpreter: A Journal of Mormon Scripture*,[283] provides a perceptive and useful account of the field:

> Mormon studies simply involves studies of things Mormon, including the Mormon people and their history but also their scriptures and their doctrines. Nothing in the term privileges, say, research into the reception history of the scriptures over philological, archaeological, and historical approaches linked to their claimed origin or *Sitz im Leben* even if, as in the case of The Book of Mormon, that origin is controversial.[284]

All of the approaches highlighted here can only give a certain sense of the religious tradition of the Mormons, their theology, history, rituals, institutions, and everyday life. The works are linked by their common focus on the LDS, mainly because it is formed by the largest single grouping of Mormons. The information on that community is evidently comprehensive and enriching.

This chapter has provided insight into the different approaches that can be taken to the study of Mormon culture, and into what the aim of each perspective might be. Additionally, these introductory considerations not only leave a strong sense of the diversity of Mormon studies but also highlight particular aspects of Mormon culture, worldview, and history. This multi-perspective omnium gatherum therefore can stand as a very useful backdrop for the current study; additional literature relevant to the field of Mormonism and media is then included and discussed in the relevant subsequent chapter.

---

[283] "Journal," The Interpreter Foundation, accessed July 26, 2017, http://www.mormoninterpreter.com/journal/.

[284] Daniel C. Peterson, "'Let a Hundred Flowers Blossom': Some Observations on Mormon Studies," *Mormon Studies Review*, no. 1 (June 2014): 80.

Part II: Interactions between the Communication Spaces of Documentary Media and Religion

4. The (Ex-) Mormon Image Campaigns

The money spent on public relations campaigns in the run up to elections is telling evidence of the media's ability to mold an image. The discussion in this chapter focuses on the spaces of communication of two series that are in effect commercials and on the modes in which they can be read. In *I'm a Mormon* (US 2010–2015) and *I Am an Ex Mormon*[285] (US 2010–2015), members and former members of The Church of Jesus Christ of Latter-day Saints (LDS) respectively promote their world views. In the *I'm a Mormon* video series LDS Church members advertise on behalf of their church by presenting themselves as model Mormons. In the *I Am an Ex Mormon* video series former LDS Church members defend their decision to leave by highlighting the advantages of no longer belonging to the institution. While in both series social actors provide personal insights into to their lives and worldviews, different self-representation strategies are applied in the videos, which last between two and five minutes.

Self-representation by the LDS Church in the media has a long history. In Mormon film productions, where members of the LDS Church employ media to particular ends, self-representation strategies often seek to outweigh representations by others. In the *Encyclopedia of Religion, Communication and Media*[286] and in a comprehensive work in progress,[287] Sherry Pack Baker, a historian of communication, has traced the now-distant roots of Mormon engagement with the media, providing an overview of an intensive relationship throughout the history of the Mormons. Baker points out that since its foundation in 1830, the LDS Church has had a positive attitude toward the media, often employing the most current technological innovations. Today the LDS Church continues that tactic, using print, images, audiovisual media, and the Internet to spread its message, recruit members, and transmit information.[288]

---

285 'Ex-Mormon' is used here to describe former members of the LDS Church; the unhyphenated 'Ex Mormon' refers to the video campaign *I Am an Ex Mormon*.
286 Pack Baker, "Mormonism."
287 Sherry Pack Baker, "Mormon Media History Timeline, 1827-2007," *Brigham Young University Studies* 47, no. 4 (2008): 117–23.
288 See part I, chapter 3.1.

Part II: Interactions between Communication Spaces and Religion

4.1. Two sides of an image campaign

The current chapter compares the videos of two different production spaces, putting them in conversation with each other. On one hand, I interrogate the media strategies found in the commercials *I'm a Mormon*, a series launched – and produced by the LDS chruch. On the other hand, I explore the *I Am an Ex Mormon* video series, produced by former LDS Church members in response to the LDS Church campaign. The self-definition by LDS Church members found in the former series is communicated in specific reading modes, to which the Ex-Mormons respond in the latter. Both series promote worldviews that are religiously defined in terms similar to the relationship between brand and consumer in a secular context of markets and goods. Assessing the relationship between brand and consumer in a faith-based context, Mara Einstein has noted,

> consumers take on brands as part of their personal identity and in turn become evangelists for the product. The irony is that conversion and evangelizing have traditionally been religious processes, and now that religious institutions are reclaiming the concept of self-promotion, they are being chastised for being marketers.[289]

In the case of the *I'm a Mormon* series, members of the LDS Church promote their church through self-representation; they are their own "marketers." The counter-campaign of *I Am an Ex Mormon* is, by contrast, reactive.

My approach is shaped by three questions that scrutinize aspects of the two series. The first question concerns the self-representational strategy: how can we characterize that self-representation in the spaces of communication of the *I'm a Mormon* videos and in the response of the *I Am an Ex Mormon* videos? This first part of each subchapter contextualizes the video clips, embedding them in the communication spaces of the broader media campaigns. The second part of each subchapter considers a single episode from each series in light of the second question: how do the commercials communicate their message? The third question, addresses reading modes: in which reading modes, constructed and shared by all participants, from makers to audience, do the series participate? This subchapter is framed by

---

289 Einstein, *Brands of Faith*, 85. Einstein's monograph provides a concise and rich overview of marketing strategies by religious communities or religious practices. The result is a ground-breaking study of religion and advertising that analyses marketing vocabulary as employed within religious spheres.

the semio-pragmatic model of the communication spaces of production, consumption, distribution/circulation and reading modes.[290]

A semio-pragmatic approach considers a variety of situations, or modes, by which the audience reads the sources. Reading modes are steered by the audio-visual source itself, which provides information in the space of representation, and the source's communication spaces. Fleshing out possible reading modes is a heuristic tool that embraces different audiences in the space of consumption of an audio-visual source. The idea behind this approach is that an audio-visual source's meaning is generated in the tension between the space of consumption, where different audiences receive the same source, and the space of representation, which interacts with the other spaces of communication.[291] By no means exhaustive, such an approach seeks to explore a source's possible reading modes. If the same reading mode is applied by different spectators (including the producers), the meaning of the audio-visual source is located on the same "axis of relevance."[292]

The conclusion of the chapter compares the reading modes generated by the series' different communication spaces of production, representation, circulation/distribution and consumption.

4.2. I'm a Mormon campaign

Initially the *I'm a Mormon* video series was part of a bigger image campaign. The aim of the LDS Church was to relaunch its media presence in an updated and refreshed form. The new media strategy was presented in 2010 via the Internet, television, and billboards, with the Missionary Department in charge of the multi-million-dollar campaign. The following analysis of the series first on a macro-level draws all 184 commercials under the microscope in their space of production and distribution. Then, a close reading of one single video focusses on the space of representation. Finally, the campaign's space of consumption is discussed by mean of its website and how it enhances online activities. The analysis aims at defining possi-

---

290 For a detailed discussion of the semio-pragmatic model of communication spaces see part I, chapter 2.2.
291 Marie-Therese Mäder, "Auf den Spuren eines Stummfilms. Zwei Filme eine Geschichte," in *Leid-Bilder. Eine interdisziplinäre Perspektive auf die Passionsgeschichte in der Kultur*, ed. Natalie Fritz et al. (Marburg: Schüren, 2018), 52–54; Odin, "Spectator, Film and the Mobile Phone," 155.
292 Odin, *Les espaces de communication*, 39.

ble reading modes for the videos, whose self-representation strategy becomes evident.²⁹³

Space of production and distribution of a global campaign

Between 2010 and 2015, 184 commercials using the tagline "I'm a Mormon" were produced, with each lasting between two and four minutes. The shorts were principally distributed through the Internet, and the LDS Church Public Affairs Department assisted with their promotion. All this material can be accessed through the official LDS Church webpage, but it also appears on YouTube and other Internet platforms. Between 2010 and 2012 individual clips were also aired on a number of television channels all over the United States, in consort with a poster campaign on bus platforms and the interior of public transportation in the following cities: Minneapolis-St. Paul, St. Louis, Baton Rouge, LA, Colorado Springs, CO, Rochester, NY, Pittsburgh, Oklahoma City, Tucson, AZ, and Jacksonville, FL. After the success of the Broadway musical *The Book of Mormon* in New York City, the campaign was launched in June 2011 with prominently placed billboards at Times Square, signs on taxi roofs, and advertisements in the subway.²⁹⁴ The media scholar Chiung Hwang Chen suggests that many observers speculated the campaign paved the way for Republican presidential candidate and Mormon Mitt Romney to repair the image damage from Proposition 8 advocacy.²⁹⁵

In the distribution space the campaign was focused on the Internet in particular, where members of the church with different cultural backgrounds were put in contact. At the end of each short film, a link appeared that facilitated its sharing, and the commercials can easily be downloaded too. In March 2019 the church launched a completely new website, with the *I'm a Mormon* campaign's webpage reduced to the videos, which are

---

293 As of June 2019, only 162 of these commercials were available through the Mormon Channel Web site (see Mormon Channel). "I'm a Mormon," accessed May 19, 2019, https://www.mormonchannel.org/watch/series/im-a-mormon/sort:latest/page:6. The present considerations refer to the 184 videos available in 2015.

294 Chiung Hwang Chen, "Marketing Religion Online: The LDS Church's SEO Efforts," *Journal of Media and Religion* 10, no. 4 (November 18, 2011): 199.

295 Proposition 8 was the successful campaign financed by the Catholic Church and the LDS Church to abolish the law that legalized gay marriage in California. See also the documentary *Proposition 8* (Reed Cowan, Steven Greenstreet, US 2010).

also presented on the LDS Church's YouTube channel, ComeUntoChrist.org.[296]

One of the biggest stigmas faced by LDS Church members is the widely held view that they are not Christians but rather members of a secret cult. With the results of a survey carried out in 2010 in mind, the church wanted to overcome a "problem of perception" in the United States. Opinions expressed by Americans about the LDS Church were largely negative, with adjectives such as secretive, cultish, sexist, controlling, pushy, and anti-gay dominating descriptions of the church in 2010.[297] The *I'm a Mormon* campaign also tried to direct attention away from Mormon theology and toward Mormon people, as Elder S. Hickley explained: "During the past several decades we've used media focusing primarily on what we believe. This effort focuses more on who we are *because* of what we believe."[298]

Mitt Romney's involvement in the US presidential race in 2012 provided one reason for the campaign.[299] Romney's membership of the LDS Church was a significant biographical handicap for a future president. This media campaign sought to overcome prejudices against Mormons through a particular emphasis, as Matthew Bowman has pointed out: "Though Mormonism still embraces personal self-discipline and a certain degree of conformity, the great strategy of mormon.org is instead to project a wholesome diversity, to reflect back to a pluralistic America itself revitalized by the fruits of Joseph Smith's revelations."[300] As we shall see, the diversity mentioned in the campaign has its limits, even though the campaign focuses not only on American members but also on Mormons scattered all over the globe.

---

296 A short text about the protagonist is listed below the video and an inactive link is given for more information. The copied link leads to the new webpage "Discover What's inside | ComeUntoChrist.Org," accessed May 20, 2019, https://www.comeuntochrist.org/beliefs/book-of-mormon/discover.
297 Laurie Goodstein, "Mormon Ad Campaign Seeks to Improve Perceptions," *The New York Times*, November 17, 2011, sec. U.S., https://www.nytimes.com/2011/11/18/us/mormon-ad-campaign-seeks-to-improve-perceptions.html.
298 "Mormon.Org 'I'm a Mormon' Effort Launches in New York City," www.mormonnewsroom.org, June 16, 2011, http://www.mormonnewsroom.org/article/mormon-ads-new-york-city.
299 Haws, *The Mormon Image in the American Mind*, 207–281.
300 Bowman, *The Mormon People*, 2012, 248.

Part II: Interactions between Communication Spaces and Religion

The limits of diversity in the space of representation

In the first year of the campaign, 45 short films were produced, of which 38 portrayed Mormons resident in the United States. The following year only 18 of the 45 members portrayed lived in the United States. The year 2012 saw 58 commercials produced, featuring 40 individuals not resident in the United States. The number of non-US residents featured in the campaign thus rose through these first three years. In 2013 fewer commercials were produced, only 21, with 9 American representatives. As these figures show, even after the 2012 presidential race was over, the church continued its production of the series, and an additional nine *I'm a Mormon* shorts appeared in 2014 and 10 in 2015. Since 2013 the goal of the series has not been to foster one member's presidential campaign but to enhance the Mormon public image in general. And the campaign is also intended to provide support for missionary efforts, to convince non-members to join the church.

An overview of these 184 short films makes the impressive diversity of the people portrayed evident on a number of levels. The geography of the social actors is very broad: they live in twenty-three different countries located on five continents – Europe, North America, South America, Asia, and Australia (table 1).

A closer look at these figures allows us to establish that ninety-four social actors are from the United States and ninety from other countries (table 2). Also worthy of our attention is the fact that seventeen of the ninety-four social actors portrayed in the United States have non-American cultural roots. Overall, therefore, almost two-thirds of the Mormons depicted in this material do not have a U.S. background. The LDS Church seems eager to show its international character or, more accurately, its global diffusion and anchoring throughout a worldwide community. The many languages spoken in the episodes, languages that include Spanish, French, German, Japanese, Portuguese, Italian, Russian, Japanese, Taiwanese, and Mandarin, also demonstrate this globalized self-representation.[301]

Each clip places a single member of the LDS Church in his or her own context by highlighting one specific aspect of that individual's life, perhaps a particular skill. The series not only seeks to show the diversity of the life plans possible within Mormonism but also draws a multifaceted picture of

---

301 In additional to nationality, spoken language, and cultural background, the gender roles displayed could also be drawn into the discussion, as they give insight into the gender diversity within the clips.

4. The (Ex-) Mormon Image Campaigns

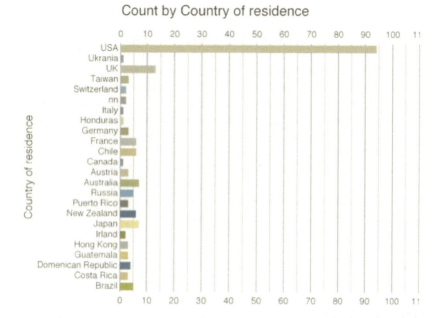

Table 1 Countries of residence.

Year	Number of videos	Country of residence US	Country of residence not US	US residence with non-US cultural background
2010	40	38	2	8
2011	45	18	27	4
2012	58	18	40	2
2013	22	10	12	1
2014	9	8	1	2
2015	10	2	8	0
Total	184	94	90	17

Table 2 Cultural background of the social actors in the I'm a Mormon series.

the race, age, and family situations of the church's members. Yet even though the series portrays the great diversity of the Mormon people, its aesthetic strategy and the dramaturgy of the portraits reveal a subtle unity of attitudes and values.

In October 2011, the LDS Church Public Affairs Department announced in the *Mormon Faith* blog that the campaign would be run in

Part II: Interactions between Communication Spaces and Religion

twelve major cities in the United States and Australia. The director of the LDS Church Public Affairs Department, Michael Otterson, suggested that the advertisements were successful "because they show Latter-day Saints as they really are – average people who try their best to follow Jesus Christ."[302] The second part of this analysis considers whether the people portrayed are really as average as Otterson proposes. Both the narrative of the *I'm a Mormon* series and its context are part of a self-representational strategy that seeks to bridge the gap between individual members and a potentially global audience.

In the following case study of the video *I'm a Mormon, Parisian, and Mother of 7* (LDS, US 2012, 2'42) the communication strategies of one commercial are scrutinized on a micro-level to determine how the LDS Church places its self-representation strategy within the logic of the media and how the process of mediatization works.[303]

The space of representation in *I'm a Mormon, Parisian, and Mother of 7*

At a micro-level, analysis of the commercial *I'm a Mormon, Parisian, and Mother of 7* gives further insights into the representation strategy. The main social actor in our example is Nadja Pettitt, a mother of seven children who lives in Paris. Pettitt was raised in Switzerland and has lived in the United States, the Netherlands, and France. Pettitt explains that she speaks Swiss German and High German, French, Spanish, English, and Dutch. She is constantly on the move, seen to be very busy throughout the whole episode. The editing is fairly fast and includes a cheerful and dynamic music score, and the bright and clean colors support the affirmative atmosphere. Pettitt is represented as a multitasking and vivacious mother who is equipped with endless energy. Her husband and their children are visible mostly in the background and whirling around her, but they stay mute. The analysis here follows the takes in chronological order.

Pettitt is not "only" a mother; she is her children's chauffeur (fig. 12), a freelance translator, a cook, a housekeeper, and a violin teacher (fig. 13): "Playing or not playing was not an option. But what to play was an option for my children," she explains. She prepares meals and is the manager of

---

302 "'On Faith' Blog: The Real Mormons Behind TV Advertising," www.mormonnewsroom.org, October 31, 2011, http://www.mormonnewsroom.org/article/on-faith-blog-real-mormons-behind-tv-advertising.
303 A detailed discussion of mediatization is provided in chapter 2.2.

her children's education (fig. 14). For much of the episode her children are visible in the background.

Fig. 12 Busy mother Nadja Pettittt as chauffeur (I'm a Mormon, Parisian, and Mother of 7, 00:00:17).

Fig. 13 Busy mother Nadja Pettitt as violin teacher (I'm a Mormon, Parisian, and Mother of 7, 00:00:09).

Fig. 14 Busy mother Nadja Pettitt as family manager (I'm a Mormon, Parisian, and Mother of 7, 00:00:33).

Fig. 15 Busy mother Nadja Pettitt explains: "I could never imagine that somebody else could essentially raise my children" (I'm a Mormon, Parisian, and Mother of 7, 00:00:53).

But there are three exceptions – in shots at the beginning, in the middle, and at the end – when Pettitt is not moving and speaks directly into the camera. During the first of these moments she explains that she works freelance because, she states, "I could never imagine that somebody else could essentially raise my children." This statement is filmed in a close-up, with the social actor addressing the audience. The fixed camera frame and the distance mark the shot aesthetically as the central message (fig. 15).

Another vital moment is found in the viewer's encounter with the family on the football field. One child is absent, but the remainder of the hap-

Part II: Interactions between Communication Spaces and Religion

Fig. 16 The happy family poses for a portrait (I'm a Mormon, Parisian, and Mother of 7, 00:02:30).

Fig. 17 "Je suis Maman. Je suis linguiste épanouie. Mon nom est Nadja Pettittt et je suis Mormone" (I'm a Mormon, Parisian, and Mother of 7, 00:02:36).

py family is staged in a grouping typical of a photo shoot (fig. 16), with mother and father positioned in the middle and their children around them. The scene is filmed in slow motion and the atmosphere changes from vivid and funny to emotional with a serious undertone. The family picture seems perfect, shot in sharp, bright colors.

Then we hear Nadja Pettitt saying in the voice-over, "Je suis Maman," and simultaneously the English words fade in, in bold white letters. The shot changes. Pettitt exits an office building through a glass door. Still in voice-over, she states, "Je suis linguiste épanouie." In the next shot, Pettitt is sitting in the room where the clip started. She is placed on the right side of the frame and filmed in close-up. Again she looks and speaks into the camera, toward the audience (fig. 17): "Mon nom est Nadja Pettitt et je suis Mormone." The translated words are on the left side of the frame: "I'm a mom. I'm a blossoming linguist. My name is Nadja Pettitt and I'm a Mormon."

After this statement, the camera zooms even closer and the words fade out. In this moment, for the first time during this clip of 2 minutes and 40 seconds, we see busy mother Nadja Pettitt motionless, and she is not talking. A final smile appears on her face. That smile is warm and authentic. Her confession has been staged most effectively, with its focus on a sympathetic social actor and her statement.

The depiction of Nadja Pettitt confirms and justifies how the everyday life of a successful Latter-day Saints mother looks. According to Chiung Hwang Chen the mother role depicted here affirms a traditional image of motherhood.

> Motherhood is portrayed as a major element of women's identity; most show motherhood in action. Women cook, clean, teach, sing,

and play with their children; they photograph and paint their little ones; they blog about motherhood; and they talk about the joy, worries, and frustration of being mothers.[304]

Chen's accurate observation analyses the series' narrative of mothers and exactly expresses Nadja Pettitt's attitude. The mothers in the *I'm a Mormon* videos seem to take their joy at being a mother as their highest goal. But women without children are also depicted. In these instances the women are incorporated into proxy families, whether in caring for their sibling's children as passionate aunts (*I'm a Mormon, Viennese Violinmaker, and Fantastic Aunt*, US 2011), in taking care of orphan children (*I'm a Mormon and Mother to 79 Orphaned Children*, US 2012; *I'm a Mormon, Mother, and Caretaker of Bulgarian Orphans*, US 2012), or at least in being happy about the marriage of other couples, who will soon themselves be parents (*I'm a Mormon Wedding Dress Maker and Patron of Beauty*, US 2015).

The aesthetic strategy is similar across all the episodes in this series, providing a recognition factor. The social actors are diverse, but all are photogenic, pleasant, efficient, and successful in their occupations. At first glance the narrative presents them as people like you and me. But in some ways the people in these episodes are also not average. All the Mormons who are depicted in the series are in some respect exceptional, and all are seeking to make a maximal contribution. Thus Nadja Pettitt is no common mother, for she is mother to seven children who are all involved in different activities managed according to Pettitt's impressive schedule.

The *I'm a Mormon* videos show the social actors at work, enjoying their leisure time, and in their homes. These representative Mormons are often presented to us along with their spouses, children, parents, or other relatives. Beyond motherhood, families are themselves key. If there is no family, we see close friends instead. Yet what we are not given, either visually or aurally, is an articulation of their religious community or their religious practices. We do not encounter these social actors when they are involved in church activities, preaching, or addressing theological topics. These activities are kept private. Family, work, and hobbies are public matters; religious practice is not on display. Based on this micro-analysis of a single video and the information gathered in the spaces of production and distribution, we can now explore possible reading modes for this series.

---

304 Chiung Hwang Chen, "Diverse Yet Hegemonic: Expressions of Motherhood in 'I'm a Mormon' Ads," *Journal of Media and Religion* 13, no. 1 (January 2, 2014): 39.

Part II: Interactions between Communication Spaces and Religion

Controlling the reading modes in the space of consumption

In the case of the *I'm a Mormon* series, which is produced by a religious institution, the documentary and moral modes rely on the credibility of the social actors, who are portrayed as likable people with positive personalities.³⁰⁵ They all appear honest, although they have conspicuously similar attitudes as happy, successful people and role models for the LDS Church. Their moral message is that their being a member of the church is the best thing that could have happened to them and that as a result every other issue in their lives is solvable.

Beside these constitutive modes of documentary media, three other reading modes can be identified within the communication spaces: the advertising mode, the identity mode, and the performative mode. These modes, although not shared by every spectator, make up a possible "axis of relevance" that embraces the diversity of the communication space formed within a framework determined by institutionalized religion.

First, the series applies the advertising mode steered by the production space, for it has been produced by the LDS Church specifically to shape its image. The social actors in front of the camera are outstanding representatives of the church who are willing to step up for an institution to which they belong. Most probably they see benefits in presenting parts of their life and sharing their worldview with a broader public. On its webpage the Public Affairs Department of the LDS Church provides additional information on and guidance to the *I'm a Mormon* campaign, explaining:

> The ads give a glimpse into the lives of Latter-day Saints from all over the world and refer people to the mormon.org website, where they can read the profiles of tens of thousands of Mormons, chat live with representatives who will answer questions about the faith and watch dozens of videos about members of the Church.³⁰⁶

The quote shows how the producers have sought to shape the consumption space in order to facilitate a communication process in which the audience will share the axis of relevance intended by the producers. The instructions are informal and functional. They appear to operate as a manual

---

305 Documentary media are defined by applying the documentary and moral modes. See for more detail part I, chapter two.
306 "'I'm a Mormon' Campaign Provide Glimpse into Lives of Latter-Day Saints," www.mormonnewsroom.org, accessed May 21, 2019, http://www.mormonnewsroom.org/article/-i-m-a-mormon-campaign.

4. The (Ex-) Mormon Image Campaigns

rather than as elucidation, an intention that seems all the more reasonable in light of the complexity of a campaign that consists of a variety of commercial forms such as television spots, billboards, and advertisements on buses and on the Internet.

Secondly, the series adopts an identity mode, whereby LDS Church members can identify with the social actors who are portrayed. Here, then, we find self-affirmation, as boundaries are defined between LDS Church members and others, as the title *I'm a Mormon* indicates. The social actors in the campaign's videos offer different life concepts with which an LDS Church audience can identify. Despite the cultural and geographical differences, the narrative suggests that the social actors who are presented are all the same by ending each video with the protagonist introducing him- or herself, while looking directly at the audience, with the sentence "My name is XXX and I'm a Mormon." By drawing symbolic boundaries between the Mormon and the non-Mormon world in the space of consumption, the self-affirming communication strategy of the video makes identification with the represented LDS Church members possible.[307]

The identity mode was promoted by online interactions between members at least until the webpage was updated in spring 2017. LDS Church members who were registered members of the relevant forum were able to leave comments about the commercials on the LDS Church webpage. These online comments were organized according to "Frequently Asked Questions" selected by the webmaster and then answered by the members themselves. These FAQs referred to Mormon theology and teachings on issues such as the eternal marriage, the afterlife, and the role of husband and wife in a family. The answers originated from "common church members," and we can assume that LDS Church officials – probably from the Membership Department in this particular case[308] – had selected and organized the comments. This communication strategy ensured the online discussion involved only members, deliberately excluding non-members. Since spring 2017 these comments have no longer been available. The LDS Church website became less interactive, with more limited possibilities for virtual

---

[307] For more on the distinction between symbolic and social boundaries see Michèle Lamont and Virág Molnár, "The Study of Boundaries in the Social Sciences," *Annual Review of Sociology* 28, no. 1 (August 1, 2002): 138. "But symbolic and social boundaries should be viewed as equally real: The former exist at the intersubjective level whereas the latter manifest themselves as groupings of individuals" (169).

[308] According to the interview with a media professional (SA5, 4:108) in Salt Lake City/UT, June 25, 2015. See part II, chapter 6.2.

exchanges between members, and now provides an even more controlled setting.

But the identity mode elicited by online comments can still be processed outside the official church website. The extended links to other commercials that can be accessed through the official website are on YouTube, where both members and non-members can leave comments. For example, by 19 May 2015 *I'm a Mormon, Polynesian Father, and Former NFL Player* had received 2,607 comments,[309] with the first two, and therefore the most recent, posted by Mormon.org. By posting regular comments, the LDS Church can ensure its responses remain at the top of the list, together with those of LDS Church members. An overview of the comments suggests that the commentators tend to express either approval or disapproval of the lifestyle and portrayal of ex-NFL player Gabe Reid. Non-Mormons sometimes mention their own religious affiliations or their broader opinions on Mormons or LDS Church members and feel their religious context affirmed through the commercials. The identity mode makes evident the crucial tension between exclusion and inclusion that constructs boundaries.[310]

The series also provides a third mode, a performative mode, in which the social actors participate in the production process. They perform their values, worldviews, and lifestyles in a self-portrait that is then received by friends and strangers, by Mormons and non-Mormons. An impressive number of Latter-day Saints appear before the camera. Prior to the re-launch of the webpage, that number had been extended by profiles that appeared online but without a video. A search mask on the right-hand side of the webpage made it possible to search for Latter-day Saints according to gender, age, and ethnicity (fig. 18); with a click on "more options" that search could be refined to a specific member profile according to criteria such as "gender," "age," "ethnicity," and "previous religion," general keywords, or "first or last name," "heritage," or "country/state/region" (fig. 19). The section "previous religion" lists diverse Christian denominations as well as Atheist, Agnostic, Buddhist, Muslim, Jewish, Hindu, or "no religious background."[311]

---

309 "Gabe Reid – Former NFL Player, Polynesian Father, Mormon," accessed December 5, 2017, https://www.mormonchannel.org/watch/series/im-a-mormon/gabe-reid-former-nfl-player-polynesian-father-mormon.

310 This discussion will be followed up in the section on the *I Am an Ex Mormon* series.

4. The (Ex-) Mormon Image Campaigns

Fig. 18/ Fig. 19/ Fig. 20/ Fig. 21/ Fig. 22 The search mask of the former I'm a Mormon webpage enhanced a performative mode in which Latter-day Saints represented themselves.

The webpage on which the commercials were embedded visually connected the videos with the wider Mormon community to suggest that these portraits are of outstanding representatives of an even bigger community (fig. 20). The webpage provided space in which less prominently portrayed Mormons also presented themselves with photo portraits (fig. 21) that are similarly accompanied by a Q&A section (fig. 22).

Another positive impact of these extended profiles created by Latter-day Saints was that they directed traffic to the mormon.org site, increasing the church's search ranking. The campaign not only presented its members in a positive light but also enhanced the LDS Church's activity according to Search Engine Optimization (SEO).[312]

The relaunch of the web site on which the *I'm a Mormon* videos were presented fundamentally changed the performative mode. In the former version the web site not only had the potential to strengthen the community experience but also increased the possibility that non-Mormons would meet Mormons online with whom they shared similar attributes, such as heritage, (previous) religion, or geographic origin. On the new site, as noted, these options are no longer available. The performative mode in the current version thus provides few bottom-up activities whereby the members of the church can engage individually in online conversations with other members.

Currently the *I'm a Mormon* videos appear followed by other Latter-day Saint portraits on non-transparent algorithms.[313] The webpage of the videos provides only sparse information and refers visitors to the relaunched site, www.comeuntochrist.org, which embraces the church's on-

---

311 As a side note: most converts to the LDS church were previously affiliated with another Christian denomination. The predominance of members in historically Christian countries comes, according to Rodney Stark, because "people want to preserve their religious capital" (25). Stark's approach is based on rational choice theory. He explains that people with a Christian background but with few or no active connections to any religious group are most likely to convert to Mormonism. Most conversions take place in a private setting, with few a result of missionaries' approaching people on the street by chance. A more detailed discussion of Stark's rational choice argument is provided in chapter 3.4. See Stark, *The Rise of Mormonism*, 25.
312 Chen, "Marketing Religion Online," 200.
313 "I'm a Mormon," accessed November 6, 2017, https://www.mormonchannel.org/watch/series/im-a-mormon.

line mission.³¹⁴ On some pages a form appears where visitors can fill in a name and phone number to order a free copy of *The Book of Mormon* and are informed that they will be contacted by church representatives. A pop-up menu allows visitors to schedule a visit with a missionary, to chat online with church representatives, or to use a search to locate a nearby church. This new way of communicating controls the interactions between church representatives and visitors to the website, be they Mormon or non-Mormon.³¹⁵ Compared with the older version, it reduces the possibilities of the performative mode to a rather passive endeavor.

To sum up: the identification of communication spaces and reading modes in the *I'm a Mormon* campaign enables us to flesh out different axes of relevance present in the media. In the case of the LDS Church video series, the advertising, identity, and performative modes explain the various practices and attitudes performed within the spaces of communication. As we shall now see, the less generously produced *I Am an Ex Mormon* video series engages the reading modes differently.

4.3. I Am an Ex Mormon initiative (US 2010–15)

With its 44 videos produced between 2010 and 2015, the *I Am an Ex Mormon* can be understood as an answer to the LDS Church's image efforts and in particular to its global campaign *I'm a Mormon*. In light of this purpose, the analysis of the communication spaces of the *I Am an Ex Mormon* videos focuses more fully on the interactive dimension. This is done by examining in detail the online discussion about the video, analyzed in the close reading section, and an additional analysis of a video that addresses possible participants in the Ex-Mormon series. The analysis of the communications spaces that follows fleshes out the reading modes: the advertising video seeks to recruit future protagonists and the data collected in the process of systematizing the videos gives access to the production space. A single video is analyzed in the space of representation and, finally, the space

---

314 The LDS Church seeks to highlight the presence of 'Jesus Christ' within the official name of the church as a means of fostering Christian associations and at the same time deemphasizing the term 'Mormon'.
"The Correct Name of the Church," accessed June 11, 2019, https://www.churchofjesuschrist.org/study/general-conference/2018/10/the-correct-name-of-the-church?lang=eng.

315 The church has promoted its online efforts by changing the webpage's address to ChurchofJesusChrist.org.

of consumption is characterized by evaluating the online comments about this specific video on the series' website.

Space of production as a private initiative

The producers of the *I Am an Ex Mormon* initiative provide information about their activities in a post from May 21, 2011, that announces more videos:[316] "We are currently filming in Utah – in the meantime ... enjoy a missionary story with Stuart."[317] A social actor named Stuart then tells a story about his time as a missionary in England in which he criticizes the way in which missionaries all but walked into houses uninvited and turned on their projectors to show a film about Mormonism. According to Stuart, this method was called "being bold" and was typical of how he was taught to proselytize. At the end of Stuart's mission story, the producers thank viewers for their support of the video series and the end credits announce new videos that will be available in June.

Below the video, an announcement of and a link to a mini-series about sexuality in Mormonism is provided. Stuart and his wife Kerri talk very openly about the repressive sexual policies of the church. Here the Ex-Mormon platform is used in a performative mode. Stuart and Kerri not only recount their experiences of sexual repression in the LDS Church but also explicitly explain how that policy can be improved. Another video, entitled *Seeking participants*, on the webpage is indicative of how the producers look for participants by applying an advertising mode (fig. 23).[318]

The video compiles clips from the *I Am an Ex Mormon* series and short statements by the social actors. Statements like "the depressions I had suddenly went away" are combined with titles used by the producers to summarize their message: "Life after Mormonism" (shot of social actor 1) "can be full of joy" (shot of social actor 2) "can be full of growth" (shot of social actor 3) "full of hope" (shot of social actor 4) "full of beauty" (shot of social actor 5) "full of discovery" (shot of social actor 6) "full of healing" (shot of social actor 7) "full of ... love, fulfillment, truth charity, peace free-

---

316 The campaign is financed by donations, as indicated on its webpage: "Help us create more videos!" with a button that links to PayPal.
317 "Filming in Utah – More Videos in June! | I Am an Ex Mormon," accessed December 4, 2017, http://www.iamanexmormon.com/2011/05/filming-in-utah-more-videos-in-june/.
318 "Seeking Participants | I Am an Ex Mormon," accessed December 5, 2017, http://www.iamanexmormon.com/2011/04/seeking-participants/.

4. The (Ex-) Mormon Image Campaigns

Fig. 23 Image from the webpage i-am-an-ex-mormon.com, where further participants are sought.

dom, balance, conviction, opportunity, enthusiasm, excitements...authenticity [...]." Many positive terms are quickly superimposed one after the other, making it impossible to catch them all. Then comments fade in with references to the website or the video series such as, "'Love the series ... they've been a great source of comfort and support me.' -Anonymous" or "Sometimes I still feel alone," the title superimposes "Thank you" then "for creating this website", then "It gives hope. – Jeff." The protagonists highlight how much the series has helped them overcome the difficulties and fears associated with leaving the LDS Church. At the end of the video the title suggests: "Our purpose is not given to us", superimposed by "by authority – our purpose comes", superimposed by "comes from within." Then a wipe with light bubbles in green white introduce the title "i-am-an-ex-mormon.com – now seeking participants – go to iamanexmormon.com/join-us." When the link is clicked, the production explains its aims and the concept behind the series. The instructions reveal how the producers intend to shape the function and effect of the videos:

If you want to be in a video, please keep in mind the following:
- We want to highlight personal struggles and success about your exit story from Mormonism.
- We are not trying to focus on doctrinal issues, although we will not shy away from them if you feel it is important to your story.
- We want our videos to avoid the tone "this is why the church isn't true" but rather "this was my experience and this is what I struggled with."

Part II: Interactions between Communication Spaces and Religion

– We want to highlight areas that many Ex-Mormons struggle with during their transition out of the church. Divorce, shunning, loneliness, fear etc. How did you deal with these things?[319]

As the first three instructions show, the producers are not interested in theological argument. Their focus is on personal and psychological experiences. The reason for leaving that is most often mentioned in the video is that the church is not true (17 times). At the same time the protagonists recount their personal challenges and the fears surrounding their departure. Ex-Mormons who were educated in the church and served the mission would likely feel secure talking about doctrinal issues, but that rhetoric would not have the same personal edge. Personal struggles and experiences provide an emotionally richer narrative that is at the same time also more engaging for the audience.

"What have you gained from leaving the church? What advice do you have for others going through this transition? We want to give hope to those who might feel there is no joy in life after Mormonism."[320] These questions show one of the purposes of the videos. The participants should be role models and experts with experiences from which others can benefit. This idea is supported by the search mask on the webpage which lists church functions: *BYU student, Mormon Institute Teacher, Relief Society Instructor, Stake Mission Presidency, Ward Clerk, Young Men's Counselor, Veil Worker*, and *Young Women's Teacher* are only a few of the 83 categories. The aim of the videos is not only to communicate how life is after Mormonism but also to accompany Latter-day Saints as they leave the church. On that score, the videos may support the detachment process by applying the performative mode intended to activate their audience.

The comments section on the webpage allows additional exchanges about the videos and reinforces their counseling function. The audience consists not only of Ex-Mormons but also of doubting Latter-day Saints: "We want our videos to help Mormons avoid stereotyping 'Ex Mormons' and we want to provide strength and support to those exiting the church or just beginning to have doubts."[321] What is the stereotype of an Ex-Mormon? The stereotypical Mormon is the Mormon missionary with white

---

319 "Be in a Video! | I Am an Ex Mormon." Accessed December 23, 2017. http://www.iamanexmormon.com/join-us/.
320 "Be in a Video! | I Am an Ex Mormon," accessed November 6, 2017, http://www.iamanexmormon.com/join-us/.
321 "Be in a Video! | I Am an Ex Mormon."

shirt, tie, neat haircut, and a friendly smile.[322] The stereotypical Ex-Mormon maybe then be drawn ex negativo, as lonely, excluded and lost, or in any other way the opposite of the image propagated by the *I'm a Mormon* campaign. That preconception is a fear that might hinder Mormons from leaving the church and provides the axis of relevance that the campaign wants to counter, as analysis of the videos reveals.

A close look at Ex-Mormons in the space of representation

These videos usually portray one social actor – the exceptions are two couples and one family with two children – in single setting, for example, in front of an LDS Church temple, in their home, or in an unspecific outside area. They mostly speak into the camera, without any further activities shown. The videos are in a testimonial style, in which social actors provide witness of their personal experiences.[323] The Ex-Mormons are filmed in close-up or at least in a medium shot that shows the upper half of their bodies including their arms. The straight camera angle gives the impression that the person is in front of the spectators addressing them directly. Their words provide a direct explanation, without detours, as to why they left the church.

The videos cover four distinct age groups.[324] Those aged 18–29 are represented by 10 social actors; the age range 30–45 is the biggest group, with 19 Ex-Mormons; 10 people aged 46–65 speak about having left the church; only two protagonists are older than 66. Two social actors have wished to remain anonymous. The professions of the social actors – they include students, mothers and fathers, nurses, and musicians – are not deemed significant and sometimes are not even mentioned. The gender distribution is more significant, with 27 male and 14 female Ex-Mormons taking part, along with two heterosexual couples and one family with two children (boy and girl). The lack of ethnic diversity is striking. Only one person is non-Caucasian – Michelle from the Caribbean, as she introduces herself – and three protagonists are not US Americans (German, Canadian, British).

---

322 One of many examples of stereotyping Mormon missionaries is found in the series *Breaking Bad* (AMC, US 2014–16) when one of the protagonists, high on crystal meth, considers Mormon missionaries to be Hells Angels (*Cancer Man*, season 1, episode 4).
323 Nichols, *Introduction to Documentary*, 151.
324 The age of the protagonists has been estimated on the basis of their appearance.

Part II: Interactions between Communication Spaces and Religion

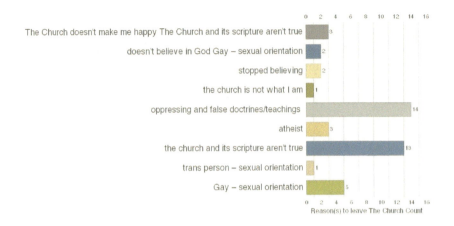

Table 3 Reasons given for leaving the LDS Church.

Finally, most of the participants (33 in total) were born into the church, with three converting as children, one as adult; in 7 instances we are not told with certainty.

The reasons for leaving the church are also diverse, but they do intersect. As table 3 indicates, most of the participants mention "The church and its scripture aren't true" combined with "The church doesn't make me happy" or as single reason "The church and its scripture aren't true" (13+3). "Oppressing and false doctrines/teachings" is a similar claim and is cited by 14 social actors. In six of the 44 videos sexual orientation is given as a reason for leaving the church, with gay and trans people having felt excluded, suppressed, and discriminated in the LDS Church. In such instances, the social actors use their appearance in the *Ex-Mormon* videos to reveal not only that they have left the church but also their sexual orientation. Some of these social actors are using the public platform of the video to inform family and friends of their decision.

The Ex-Mormons often mention that they started to doubt the church's teachings and to question its history but found the church leaders unable to answer their questions. Other similar reasons, as illustrated in table 3 are the loss of belief in the truth of the church, inconsistencies in the scripture that the church is defending, or beginning to learn and read about the church that result in realizing that the church isn't true. The decision to leave the church was usually the participant's own, although sometimes they speak of being motivated by others.

Some general observations reveal strategic traits that might be part of the broader concept behind the videos. For example, the social actors never cry. While a few seem moved as they narrate their experience, they largely describe their happiness after leaving the church. Family is a vital issue. Many of the Ex-Mormons fear losing their family and friends, which is also the reason for two of them staying anonymous. They also fear losing their jobs or being excluded from their universities because their education is supported by the church or they study at the LDS Church-affiliated Brigham Young University. In the following section, a close reading of one Ex-Mormon video will consider the documentary strategy of the series.

The space of representation in *My Name is Heather and I'm an Ex Mormon*

The title of the video (LDS Church, US 2015) on YouTube and on the webpage http://www.iamanexmormon.com/ summarizes the main message of Heather's story: "I'm happier than I've ever been in my entire life and I am an Ex Mormon." [325] In most of the narratives, indeed, the social actors talk about their life after leaving the church and of how this life change improved their personal and emotional well-being. The bottom line is that because life without the LDS Church is so much better, it is worth leaving the community. The social actors present themselves as "cured", as feeling now very different from how they felt as members of the LDS Church.

The video and the webpage text provide biographical information that is part of Heather's narrative.[326] Heather is about forty years old, a mother of six children aged between seven and eighteen. She and her ex-husband left the church at the same time and then divorced. Four years before the video was produced she remarried, with her husband Jeff another Ex-Mormon whom she met on the Ex-Mormon online message board. At the time Jeff was also in the process of divorcing. Heather writes on the webpage: "We have just celebrated our four years anniversary and are living an authentically happy, family-centered life."

The video's editing pace is rather fast. There are forty cuts in 190 seconds, which results an average shot length of 4.75 seconds. Heather tells

---

325 iamanexmormon, *I'm Happier than I've Ever Been in My Entire Life and I'm an Ex Mormon*, accessed November 24, 2017, https://www.youtube.com/watch?v=vW-p9l0qTFC0.

326 "My Name Is Heather and I'm an Ex Mormon | I Am an Ex Mormon," accessed November 26, 2017, http://www.iamanexmormon.com/2011/07/my-name-is-heather-and-im-an-ex-mormon/.

her own story and is the only voice heard during the video. In one half of the takes she speaks to the camera while sitting on her sofa, and during the other half she is preparing a barbecue dinner, grilling sausages and hamburgers and setting the table with her children helping. These two situations alternate in the editing. During the preparation for dinner, Heather continues her story off screen in the voice-over and becomes the first-person narrator.[327] In contrast, she talks on screen while sitting on the sofa. The extra-diegetic music score, where the sound source is not in the image, supports the emotional atmosphere of Heather's story. When she talks about her difficult time during her marriage and about how unhappy she was, the sound slows down and is melancholic. As soon as she starts to talk about her newfound happiness, the music changes to a faster pace and becomes cheerful. Music plays in the background during the whole video, linking the shots and supporting the rhythm of the editing.

In the last 50 seconds of the video, the editing, frames, and Heather's performance communicate a story of success with a happy ending. Sitting on a sofa in her living room, Heather recounts that she finally left the church. The following 12 film stills and quotes show how the takes are combined with Heather's story in the voice-over and on-screen (fig. 24–35):

The video puts Heather at the center of the narration and makes the audience believe that her story is authentic and find it compelling. There are six close-ups showing her face (fig. 27) and two extreme close-ups (fig. 31). The close-ups enhance the intimacy and immediacy with the protagonist at the end of the video. She looks into the camera lens over and over again and by doing so remains in eye contact with the audience. The viewer is sitting across from Heather in her living room and follows her into the kitchen. Heather and the viewer are like close friends.

Her children are present in the harmonious kitchen setting and warmheartedly interact with their mother. The situation shows Heather as a relaxed, caring, and loving mother. She cooks and sets the table for her children, who bustle around her and are obviously happy. We see how tenderly Heather interacts with them. The following situation is typical. Her daughter, helping her mother in the kitchen, gazes into the camera with a smile (fig. 36). She looks at her mother. Heather is smiling back (fig. 37) and approaches her, wiping a piece of hair from her face (fig. 38).

The audiovisual dramaturgy sells the Ex-Mormon message efficiently and emotionally. It is supported by the music score, rhythm of the editing,

---

[327] Sarah Kozloff, *Invisible Storytellers: Voice-over Narration in American Fiction Film* (Berkeley: University of California Press, 1988), 43–49.

4. The (Ex-) Mormon Image Campaigns

Fig. 24 "And I was allowed to act for my own happiness ... (My Name is Heather and I'm an Ex Mormon, 00:02:19).

Fig. 25 ... and so I ended my fifteen-year marriage (My Name is Heather and I'm an Ex Mormon, 00:02:23).

Fig. 26 [voice-over by Heather] And I've never been happier, mmh ... (My Name is Heather and I'm an Ex Mormon, 00:02:25).

Fig. 27 I got married four years ago to the man of my dreams. He is wonderful. He loves me in a way I never knew people could be loved. And he has made me happier than I ever could have imagined. I can't imagine ... (My Name is Heather and I'm an Ex Mormon, 00:02:30).

focus, and use of blurred images to signal her despairing search for happiness. The person-centered narration obscures that the video is part of a campaign which has its own aims. As first-person narrator Heather is in charge of the narrative. The film theorist Sarah Kozloff explains the function of a first-person narrator:

> films often create the sense of character-narration so strongly that one accepts the voice over narrator as if he or she were the mouthpiece of the image-maker either for the whole film or for the duration of his or

143

Fig. 28/ Fig. 29 [voice-over Heather] ... still being in that place where I had to endure being in a marriage that makes me unhappy. I did not think that this ... (My name is Heather and I'm an Ex Mormon, 00:02:48/ 00:02:55).

Fig. 30 ... type of marriage existed. I really didn't. And I have it now (My Name is Heather and I'm an Ex Mormon, 00:02:56).

Fig. 31 My name is Heather (My Name is Heather and I'm an Ex Mormon, 00:03:00).

Fig. 32 [voice-over Heather] I am a nurse, I am a mother, I am happier than I have ever been in my entire life ... (My Name is Heather and I'm an Ex Mormon, 00:03:03).

> her embedded story. We put our faith in the voice not as created but as creator.[328]

Heather brings credibility to the *I Am an Ex Mormon* campaign, which is a crucial mode for the documentary advertisement series. The audience believes her story even though they may not share her opinions. Only at the end of the narration, when reference to the *I'm a Mormon* series is made with the statement "I am a nurse, I am a mother, I am happier than I have ever been in my entire life and I am an Ex Mormon", does the video reveal that its reading mode is to counter the LDS *I'm a Mormon* campaign. The

---

328 Kozloff, 45.

4. The (Ex-) Mormon Image Campaigns

Fig. 33/ Fig. 34 … and I am an Ex Mormon (My Name is Heather and I'm an Ex Mormon, 00:03:07/ 00:03:08).

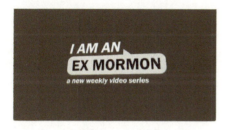

Fig. 35 Finally, the logo of the campaign is superimposed. (My Name is Heather and I'm an Ex Mormon, 00:03:11).

Fig. 36/ Fig. 37/ Fig. 38 The audiovisual dramaturgy highlights the warm relationship between Heather and her children (My Name is Heather and I'm an Ex Mormon, 00:02:12/ 00:02:14/ 00:02:17).

comment section on the webpage below each video allows us to access viewer reactions.

Online comments in the space of consumption

The YouTube comments on *My Name is Heather and I'm an Ex Mormon* have been posted steadily since the video was published in July 2011. By

145

	female	male
#opposing/reacting to previous comment	23	11
Contra LDS Church		
contra: affirmative comment	11	5
contra: congrats Heather	1	1
contra: critic of LDS/Mormonism in general	16	5
contra: defends Heather	4	2
contra: Ex-Mormon	2	1
sum contra	34	14
Pro LDS		
pro: critics of Heather	2	1
pro: critics of the video	0	1
pro: defends LDS	10	6
pro: LDS Church affiliated	6	2
sum pro	19	10
sum of all comments	76	35

Table 4 Pro and contra comments.

November 22, 2017, the video had received 42,985 views, 709 comments, 480 likes and 66 dislikes. Commenting on YouTube is still possible, whereas the comment section on the *I Am an Ex Mormon* webpage below the video has been closed since July 11, 2016. The comments on the latter site are in general more differentiated and more comprehensive than on YouTube, and in comparison with other videos, Heather's video received a more substantial number of comments, with, according to the webpage, 111 responses.

a) More female participants in the online comments

The overview of the comments (table 4) reveals that entries made by women are more engaged, both in terms of number and content. 76 contributions by women stand against 35 contributions by men. Women reacted twice as often (23 times) with an immediate response that resulted in a conversation, were three times more likely to criticize Mormonism (16 female/5 male) and at the same time also defended the LDS Church more often (10 female/6 male). In sum female participants criticized Mormonism and/or the LDS Church 34 times, whereas male participants wrote 14 critical comments.

Less difference is reflected in the pro LDS/Mormonism section, with 19 comments by women and 10 comments by men. That Heather's story revolves around her role as a wife and mother is mirrored in the comments. The video's target audience is obviously female Ex-Mormons and Mormons. It is not necessarily clear whether the 19 women who defend the LDS Church are Mormon, but they seek to spare the LDS Church from responsibility for Heather's miserable marriage:

> Karen, JULY 6TH, 2011 AT 12:08 AM
> First of all, there are many happy marriages within Mormonism, so the fact that you married the wrong guy has nothing to do with the religion you chose. Second, I find it difficult to believe 5 bishops told you to stay in a miserable marriage. I know of plenty of bishop-supported Mormon divorces, and people find happier relationships, and stay happily Mormon. Maybe you were telling your bishop you wanted to work things out and he expressed what he felt you needed to hear to that end? You seem to be faulting your former chosen religion for your happiness or lack of happiness. If you are happy now, it might just be something else entirely, but this is a straw-man soft-gloved attack of Mormonism which you blame as the cause of your unhappiness, rather than seeing your choices as your own all along.[329]

Karen calls Heather's explanation for her happiness a "straw-man soft-gloved attack of Mormonism." Her argument is rather defensive but impressively elaborated. She provides a well-crafted explanation of various reasons for unhappiness in marriage, an argument that is surely valid. Heather's reasoning is weakened, for a divorce can be multicausal. As additional pro-Mormonism comments argue, there are many happy Mormon couples too. Strictly speaking, Heather's video does not prove a case against Mormonism; it simply shows a very happy Ex-Mormon mother who encourages doubting church members to quit the institution in search of a happy ending like hers. The video works less on the basis of sound argument and more as an emotional and authentic message in support of Ex-Mormons and doubting Mormons.

---

[329] "My Name Is Heather and I'm an Ex Mormon | I Am an Ex Mormon."

b) Drawing religious and social boundaries

Comments by women are more likely to support and affirm Heather's story, as in the case of the following comment by Jean, which congratulates Heather for her courage:

> Congrats Heather for having the courage to leave both an unhappy marriage and the LDS Church. We are coerced as human beings to comply with our tribe's expectations and it looks as though you did a good job. You stayed active and believing in the LDS Church and stayed in an unhappy marriage just because it was 'the right thing to do'. It wasn't right for you; you recognized it and got out. That takes so much courage especially when you have 6 children. I imagine there were times when you said to yourself, "what the heck am I doing?"
> We cannot predict with certainty where any decision will take us, but we can be reasonably assured that if what we have 'been doing' has brought us doubt and unhappiness that it will continue unless we make some scary changes. You did it! Congratulations are as much in order for you as they are for someone who overcomes an addiction.[330]

The focus of Jean's affirmative reaction is not criticism of Mormonism, although she does congratulate Heather for having the courage to leave the church. This type of supportive and diplomatic comment, of which there are 16, is not so much critical of the LDS Church as enthusiastic about leaving the church. This approach is in accord with the producer's concept in seeking to show the advantages of living as an Ex-Mormon rather than focus on blaming the LDS Church for a miserable existence. But there are also many harsh critics of TBM ("true believing Mormons"), like Shantenelle

> When you don't believe something is true, you generally distance yourself from it. TBM's tend to not open their minds enough to realize that those of us who use our free agency to live a life outside of Mormonism have a new, grander perspective on life as well as the afterlife. It's not limited to commandments and kingdoms! Heather will be with her new husband and all of her children forever if that is what she wants/desires/believes. She "gets it" even more now that she doesn't have the filter of Mormonism clouding her spectacles!

---

330 "My Name Is Heather and I'm an Ex Mormon | I Am an Ex Mormon."

Don't you see? After realizing the falseness of the church, her temple sealing, the covenants, the endless hours of dutifully fulfilling a variety of callings over the years seems so unimportant and meaningless in hindsight. Not that those things should be unimportant and meaningless to you! Because maybe you need the church. But Heather doesn't. And so many like her do not.[331]

Shantenelle accuses TBMs of being narrow minded. She also speaks of "those of us who use our free agency to live a life outside of Mormonism" and locates herself in the Ex-Mormon group. The "us" is important in the conversation, which is largely framed by two opposing groups. The comment section serves to define in-groups and out-groups, with commentators identifying with one of them and readers' own identifications supported by the content of the comments. The Swiss anthropologist Andreas Wimmer ascribes these characteristics to the practice of boundary making:

> A boundary displays both a categorical and a social or behavioral dimension. The former refers to acts of social classification and collective representation; the latter to everyday networks of relationships that result from individual acts of connecting and distancing. On the individual level, the categorical and the behavioral aspects appear as two cognitive schemes. One divides the social world into social groups – into "us" and "them" – and the other offers scripts of action – how to relate to individuals classified as "us" and "them" under given circumstances. Only when the two schemes coincide, when ways of seeing the world correspond to ways of acting in the world, shall I speak of a social boundary.[332]

The comment section can be understood as a field in which religious and social boundaries are defined. The participants describe what it means to no longer practice Mormonism in a particular social dimension: Shantenelle, for examples, writes of what it is "to live a life outside Mormonism." The categorical dimension is expressed with the use the first-person plural "us" or in statements such as: "Because maybe you need the church. But Heather doesn't. And so many like her do not." Shantenelle highlights that Heather is not alone, for she is embedded in a wider group of like-minded people. They are different in that they no longer need the

---

331 "My Name Is Heather and I'm an Ex Mormon | I Am an Ex Mormon."
332 Andreas Wimmer, "The Making and Unmaking of Ethnic Boundaries: A Multi-level Process Theory," *American Journal of Sociology* 113, no. 4 (2008): 975.

Part II: Interactions between Communication Spaces and Religion

church. Most of the comments are located within one of these two groups. The definition of boundaries in the comments steers an identity mode that is similar to that in the *I'm a Mormon* series and is dominant in both series. But other communication modes are also engaged.

c) Linking Ex-Mormons and Mormons in the comments

My Name is Heather and I'm an Ex Mormon is linked to other videos structured by the participant's function in the LDS Church:

> posted by D. William Johnson (admin) on Saturday, July 2nd, 2011 at 7:50 am in Home Making Leader, Mormon Mother, Mormon Primary Presidency, Mormon Primary Teacher, Nursery, Relief Society Instructor, Uncategorized, Visiting Teaching Coordinator, Young Women's Advisor, Young Women's Teacher[333]

The keywords determined by function in the LDS Church allow former members to find people in similar situations or with similar experiences of activities within the church. The webpage thus seeks to connect non-Mormons with doubting LDS Church members. Additionally, the social actors from the videos participate in the online discussion. Heather provided six detailed comments on July 10 and August 18, 2011. One of her comments fed the discussion with further details about her reason for leaving, the process that led her to this decision and why she participated in the video series:

> Those of you who think that my point is "the church made me do it" didn't really listen to what I was saying in my story. Leaving the church happened because I found out that it wasn't true. I prayed for TWO years to regain my testimony. I was a choice daughter. I was living a genuinely LDS life. I attended the temple regularly, and I faithfully exercised the callings that were handed to me (when I was a mother with babies who worked full time). I BEGGED for my testimony to come back to me, literally. But if Joseph Smith and Brigham Young were child molesters and exploiters of women and families, in my mind, they can't be prophets. What you see in this video is a fortunate side effect, for me, of leaving Mormonism … genuine happiness. Those of you who say that the church did not make me marry a dis-

---

333 "My Name Is Heather and I'm an Ex Mormon | I Am an Ex Mormon."

gusting idiot when I was nineteen are correct but the culture and DOCTRINE of the church pushes you in that direction as soon as you feel any love toward a possibly viable candidate. President Benson's talks were very strongly worded in that direction as was the recent talk in General Conference encouraging young singles not to wait for their perfect soul mate but to get to the business of breeding ASAP.

The entire reason I volunteered to do this is to illustrate that people can be happy when they leave the church. We can become our genuine selves. We can make the right decisions based on who we are and not based on what the prophet or the scriptures say. We are GOOD PEOPLE and not evil, lost souls who will burn in hell. My quest for happiness was not my reason for leaving the church, but gaining it was a really fabulous side effect.[334]

Again, Heather describes the fortunate side effect of leaving Mormonism as "genuine happiness." She also criticizes Joseph Smith and Brigham Young, first and second prophets of the church, as "child molesters" and "exploiters of women" and the church's practice of encouraging members to marry at a young age. Administrator Dan Johnson also contributes to the comments, defending Heather's position by condemning the church's practices or moderating the conversation. His nine comments are on the following model:

> Karen, you can't possibly know Heather and the details of her story. I find it interesting that you seemed to have jumped to your own judgement of the situation regardless of this obvious lack of information.[335]

Each video is tagged to link it with similar narratives from the series. Heather's video is tagged with the following keywords: *church, Church of Jesus Christ of Latter-day Saints, deconversion,*[336] *Ex Mormon, exmormon, God, Latter-day Saints, LDS, Marriage Equality, Mormon, Religion.*[337] These keywords allow viewers to find other videos that include the same topics and

---

334 "My Name Is Heather and I'm an Ex Mormon | I Am an Ex Mormon."
335 "My Name Is Heather and I'm an Ex Mormon | I Am an Ex Mormon."
336 Most of the tags are self-explanatory; only "deconversion" requires explanation. Heather converted to become a Latter-day Saint. "Deconversion" in this context means that she left the church after having converted. The tags and keywords help visitors to the site to orient themselves and to be redirected to videos with the same topics.
337 "My Name Is Heather and I'm an Ex Mormon | I Am an Ex Mormon."

Part II: Interactions between Communication Spaces and Religion

promotes the performative mode that encourages interaction between the participants.

Eliciting sympathy in the reading modes

To sum up: the *I Am an Ex Mormon* series engages the documentary mode with references to credibility and authenticity to elicit sympathy through additional reading modes in its spaces of communication. With the series a private initiative, the social actors do not have institutional support for their participation and therefore take a significant risk. For this reason, a few prefer to stay anonymous, fearing the response of their family and friends.

In light of the risk of such significant consequences of participation in this series, such as exclusion by families and Mormon friends, the moral mode is very present in the series' space of representation. The message is: "Because this church is so bad, I am ready to take a big risk and inform people about what really happens there." In voluntarily shouldering this responsibility and taking a personal risk, the participants bring a significant credibility to the production. The Ex-Mormons take on an authority that enables them to control their future lives, activating an identity mode in which they redefine themselves as Ex-Mormon and distinguish themselves from Mormons.

An emotional mode comes into play in the space of representation and consumption. Two of the close-ups of Heather are extreme close-ups, connecting audience and protagonist. This specific frame advances Heather's newly found happiness. The same is the case with the music score, which works simply but effectively in the background and amplifies the narration's emotional undertone. When Heather talks about her unhappy marriage, which she sees as a result of being forced to marry too young, the music is slow and the melody sad; when she talks of her life after the LDS Church, the music carries a brighter rhythm. The emotional mode is also employed in the space of consumption. Participants in the comment section recount their own feelings as members of the church and after leaving. All of them seek to show how their lives without the church are more satisfying and happier than before. They highlight that it was worth taking the risk to quit and start a new life. With the institutional church less evident as a defining presence, the emotional mode in the online comments is instead personal and individual.

And, finally, the identity mode is also applied in the space of consumption. As demonstrated, the comments distinguish their writers as pro or contra the video. The comment section allows these writers to be involved in a public discussion. Technically, the comments are anonymous, as real names are not required nor evidence of the author's identity. But in being vocal about their opinion, the commentators draw boundaries between members, non-members and ex-members. The comment section groups people with the same views and provides space in which individual opinions can be expressed. For obvious reasons, the space of the *I Am an Ex Mormon* website privileges the aims of Ex-Mormons and their reading modes.

4.4. Spaces of communication in competition

Where does the experience of watching the whole series of 184 *I'm a Mormon* and 44 *I Am an Ex Mormon* video-ads leave us? In the conclusion of this chapter, the differences and possible interactions between the advertisement series will be explored by comparing the diverse reading modes in the communication spaces of production, representation, circulation / distribution, and consumption.

Four aspects define the reading modes of both series. While the documentary and moral modes evidently belong to the generic strategy of the videos, the identity, advertising, emotional, and performative modes embrace the specificity of each series, on which the concluding thoughts will focus.

In the space of representation two differences are notable. The family, a core unity of the LDS Church, is consistently at the center of the narration of the *I'm a Mormon* series.[338] While also part of the workforce, every man or woman stresses the importance of family, of having a husband or wife and of being a mother or father. If the portrayed members are not (yet) parents or married, they are often shown with their parents and sometimes with close friends who function like family. The relationships are consistenct with the core beliefs of the church, which exclusively supports heterosexual marriages. Here the series specifically engages an advertising mode that praises the religious institutions by promoting their member as role models who, hopefully, will evoke an identity mode.

---

338   Chen, "Diverse Yet Hegemonic."

The *I Am an Ex Mormon* videos are less concerned with the core family. The protagonists often refer to family in a negative way, fearing exclusion because they no longer belong to the church. Beside Heather's story, only one additional family (*We are the Leavitt Family*, US 2011) and two couples are depicted, one with children (*Our Marriage Has Survived a Crisis of Faith*, US 2011) and one in which the wife is pregnant (*Maria and Henning Schnurr – We are German Ex Mormons*, US 2011). In the latter video, the German couple Maria and Henning Schnurr state that one reason for their decision to leave the church was that they had started to question their faith that they wanted to hand down to their child(ren). The reference to family in the *I Am an Ex Mormon* videos therefore seeks to elicit an emotional mode that raises the audience's sympathies for the protagonist's decisions.

Secondly, Mormon beliefs are not discussed in the *I'm a Mormon* ads and religious practices are absent from both series. The former series shows many other forms of activity, often leisure based. The life of members of the LDS Church seems very busy and involves sports and many activities out of doors. They are healthy, energetic, and optimistic people. They are successful not only in their work but often also in their leisure time. Many representatives are current or former professionals in sports, the arts, or entertainment. Religion is presented as a lifestyle and as an attitude and, implicitly, as a reason for their success. Here lies a vital strategy for communicating the LDS worldview, one that engages the performative and advertising modes in terms of what is included and what is left out. As we have seen, the videos share an audio-visual style and the social actors' lifestyles are standardized too. Presented as role models, the protagonists advertise for and recruit followers who would like to adopt and perform their lifestyle as members of the church.

By contrast, the *I Am an Ex Mormon* initiative is focused on the narrative of why its social actors left the church. The narrative engages identity and emotional modes. The social actors often refer to the teachings, doctrines, and also the history of the church to explain why they no longer were able to believe in the church. We don't see them extensively with their families or enjoying leisure time. Some are filmed during a walk or while they are cooking at home, but they are rarely filmed at work or in the public sphere. It almost seems as if they have to confess in a private or even hidden setting.

Thirdly, a colonization strategy is evident in the production space of the *I'm a Mormon* commercials. On this level the performative and advertising modes interact to build a uniform LDS image. The Mormon lifestyle is transferred into and implemented within other cultures and other countries. Even though the cultural background of the members who are presented is diverse, their representation tends to conform to a repetitive pattern. A recognition factor is crucial if the commercials are to carry a corporate identity. The portrayed individuals function as signifiers of the unique LDS Church. The episodes relate an image and sell a product. That product is the church, represented by individual members who are buttressed by their families and friends. The social actors perform the LDS image as a norm within a greater geographical diversity. Within that diversity, the episodes recount a remarkable unity in the lives portrayed and the attitudes of the social actors. This unity is reinforced in a variety of ways that include an aesthetic strategy that produces familiar camera work, scoring, lighting, and staging across the episodes. This uniformity in style leaves less freedom of expression to the Mormons on-screen, with the Missionary Department apparently in control of the production from beginning to end.

In contrast, the *I Am an Ex Mormon* campaign is more diverse in the space of representation and applies an emotional mode in addressing its audience. The protagonists played an active part in the production process that adapted the audio-visual narrative to the protagonist's story. This resulted in the videos diverging in terms of length, film style, and narration. Diversity also comes into play in sexual orientation, but to a lesser extent with race, for the social actors are mainly Caucasians. As noted, seven of the Ex-Mormons are gay or transgender persons. Furthermore, the space of production is more transparent than the space of production generated by the LDS Church, providing further support for the emotional mode. The advertisement video, the only video on the website that applies an advertising mode, is frank about its own strategy and provides evidence of the difficulty of finding participants for the project, with only 44 videos having been made since 2010.

The advertising mode of the *I'm a Mormon* campaign in the space of production seems to have great chance of success, for a number of reasons. The LDS Church could finance the campaign generously, a financial viability not replicated for the *I Am an Ex Mormon* series: Mormons tithe; Ex-Mormons and their supporters only donate. Further the social actors for the former production are socially and psychologically rewarded by the large community of Mormons. The LDS Church has more members than there are ex-members, and the ideological support for its campaign is therefore greater. Additionally, participants in the *I Am an Ex Mormon* series are taking risks and surrendering something, as we have seen in the discussion of the emotional and identity modes. The Ex-Mormons who appear in the series are certainly appreciated by other Ex-Mormons, but they may be ignored or even despised by Mormons.

And, finally, in both series happiness plays a key role, as we have seen in the discussion of the reading modes. In the LDS Church campaign happiness is a product of being a Mormon, and in the counter campaign happiness is a product of being an Ex-Mormon. Only outstanding people find a place in the standardized religious communication space created by the LDS Church-produced videos. We encounter no one who has failed or is unhappy, no one who talks of discrimination. Success is defined differently in the *I Am an Ex Mormon* series. The participants' main achievement is their decision to leave the church. The Ex-Mormons often comment that their lives altered completely with that decision, from being unsatisfying and fearful into being buoyant and happy.

With the *I'm a Mormon* videos the LDS Church's missionary department efficiently and professionally created a person-centered campaign using documentary media and the possibilities of digital technology to relaunch the public appearance of the LDS. This new face of the religious community reflects how existing ideas and values could be adapted and communicated through mediatization. In the case of the *I'm a Mormon* campaign, performative, advertising, and identity modes shape a religion and its community, which need to adapt to the rules of a Westernized neoliberal society and its public sphere. The *I Am an Ex Mormon* initiative takes part in this media discourse and provides its own version, of being an ex-Mormon, by applying emotional, identity, and performative modes. And as the term Ex-*Mormon* indicates, Mormonism remains its point of reference. The initiative is legitimized by reference to the LDS Church campaign. The stylistic allocations in the title, the person-centered dramaturgy, other style elements like music, and the happy performance mode are significant enough to put the two accounts in conversation. Each side can profit from and is limited by the other. Although the LDS Church does not allow comments on its webpage, the Ex-Mormon page provides space for conversations between Mormons and Ex-Mormons. Here they are connected to each other in the space of communication as they overlap on each level of production, circulation / distribution, representation, and consumption to a certain extent. By identifying the partly overlapping and specific reading modes, it has been possible to examine the aims and audience response of both series.

This chapter demonstrates how the *I'm a Mormon* image campaign is shaped by the consumption space within which it is received. It further highlights how the consumption space responds to the space of representation by applying different reading modes. One of these numerous reading modes is articulated in the production of the *I Am an Ex Mormon* videos, which produced further reading modes. These complex processes of producing, distributing, circulating, consuming, and reproducing documentary media are located in spaces of communication that efficiently exchange, transform, and reproduce religious worldviews. New forms of religious communication will influence and alter a community and its aims. In the current case, that transformation includes the targeted audience of members, non-members, and ex-members who take part in the mediatization processes of growing religious communication spaces.

5. The Private is Public in Reality Shows about Religion

What do a reality show about a polygamist Mormon family produced by a private television channel and a reality show about Mormon missionaries produced by a religious institution have in common? The answer: a great deal. Both productions depict practicing Mormons and they also share the reality television (RTV) format, with its distinct aesthetic conventions, production framing, and reading modes. In *The District* (US 2007–13) The Church of Jesus Christ of the Latter-day Saints (LDS Church) provides instruction in the training of missionaries; *Sister Wives* (US 2010–19) is produced by Discovery Inc., a US American company that specializes in real-life entertainment, for the US TV network TLC, where it is shown to entertain. The distinction between the two is not, however, clear cut. *The District* aims not only to teach its audience but also to entertain, and the polygamous family in *Sister Wives* uses the show to defend and teach about their polygamous lifestyle, seeking greater acceptance and perhaps eventually legal status.[339]

The current chapter explores the interface between religion and reality television and demonstrates how the boundaries between the private and public spheres of religion are blurred. To show how the public and private interact, it addresses the shows' different reading modes in relation to how they address their audiences. *The District* instructs its audience in missionary work by applying an entertaining mode. By contrast, *Sister Wives* entertains its audience with instruction about a religious lifestyle, that of a polygamist family. In so doing both RTV shows communicate religious issues that link the private with the public.

---

339 Maura Strassberg has discussed the legal situation of the polygamous family portrayed in *Sister Wives*. The five adults brought their case to court on the grounds that Utah's criminalization of polygamy was unconstitutional. See Maura Strassberg, "Scrutinizing Polygamy: Utah's Brown v. British Columbia's Reference Re: Section 293," in *Beyond Same-Sex Marriage: Perspectives on Marital Possibilities*, ed. Ronald C. Den Otter (Lanham: Lexington Books, 2016), 167–203.

Part II: Interactions between Communication Spaces and Religion

5.1. Image cultivation

How can we define the relationship between reality television and religion and how might it be characterized? What role does religion play in this type of documentary media and how does the RTV style shape and communicate religion? Picking up on the definition given in part I, religion is understood here as a specific form of communication often dealing with human contingency. The term religion is also closely connected to its agents and to how they understand the concept.[340] They give meaning to religious symbols, practices, and narratives, with those practices including media practices that are embraced by the term "mediatization".[341]

The semio-pragmatic approach applied here considers how religious actors interact with the media and thereby define their own meaning and, vice versa, how media professionals depict religion and its practices in light of their own perspectives. These interactions have in common the variety of ways they communicate about religion, be it from a perspective that is inside, outside, or a mixture of both. Religious communication is influenced by the institutions involved, so in this instance not just by the church but also by a private television channel. The institutional framing, whether church or television network, influences how religious representations are expressed and how they interact with the communication spaces of production, circulation/distribution, and consumption. In these spaces, a diversity of social actors, religious and non-religious, actively shape the meaning-making processes of religious representations and practices.

RTV as documentary media

In this study, RTV is understood as a specific type of documentary media that is defined by a characteristic audio-visual style in the space of representation, by particular production and distribution processes, and by its intended audiences and reading modes in the space of consumption. Stylistically, RTV is conceptualized as an (almost) unscripted show with "ordi-

---

340 See chapter part I, chapter 2.
341 Hjarvard, "Three Forms of Mediatized Religion. Changing the Public Face of Religion"; Hjarvard, "The Mediatisation of Religion: Theorising Religion, Media and Social Change.".

nary" people in the sense of "non-elite".[342] The producers claim to be entering into a private sphere, where they observe people through the camera lens. But the everyday life they record has to be more captivating and more spectacular than the lives of the viewers. Why would they watch something on TV that might take place in their own everyday lives? In the space of representation RTV therefore seeks to depict a combination of entertainment and "the self-conscious discourse of the real" as Laurie Oulette and Susan Murray point out. They describe RTV as

> an unabashedly commercial genre united less by aesthetic rules or certainties than by the fusion of popular entertainment with a self-conscious claim to the discourse of the real. This coupling ... is what has made reality TV an important generic forum for a range of institutional and cultural developments that include the merger of marketing and "real life" entertainment, the convergence of new technologies with programs and their promotion, and an acknowledgement of the manufactured artifice that coexists with truth claims.[343]

Truth claims only work if the audience agrees to believe that what they are seeing is genuine. Therefore RTV must convince the viewer that what is depicted really happened in the space of production. These "real" events are further combined with an entertaining mode. One can argue that RTV mediates the everyday lives of common people to divert viewers from their own everyday lives. The potential paradox in this approach is dissolved when we recognize that it is easier to be disgusted or fascinated by other people's lives than to engage our own lives. Watching the struggles and joys of others may distance viewers from their own burdens.

Thus RTV spaces of communication combine strong references to the "real" with an entertaining mode. In the space of production and distribution, RTV performs as a commercial genre, seeking to acquire potential customers and be able to sell advertisement time and product placements.[344] The space of representation is focused on presenting the real as spectacularly as possible, to keep the audience, potential consumers of the advertised products, watching. The relationship between audience and the

---

342 Anita Biressi and Heather Nunn, *Reality TV: Realism and Revelation* (London, New York: Wallflower, 2005), 154/155.
343 Susan Murray and Laurie Ouellette, *Reality TV: Remaking Television Culture*, 2nd ed. (New York: New York University Press, 2009), 3.
344 June Deery, "Reality TV as Advertisement," *Popular Communication* 2, no. 1 (March 2004): 1–20.

depiction of the real places a levy on the social actors and may result in their exploitation.[345] RTV productions profit from personal dramas involving the social actors, who may feel forced to reveal as much as possible. The pressure to express themselves can lead to competition for attention among the social actors that encourages them to expose their individual goals and personal interests.

These conditions provide viewers with spectacle, which can include intimate moments, with immediacy, and with a promise to present "social, psychological, political and historical truths and to depict the rhythms and structures of everyday life with the least recourse possible to dramatisation and artifice."[346] Participants in reality shows earn money by selling the right to represent their private lives and as a result their lives become public. The media institutions, in this instance television channels, then in turn sell commercial time. Yet what if the viewer simply changes channel while the commercials are shown and fails to return? The show has to offer something that keeps the viewer tuned in during breaks for advertisements. When it needs to compete with other media suppliers, RTV must adopt the rules of the market.

RTV between private and public

RTV meanders between private and public spaces, almost dissolving their borders. In its spaces of communication RTV even challenges the right to privacy and autonomy. Whether privacy and autonomy are respected depends on the interactions between the spaces of production and representation. While it might be argued that potential social agents are free to decide whether to participate and what to reveal, the situation is more complex. What of the involvement of children – frequent participants in RTV shows about polygamy – who are not able to give permission on their own behalf? As Michel Foucault has demonstrated, relations between human beings always involve power. There are dependencies between producers and social actors.[347] The exercise of such power defines the production and representation processes, but ruler and subject also maintain each other

---

345 Murray and Ouellette, *Reality TV*, 4.
346 Biressi and Nunn, *Reality TV*, 2005, 3.
347 Michel Foucault, *Sexualität und Wahrheit*, [Versch. Aufl.], Suhrkamp-Taschenbuch Wissenschaft (Frankfurt/M.: Suhrkamp, 1977), 93–95.

5. The Private is Public in Reality Shows about Religion

and thereby sustain the power network.³⁴⁸ For the media scholar Swantje Lingenberg, the central question concerns who draws the boundaries between the private and the public and whether individuals can maintain their autonomy within their private sphere or are defined by economic and political rules.³⁴⁹ German media scholar Friedrich Krotz's work on the Internet allows us to recognize that rather than concentrate on the extent of the privacy or publicity RTV facilitates, we might look at how the boundary that manifests in the social and cultural sphere is drawn between the private and the public. That boundary cannot be defined solely by the media, in this instance by RTV.³⁵⁰

Krotz explores three discourses about the public and the private.³⁵¹ First, with reference to Jürgen Habermas he defines the political dimension of the public, where power can be controlled. Democracy exists only in the public sphere and privacy is an individual human right. Secondly, the medial dimension addresses the need for publicity, which may run counter to, or even override, the rights of the individual because the media are less concerned with a single human being and more concerned with their target audience. And, finally, the third approach emphasized by Krotz requires the media to be assessed not in relation to their role in democratic processes but rather according to their practices, which make evident that the media, including RTV, have purposes beyond providing publicity for democratic processes.

RTV productions must be financially successful; to be financially successful they need to preserve their audience; to preserve their audience they need to keep their viewers entertained. Krotz highlights that the lives filmed by the camera are not the private lives of the participants. The social actors stage themselves and their lives, enabling a spotlight to be shone on intimate and private moments.³⁵² This blurring of the public and private has telling implications for the depiction of religion in reality shows.

---

348 Fritz et al., *Sichtbare Religion*, 122–126.
349 Swantje Lingenberg, "Öffentlich(keit) und Privat(heit)," in *Handbuch Cultural Studies und Medienanalyse*, ed. Andreas Hepp et al. (Wiesbaden: Springer Verlag, 2015), 177.
350 Friedrich Krotz, "Die Veränderung von Privatheit und Öffentlichkeit in der heutigen Gesellschaft," *Merz: Medien + Erziehung. Zeitschrift für Medienpädagogik* 8/09, no. 53 (2009): 2/3.
351 Krotz, 4–8.
352 Krotz, 7.

Part II: Interactions between Communication Spaces and Religion

Religion in the public sphere of the media

In recent years the positioning of religion in the tension between private and public has been much debated. The application of these dichotomic terms in the study of media and religion has been marked and has borne fruit. Traditional religious practice now competes in parts of Europe and North America in particular with leisure-time activities.[353] The authors of a socio-empirical study in Switzerland have concluded that with leisure time traditionally located in the private sphere, religion has become a rival for that time within that market.[354] Additionally, with increasing secularization, the presence of traditional religion in the public sphere is diminishing.[355] Political debates surrounding religious symbols in the public sphere confirm a tendency particularly marked in Europe for traditional religious identity markers to be exhibited only in private and not in public: thus, for example, in 2009 the Minaret Initiative in Switzerland achieved a ban on the construction of minarets.[356] In Denmark, Belgium, Germany, France, part of Switzerland (Ticino), and the Netherlands the wearing of the full face veil is prohibited.[357] Legal restrictions are often aimed at Muslim clothing that traditionally covers the female body, including the face.[358] Other debates have questioned whether public servants should be allowed to wear a head scarf, if crucifixes should be displayed in public buildings (in Bavaria),[359] or if schoolboys should be permitted to refuse to shake the

---

353 Chapter 1.1 discusses this aspect further.
354 Stolz et al., *Religion und Spiritualität in der Ich-Gesellschaft*. See detailed discussion in the chapter "Religious lifestyles in the media" in part I.
355 Wim Hofstee and Arje Van der Koij, "Introduction," in *Religion beyond Its Private Role in Modern Society*, ed. Wim Hofstee and Arje Van der Koij, vol. 20 (Leiden: Brill, 2013), 1–14.
356 Fritz et al., *Sichtbare Religion*, 1/2.
357 Radhika Sanghani, "Burka Bans: The Countries Where Muslim Women Can't Wear Veils," *The Telegraph*, July 8, 2016, https://www.telegraph.co.uk/women/life/burka-bans-the-countries-where-muslim-women-cant-wear-veils/.
358 Reyhan Şahin, "Symbol of Islam, of Emancipation, or of Oppression? Various meanings of Muslim Head Coverings in Germany," *Journal jüdisches Museum Berlin*, no. 16 (2017): 47–54.
359 Kate Connolly, "Bavarians Wary of New Law Requiring Crosses in All Public Buildings," *The Guardian*, May 31, 2018, sec. World news, https://www.theguardian.com/world/2018/may/31/bavarians-wary-of-new-law-requiring-crosses-in-all-public-buildings.

hand of a female teacher for religious reasons.[360] These recent debates around religious symbols in the public sphere were intensely covered by the media.

Some prominent academics contend that religion is returning[361] or has never left or deem secularization to be a European special case.[362] Linda Woodhead has adopted a middle way in this debate, noting that the tension between the private and the public is integral, for "spirituality – like a great deal of religion – therefore has both public and personal aspects. These aspects are analytically separable but not distinct, and should not be pulled apart as sharply as the public/private binary would have us to do."[363] The private – or according to Woodhead "personal" – and the public are intermingled in the religious realm and are therefore useful categories on a systematic level only. We can, however, deploy these concepts as analytical tools as we explore the interface between reality shows and religion.

RTV as interface between the private and public sphere of religion

Why should we be concerned to know whether religion must be considered private or public and how those roles might be changing? The distinction between these two spheres has long been formative for scholarly research about religion, and, as we shall see, scholars need not fear that this defining rationale is about to disappear. As discussed there are different opinions about the private and the public sphere of religion but the authors mainly agree that there is something going on between these realms. And it makes sense to look at specific cases to work out this complex relationship. The binary terms are on several levels interwoven in the RTV and the analysis of this fabric provides rich insights into a relevant dimensions of religion.

---

360 "Swiss Parliament Will Not Enforce Handshakes in School," SWI swissinfo.ch, accessed February 8, 2019, https://www.swissinfo.ch/eng/business/religion-in-the-classroom_swiss-parliament-will-not-enforce-handshakes-in-school/43549838.
361 Taylor, "Why We Need a Radical Redefinition of Secularism."
362 Casanova, "Eurozentristischer Säkularismus und die Herausforderung der Globalisierung," 33–37.
363 Linda Woodhead, "New Forms of Public Religion: Spirituality in Global Civil Society," in *Religion beyond Its Private Role in Modern Society* (Leiden: Brill, 2013), 49.

Part II: Interactions between Communication Spaces and Religion

The media have a central role to play in the debates about religion in the public and the private spheres. As we have seen (chap. 2, part I), newspapers, radio, television, and the Internet all participate in the diffusion of religion in the public sphere. For Jürgen Habermas their participation is characteristic of a post-secular society where religion is involved in meaning- and decision-making processes.[364] As a type of documentary media, reality shows that engage religion contribute in a particular way, relocating religion from the private to the public sphere. The staged images of religion in the private sphere that are broadcast on RTV are circulated back into the private sphere through the space of consumption. In this case RTV functions as a multifaceted interface: individual and private actions become public and public actions become private. If reality shows are not actually depicting private religion, as Krotz argues, but rather religion staged as private, the complexity of the interface is intensified. The distinction does not disappear, as philosopher of law Bart C. Labuschagne contends,[365] but the media define their own rules in the spaces of production, representation, circulation/distribution and consumption and these rules are relevant for the perception of religion.

Using a single form of documentary media, *The District* and *Sister Wives* depict very different Mormon experiences. Those different lives enable a multilayered investigation of the private and public dimensions of religion. Both polygamous Mormons and members of the LDS Church are depicted in private spaces, where they defend their lifestyle, their religious institution, or even the nature of their family unit. This chapter will now explore how RTV shapes religion and how religion shapes RTV, first through discussion of the spaces of communication and then through a close reading of a number of central sequences.

---

364 Jürgen Habermas, "Religion in der Öffentlichkeit der 'postsäkularen' Gesellschaft," in *Nachmetaphysisches Denken II. Aufsätze und Repliken*, vol. 2 (Berlin: Suhrkamp, 2012), 313.

365 Bart C. Labuschagne, Wim Hofstee, and Arje Van der Koij, "Religion and Politics in Post-Secular Society: Beyond the Public / Private Divide," in *Religion beyond Its Private Role in Modern Society* (Leiden, Boston: Brill, 2013), 27.

5.2. Entertainingly instructing the audience in The District

In October 2012 the *Deseret News*, a Salt Lake City-based newspaper, ran the headline "LDS missionaries are stars of new reality TV series."³⁶⁶ The wording was accurate in capturing the nature of the show – the spotlight is turned on missionaries and their work (fig. 39). But the show also actively supports the work of mission, potentially motivating young Mormons to go on mission or encouraging a friendly response from non-Mormons visited by missionaries. The missionaries who later became "stars" of *The District 2* (US 2012/13) had originally been filmed for an instructional video made in 2009 in San Diego/CA to prepare missionaries for service. The show is collaboratively produced by BYUtv and the LDS Church's Missionary Department. Established in 2000, BYUtv is a satellite TV station of Brigham Young University (BYU). By 2004 its programming was reaching an audience of 26 million and 15 years later more than 53 million US households.³⁶⁷ The webpage for the series announces the show as follows: "These video segments show real missionaries, members, and investigators in non-scripted, unrehearsed, actual missionary situations."³⁶⁸

The production history tells us something of the interplay between RTV and religion. During three months in 2007, a film crew recorded four male and two female missionaries at the Mormon mission in San Antonio, TX. The film footage was edited and used as training material, supplementary to the standard mission curriculum of the mission book *Preach my Gospel*, which had been recently introduced, in 2004.³⁶⁹ This footage later became *The District 1*. Church leaders had seen the video as a way to help missionaries implement the new approach to mission outlined in *Preach my Gospel*, for example in relation to their daily schedule:

---

366 Jamshid Ghazi Askar, "LDS Missionaries Are Stars of New Reality TV Series," DeseretNews.com, October 12, 2012, https://www.deseretnews.com/article/865564309/LDS-missionaries-are-stars-of-new-reality-TV-series.html.
367 BYUtv Giving. "What We Do."
368 "The District," accessed February 8, 2019, https://www.mormonchannel.org/watch/collection/the-district.
369 Intellectual Reserve, Salt Lake City/UT, US 2004. The book has been translated into 42 languages.

Part II: Interactions between Communication Spaces and Religion

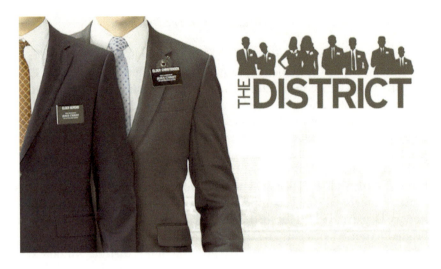

Fig. 39 A poster for the reality show The District 2 shows two business suits, an identify marker for Mormon missionaries.

Missionary Daily Schedule

6:30 a.m.	Arise, pray, exercise (30 minutes), and prepare for the day.
7:30 a.m.	Breakfast.
8:00 a.m.	Personal study: *The Book of Mormon*, other scriptures, doctrines of the missionary lessons, and other chapters from Preach My Gospel, the Missionary Handbook, and the Missionary Health Guide.
9:00 a.m.	Companion study: share what you have learned during personal study, prepare to teach, practice teaching, study chapters from *Preach My Gospel*, confirm plans for the day.
10:00 a.m.	Begin proselyting. Missionaries learning a language study that language for an additional 30 to 60 minutes, including planning language learning activities to use during the day. Missionaries may take an hour for lunch and additional study, and an hour for dinner at times during the day that fit best with their proselyting. Normally dinner should be finished no later than 6:00 p.m.

9:00 p.m.	Return to living quarters (unless teaching a lesson; then return by 9:30) and plan the next day's activities (30 minutes). Write in journal, prepare for bed, pray.
10:30 p.m.	Retire to bed.[370]

Criticism of *The District 1* noted that the footage seemed too perfect; the reality of tough missionary work was lacking.[371] More flaws would give a greater sense of the reality. The next version would also contextualize the missionaries, who through self-reflection present their stories on-screen in black and white, with personal material such as photos of their family and from their childhoods included. They were also allowed to talk about more intimate and emotional topics during interviews.

The District 2 was filmed in San Diego/CA with six male and two female missionaries. Now BYUtv creative director Scott Swofford, the former media director at the Missionary Department responsible for the production of training videos and for initiating the *I'm a Mormon* campaign, proposed the material be used for a reality show.[372] For the second season more time was invested in preparing the missionaries. The filming itself was more elaborate and took five times longer.

The videos of *The District 2*, with the title *8 Stories*, are permanently shown at the theatre of the LDS Church visitor center in Salt Lake City (UT), located in the temple district. Behind three dark glass doors three monitors, on which the show is screened, are visible from the outside (fig. 40). To the left and right of the doors eight posters present the protagonists in oversized and illuminated posters, where they are posed as upright role models for the perfect missionary (fig. 41). Inside the theater the eight young people are again present on huge images displayed on the wall, but now they, or at least the men, are dressed in casual clothing. The male members of the group wear jeans and a checkered shirt; the women are wearing prudish Mormon-missionary-conforming blouses (fig. 42). The elegant theater in which *8 Stories* is presented is indicative of how important the mission is for the LDS Church. The investment is not surprising: today members of the LDS Church are more likely to be converts than cradle Mormons.[373]

---

370 Preach My Gospel, 2004, viii.
371 Bridget Kreis, "'The District': Where Are They Now?," *Third Hour* (blog), March 16, 2015, https://thirdhour.org/blog/hasten/district-now/.
372 The campaign is discussed in detail in part II, chapter 1.
373 Stark, *The Rise of Mormonism*, 136. See also chapter 3.4 for more details.

Part II: Interactions between Communication Spaces and Religion

Fig. 40/ Fig. 41/ Fig. 42 The show is prominently presented at the Temple Square North Visitors' Center in Salt Lake City/UT (Images: Marie-Therese Mäder, US 2015).

The two series can be streamed online or watched on two DVDs, which include further instructional material. The DVDs have different titles that suggest their purposes: "Demonstrating Principles of Planning, Finding, and Working with Members" (*The District 1*) and "Demonstrating Principles of Teaching" (*The District 2*).[374] Each DVD case contains two DVDs, with the series' episodes on disc one and the training segments on disc two. The space of consumption of this LDS Church reality show demonstrates how a single product can be used for different purposes. The production tapped *The District*'s full potential, for it is used to instruct future missionaries, to explain to their parents and families to what it means for their sons and daughters to be sent on mission, and to inform non-Mormons who might encounter missionaries in the street or on their doorstep.

---

374 The DVD is produced by the LDS Church and officially distributed by Intellectual Reserve (US 2007, 2010), a non-profit corporation owned by the corporation of the president of the church.

Communication strategies of *The District 1* and *The District 2*

In additional to the different social actors, there are obvious stylistic differences between the two seasons. *The District 1* works with more instructional means and is therefore less entertaining than *The District 2*. For example, *The District 2* introduces the social actors with their names and each episode has its own title, whereas *The District 1* prosaically calls its three episodes simply *Planning*. The narrative of *The District 1* also focusses less on the missionaries and their personalities and more on the processes of mission work; a shift in emphasis sees the former more central in *The District 2*. This shift is replicated with the deployment of an entertainment mode and other specific stylistic elements of (reality-) shows: each episode of *The District 2*, for example, begins with recurring opening titles and each finishes with a "cliff hanger", intended to rouse curiosity about the next episode.

Both seasons, we should note, explicitly but in somewhat different ways refer to the documentary media genre. Season 1 of the *District 1* starts with a title on a black background accompanied by suspenseful electronic music that simulates the rhythm of a heartbeat. The male voice-over comments: "What you are about to see is real and unscripted." Then the series' title is superimposed and the voice resumes: "The missionaries, investigators, and members in this program are not actors." In the first episodes of *The District 1* the title is still visible as two missionaries are filmed from behind as they walk through the streets (fig. 43). It is night. Suddenly one missionary sees some passers-by and starts to run, saying: "Huh, there is a man, let's go talk to him" (00:00:16–00:00:19).

Although in both seasons each episode provides a short summary of the previous episode, *The District 2* follows a new path in introducing its narrative.[375] The episodes in the later series open with the theme music and scenes from sunny San Diego, longshots of the beach, surfers under a blue sky, skaters in the street and a typical white Mormon temple. Then the voice-over explains (00:00:08–00:00:15): "San Diego, California. This is our home for eighteen months to two years." Short scenes from the series follow, with

---

375 The discussion refers to the six episodes of *The District 2* that are available on the webpage "The District." Accessed March 1, 2019. https://www.mormonchannel.org/watch/collection/the-district. The episodes can be downloaded in different sizes, indicative of the church's desire to ensure the episodes can be widely dispersed. Surprisingly, the downloaded files for epodes 1–3 differ from the embedded sources. They are longer and contain partly different footage.

Part II: Interactions between Communication Spaces and Religion

Fig. 43 The District 1 introduces its protagonists proselytizing in the streets in a suspenseful nighttime atmosphere (The District 1, Planning, 00:00:09).

the missionaries commenting on their experiences. The commentary continues – "This is the story of eight missionaries who are called to serve" – as the eight missionaries are introduced visually with a split-screen of a close-up on one side and a single shot on the other side (fig. 44–51).

"What you are about to see is real and unscripted. The missionaries, investigators, and members in this program are not actors. This is the story of *The District*."[376] The opening credits, accompanied by uplifting piano music, include scenes from different episodes and finish with the title of the show on a black background. The commentary announces: "Last time on the district" and then earlier events are summarized to refresh the audience's memory (00:01:19–00:01:55). The ending of each episode adopts a similar model, this time providing glimpses of the next episode. The audiovisual devices applied to the opening and ending of each episode of *The District 2* correspond with conventional RTV narration. To this point, the narration of *The District 2* has addressed the audience in an entertaining reading mode, with an instructional mode not yet apparent.

---

376   *The District 2*, 00:00:34–00:01:18.

5. The Private is Public in Reality Shows about Religion

Fig. 44/ Fig. 45/ Fig. 46/ Fig. 47/ Fig. 48/ Fig. 49/ Fig. 50/ Fig. 51 The social actors are introduced with a split screen that presents them in portrait on one side and at work on the other side (The District 2, Turning Point, 00:00:27–00:00:34).

Success stories

One particular characteristic of the episodes is not typical of RTV style: the dialogue, in part unscripted, is conspicuously standardized to follow the missionary guide *Preach my Gospel*. Although the scenes are pronounced to be unscripted, for several weeks in advance, the missionaries had been prepared for the shooting, alongside the basic missionary training with which each mission begins. The missionaries' behavior is therefore not entirely spontaneous and seems somewhat rehearsed.

Turning Point, the sequence from episode 7 to which we will now turn and which tackles the missionaries' work and successful proselytization and contains reflection by the missionaries, addresses as already mentioned three consumption spaces. First, it is intended for future missionaries, who are instructed in how to proselytize. Secondly, it helps their family members and friends understand what they experience during the 18–24 months of their absence. And thirdly, candidates for baptism, "investigators" as they are known, are informed about the process of conversion. The term "investigators" is intended to convey that the work of learning about the church is done by the potential converts, who are to establish for themselves the truth of the church's teachings. The episode has an emotional arch that shows doubts and frustrations on both sides, by missionaries and possible converts, but reaches a happy ending (00:20:37–00:24:14), at least for two missionaries and their convert. The narrative is built around a Jynx, a candidate who is not easily persuaded and whose stubborn unwillingness to accept everything the missionaries say is charming and winning. The close reading that follows here considers the reading modes of the narration and how it connects to the public and private dimensions of religion.

Proselytizing in private

A short visual insert of a red rose marks the beginning of a new sequence, with Jynx and the missionaries in a private space, her living room. Jynx is obviously not thrilled to hear that Mormons do not drink coffee. Elder Moreno tries to find the right words to make the rules clear without being too overbearing or too strict. The camera is very close to Jynx (fig.52), showing her surprise and indignation as she reacts to the idea that she might stop drinking coffee.

5. The Private is Public in Reality Shows about Religion

Fig. 52 "Coffee!?" Jinx finds it hard to grasp that as a Mormon she would have to give up drinking coffee (The District 2, Turning Point, 00:20:41).

Fig. 53 Elder Moreno leads the conversation while Elder Christensen listens attentively and supports his colleague with his presence (The District 2, Turning Point, 00:20:43).

The two elders, Moreno and Christensen, are filmed in a medium close shot. The scene applies the reverse-shot principle, with the camera located in the middle of this private conversation space, filming the social actors from the front as they talk and listen to each other. The scene gives the impression that the camera, or viewer, is participating in this private conversation. When Elder Moreno seeks to explain why Jynx should give up coffee, the camera moves closer. The elder is now in focus, challenged to explain the rules (fig. 53): "Why do you think the Lord would want us to stay away from these types of things?" (00:20:43–00:20:46).

Jynx' hesitation is emotional and inscribed in her facial expressions. She defends her reluctance to stop drinking coffee and beer, surprised and also somewhat indignant at the suggestion: "I can understand harmful or addictive substances and illegal drugs and tobacco. But I love my beer and I like my coffee every morning." She laughs at the absurdity of the rule. At first the viewer may assume she is arguing with a single person, but a two shot reveals two people are sitting across from here – Elders always proselytize in pairs. Later we see that four people are in fact present: a two shot shows her friend Joan sitting next to her on the sofa (fig. 54). Joan is herself a Mormon and supports the missionaries' arguments about living according to the rules of health of the "Word of Wisdom".[377]

---

377 "Word of Wisdom" is part of the scriptural canon of the LDS Church. It includes instruction on what should be eaten and drunk and prohibits the use of tobacco and drugs. These rules are based on revelations by Joseph Smith and are part of Mormon teachings. See section 89 in Orson Pratt and Church of Jesus

175

Part II: Interactions between Communication Spaces and Religion

Fig. 54 Joan proposes to Jynx that she should start by giving up just one thing (The District 2, Turning Point, 00:21:27).

Elder Moreno proceeds with his instruction, with Jynx so far making no commitments (00:21:00–00:21:44): "You are getting a confirmation that it's true, it would have to come through experience and maybe living it to try to find out if this really is inspired from God." Jynx is shown in a close-up. Elder Moreno proceeds: "Just like if you wanna find out Joseph Smith was a prophet you have to read *The Book of Mormon*. Likewise, we invite you ..." The two elders are again shown, with Elder Moreno continuing, "... to see the fruits of living the Word of Wisdom." A two-shot of Joan and Jynx follows and Moreno continues off-screen: "Will you live the Word of Wisdom so that you can prepare yourself for baptism?" Jynx is surprised: "You mean start now?" Moreno affirms: "Uh huh." Now Joan intervenes: "Pick one thing, one thing." Jynx answers with obvious hesitation: "Ok, I give up tobacco." Now everybody is laughing. But Joan and Elder Moreno don't give up. Joan adds: "That you do!" Again the group laughs. Moreno presses further; he wants a commitment: "No, just live the commandment now." The first part of the conversation ends with a joke when Jynx answers that she will give up "illegal drugs" which she obviously doesn't consume. After a cut Jynx is shown in an interview situation; she is holding a copy of *The Book of Mormon* and reflecting "on the sofa" on

---

Christ of Latter-day Saints, *The Doctrine and Covenants of The Church of Jesus Christ of Latter-Day Saints* (LaVergne/TN: Kessinger, 2009).

5. The Private is Public in Reality Shows about Religion

Fig. 55 Brother Hunt, a LDS Church member, is supervising the discussion. He is in the middle of the frame, sitting in the highest position (The District 2, Turning Point, 00:21:58).

her possible conversion to Mormonism. Framed in a medium close-up, she talks to an invisible interviewee who appears to be at a 45 degree angle from the camera. Her pronouncements now seem less trenchant and direct (00:21:47–00:21:58): "My big concern was all these little rules. Maybe when I read this I will see that God says in here that all these D&A [deals and allowances] are necessary."

Finally, in a medium long shot we see all five of the social actors who are participating in this conversation. Church member Brother Hunt is centrally positioned in the shot, with Jynx and her friend on his right and the two elders on his left. His position in the middle of the space acknowledges his privilege, as a supervisor in the LDS Church (fig. 55).

Elder Moreno persists: "So will you commit to the Word of Wisdom?" Jynx remains stubborn: "Ok, I won't drink beer." Joan is laughing, and Jynx continues: "But I have to keep my coffee going this week." The camera zooms in to Jynx as she makes this pronouncement; she too is now laughing. In a close-up Elder Moreno says insistently: "Ok, and next time when we meet will you give up coffee?" Jynx is not persuaded and will not make any promises. She looks Moreno in the eye and says (fig. 56): "We will see." The camera returns to Moreno after a cut and the audience see a certain disappointment in his facial expression as he answers with a curt "ok", and nods disappointedly (fig. 57). Jynx' resistance obviously challenges Moreno; at the same time her reaction is relatable.

Fig. 56 Asked to agree to stop drinking coffee at their next meeting, Jynx looks Moreno in the eyes and declares: "We will see." (The District 2, Turning Point, 00:22:15).

Fig. 57 Moreno's disappointment at Jynx' resistance is obvious (The District 2, Turning Point, 00:22:19).

Fig. 58 Evidently Jynx does not like the rules she would have to follow as a baptized member of the LDS Church (The District 2, Turning Point, 00:22:26).

Apparently Jynx does not agree with all the rules she will have to abide by: "It's just that I have so few vices and that little cup of coffee in the morning." She nods almost sadly. Joan tries to cheer her up (fig. 58): "But you can..." She is quickly interrupted by Jynx' comment: "That isn't nice!"

5. The Private is Public in Reality Shows about Religion

Baptism in public

The episode finishes with a successful conversion story: the baptism of Eric (00:22:29–00:24:07). This, the narration proposes, is the outcome awaiting Jynx. Eric has refrained from cigarettes, alcohol, and coffee in order to become a member of the church, as he mentions in the interview at the end of the episode. The sequence comes after that with Jynx and takes place in a public space, within the church at the baptismal font.[378] Off-camera Eric explains his decision to convert. Mormon priests bless him, a rite that follows the baptism. The whole sequence is accompanied by uplifting guitar music (00:22:35–00:24:05). Eric proceeds with his story off-screen: "I wasn't drinking anymore, I wasn't smoking. And it gives me more energy and I try to think of good things rather than thinking of bad things that happened to me because a while back I'm kind of like full of anger and hate every time, but now I kind of let go." We hear the priest say "Amen" (fig. 59), and Eric replies "Amen." After the second "Amen" a black is superimposed and the title *The District* fades in.

Fig. 59 The camera is very close on Eric during the blessing rite (The District 2, Turning Point, 00:24:05).

---

[378] Baptisms are public events in the LDS Church, to which non-Mormons are welcome. They differ from rites such as the sealing ceremony of couples (marriage) or the baptisms for the dead. They take place in the temple to which only Mormons officially recommended by the bishop have access.

The end sequence provides detailed information about how a Mormon baptism is performed. It is also an opportunity for Elder Murray and Elder Tuituu to speak about persistence. They describe the process of proselytizing during an interview that continues in the voice-over during the baptism. Eric, wearing the white baptism garment, and Murray are posing for pictures in front of the baptismal font. Elder Murray slaps Eric on the back and talks to him. Elder Tuituu comments: "This man has a strong desire to follow Christ and makes sure that he is in his life and he is willing to trust God and willing to follow him. But even though it can than result … " Elder Tuituu stops briefly and proceeds again when the baptism group is shown, with the priest, Elders Murray and Tiutuu, and Eric: "My companion and I were able to see a result for him. We knew what might be ahead of him. We were so excited."

The whole baptism is depicted largely as instruction. First the rite is rehearsed outside the pool, where the priest explains to the person to be baptized what exactly he will do in the font (fig. 60). After a group picture with the Elders, the priest and the baptism candidate Eric (fig. 61), the actual baptism inside the pool follows (fig. 62), filmed with an underwater camera (fig. 63). The audience enters virtually into the baptism font and observes the rite closely, able to witness the moment when the priest and the newly born Mormon shake hands in the pool right after the act of immersion (fig. 64). Before the next part of the rite starts, the missionaries congratulate and hug Eric (fig. 65). They are very proud of the baptism, and the perspective provided by the camera seems to suggest that they are congratulating themselves on this achievement: when Elder Tuituu hugs Eric, Eric is visible only from the back.

During this rite of passage, Murray comments, mostly in the voice-over, on his experiences during missionary work. In the course of the interview in the baptism sequence he is shown in close-up in two short cutaways as he comments (00:23:13–00:23:47): "But I've followed that prompting to go just a little bit more and it came. And so now I have a testimony that whenever you do all that you can, Murray, to bring about the good, to have success, it will happen, it may not happen in your timetable or the way you want it to do. But it always happens and I know that." During the blessing rite the voice of the priest is audible in the sound bridge (fig. 66): "We lay hands upon your head and confirm you a member of The Church of Jesus Christ of Latter-day Saints."

The episode ends with a baptism and the blessing of the community by the priests, as is also the case at the end of the seven other episodes. The structural analogy highlights that the efforts of the missionaries are always

5. The Private is Public in Reality Shows about Religion

Fig. 60/ Fig. 61/ Fig. 62/ Fig. 63/ Fig. 64/ Fig. 65 The performance of a baptism is instructional for both missionaries and potential candidates for baptism (The District 2, Turning Point, 00:22:42/ 00:22:56/ 00:23:06/ 00:23:08/ 00:23:12/ 00:23:23).

Fig. 66 Eric is now a member of the LDS Church and receives a blessing. He is accepted into the community surrounded by Mormon priests, who welcome him and care about him, the scene suggests (The District 2, Turning Point, 00:24:01).

rewarded by God, evident in baptisms that result from the missionaries' persistence.

Part II: Interactions between Communication Spaces and Religion

Reading modes of proselytizing in private to be baptized in public

The close reading of the two sequences reveals how the public and private dimensions structure the narration and its communication spaces. It also shows how an informational mode is combined with an entertaining mode. The first sequence takes place in Jynx' private home, a private space, where the missionaries are invited to proselytize. Elder Moreno intervenes in her private preferences related to eating and drinking; Jynx reacts with indignation. His instructions are felt by Jynx as intrusions into what is private. The audience are not only invited to observe the conversation, but the use of the shot-reverse-shot rule also locates them at the heart of Jynx' living room, where they experience these delicate and personal interactions. Jynx' attitude is transparent and therefore remarkably readable. The private decision to become a Mormon becomes a public event, a shift that is reinforced when the image reveals the presence of a supervisor from the church.

The second sequence, depicting the baptism, takes place in a public space. Baptisms are carried out in the church, to which everybody has access, Mormon and non-Mormon alike. The filming of Eric's baptism carries an informational mode for future converts, missionaries, and non-Mormons. The missionaries' statements are intended to encourage other elders and sisters to persist, even though finding candidates for conversion is not an easy task. The narrative attributes the responsibility for a successful mission to the missionaries, as a product of their abilities and efforts. Many aspects of the mission are left out of this reality series: we do not see, for example, self-critical reflection on whether proselytizing is always justified, nor does anyone asks more deeply about responsibility in relation to a candidate who is in a personally difficult situation but is given hope in the form of a potential conversion. In a few instances we see no-longer active members brought back to the church, but the show's ultimate goal is to portray baptisms that provide evidence of a successful mission.

The District also is an opportunity for the LDS Church and its Missionary Department to define their own narrative about missionaries and their service. Here they frame a response to critical and often damaging representations of the LDS Church mission. The RTV format is applied in the interests of the church, to establish and communicate a positive image. The young and likable social actors are used for exactly these purposes. We do not know if they will profit in the long term from their participation in the series. We can expect that they will be seen positively by other church

5. The Private is Public in Reality Shows about Religion

members and that their church-based networks will be strengthened. But we cannot know, for example, of any personal consequences.

The implications for social actors who reveal their private lives through participation in the public space of the reality show are particularly profound in the case of polygamous families. The religious institution is less relevant in these shows than in *The District*. The focus is on the social actors' private lives within their own homes and on legal issues related to their lifestyle, as we shall now explore.

5.3. Instructively entertaining the audience in Sister Wives

Reality-shows love polygamy. The depicted families usually consist of a single husband, several wives, and an impressive number of children and sometimes grandchildren. The show *Three Wives, One Husband* (Channel 4, UK 2017) is about three polygamous families living in houses built into a rock in the Utah desert. The families look very contemporary and in many ways not unlike other families – except that several wives are married to one husband and they live largely secluded from other communities. In the RTV show *#Seekingsisterwife* (TLC, 2018) the search for another wife is the focus of the narration. *Polygamy, USA* (National Geographic, US 2013) shows a whole community living a polygamous lifestyle in the secluded Centennial Park community, where cameras were permitted to record their daily lives for the first time in 2012.[379] *My 5 Wives* (TLC, US 2013–2016) was a less successful RTV show and was canceled after two seasons, perhaps because the show is very similar to *Sister Wives*, which is produced by the same channel.[380] The latter more successful show has run for 14 seasons so far and depicts the lives of the Brown family, with one husband, four wives, 18 children and at the moment two grandchildren. It has been aired in the United States since 2010 and in German-speaking European countries since 2014, with the title *Alle meine Frauen*. At the beginning of the show the Browns live in Utah, but during the first season they flee from Utah to Las Vegas, fearful of the legal repercussions of their polygamy.[381]

---

379 Chapters 7 and 7.1 discuss this series in more detail.
380 Wives married to a single husband in a polygamist setting are called sister wives.
381 Kelly O. White, "The Sister Wives: Has Incest and Sexual Assault Become the New Reality? The United States District Court for the District of Utah Grants

183

In almost all these shows the social actors self-identify as Mormons, although they are affiliated with different churches.[382] These shows have had a marked influence on public perceptions of polygamy, as Jane Bennion has recorded: "Because of shows such as *Big Love*[383] and *Sister Wives*, polygamy has become part of prime-time culture, no longer relegated to the hidden cultish confines of southern border towns and western desert wastelands."[384] While such shows about polygamy focus on the family unit, they also revolve around religion, as I will demonstrate in the case of *Sister Wives*.

Here are the Browns

The Brown family – husband Kody, his four wives, Meri, Janelle, Christine, and Robyn, and their 18 children – are members of the Apostolic United Brethren, a fundamentalist church within the grouping that identify as Latter-day Saints.[385] During the course of the show, the family's younger generation gradually leaves home for college and the numerous family members are less often all together. They do reunite for weddings, however, and four weddings have been depicted so far (fig. 67).

Polygamists the Holy Grail," *Creighton Law Review* 48, no. 3 (June 2015): 681–708.

382 In *Seekingsisterwife* depicts a family that is not religiously motivated to live in a polygamous family setting.

383 *Big Love* is an acclaimed fiction series produced by HBO (2006–2011) about one husband and his three wives.

384 Janet Bennion, *Women of Principle: Female Networking in Contemporary Mormon Polygyny* (New York, N.Y.: Oxford University Press, 1998), 129–142. The anthropologist Bennion lived for two years in a polygamist group undertaking field work. Her research focusses on the strong female network within this grouping.

385 J. Gordon Melton, ed., "Polygamy-Practicing," in *Melton's Encyclopedia of American Religions*, 8th ed. (Detroit, MI: Gale, 2009), 646–51.

5. The Private is Public in Reality Shows about Religion

Fig. 67 A family portrait taken at the wedding of Kody and Christine's daughter Aspyn in 2018. The series portrays several weddings very prominently, including Kody Brown's marriage to his fourth wife, Robyn (Image: https://www.tlcme.com/shows/sister-wives/photo-galleries/sister-wives-daughter-aspyn-browns-wedding-photos, accessed March 17, 2019).

The series communicates a religious worldview in combination with theological ideas as presented by the Brown family and shaped by RTV style. Even though RTV is per definition an unscripted show format, it exhibits a standardized audiovisual language with editing key to conveying a consistent but also entertaining narration. For example, the repetition of takes within the narration of *Sister Wives* highlights situations or stresses specific statements by the social actors. The soundtrack often emotionalizes the narrative as happens in mainstream fiction shows. The sofa discussions are another repeated element of RTV, with different combinations of family members reflecting about past and future events while sitting on the sofa. The individual branches do not participate in family sofa sessions; rather these occurrences involve the wives, with or without Kody and in different combination, and on some occasions solely the teenagers in the family. The youngest children usually appear in the final episode(s) of each season, which carry the recurring title *Sister Wives Tell All*. Only in the four episodes that each focus on a single wife – *Meri Behind the Scenes, Robyn Behind the Scenes* (Sister Wives, season 8, special episodes), *All about Janelle* and *All about Christine* (*Sister Wives*, season 9, episodes 4 and 6, US 2015) – are the wives interviewed on their own.

All the adults in the family have a Mormon background: Kody and Janelle were formerly members of the LDS Church; Meri, Christine, and

Robyn were raised in Mormon polygamist families. Over the course of 14 seasons and nine years, the Brown family starts several new lives, with new jobs, schools, and housing. The audience watches them going on holiday, struggling with relationships, meeting friends and the extended family, attending church services, expanding their businesses, building houses, and having more children. We see the adults as parents and watch the children graduate from high school or start college. We follow the engagements of daughters Maddy, Mykelti, and Aspyn, including their marriage festivities, and the coming out of Meri and Kody's only child, Mariah, as a lesbian. During the recurring interviews on the sofa, the five adults and from time to time also their children talk about events that have been emotionally challenging. The family members also reflect on their religious worldview, among other topics, and its impact on their lives.

The representation of the Browns' religious worldview is conspicuously connected to gender roles within the family.[386] There are several reasons for this focus. First, as the name of the show, *Sister Wives*, suggests, the relations between the wives are at the core of the narrative. Secondly, the polygamous lifestyle is key to the cosmology of the church to which the Browns belong, which is, thirdly, theologically based on a clearly heteronormative gender division. The gender-studies scholar Brenda R. Weber poses a challenging question in wondering "if the very shows that are the most ridiculous in their gender imperatives…,"[387] like for example *Sister Wives*, "…actually provide the most provocative and, often, progressive models for thinking about the workings of pleasure, power, and oppression in a twenty-first century that is governed by the image?"[388] We might well assume that in a polygamist setting, here with one husband and four wives, the gender roles specify a subjugated position for the women. But as I will demonstrate, the differentiation of labor amongst the family members allows not only variety across gender roles within the Brown family but also multiple positions for female viewers, which might in turn encourage the latter to question their own position within their private rela-

---

386 Myev Rees calls the interpretation of religion in *Sister Wives* a "Protestant Project" (114), as the family rejects the established LDS Church and seeks religious freedom. See Myev Rees, "Sister Wives. The Protestantization of Mormon Polygamy," in *Religion and Reality TV: Faith in Late Capitalism*, ed. Mara Einstein, Diane Winston, and Katherine Madden (Milton: Routledge, 2018), 107–120.
387 Weber, "Trash Talk: Gender as an Analytic on Reality Television," 10.
388 Weber, 10.

tionships. The husband in these depictions is almost entirely restricted to the traditional role of the head of the family.

The interactions between the public and private realms in *Sister Wives* are a key component of the relationship between RTV and religion. We will see how the spaces of communication and its reading modes address the private sphere through the depiction of binary gender relations and how the religious worldview and the theology of AUB can be deployed for public justification of the polygamous lifestyle. Additionally, however, we shall explore how the TLC reality show questions these religiously justified binary gender roles in the public spaces of circulation and consumption.

Binary gender roles in *Sister Wives*' four spaces of communication

At first sight *Sister Wives* appears to be based on a patriarchal and heteronormative value system in the space of representation, for how else can polygamy be understood? Weber describes the attitude underlying the show:

> *Sister Wives* … relies on a homo/heteronormative logic in valorizing the idea that consenting adults can form whatever form of families they choose, as long as those families seem different rather than "weird". (On *Sister Wives*, this means that four wives can have a separate sexual relationships with one man, but they cannot sleep with one another or altogether).[389]

Referring to its space of consumption, TLC notes on its German-language website that the target audience comprises women aged between 20 and 49. The Prime Media network demographic for 2014 confirms that the primary US audience was aged between 25–54 and 75% female and that TLC is the most-watched cable network for female viewers on Friday nights.[390] Furthermore the channel is ranked as a top five cable network for female

---

389 Brenda R. Weber, ed., *Reality Gendervision: Sexuality & Gender on Transatlantic Reality Television* (Durham and London: Duke University Press, 2014), 28.
390 "TLC," Comcast Spotlight, January 26, 2010, https://comcastspotlight.com/content/tlc; "TLC Rings in Records Ratings for 2018; A Top Three Cable Network for Women – Discovery, Inc.," accessed June 13, 2019, https://corporate.discovery.com/discovery-newsroom/tlc-rings-in-record-ratings-for-2018-a-top-three-cable-network-for-women/.

viewers on Tuesdays, Thursdays, Fridays and Sundays. These numbers suggest that the channel is indeed reaching its target audience.[391]

Weber's exploration of gender in the space of consumption recognizes that RTV is gendered not only in light of the female social actors who appear on screen but also in being defined as lowbrow culture produced for a female audience:

> It is not just the producer (the female author / the television producer) or the product (the novel / Reality TV) itself that is gendered and, through this gendering, coded as subordinate and less valuable; it is the very way value itself is referenced.[392]

While RTV is indeed associated with certain gendered values, *Sister Wives* contests those connotations with its dislocation of the traditional ties between sex and gender, a reality that is in line with argumentation by Jackey Stacey in her thoughtful chapter "A Certain Refusal of Difference: Feminism and Film Theory", written in 1989.[393] In considering the relations between representation and audience, Stacey stated that biological essentialism underlies feminist film theory and contended that "we need to separate gender identification from sexuality, too often conflated in the name of sexual difference."[394] As soon as we separate gender from sexuality new reading possibilities for *Sisters Wives* open up. Thus the non-sexual relationships between the wives have a validity that parallels the sexual relationships between each wife and Kody. Courtney Bailey even attributes a "slippery and contradictory quality of queerness"[395] to the show, arguing that *Sister Wives* questions the simple heteronormative gender narrative by performing repeated heterosexuality.

---

391 The audience demographic in Germany is quite similar, although TLC is not yet as successful as in the US. The channel has been present in German-speaking European countries only since 2014, making its success still remarkable.
392 Weber, "Trash Talk: Gender as an Analytic on Reality Television," 15.
393 Constance Penley, *The Future of an Illusion: Film, Feminism, and Psychoanalysis*, vol. 2, Media and Society Series (Minneapolis: University of Minnesota Press, 1989), 41–56.
394 Jackie Stacey, "Desperately Seeking Difference: Jackie Stacey Considers Desire Between Women in Narrative Cinema," in *Reading Images*, ed. Julia Thomas (London: Macmillan Education UK, 2001), 53.
395 Bailey, Courtney. "Love Multiplied: Sister Wives, Polygamy, and Queering Heterosexuality." *Quarterly Review of Film and Video* 32, no. 1 (January 2, 2015): 38–57.

The show accomplishes this queering of heterosexuality most obviously by highlighting continuities between the experiences of polygamists and the experiences of LGBT individuals in a heteronormative world. In less obvious ways, the show also queers gender and sexual norms by validating an alternative vision of civic intimacy based on public advocacy, female homosociality and non-normative bodies.[396]

Female "homosociality" is part not only of the everyday life of the family but also of their religious worldview, for the relationships between the sister wives are theologically legitimized. How then does their religious worldview influence the binary gender roles in *Sister Wives* and how might the private and public spaces of religion add to the dynamic of "deconstructing sexual normativity beyond just heteronormativity"? To answer these questions let us first look at the religious context.

Polygamist Family Brown and the Apostolic United Brethren (AUB)

The Apostolic United Brethren (AUB), the religious community to which the Brown family belongs, is a splitter group of the FLDS[397] founded by Lorin C. Woolley in 1912. When Joseph White Musser, later the first AUB prophet, joined the FLDS he compiled and published various accounts of the 1886 revelation about plural marriage and about denying blacks admission to the priesthood by referring to descendants of Cain. The AUB believes that the LDS Church has no claim on Joseph Smith Jr., Brigham Young and John Taylor, among others, as leaders because it has rejected their teachings. In 1954 Joseph White Musser, after suffering a stroke, he appointed two new members, Margarito Bautista and Rulon C. Allred, to guide the community. The Apostolic United Brethren, which finally split

---

396 Bailey, Courtney. "Love Multiplied: Sister Wives, Polygamy, and Queering Heterosexuality." *Quarterly Review of Film and Video* 32, no. 1 (January 2, 2015): 41.
397 The most prominent example of the FLDS in Colorado is the group around Warren Jeffs, prophet of the largest polygamist community, known also as United Order Effort. Jeffs was convicted on two counts of being an accomplice to rape, a result of his arranging the marriage of an unwilling 14-year-old female. He was sentenced to life in prison plus twenty years. Although he is imprisoned, the community continues to treat him as their leader and prophet. For more detail see Cardell K. Jacobson and Lara Burton, "Prologue: The Incident at Eldorado, Texas Cardell K. Jacobson and Lara Burton," in *Modern Polygamy in the United States: Historical, Cultural, and Legal Issues*, ed. Cardell K. Jacobson and Lara Burton (Oxford, New York: Oxford University Press, 2011), xvii–xxvi.

from the FLDS, is therefore often referred to as the "Allred Group". Under Allred's leadership membership of the group grew. With approximately 10,000 members, the AUB, informally also known as The Work, The Priesthood or The Group, is now the largest polygamist group in the US; its headquarters are in Bluffdale (UT).[398] It essentially follows the principles, doctrines, and theology of the LDS Church as they were prior to the denunciation of polygamy 1890. [399] The AUB therefore rejects most of the revelations of the LDS Church from the twentieth and twenty-first centuries.[400]

In general AUB members are more progressive than other FLDS groups.[401] For example, they make it possible for teenage girls to decline to marry and require the wives in plural marriages to be treated equally. According to extensive field research undertaken by Jane Bennion in the 1990s, AUB members also maintain a more progressive gender model, specifically in terms of the intensive cooperation between wives. Bennion recorded, "I had expected to find rampant child sexual molestations and beaten and cloistered women [...]. Instead I found feminism, female autonomy, and widespread sharing."[402] Bennion even described the husband's position within the family structure of AUB members as weak and as much less relevant in daily life, with the husband performing essentially as a visitor to the core family.

The organization of daily life within such polygamous units appeared to Bennion to be particularly supportive of women: "This matrifocal network provided these women with shared childcare that enabled them to pursue an education or a career outside the community. It offered them relief in companionship and solidarity when they were abandoned by their hus-

---

398 Janet Bennion, "History, Culture, and Variability of Mormon Schismatic Groups," in *Modern Polygamy in the United States: Historical, Cultural, and Legal Issues*, ed. Cardell Jacobson and Lara Burton (Oxford, New York: Oxford University Press, 2011), 104.
399 Hammarberg, *The Mormon Quest for Glory*, 256.
400 The LDS Church, the biggest Mormon group, officially ceased practicing polygamy in order that Utah might be admitted into the Union in 1896. See Melton, "Polygamy-Practicing."
401 Janet Bennion, "Progressive Polygamy in Western United States," in *Beyond Same-Sex Marriage: Perspectives on Marital Possibilities*, ed. Ronald C. Den Otter (Lanham: Lexington Books, 2016), 28–36.
402 Janet Bennion, *Polygamy in Primetime: Media, Gender, and Politics in Mormon Fundamentalism*, Brandeis Series on Gender, Culture, Religion, and Law (Waltham, Massachusetts: Brandeis University Press, 2011), 56.

bands."[403] To a certain degree the RTV show *Sister Wives* portrays just such matrifocal network, justified in this instance by a religious doctrine, with a variety of roles performed by women within both the private and public spheres. Sister wives Robyn, Christine, Janelle, and Meri split the diverse responsibilities of family organization and employment in various constellations as they stay at home, continue their education, or support the family financially by working outside the home.

The following discussion looks at Mormon doctrines addressing gender to which the narrative of *Sister Wives* explicitly refers. It also considers how the show's gender concepts question, reverse, or transcend the divide between the public and private realms of religion by steering different reading modes.

AUB theology reloaded in "Sister Wives"

Only 30%–40% of Mormon fundamentalists practice polygamy.[404] Even though the AUB believes that polygamy is a requirement for exaltation, it also permits monogamy and grants woman the right to denounce a partner. Four core beliefs define AUB theology and its religious practice: plural marriage, which is also called "celestial marriage", the Adam-God doctrine, the Law of Sarah, and the doctrine of consecration. These beliefs are expressed in different ways during the show, with plural marriage referenced most conspicuously. Polygamist groups like AUB justify plural marriage with reference to the Old Testament. Their prime model is Abraham, who because his marriage to Sarah remained childless had sexual relations with Hagar, which resulted in the birth of his son Ishmael (Genesis 16). Solomon had 700 wives and 300 concubines (1 Kings 11, 3). Reference is also made to other male figures of the Old Testament, including Moses and Jacob, having several wives.

The Adam-God doctrine and the Law of Sarah

The two principles of the Adam-God doctrine and the Law of Sarah are crucial to all Mormon fundamentalists and influence their everyday religious practices with a connection to the afterlife. All Mormons consider

---

403 Bennion, 57.
404 Bennion, 112.

themselves not only as Adam and Eve's descendants but also, figuratively and conceptually, this couple. The Adam and Eve concept is significant to the endowment ceremony in the temple.[405] Mormons believe that Adam became a god after his earthly life with Eve and their children. The Adam-God doctrine authorizes every man to build his own kingdom on earth and teaches them how to become gods on earth. One of their duties is to establish an extended family during their lifetime and follow Mormon doctrines, whereby they will finally become gods. Worthy men will be kings and all of their family members will become gods in the afterlife if they lived a righteous life.[406]

The Law of Sarah regulates the process that leads from monogamy to polygyny.[407] A woman who is her husband's first wife can decide whether she will accept her husband having an additional wife or wives. Her husband must first ask her; ideally, indeed, she will choose the second wife herself. If she approves the marriage, it will take place, but even if she disapproves, the Law of Abraham[408] still allows her husband to take another wife. The marriage ceremony, in which the wives are linked together for eternity, is carried out in reference to the Law of Sarah. Bennion has summarized the impact of the law:

> Through this eternal bond, women are encouraged to work together economically, socially, and spiritually and, in some rare cases, sexually (that is, in scheduling the rotation of their husband's nightly visits). These bonds are sometimes enhanced when women court other women as future co-wives. They are crucial during the prolonged absences of their husbands and create a strong interdependence that forces women to learn a large repertoire of domestic and mechanical skills such as dry-walling, fishing, plowing, and herding cattle. Few monogamous women experience this same, intense, training.[409]

At various points the show *Sister Wives* negotiates the women's own expectations that they will be open towards and accepting of Robyn, their hus-

---

405 Latter-day Saints conduct a series of rites called "temple endowment" when visiting a temple.
406 Valerie M. Hudson, "Mormon Doctrine on Gender," in *The Oxford Handbook of Mormonism*, ed. Terryl L. Givens (New York: Oxford University Press, 2015), 352–357.
407 Bennion, *Polygamy in Primetime*, 58.
408 "Some fundamentalists refer to plural marriage using this term. This law gives men the right to take additional wives, as Abraham did." See Bennion, 324.
409 Bennion, 98/99.

band's new wife. The divide between, on one hand their belief that through her acceptance they improve as human beings, with exaltation as their aim, and, on the other hand, the reality of their emotional struggle, is experienced by each wife differently. In the course of the seasons, all three sister wives, Meri, Christine and Janelle, explicitly admit their jealousy towards the new wife Robyn. In describing the show's impact, Christine records, "the hardest thing to see is Kody's affection with other wives."[410] Kody's fourth marriage with Robyn is thus challenging for all the wives, despite Kody's affirming that they are all marrying Robyn (season 1, episode 7, *Four Wives and Counting*). The wedding pictures inserted in the final credits appear to confirm this statement: Robyn does not wear a white dress in the pictures – she did wear it at the ceremony – so that she does not stand out from the other wives in the family portrait (fig. 68). Their dresses are differently cut, but they are all made from the same fabric, which is chocolate brown and purple in color. We learn during the show that Meri, Kody's first wife, requested that Robyn wears a dress similar to that of the other wives in the family portraits.

In the wedding pictures, all the biological families are grouped together (fig. 69–72) – a rare event during the show – with all the women wearing similar dresses. Only in the picture of the four wives Robyn is wearing a traditional, and distinctive, white bridal dress, symbolizing her marriage to the three sister wives (fig. 73).

The gender hierarchies are also conspicuously represented in the family portrait in which Kody is located in the middle of the upper row, with his first and fourth wives seated below him and his second and third wives on each side of them (fig. 68). The four eldest daughters Aspyn, Mariah, Maddy, and Mykelti, stand alongside their father, two on his left and two on his right, suggesting his centrality to them, and thereby also his control. A traditional picture of the wedding couple, so of Robyn and Kody, is missing.

---

410 *Four Wives and counting* (*Sister Wives*, season 1, episode 7, US 2010).

Part II: Interactions between Communication Spaces and Religion

Fig. 68 The separation between female and male family members and family hierarchies are conspicuously staged (Sister Wives, Four Wives and Counting, 00:20:32).

Fig. 69/ Fig. 70/ Fig. 71/ Fig. 72 The four biological families are grouped together. Robyn (fig. 72) brings three children into the family from a former marriage. The wives, including the bride, and some of the children are all wearing dresses of the same chocolate-brown and purple fabric (Sister Wives, Four Wives and Counting, 00:20:30–00:20:50).

5. The Private is Public in Reality Shows about Religion

Fig. 73 The sister wives Janelle, Meri, Robyn, and Christine (f.l.t.r.) gather for a picture with Robyn at the wedding. It is the only picture in which she is wearing a white wedding dress (Sister Wives, Four Wives and Counting, 00:20:55).

The positive emotions which connote Kody and Robyn's wedding day, fostering the sensationalism of a polygamist marriage, form a rather exceptional narrative in this show. Solidarity between all the wives is rarely depicted and their cooperation is not emphasized. While amicable moments do occur, as between Meri and Robyn in the beginning of the series,[411] the focus is more often on the struggles, jealousies, and sacrifices each wife needs to pursue in order to receive the greater good of being a sister wife. One reason for this depiction is probably that cooperation and harmony elicit a less sensational reading mode; tensions and struggles tend to be more entertaining.

Reading modes of the private and public in the wedding sequence

The interplay between the private and the public in the culmination represented by the wedding is striking. The depiction of the event enhances

---

[411] After the birth of Robyn and Kody's first child, Solomon, Robyn proposed to Meri, who suffers with reduced fertility, that she could act as Meri's surrogate (*Sister Wives, Sisters' Special Delivery*, season 3, episode 12).

both the entertaining and spectacular reading modes. Kody's fourth marriage, to Robyn, is also the Brown family's "coming out", in Kody's words. The idea is repeatedly cut in during the episode, intensifying its spectacular mode. It is also emphasized that this is the first polygamist wedding to be shown on television (although the audience witnesses little of the wedding ceremony itself).

According to the show's narrative, the wedding episode serves to officially present the Brown family as polygamists in public for the first time. Of course, from its beginning this first series has been a kind of coming out. Even though the events took place in the past, by applying the documentary reading mode the show allows its viewers to believe that everything is happening in the moment. This temporal divide between real and filmic time is an ongoing dilemma, but it is particularly significant for the wedding sequence and its presence in the public sphere. The wedding has a double public presence: as a public event in the past and as a public event mediated by the show's broadcast. Indeed, the wedding has brought a new twist to the private and public divide, for much of the narrative of the show until this point has been crafted by the Browns' everyday life in the private sphere of their own homes. But the wedding takes place first within the semi-public space formed by the presence of invited guests and then is made fully public through its transmission on TLC. Some parts of the wedding remained private, however, elements such as the sealing ceremony, at which only "worthy" Mormons can be present. Elements of the wedding reception, attended by invited guests, were approved, however, for inclusion in the show.[412]

Four narrative strategies shape the wedding sequence and are applied throughout the season, generating different reading modes: (1) flashbacks, with scenes from earlier episodes, (2) the sofa section, during which the social actors reflect on the events that are depicted, (3) photos of the socials actors' lives before the show, (4) the actual event. These narrative strategies principally communicate two modes: informational and emotional. Thus, in the informational mode, photos from Kody's other three marriages are shown, commented upon by the relevant wife. They describe comparatively their weddings and relationships with Kody and how they joined the family (00:16:38-00:17:20). Meri's wedding involved a big party, whereas

---

412 The sealing ceremony traditionally takes place in a temple, to which only worthy members have access. The Brown family probably conducted the marriage rite for time and eternity at home. See more about the "celestial marriage" in Hammarberg, *The Mormon Quest for Glory*, 256–259.

Janelle's and Christine's weddings were very simple. Janelle wore a black dress, as the viewer sees in a photo. She explains that her wedding was so small because most of her family and friends refused to attend – she has lost touch with most of her family members and friends because they were "appalled" at her decision to marry a Mormon polygamist. As they sit on the sofa, the adults discuss the meaning of marriage in a polygamous context and why the spiritual element will not be depicted as part of the show – it is deemed "sacred".

The wedding reception sequence applies an emotional reading mode, evoked by the interactions between the adults, which surely catch the viewers' attention. One unstated question drives this reading: how do the other wives deal with the idea that their husband will be spending the night with his beautiful new wife, with whom he will likely have sexual intercourse. Sister wives Meri, Janelle, and Christine discuss their ambivalent feelings about their husband's new wife in depth as they sit on the sofa. Another emotional moment comes when the first three wives and their children leave the reception. Kody says goodbye to each of his other wives before leaving with his bride, claiming a private moment with each of them. He tells each wife that he loves her and will miss her.

Sitting on the sofa and with tears in her eyes, Robyn stresses that it was wonderful that Meri included her in her leave taking from Kody. These scenes with each wife highlight that Kody is required to treat all his wives equally. He seeks to demonstrate that he cares about them and is in a loving relationship with each of them. While the wedding acknowledges the multiple relationships within the family, it also unites the large family not only emotionally but also visually. This family unity is expressed in an extreme longshot of the party from a high angle (fig. 74), as if someone is looking down on them. Or, in Christine words (00:17:43–00:17:46), "It's a blessing, an absolute blessing! And that's what the reception was."

Part II: Interactions between Communication Spaces and Religion

Fig. 74 The core Brown family and some guests are dancing together. The long-shot from a high angle accentuates their unity and its religious dimension, as if someone is watching over them from above (Sister Wives, Four Wives and Counting, 00:17:50).

The reception sequence includes additional emotion-inducing features. The dancing guests are shown in slow motion, including Kody as he dances with each wife, accompanied by emotional diegetic and extra-diegetic music. Inserts of flowers and of the almost-full moon emphasize the atmospheric surroundings. The RTV style emotionalizes the polygamist marriage and thereby communicates the Brown family's coming out in a romantic and bonding atmosphere for themselves, their guests, and also for the audience, applying an emotional reading mode that encourage the viewers to tune in again for the coming second season. The decision to "come out", a term originally used by homosexuals about first speaking of their sexual orientation in public, will have real-life consequences for the family. In the next season the family moves to Nevada, fleeing potential legal prosecution for polygamy.[413]

---

413 Strassberg, "Scrutinizing Polygamy."

The doctrine of consecration

The doctrine of consecration is another polygamist principle that shapes the show's narrative. Bennion explains: "Some fundamentalist groups ask or require members to consecrate, or give, money and legal ownership of property to church leaders."[414] The law of consecration supports the idea of a voluntary communalism, and in the case of AUB, the United Order controls and redistributes the wealth. The practice is an expression of the equality of members. Male and female members have different stewardships, the tasks undertaken to earn money for the community. New members are often asked to consecrate their property and assets as a sign that they are worthy members.

The Brown family, which functions as the smallest community unit, applies the doctrine of consecration. All income and expenses are administered within a single family budget. The financing of the four houses built for the four wives in a cul-de-sac in Las Vegas is undertaken communally. When the financing of the houses proves difficult, the adults discuss whether Meri, who has only one child, who is almost old enough to leave for college, really needs such a big house; in the end, however, they all accept that they will have houses that are the same size.[415]

The communal principle is also applied in terms of family needs and organization. Some adults contribute in a private space, while some earn in a public space. Thus, Janelle works fulltime; Christine has always been a stay-at-home mom, home schooling the children and running the household; Meri works part-time; Robyn is the driving force behind the online store *My Sisterwife's Closet*, which sells jewelry, clothes, and accessories among other items. Season six revolves in particular around discussion of how to launch *My Sisterwife's Closet*, how to ensure its success, and who will be responsible for it.[416] The references to this online store strongly define the show's public dimension, as a point of contact with anyone who can go online and is ready to shop.

In season 11 another shared business is introduced: Meri plans to open a bed-and-breakfast in a house that once belonged to her great grandmother.

---

414 Bennion, *Polygamy in Primetime*, 323.
415 Financing the house is at the center of the narration in seasons 5 and 6 of *Sister Wives* (TLC, US 2012/14). In the same seasons *My Sister Wife's Closet* is also discussed (intensely in season 6, episodes 1 and 2).
416 "My Sister Wife's Closet," My Sisterwife's Closet, accessed March 19, 2019, https://mysisterwifescloset.com/.

She looks not only for financial support from the sister wives and Kody but also for their permission, although she is legally divorced from Kody and could decide by herself to start a new business.[417] In following the law of consecration, she needs the agreement of the adults, in particular of her "spiritual" husband, as head of the family. The show included the story about the new business in January 2019, with the three other sister wives depicted supporting Meri's idea but Kody seeming reluctant. However, according to its webpage, the bed-and-breakfast Lizzie's Heritage Inn had been owned by Meri and the Brown family since 2017.[418] The temporal discrepancy between representation and actual event in the space of production challenges the illusion of realness. The depiction could be read as a "making-of" account of a new business, portrayed in effect in flashback, a perspective that holds entertaining qualities even if the outcome is already known. Lizzie's Heritage Inn might also profit from its owner's celebrity, with fans perhaps eager to stay overnight in hope of meeting Meri in person.

To sum up: the show's communication spaces of production, representation, circulation/distribution, and consumption both affirm the traditional binary gender concept of male and female and promote female agency within the public and private spheres. They embrace a religious worldview that is communicated primarily in two reading modes: the emotional and the informational, mediated through RTV culture, as we shall now see.

The gendered and mediated religious worldview of *Sister Wives*

Religion is largely absent from the production spaces, contained only within the private family sphere. The RTV format of the TLC channel provides an institutional and public framing for the Brown family's religious affiliations. The AUB church as an institution is completely absent; only the LDS Church is discussed from time to time, for example when Maddy's LDS Church membership is denied or when the Brown family meets friends who are LDS Church members. Additionally, the patriarchal struc-

---

417 As the first couple to marry, Meri and Kody were married legally. Kody's marriages to Janelle, his second wife, and Christine, his third wife, are spiritual only. He divorced Meri in order to marry his fourth wife, Robin, legally, which enabled him to adopt her three children from an earlier marriage. See *Sister Wives* season 8, episode 7 *Divorce* (TLC, US 2015).

418 "Lizzie's Heritage Inn," Lizzie's Heritage Inn, accessed March 20, 2019, https://lizziesheritageinn.com/.

ture of AUB theology is not entirely in alignment with the gender concept of the show. As we have just seen, with its matrifocal network and homosocial gender concept the show is about women and is intended for a mostly female audience. The male dominance of the religious worldview is challenged by the overwhelming presence of female social actors on screen and the female target audience.[419]

In the space of representation, for purposes of entertainment the show establishes a tension between male and female positions within the private space of the family. Although Kody is ruler of his family kingdom on earth, the relations between the adults transcend the binary gender roles of heteronormativity, reaching towards homosociality. The show often puts Kody at the center of the narration: thus, for example, he always sits in the middle of the sofa with his wives around him and he frequently closes a scene, topic, or sequence with concluding comments. Yet his wives obviously spend more time with each other than with their husband. And even though the AUB church, founded on LDS Church theology, is a male-dominated community, female social actors Meri, Janelle, Christine, and Robyn are the main organizers of the family. They care about the weddings, choose the wedding dresses,[420] cook the meals, coordinate family vacations, and organize the family's relocation to new houses. Kody often performs only as the voice of the family: thus he makes announcements during family gatherings, of a pregnancy, for example, or of the four-house project. The wives also bond on a symbolic level. Meri, Janelle, and Christine make Robyn the gift of a ring called "the Brown sister wife ring", which exclusively connects the wives. The festivities at Robyn and Kody's wedding reception include all four wives, and almost equally, with the only difference that Robyn wears a white dress during the party.

In the space of consumption, the family uses the show to fight for legal rights and public acceptance of their polygamist lifestyle. Indirectly the AUB church appears to be a female-dominated private religion, an image that mirrors the show's predominantly female audience. We see the family mostly in the private sphere, traditionally gendered as female. This private sphere becomes public when claiming religious freedom. By going public with their religious lifestyle, all the Brown adults ask for tolerance, acceptance, and legal status as a family. And finally, the RTV show *Sister Wives*

---

419 "TLC"; "FAQ," tlc.de, accessed March 21, 2019, https://www.tlc.de/info/faqs.
420 Kody finally and secretly decides the choice of dress with Robyn. The other wives are very vocal about Kody's transgression, leading to extensive discussion during the show.

and its gender concept compete with the public image of the main LDS Church, which claims the title "Latter-day Saints" for its members alone.[421] Compared to the performance of gender binaries by the Brown family, the LDS Church seems compliant, conservative, and backward.

5.4. Religion linking the private and the public sphere

As we have seen, both *The District* and *Sister Wives* blur the boundaries between the public and private spheres and both apply an entertaining and instructional reading mode, if in different ways. This interface between the private and the public is connected to the shows' reference to the historical world or "truths". Both shows have specific goals strongly connected to religious worldviews. How these RTV shows use their spaces of communication to specific ends will be discussed in the following by comparing how each production space interacts with the religious institution to which the social actors are affiliated.

The LDS Church, producer of *The District*, is officially in the foreground of that show from the start. As we have seen, the show was initially intended for the education of future missionaries, but when the producers became aware of its entertaining qualities, they decided to air it on television and thus bring it to a wider public. The instructional mode had been applied to the private space of the church's education purposes; the entertaining qualities related to its broader public presence. Implicitly the show's purpose was public from the start, as the education of missionaries is intended to enable them to address people in public spaces to arouse their interest in the church. The presentation of the RTV product to the broader public was a different strategy, but it was related to the first, as also a means to win understanding for the church, and for its missionary endeavor. *The District* thus refurbished the LDS Church image through its portrayal of happy and successful missionaries on two levels: attracting missionaries to the church and attracting sympathy for existing missionaries, and by extension for their church. The success of the show in the space of consumption can be then based both on having more young people go on mission in the public sphere and on having more people view the LDS institution in a positive light, and perhaps even become members, through watching the show in a private space.

---

421 "Style Guide — The Name of the Church," www.mormonnewsroom.org, April 9, 2010, http://www.mormonnewsroom.org/style-guide?lang=eng.

Sister Wives' entertaining mode is necessarily prominent because TLC is a private TV channel that sells advertising time. The price of the advertisements is determined by viewer and household numbers, as potential consumers of the products advertised. That economic concern is initially prominent in the production. In the first episodes the religious affiliation of the polygamous family is kept private. Although members of the AUB church, the Brown family are interested neither in proselytizing nor in selling their church. The religious institution remained in the background, as a private matter. But in the course of the first season, the reference to their religion slowly changes. When Kody Brown marries his fourth wife, Robyn, the family's religious lifestyle becomes public, both in the historical world depicted by the show and in the present when the show is broadcast. Two principal reasons determine this shift. First, the private-public tension and within it the legal, social, psychological and religious dimensions make the show very attractive. The family was invited onto other shows and was discussed in the media, which generated more viewers to be entertained and added to viewer figures.

The Brown family have a second, more personal reason for approving the public depiction of their polygamy. In 2010 the adult Browns brought Utah's criminalization of polygamy to the United States District Court for the District of Utah, claiming that it was unconstitutional. The state was declared to be "failing to submit any admissible evidence on the social harms of polygamy and largely failing to substantively oppose the constitutional claims."[422] In 2016 the court vacated the district court decision as moot once the Browns moved to Nevada and also in light of the Utah county attorney's "adoption of the policy limiting bigamy prosecutions to cases involving fraud, minors, or abuse."[423] The Brown case informally resulted in the decriminalization of polygamy in Utah, which is of public interest and opened up the possibility that the Brown family might move back to Utah, where the headquarters of the AUB are located. Going public with their lifestyle and claiming before the court that this lifestyle was not criminal connected private and public interests, with other polygamist families in the state of Utah also benefitting.

Although the court decision is not widely discussed during the show, the adults mention on occasion that the law does treat plural families unfairly.[424] The Browns use their celebrity status to publicity related ends.

---

422 Strassberg, "Scrutinizing Polygamy," 168.
423 Strassberg, 168.
424 See season 9, *Tell All*, part 2.

The success of the show is a win-win situation for both sides, the social actors and the television network. Viewer are eager to see the private lives of a polygamist family fighting for legal acceptance, and at the same time by revealing something of their private lives, the protagonists can win the audience's sympathies for a polygamist family life. The family profits not just financially but potentially also in terms of its social and legal acceptability. Their own business, like Robyn's online shop, Meri's bed-and-breakfast, and Janelle's work as a real estate agent, gain a boost from their participation in the show, in additional to the payment received from TLC for each episode (a sum that has never been made public). One might say the Browns sell a version of their private lives to drive their public business. In this private-public divide, religion connects actual events with legal, political, economic, and social "discourses of the real", to return to Murray and Ouellette's terminology.[425]

The interface between the private and the public in the two RTV shows refers in different ways to religion. It demonstrates that reality shows not only draw on but also shape events by applying reading modes, in these instances entertaining and instructional modes. The mediatization of religion can be an asset for the institutions involved, be they churches or television networks. The economic value of the shows, expressed in viewer figures, is indicative of the number of potential new church members or consumers of advertised products. The parallels between the shows are conspicuous.

RTV shows are a commercial genre that commodifies not only its social actors but also, in these instances, religion.

---

425 Murray and Ouellette, *Reality TV*, 5.

6. Researching Spaces of Production and Consumption of Latter-day Saints Media

Various strategies can be deployed in researching the four communication spaces of documentary media – production, representation, consumption, and distribution/circulation – in a semio-pragmatic perspective.[426] Throughout this book, the media's *context* is addressed in order to establish and investigate reading modes. In this chapter the communication spaces of production and consumption are analyzed using both quantitative and qualitative methods – an audience study[427] on one hand and interviews with Latter-day Saints media and communication professionals on the other.

The first part of the chapter examines how the semio-pragmatic approach can be combined with an audience study to understand its effectivity in communicating values, opinions, and attitudes about Mormonism. With the audience study conducted in Switzerland (Zürich) and Spain (Barcelona), we can also explore cultural differences in the space of consumption. The second part of the chapter considers how media professionals affiliated with The Church of Jesus Christ of the Latter-day Saints (LDS) frame their own work in light of their religious affiliation. Finally, in the last section of this chapter, the results of both approaches and their methodological implications and limitations are brought together and reflected upon. The overall aim is to illuminate the intentions and experiences of media producers and media consumers in the case of documentary media produced or shaped by religious actors with connections to the LDS Church.

This chapter differs from other chapters in this book not only in its methodological approach but also in the presentation of its results, which

---

426 The theoretical horizons of the communication spaces are introduced in part II, chapter 2.
427 The audience study was conducted in cooperation with Maria Teresa Soto Sanfiel of the Universitat Autònoma de Barcelona. See Marie-Therese Mäder and María T. Soto-Sanfiel, "'We Are Open-Minded, Tolerant, and Care for Other People': Comparing Audience Responses to Religion in Documentaries," *Journal of Media and Religion* 18, no. 3 (July 3, 2019): 98–114; María T. Soto-Sanfiel and Marie-Therese Mäder, "Identifying with a Religious Character," *Journal of Religion in Europe*, 2020, 1–31, https://doi.org/10.1163/18748929-20201471.

here involves tables, numbers, and quotations from interview sequences. The narrative created from these findings recounts how producers and consumers understand the interface between documentary media and religion and illuminates how it is constructed by the researcher. The approach follows the crystallization concept developed by Laura L. Ellingson, professor of women's and gender studies, which "problematizes the multiples truth it presents. [...] since researchers construct knowledge and representations (narratives, analysis, etc.), all accounts are inherently partial, situated, and contingent. Rather than apologizing for this partiality as a limitation, scholars using crystallization can celebrate multiple points of view of a phenomenon across the methodological continuum."[428] This chapter thus also expands the methodological approach of our project by taking up tools from qualitative and quantitative research in combination with knowledge gained through semio-pragmatics.

6.1. A semio-pragmatic analysis combined with an audience study

The current sub-chapter deploys a semio-pragmatic analysis in combination with an audience-study to assess the effectiveness of the communication of religion through documentaries. It also considers how cultural differences impact the documentary reception process. To these ends, a semio-pragmatic analysis was applied to the documentary *Meet the Mormons* (Blair Treu, US 2014, 78') and subsequently a reception study was conducted with undergraduate participants from Spain (N= 103, $Mean_{Age}$ = 21.21, SD = 3.40) and Switzerland (N=104, $Mean_{Age}$ = 21.54, SD = 2.34), using questionnaires that had been produced with the results of the semio-pragmatic analysis. The participants watched the documentary and completed the questionnaires, which highlight the perceived values of the documentary and provide opportunity for the expression of opinions about the documentary and attitudes towards it. The results show that the semio-pragmatic tool can enable an understanding of how religion is mediatized in documentaries and that cultural context can significantly influence the perception of values, attitudes, and opinions.

---

428 Ellingson, *Engaging Crystallization in Qualitative Research*, 22. The concept is discussed in more detail in part I, chapter 2.

Audience responses to religion in *Meet the Mormons*

The questions of how religious communication employs media and how media change religion are certainly not new and have been extensively researched, as the scale of the literature shows.[429] Such questions address processes that are generally subsumed under the expressions "mediatization of religion", "mediatized religion" or "religious mediation", which embrace different aspects of the interface between media and religion.[430] The complexity of religious communication that employs media brings certain methodological challenges for researchers. Steward Hoover, for example, proposes that religious mediation, i.e. the "act of communication via a medium,"[431] must be understood from the audience's perspective and not in light of the religious authorities and how they want it to be understood.[432] What methodological approach might we then take to the audience's interaction with mediatized forms of religion? Picking up again on the concept of crystallisation, the audience study undertaken for this project researches how a religious worldview is communicated[433] by a documentary and evaluated by audiences.[434] Two questions guided the research process:
1. To what extent does the audience's perception endorse the values, opinions, and attitudes that are conveyed by the semio-pragmatic analysis?
2. Are there differences in the responses to the documentary that can be attributed to the audience's cultural background?

The section is structured as follows: first, the semio-pragmatic analysis, which takes into account the documentary's spaces of communication,

---

429 Danielle Kirby and Carole M. Cusack, eds., *Religion and Media. Critical Concept in Religious Studies*, Critical Concepts in Religious Studies (London: Routledge, 2017); Mia Lövheim, *Media, Religion, and Gender: Key Issues and New Challenges* (London; New York: Routledge, 2013); Stout, *Media and Religion*; Daniel A. Stout and Judith Mitchell Buddenbaum, *Religion and Mass Media: Audiences and Adaptations* (Thousand Oaks, CA: Sage Publications, 1996).
430 Hjarvard, "The Mediatization of Religion," 11; Hjarvard, "Three Forms of Mediatized Religion. Changing the Public Face of Religion." For a detailed discussion of the term *mediatization* see part I, chapter 2.1.
431 Hjarvard, "The Mediatisation of Religion: Theorising Religion, Media and Social Change," 123.
432 Hoover, "Media and the Imagination of Religion in Contemporary Global Culture," 611.
433 Fritz et al., *Sichtbare Religion*, 50–74.
434 John L. Sullivan, *Media Audiences: Effects, Users, Institutions, and Power* (Thousand Oaks, CA: SAGE, 2013), 105–186.

and its results are applied to two audience studies; secondly, the audience studies are presented in detail; finally, the results of the studies are compared and discussed.

Framing the semio-pragmatic audience study

The semio-pragmatic approach is understood as an heuristic tool that deciphers an audio-visual source's reading modes.[435] It places audio-visual media in the tension between film and the communication spaces within which media function.[436] From this it follows that "the meaning of a text changes in accordance with its context."[437] Such an approach emphasizes the institutional context within which the audio-visual sources are produced, distributed, and consumed, for it often provides reliable and accurate information about reading instructions and reading modes.[438]

For this reason, a semio-pragmatic analysis was conducted to establish the documentary and moral reading modes. The results were transposed into questionnaires to be applied as part of two audience studies conducted in 2015 in Spain and in Switzerland. The questionnaires were created in English and translated into both Spanish and German applying the forward translation method.[439] As audio-visual stimulus for the study, we selected one eleven-minute-long sequence (*The Humanitarian*) from *Meet the Mormons*. The principal reason for selecting this particular documentary was that it has been dubbed into German and Spanish, the languages of the study. Its narrative structure allowed for the extraction of a coherent and complete sequence. The extracted audio-visual narrative is representative of the whole film, which consists of six complete chapters. Although we provided a shortened version, in order that the participants' attention be retained throughout the viewing, a comprehensive sense of the aim of the documentary was still guaranteed. We noted also that the documentary depicts Mormonism, a religious grouping that is relatively unknown in Eu-

---

435 Buckland, *The Cognitive Semiotics of Film*, 77–108.
436 Kessler, "Historische Pragmatik," 106.
437 Roger Odin, *Les espaces de communication*, 15. The French original reads: ... "le sens d'un texte change avec le contexte." Translation mine.
438 A more detailed discussion of the semio-pragmatic approach is included in part I, chapter 2.2.
439 José Muñiz, Paula Elosua, and Ronald K. Hambleton, "Directrices Para La Traducción y Adaptación de Los Tests: Segunda Edición.," *Psicothema* 25, no. 2 (2013): 151–57.

rope, which meant we were more readily able to measure the effect of the film rather than prejudices against Mormons.

Extracting the represented values, opinions, and attitudes towards Mormons

Meet the Mormons is produced and distributed by a religious institution, namely The Church of Jesus Christ of the Latter-day Saints (LDS Church) and portrays six members of this church.[440] They live or work(ed) in different countries and talk about their successful lives, what they have achieved and how their Mormon belonging has influenced their lives. It can be read as a corporate video, a term that is primarily used in the context of advertising and a form that provides a deliberately positive depiction of a product or an institution – in this case of the LDS Church, which is headquartered in Salt Lake City/UT. The experienced director, Blair Treu, is a Mormon who also worked for Disney, among other production companies, during his professional career. He graduated from Brigham Young University, a Mormon affiliated university, and mainly works now for BYUtv, the Mormon TV channel located in Provo, Utah. *Meet the Mormons* has grossed $6,047,363 (between October 2014 and February 2015), according to Box Office Mojo,[441] suggesting a successful theatrical release for a documentary. The documentary was originally produced for the LDS Church's visitor center at the Joseph Smith building in Salt Lake City/UT. As a result of its overwhelmingly positive reception in preview, the church's Public Affairs Department decided it should also be presented in theatres.[442] *Meet the Mormons* is today widely distributed and available on diverse streaming platforms, including Netflix, iTunes, and Amazon Instant Video, and it has been dubbed into other languages.

The semio-pragmatic analysis categorizes the representation of religion according to four aspects. First, the social actors depicted are central, as Mormons speak about themselves and their personal experiences. Secondly, places, geographies, and cultures demonstrate that Mormonism is a

---

440 Some of the context information of *Meet the Mormons* is resumed in part II, chapter 7.2 with a detailed discussion of the documentary's ethical dimensions.
441 "Meet the Mormons (2014) – Box Office Mojo," accessed January 22, 2018, http://www.boxofficemojo.com/movies/?id=meetthemormons.htm.
442 According to the interview conducted with Mormon media professional SA6 in Salt Lake City/UT, June 24, 2015.

global religion. Thirdly, many historical and often religious buildings are prominently depicted. Even though these structures do not have specific ties to the LDS Church, they can connect Mormonism with a larger historical context, as we see in the example of the Hindu temple in Kathmandu, Nepal, that opens the sequence "The Humanitarian" (the segment chosen for the experimental audience study). The fourth aspect concerns how Mormonism is defined in the narrative. All the social actors describe Mormonism in conspicuously similar terms. Thus, for example, in the sequence used for the audience study, the Mormon Bishop Bishnu Adhikari from Nepal speaks of Mormonism changing his life and now influencing his values and priorities, concepts that are found across all the sections of the film. Adhikari also explains how he deals with his conversion to Mormonism, having been raised within the Hindu tradition.

How, then, is religion depicted? The documentary's moral reading mode promotes Mormonism on the example of outstanding social actors with above average skills in impressive geographic locations that are filmed by an empathic and supportive camera. The narrative is completely controlled by the LDS Church; no critical voices are heard. The social actors represent the church as a global institution, with people from cultures beyond the US included or other geographies referenced. The documentary suggests that Mormonism is Christian, globally dispersed, tolerant, and open to other cultures; the message is that Mormons are outstanding normal people, Christians, family oriented, open minded, and caring of others.

This broadly framed analysis of *Meet the Mormons* determined the content of the first questionnaire in the audience study, which explores how viewers evaluate the depiction of Mormon values and the Mormon character (table 5). The questionnaire used Likert scales (1 = totally disagree to 5 = totally agree).

A close reading of the sequence "The Humanitarian" (00:47:44-00:58:40) explains the content of the second and third questionnaires, on opinions and attitudes promoted by the video's documentary reading modes.

The sequence opens with a travelling shot from a bird's eye view of a Hindu temple in Kathmandu, Nepal, the city lights at night, and the Himalayas, with a traditional Hindu dancer in front of a temple and some Buddhist sites filmed similarly. The audio-visual narrative is accompanied by a music score containing modern Indian music. Then Bishnu Adhikari is introduced; he is sitting on a chair in a green outdoor setting. He enthusiastically states (fig. 75): "I love my country Nepal. The beauty that God has given to us by his creation."

Values questionnaire:

	Completely disagree				Completely agree
Mormons are outstanding	1	2	3	4	5
Mormons are common people	1	2	3	4	5
Mormons are Christians	1	2	3	4	5
Mormonism is tolerant and adaptive to other cultures and lifestyles	1	2	3	4	5
Mormons are family oriented	1	2	3	4	5
Mormons are open minded	1	2	3	4	5
Mormons care for other people	1	2	3	4	5

Table 5 The values questionnaire asked participants: Now, tell us to what extent you consider that the following conceptions related to Mormons/Mormonism were emphasized by the video. Please, remember that this question is about the depiction of Mormons/Mormonism in the video.

Fig. 75 Mormon Bishnu Ashikari explains why he loves his home country, Nepal (Meet the Mormons, 00:49:12).

His humanitarian project is then presented in detail. At the end of the sequence Adhikari meets his Hindu father and kisses his feet, as is traditional (fig. 76). The scene is played in slow motion and concludes the sequence about Bishnu Adhikari.

Part II: Interactions between Communication Spaces and Religion

Fig. 76 The humanitarian kisses his father's feet as a sign of respect (Meet the Mormons, 00:57:38).

Adhikari's daughter explains that his kissing his father's feet is a sign of the highest respect in Nepalese tradition. Additionally, Adhikari's father comments in a voice-over: "I feel very blessed to be respected like that. I feel really blessed to be respected by my son."[443] The protagonist tells the viewers that he was raised in a religious family which believed in many gods, with a faith based on fear. He decided to attend a Christian school, where he was exposed to religious practices and thinking about Jesus Christ and responded positively. He went to the US for a master's degree, then worked for a year and subsequently returned to Nepal. Feeling a responsibility to invest in his country, he founded the organization "Choice Humanitarian", a US-based organization that helps poor people and builds schools, roads, and water systems. "Education is the key to coming out of poverty," he states. Later he provides an account of his childhood, in a family with ten siblings in rural Nepalese surroundings. The narrative includes humorous and cheerful moments, for example, when his wife and three children are introduced laughing and merrily chatting with each other during dinner or when his daughter describes Adhikari as dancing "goofily".

The sequence focusses on the religious and cultural background of the protagonist. Adhikari lived and was partly educated in the US but now resides with his family, including his three children, in Kathmandu. The nar-

---

443 The original language is Nepalese; the words are given in translation in the subtitles on the DVD.

ration, both the story and its audio-visual representation, also connects the protagonist to his Hindu and Nepalese heritage. We see the LDS Church's meetinghouse after he has recounted how he experienced the presence of God on the summit of Mount Everest. Then he recalls meeting Mormon missionaries in Russia, where he was baptized, with a picture inserted depicting his baptism, which, he recounts, "made him very happy." Adhikari and his wife explain their relationship to Jesus Christ. Adhikari terms his Hindu background "cultural practices and family tradition", differentiating culture from faith, and states: "Becoming a Christian doesn't mean you abandon your culture." By contrast, his wife refers to a "different religious faith" when talking about her former Hindu affiliation.

The sequence explains how to think about conversion to Mormonism from a different, specifically non-Western, cultural and religious background. The narrative argues that LDS Church members are able to accept and care for family members who are not Mormon. The idea of Mormons as Christians is emphasized, but their religious practices are by and large not depicted, for they take place in the temple, to which non-Mormons do not have access. We do see a picture of Adhikari's baptism, because baptisms take place in the church, where non-members are welcome.[444]

These results from the semio-pragmatic analysis provided the items for two further questionnaires that explore viewer opinions on (table 6), and attitudes toward (table 7) the depiction of Mormonism and Mormons, as steered by the film's documentary and moral reading mode. All the questionnaires used Likert scales (1 = totally disagree to 5 = totally agree).

As a next step, in addition to testing the results of the semio-pragmatic analysis in relation to values, opinions, and attitudes, we also investigated cultural differences across the audiences in their responses to *Meet the Mormons*. To research this question, we designed a cross-cultural quasi-experimental study that was conducted simultaneously in Barcelona and Zürich. The data collected was analyzed in light of variations by country. The cross-cultural and quasi-experimental study assigned at random one hundred undergraduate students from each country, Switzerland (University of Zürich) and Spain (Universitat Autònoma de Barcelona), to the experimental condition of watching the video about Mormonism. The students'

---

[444] The LDS Church uses the term *temple* for the most exclusive of church structures; once dedicated these structures can only be entered by worthy members. The terms *church* and *meetinghouse* are employed for buildings used for regular public worship.

Opinion questionnaire:

	Completely disagree			Completely agree	
The video was credible	1	2	3	4	5
The video was interesting	1	2	3	4	5
The video was entertaining	1	2	3	4	5
The video was educational	1	2	3	4	5
The video was informative	1	2	3	4	5
The video was commercial	1	2	3	4	5

Table 6 The questionnaire about opinions asked: Now, we need your personal opinion about the movie and its content. Please, tell us the extent you agree with the following statements.

involvement was voluntary; as acknowledgement participants received a T-shirt imprinted with the logo of their university.

The descriptive statistical analysis shows that the majority of the answers were located in the positive part of the Likert scale (above the neutral point 3). Participants agreed that during the reception process they had perceived the values (table 5), opinions (table 6) and attitudes (table 7) highlighted by the semio-pragmatic analysis. Even though the study confirmed the results of the analysis, the t-Student test indicated also some significant differences between the two countries.

Differences between the two samples on the values represented by the Mormons' documentary:
The Swiss and Spanish audiences differed on three out of seven items regarding the values represented in the film (see grey rows in table 8). The Spanish participants considered to a greater extent than the Swiss that Mormons are Christians, family oriented, and open minded. This evidence suggests the influence of the hermeneutic horizons of the audience, which can be understood as a product of the cultural setting in which the presented values are perceived,[445] or, in the words of Ralph Potter, of "the wider context of understanding within which men define and ponder their opin-

---

[445] Religious belonging, education and experiences, values, and moral concepts also shape hermeneutic horizons.

6. Researching Spaces of Production and Consumption of Latter-day Saints Media

Attitudes questionnaire:

	Completely disagree				Completely agree
(1) The depiction of Mormonism and Mormons of the video is true reflection of the reality	1	2	3	4	5
(2) The purpose of the video is to present a favourable perspective of Mormonism and Mormons	1	2	3	4	5
(3) The video reflects traditional events, places, people and experiences associated to Mormonism practices	1	2	3	4	5
(4) I learned about Mormonism and Mormons with the video	1	2	3	4	5
(5) The video has changed my mind about Mormonism and Mormons	1	2	3	4	5
(6) The video is a good representation of Mormonism and Mormons	1	2	3	4	5
(7) I would like to know more Mormonism and Mormons thanks to the video	1	2	3	4	5
(8) I will search for more information about Mormonism and Mormons after watching the video	1	2	3	4	5
(9) The video is intended to persuade people about the good aspects of being Mormonism and Mormons	1	2	3	4	5
(10) The video has made me reflect on Mormonism and Mormons	1	2	3	4	5
(11) I will try to get in touch with Mormons to know more about their religion	1	2	3	4	5
(12) The video is a one sided depiction of Mormonism	1	2	3	4	5
(13) The video was produced by Mormon authorities	1	2	3	4	5
(14) The video should be shown at television	1	2	3	4	5

Table 7 The attitudes questionnaire stated: Also, tell us your personal opinion about next statements.

ions."[446] The major difference in the responses was on the issue of open-mindedness, where the Swiss agreed less than the Spanish that Mormons were portrayed as "open minded." Additionally, the Spanish participants considered the documentary entertaining, educational and informative to

---

446 Ralph B. Potter, "The Logic of Moral Argument," in *Toward a Discipline of Social Ethics: Essays in Honor of Walter George Muelder*, ed. Paul Deats (Boston: Boston University Press, 1972), 108. Ralph Potter developed four elements of a moral argument of which the wider context is one. He considers disputes in this realm to be more difficult. See Potter, 108–110. For a detailed discussion of the term see part III, chapter 7.1.

	n		M (SD)		t
	Spain	Switzerland	Spain	Switzerland	
Mormons are outstanding [a]	100	101	2.87 (1.12)	2.65 (1.19)	1.33
Mormons are common people [a]	99	101	3.87 (1.04)	3.85 (1.06)	0.11
Mormons are Christians [a]	99	101	3.73 (0.96)	4.21 (1.00)	-3.47**
Mormonism is tolerant and adaptive to other cultures and lifestyles [a]	99	101	4.10 (0.86)	4.02 (0.95)	0.63
Mormons are family oriented [a]	100	101	3.94 (0.91)	4.27 (0.82)	-2.68**
Mormons are open minded [a]	99	101	3.43 (1.05)	3.96 (0.95)	-3.72*
Mormons care for other people [a]	100	101	4.22 (0.82)	4.32 (0.84)	-0.83

Note. *$p<0.05$;** $p<0.001$; [a] = equal variances; [b] =different variances.

*Table 8 Significant differences in items in the values questionnaires are marked * or **.*

a greater extent than the Swiss audience, whereas the two audiences rated "credible", "interesting", and "commercial" (table 9) similarly.

We can hypothesize that the Spanish perceived the video entertaining, educational and informative to a greater extent because they were less critical of the video and its depiction of Mormonism. The more positive evaluation might be related to their generally more positive responses to the documentary, with the Swiss participants responding more skeptically to *Meet the Mormons*, as table 9 shows.

The differences in the values and opinions questionnaires can be read as consistent with the results of the attitudes questionnaire (table 10, table 7). The Spanish participants hold to a greater extent than the Swiss participants that they learned about Mormonism and Mormons from the video (attitude 4, table 7) and that the video is a good representation of Mormonism and Mormons (attitude 6). The Swiss audience evaluated higher than the Spanish audience the statement that the depiction of Mormonism and Mormons in the video is a true reflection of the reality (attitude 1, table 7). The Swiss also indicated to a greater extent they would try to get in touch with Mormons in order to find out more about their religion (atti-

Opinions about the episode from the documentary:

	n		M (SD)		t
	Spain	Switzerland	Spain	Switzerland	
The video was credible[a]	100	101	3.76 (1.04)	3.50 (1.00)	1.77
The video was interesting[a]	100	101	3.93 (0.93)	3.83 (0.99)	0.72
The video was entertaining[a]	100	101	3.72 (1.02)	3.39 (1.15)	2.18*
The video was educational[a]	99	101	3.53 (0.98)	3.14 (1.16)	2.54*
The video was informative[a]	100	101	3.84 (0.98)	3.43 (1.13)	2.78**
The video was commercial[b]	100	101	3.09 (1.43)	3.14 (1.20)	-0.62

Note. *$p<0.05$;** $p<0.001$; [a] = equal variances; [b] =different variances

Table 9 The results of the opinions questionnaire show that the Swiss and Spanish samples perceived 3 out of 6 aspects similarly. Significant differences are marked * or **.

tude 11, table 7) and they indicated a little less, but still with significant difference, than the Spanish that the video is a one-sided depiction of Mormons (attitude 12, table 7). The differences between the countries in responses on the attitudes questionnaire suggest that the Swiss audience is more critical of the Mormon documentary, although they estimate the video to be a true reflection of reality to a greater extent. The attitude that the video is a "one-sided depiction of Mormons" in combination with the attitude that the video is a "true reflection of reality" shows that the Swiss audience was more aware of the video's intended effect, namely, to present Mormons as they would like to be perceived by their audience. The Swiss audience is therefore more conscious than the Spanish audience that the video does not provide a neutral perspective on Mormonism. Notably, while the Swiss assess the portrayal of Mormons more critically, they are more likely than the Spanish participants to express an interest in knowing more about Mormons (attitude 7, table 7).

Part II: Interactions between Communication Spaces and Religion

Attitudes about Mormons:

	n		M (SD)		t
	Spain	Switzerland	Spain	Switzerland	
I learned about Mormonism and Mormons with the video [a]	100	100	2.91 (1.18)	2.02 (1.06)	5.60**
I will try to get in touch with Mormons to know more about their religion [a]	100	101	1.71 (0.88)	2.36 (0.95)	-4.99**
The video is a one-sided depiction of Mormonism [a]	99	101	3.07 (1.10)	3.77 (1.05)	-4.62*
The depiction of Mormonism and Mormons of the video is true reflection of the reality [a]	100	100	2.60 (0.72)	2.82 (0.81)	-2.02*
The video is a good representation of Mormonism and Mormons [b]	100	100	2.68 (0.89)	2.41 (1.06)	1.94*
The video should be shown at television [b]	100	101	2.58 (1.13)	2.82 (1.14)	-1.50
The video reflects traditional events, places, people and experiences associated to Mormonism practices. [b]	100	100	3.17 (1.02)	2.97 (1.20)	1.27
The purpose of the video is to present a favourable perspective of Mormonism and Mormons [a]	100	101	4.19 (0.83)	4.02 (1.12)	1.22
The video has changed my mind about Mormonism and Mormons [a]	100	100	2.45 (1.05)	2.28 (1.14)	1.10
I would like to know more Mormonism and Mormons thanks to the video [a]	100	100	2.55 (1.19)	2.73 (1.29)	-1.02
I will search for more information about Mormonism and Mormons after watching the video [a]	100	101	2.62 (1.36)	2.44 (1.22)	1.01
The video is intend to persuade people about the good aspects of being Mormonism and Mormons [a]	100	101	3.75 (1.18)	3.84 (1.05)	-0.58
The video was produced by Mormon authorities [a]	100	100	3.39 (0.98)	3.31 (1.04)	0.55
The video has made me reflect on Mormonism and Mormons [a]	100	100	2.83 (1.07)	2.75 (0.96)	0.14

Note. *$p<0.05$; ** $p<0.001$; degrees of freedom =203 [a] = equal variances; [b] =different variances.

*Table 10 The results of the attitude questionnaire reveal significant differences in 4 out of 14 instances, marked * or **.*

Audiences perception of a Mormon world view

The results of the audience study suggest that the semio-pragmatic analysis provides an effective tool for establishing a film's reading modes and for predicting possible responses to a documentary about religion. The semio-pragmatic analysis shows that *Meet the Mormons* focusses on likable actors, the depiction of historical and religious buildings, global geographical settings, and a narrative that promotes the positive aspects of Mormonism by omitting critical reading modes. The documentary and the moral reading modes of *Meet the Mormons* could be observed by establishing the internal and external reading instructions.

Secondly, the results of the analysis were successfully transformed into scales and tested in the audience study. But the study also disclosed significant cultural differences across the reception of the values, opinions, and attitudes presented by the audio-visual message. The differences may have originated in lack of knowledge about Mormonism or in different conceptions of the specific religion or of the documentaries themselves. [447]

The audience study showed that the reception context for documentaries about religion is significant and is related to the audience's perception of values, opinions, and attitudes in the narration of a documentary. The responses measured in the study are indicative of how documentary viewers from different cultural backgrounds, namely Switzerland and Spain, perceive Mormonism. But the study also sheds light on how effectively documentaries can promote religion. *Meet the Mormons* efficiently communicates an overall positive depiction of a religious group, as the results demonstrate.

The research design further points out the importance of a multidisciplinary approach in the field of media and religion that considers sources

---

[447] To contextualize the results of the questionnaire on the Mormon documentary and to explore the differences between countries, a second documentary, representing another religion (Islam), has been similarly tested. The same procedure as with *Meet the Mormons* was applied, involving semio-pragmatic analysis that produced questionnaires on values and attitudes. To allow direct comparison, the same opinion scale was adopted in this second instance. The demographic data of the whole study, including both documentaries, is: Zürich (CH): 205 participants, 50.74% female and 45.4% male, $Mean_{Age}$ = 20.36, SD=3.24, Rg_{Age}= 18-40). Barcelona (ES): 203 participants, 62.6% female and 36% male, $Mean_{Age}$ = 22.16, SD = 2.76, Rg_{Age}= 17-37). The samples' demographics are similar and therefore ideal for comparison. See Mäder and Soto-Sanfiel, "'We Are Open-Minded, Tolerant, and Care for Other People'; Soto-Sanfiel and Mäder, "Identifying with a Religious Character".

as well as audiences. Such an approach is achieved here by combining semio-pragmatic analysis with an audience study. Drawn from communications studies, the former pays attention to the stylistic specificities of the sources, in particular of documentaries, their religion-promoting narration, and their intended reading modes. The latter is strictly concerned with quantitative data analysis. This interweaving of theories, concepts, methods, and sources allows discussion of a variety of ways in which audiences interact with the representation of religion in documentaries.[448]

The research also enables consideration of how representation and consumption interact as distinct entities. While the narration's intended meaning, its reading modes, is conspicuously stable, at the same time the reception context in which it is presented and perceived produces difference. The differences in the evaluation of the depicted religion also show the ambivalences and limitations of the semio-pragmatic paradigm. Meaning-making processes that take place between the documentary and the audience are not fully predictable. To achieve such precision, concrete audience responses need to be measured in a qualitative approach that specifies the extent of the determined meanings. A study of reception allows, however, for a comparison of audience responses through the correlation of data.

The multidisciplinary method approach is limited by its broad conception of the audiences, as "Spanish" and "Swiss", with individual or qualitative elements ignored. Future qualitive research should explore precisely such detail. In line with Ellingson's crystallization concept, the current approach is sensitive to how it constructs knowledge and representations. Again, further studies are needed, particularly to confirm or nuance these results in the context of other documentaries and religions. Moreover, future studies should observe the extent to which these representations are persuasive and can induce attitude change.

The second subsection of this chapter does not take on these challenges, which should be addressed in further research. Rather, with its qualitative approach through interviews with media professionals it adds another perspective to the interface of documentary media and religion.

---

448 Bal, "Working with Concepts," 20–22. I am aware that Mieke Bal's approach embraces interdisciplinary, which she contends is "productive", but that she dislikes "multidisciplinary", which she deems "muddled" (20). I do not share her perspective on multidisciplinary, which I believe embraces the interaction between researcher, sources, theories and methods that she is promoting.

6. Researching Spaces of Production and Consumption of Latter-day Saints Media

6.2. Qualitative interviews with LDS Church media professionals

In June and August 2015, six approximately one-hour-long interviews with eight media professionals were conducted in Salt Lake City and its surrounding area and in Frankfurt/M. (GE). The interviews were scheduled for the middle of the research process, with the groundwork on the church, its structure, and its engagement in media communication laid, but space left open for broad-ranging exploration though conversation of themes being identified and addressed by the project. All those interviewed shared two affiliations to which they were deeply committed: employment as media professionals and membership of the LDS Church. As interviewer I was curious to explore the interaction of these affiliations. While the interviews were undertaken early in the project, they were evaluated towards its end, in light of the knowledge and experiences garnered through the research.

The interviewees have been anonymized. They all are affiliated with a single religious institution, some within the hierarchy of the LDS Church and some simply as members; some are also its employees. The anonymization serves to inhibit possible repercussions from their involvement.[449] In two instances, two media professionals participated as interviewees at the same time. One of these "double" conversations was held with independent media professionals who work largely on LDS topics (SA2/SA3), as did one further interviewee who worked for the LDS Church on a contract basis (SA4). The participants in the second double interview (SA7/SA8) and a further two media professionals (SA1, SA6) were, by contrast, permanent employees of the church at the time they were interviewed. One interviewee (SA5) worked for an institution with close ties to the LDS Church. One media professional was interviewed by telephone because he (SA1) was not available for a meeting, and a telephone conversation was preferable to abandoning the interview altogether. The short overview below characterizes the professional occupations of the interviewees and their relations to the LDS Church, and provides demographical data concerning their age, gender, and whether they were born into the LDS Church or converted. The range of information varies because I was not provided with the same information for each participant.

SA1 (male, about 70 years) works for the LDS Missionary Department and is in charge of its diverse communication strategies and responsible for

---

[449] Sabina Misoch, "Qualitative Sozialforschung," in *Qualitative Interviews* (Berlin, Boston: De Gruyter Oldenbourg, 2015), 18–23.

overseeing all aspects of missionary work in the church. He graduated with a degree in Communications – Television Production and was subsequently hired as director of media at the Missionary Department, where he oversaw the production of all church advertising. He was born into the LDS Church.

SA2 (male, about 60 years) has been an independent cinematographer and producer for almost 30 years and works closely with SA3 as a co-producer for film. He was born into the church.

SA3 (male, about 60 years) is an independent writer and film producer. He graduated from Brigham Young University with a degree in Wildlife and Range Science and has a master's degree in Education from Idaho State University. He taught for almost 20 years. He worked as a radio and later film producer, now performs as moderator in these productions, and works closely with SA2 as a co-producer for film. He became a member of the LDS Church at the age of 20.

SA4 (male, about 50 years) is a filmmaker and writer. He started his career with the Walt Disney Company and directed films for the Disney Channel and other commercial companies. He received a BA in theatre from Brigham Young University. He was born into the LDS Church.

SA5 (male, about 70 years) is a film producer and director of IMAX films and other formats. He was director of media for the LDS Church Missionary Department and worked as a creative director at an LDS television channel. He was born into the church.

SA6 (male, about 65) worked for the Public Affairs Department of the LDS Church. Born and educated in England, he worked as a journalist for newspapers in Britain, Australia and Japan before joining the Public Affairs Department. He became a member of the church through conversion at the age of around 20.

SA7 (female, around 60) worked for the Europe part of the Public Affairs Department of the LDS Church.

SA8 (male, around 50) works for Europe part of the Public Affairs Department of the LDS Church. He earned a PhD in politics in Germany and actively engages in regional politics. He was brought up in a Mormon family, his parents having joined the LDS Church when he was five years old.

The first part of the interview followed a narrative-biographical, semi-structured approach and the second part was shaped by guided expert interview style.⁴⁵⁰ In light of the narrative-biographical nature of the qualitative interviews, the anonymity of the interviewees has been respected by excluding identifying information from transcribed material cited in this chapter. ⁴⁵¹ The theoretical approach was based on sociological hermeneutics of knowledge, which recognizes the singularity of each interview, understands the data as a text, and acknowledges the interpretative dimension of the evaluation process.⁴⁵² All but one of the interviews (a double interview conducted in German and not cited here) were conducted in English and transcribed word-for-word. Their consistency and often subtle language can likely be attributed to the fact that the interviewees are trained media professionals with an academic background and are used to discussing complex topics eloquently.⁴⁵³

And, finally, the interviews were coded in reference to grounded theory with the software atlas.ti.⁴⁵⁴ The coding process considered the interview sequences as closed entities in reference to the method of objective hermeneutics, which we will see in action later in this section.⁴⁵⁵ The evaluation narrative examined the main lines of each interview guided by the question, How does the religious background of the interviewees influence their work as media professionals?

---

450 Nina Baur, Jörg Blasius, and Cornelia Helfferich, eds., "Leitfaden- und Experteninterviews," in *Handbuch Methoden der empirischen Sozialforschung*, Handbuch (Wiesbaden: Springer, 2014), 570–573; Uwe Flick, *Qualitative Sozialforschung: eine Einführung*, Rororo (Reinbek bei Hamburg: Rowohlt Taschenbuch Verlag, 2016), 214–218.
451 Flick, *Qualitative Sozialforschung*, 65/66. Names used in the interviews have been anonymized.
452 Reichertz, "Objektive Hermeneutik und hermeneutische Wissenssoziologie"; Andreas Wernet, *Einführung in die Interpretationstechnik der objektiven Hermeneutik*, Qualitative Sozialforschung (Wiesbaden: VS Verlag für Sozialwissenschaften, 2009), 11–21; Andreas Franzmann, "Entstehungskontexte und Entwicklungsphasen der Objektiven Hermeneutik als einer Methodenschule," in *Die Methodenschule der Objektiven Hermeneutik: Eine Bestandsaufnahme*, ed. Roland Becker-Lenz et al. (Wiesbaden: Springer Fachmedien Wiesbaden, 2016), 1–42.
453 Wernet, *Einführung in die Interpretationstechnik der objektiven Hermeneutik*, 21–27.
454 Strübing, "Grounded Theory und Theoretical Sampling"; Boehm, "Grounded Theory - wie aus Texten Modelle und Theorien gemacht werden"; Uwe Flick, Ernst von Kardorff, and Ines Steinke, eds., "Theoretisches Kodieren: Textanalyse in der Grounded Theory," in *Qualitative Forschung: ein Handbuch*, by Andreas Boehm, Rororo (Reinbek: Rowohlt Taschenbuch Verlag, 2015), 475–485.
455 Reichertz, "Objektive Hermeneutik und hermeneutische Wissenssoziologie," 517.

Part II: Interactions between Communication Spaces and Religion

Preparation of the interviews

A short overview of the questions was distributed to the participants in advance of the interview so that they were aware of both its structure and the topics it would address. The interviews contained three sections. The first section asked about the LDS institution and how the interviewees were professionally related to the LDS Church, the position they occupied in the church hierarchy or how they and their work were related to the church, their responsibilities within the church, how active they were as church members, and how they were involved in media production for LDS related products. The list of questions below is an example and is in this case the list sent in advance to media professional SA5, who worked for a media institution affiliated with the LDS Church. The words in italics are generic replacements for the specific identifying terms used.

Institution: The Church of Jesus Christ of Latter-day Saints
- Which are your responsibilities as a producer within the LDS media production and *media institution x*?
- What is the connection between the Latter-day Saints public affairs department, the missionary department and the LDS media production and *media institution x*?
- How is the LDS presidency involved into the strategies of the LDS media and *media institution x*?
- How are the relation and the processes structured between those departments?
- Who is in charge of the Mormon channel?
- Does the Latter-day Saint Church work with an agency outside the church or is it in house?
- What is the difference between the LDS media in the US and in Europe or other countries?
- In which aspects are the LDS media, BYUtv, the missionary and the public affairs department involved in the *I'm a Mormon* campaign?

Referring to the communication spaces of production, representation, and consumption, the interviewees explained the specifics of the media productions with which they have been involved or for which they were responsible. The sample questions listed below were sent to a media professional who is an employee of the LDS Church. They illustrate the general impetus of this three-part section entitled "Media Production, Texts, Reception and Distribution":

Media Production
- In which sense are you involved in media production?
- How is the media production organized? How are the production decisions made? Is there a person or a board in charge of the productions? Who is responsible for strategic decisions according to media production?
- Do all the media professionals working for the Latter-day Saint church belong to the church?
- How many media does the church produce? What kind of? For what purposes?
- Who is in charge of the Mormon channel?

Media Texts
- *I'm a Mormon* campaign, especially the commercials and The District: What was your role in this production?
- LDS media sources on public Internet platforms like YouTube: How do you deal with the comments on and outside the LDS media platform?
- How is the interaction between those narratives for the different media (in meaning and production)?

Reception and Distribution
- Do you carry out any effect studies of the Latter-day Saint media?
- Do you dispose of figures about the media material you produce like about the consumption, audience, distribution channels, and budget?
- In which way does media reception provide positive effects and where do you see problematic areas inside and outside the Latter-day Saint community?
- Do you and how do you include other countries and cultures than the US in the media reception.

And, finally, the hermeneutic horizons of the participants, as illustrated by biographical information, were established. In this section the questions were the same for every interviewee:

Biography
- Are you born in the church or converted?
- You are a Latter-day Saint and [*name of the SA's professional activity in the field of media*]. How do you deal with these two commitments? How

do they intersect? If you do separate between these areas in which situations is this the case?
- How does the involvement in media production processes influence your experiences in the church and your attitude as LDS member in the community?
- What are your favourite television shows/series and movies?

The interview did not work strictly through the prepared questions, but they provided a guide to topics that might be touched upon during the conversation. The interviews were recorded and subsequently transcribed and then coded according to an open coding method.[456] When a code became saturated, it was sorted into inductive categories or split into subcodes.[457] The final analysis worked with the following ten categories, developed after three interviews had been coded (table 11).[458]

Categories	Description
Biographical	Concerning their private life, education and personal experiences.
Communication	Different means of communication like for example social media, statements about the purpose of their communication and LDS specific strategies to communicate.
Consumption space	Statements about the audience.
Finances	Referred to financial aspects of the LDS Church or media productions.
LDS Church related statements	When the LDS Church is explicitly mentioned.
Media production	Production titles.
Opinions	Views of Mormons formed either within the Mormon community or externally and also political opinions.

---

456 Helene Starks and Susan Brown Trinidad, "Choose Your Method: A Comparison of Phenomenology, Discourse Analysis, and Grounded Theory," *Qualitative Health Research* 17, no. 10 (December 1, 2007): 1372.
457 David R. Thomas, "A General Inductive Approach for Analyzing Qualitative Evaluation Data," *American Journal of Evaluation* 27, no. 2 (June 1, 2006): 237–46.
458 Tom Richards and Lyn Richards, "Using Hierarchical Categories in Qualitative Data Analysis," in *Computer-Aided Qualitative Data Analysis: Theory, Methods and Practice*, ed. Udo Kelle, Gerald Prein, and Katherine Bird (London: Sage, 1998), 80–95.

Categories	Description
Production space	Embraced the whole production process.
Religion	Everything referring to religion.
representation and distribution space	Statements about representation and distribution strategies of the media.

Table 11 The ten categories, developed after three interviews, had been coded.

Also during the coding process did spaces of communication (representation, distribution, production, consumption) emerge as a helpful tool for systematizing parts of the interview sequences. The multiple or partly overlapping coding of a single statement was deliberate and is indicative of possible relations between categories.

The following discussion focuses on the most salient topics and how they relate to other topics. Inclusion in this evaluation is not determined simply by the frequency of a specific code. The selection of topics has also been influenced by the questions that guided the interviews: How do the religious background of the interviewees and their work as media professionals influence each other? Are these roles interrelated or separate; do they even overlap?

Evaluation of the interviews

The evaluation of the coded interviews largely followed a text interpretation modelled on the method of objective hermeneutics.[459] This method was selected as it takes into account that the study included a relatively small number of interviews – only six, involving eight interviewees in total. In a first step, the interpretation process focused on each interview individually and its sequences that contained an argument or a statement. In a second step, these statements and arguments were analyzed by assigning codes to topic areas, which then, in a third step, were either specified in sub-codes or sorted into categories. The evaluation process applied to the

---

459 Franzmann, "Entstehungskontexte und Entwicklungsphasen der Objektiven Hermeneutik als einer Methodenschule," 26–33; Wernet, *Einführung in die Interpretationstechnik der objektiven Hermeneutik*, 21–38.

interviews therefore combines objective hermeneutics with elements of grounded theory.[460]

The results of the interview evaluation are organized into seven aspects established during the coding process when the codes were diversified or sorted into categories. Retrospectively it was evident that these aspects had been present implicitly during the interviews:
(1) Feeling alienated by mainstream media
(2) Working for the LDS Church requires sacrifices
(3) Self-definition through professional media work
(4) The "Mormonese" language
(5) Telling who we really are and being authentic
(6) LDS Church control
(7) Faith and values

The sorting of the statements into seven thematic aspects proved fruitful for the evaluation because it facilitated grouping of the statements and enabled their comparison. Although each statement was considered in its singularity, comparison revealed conspicuous parallels, as the following discussion shows.

(1) Feeling alienated by mainstream media: The interviewees very often mentioned their own experience as media consumers and a feeling of being alienated from the representational style of successful television shows and movies because of the explicit depiction of sexuality, nudity, and violence. A freelance media professional explained:

> And that's not to say I'm opposed to anybody that makes an adult driven, I'm not talking about an adult film, I'm talking about adult driven in terms of its psyche. I'm not opposed to that, I love those kinds of films. But I think because of that mindset, my manager, my agent, kinda pushed me towards the arena that was more safe for the families. And that seemed to be a good fit. Because I wasn't having to make those hard decisions about oh, I gotta pull out that scene that has nudity in it. I gotta pull, I didn't have to make those choices because this is for Disney. So you're just not gonna have those kind of choices, battles to fight. So it has impacted, so my belief system I guess is impacting the kind of stuff that I would do. And I was offered some films that were considered, I don't put a whole lot of stock in the ratings, per se.

---

460 See Wernet, *Einführung in die Interpretationstechnik der objektiven Hermeneutik*, 21–38; Reichertz, "Objektive Hermeneutik und hermeneutische Wissenssoziologie."

6. Researching Spaces of Production and Consumption of Latter-day Saints Media

> Because they're different for every country, and they're very, they don't mean a whole lot. But I was offered some films that could have probably been very good for my career but would have gone counter to my belief system, so I passed on this, decided not to do it. It's not like I'm any great saint or anything. I just didn't feel comfortable.[461]

Mormon media professionals are convinced of the harmfulness of such "adult driven" representations but those they work with are also sensitive to what their Mormon colleagues deem appropriate. Production companies therefore often do not offer them projects with potentially explicit content. Interviewees referred to their work's suitability for young people, with one interviewee explicitly referring to being discomforted by the thought of not being able to show their work to their children:

> Because I care about what my kids see, so if I have any control I'm gonna use whatever control I have, to the extent that I can. I don't have 100% control, nobody does. I'm only gonna work on things that I would feel okay about my children seeing. […]. So by and large, when I could exercise some control, I always selected products to work on that were gonna be safe for families, for kids.[462]

All of the interviewed media professionals were parents, to between four and seven children, and some had grandchildren. Their motivation for producing only family-oriented programs was heightened by an identified need for productions that entertain but are in line with their moral principles. One motivation for working in media was to fill a gap in the media market.

> They look at the television shows that are on TV right now, and they say, can't watch *Walking Dead* with my kids. I can't watch *Game of Thrones* with my kids, I can't watch *Wallander*, from Sweden, with my kids. My kids can watch either silly children's programming, or nothing. So what's in the middle? What's the sophisticated stuff that a whole family can watch together? And there isn't any. There's none. I mean, you're not going to get your five year old to watch a concert on PBS of a great orchestra, they're just not going to stay there. So, somewhere in the middle, nobody is providing this kind of program. Well,

---

461 SA4, June 22, 2015, Salt Lake City/UT, 2:28.
462 SA4, 2:27.

we believe really strongly that you should avoid things that have gratuitous violence or sexual content. But then we don't really have it.[463]

The media professionals made no mention of pressure from the church to adopt a specific attitude during the production process or to make decisions based on church-defined objectives. They described their work as driven by a desire to tell stories that matched their belief system, a means of serving a greater good.

(2) Working for the LDS Church requires sacrifices: According to the media professionals, the ability to express oneself in accord with one's religious worldview comes at a price. All of the interviewees connected their decision to abide by their moral principles with the sacrifice of a career in mainstream commercial media. They also highlighted that they could have earned much more by working for companies not affiliated with the church. They gained, they explained, in being truthful to their belief and value systems, despite the financial loss. A media professional employed by the church explained:

> I'm a journalist by training, my background is in journalism, I spent 11 years in newspaper and I always said I would never go into public relations. Because public relations seems to be all about spin. If I'm working for the Ford Motor Company I might prefer Volkswagen. So there's a certain lack of integrity in that. But when I was invited to come and work for the church in Public Affairs. I was three years in London and twelve years in Australia, and I have been here for 24 years. I realized that my passion, what I really deeply believe in my core was also going to be my job. Which is fantastic, a fantastic opportunity. Connie[464] will tell you that everyone who works here, works here because of their conviction, not because it's a job, and we can also tell you that many of us can earn a lot more working for somebody else. Working somewhere else. But we do it because we love it. So at least we feel no contradiction, at least I feel no contradiction, I think you [to Connie] get the same.[465]

Another interviewee, who was employed by a church-affiliated media institution, was even more outspoken about the consequences of choosing to work for the church. "I think everybody in this building would say, I could

---

463   SA5, June 23, 2015, Provo/UT, 5:87.
464   An alias.
465   SA6, June 24, Salt Lake City/UT, 2015, 3:102.

make three or four times the money working for someone else. I could, I took a huge pay cut to leave the freelance film making world.
So why would I do that? Only because I really believe in what we're trying to accomplish."[466] This media professional also mentioned that the employees of this church-affiliated media institution not only accepted being paid less, but also had to regulate their behavior, even if they were not Mormon: "they have to agree to abide by the Mormon principles. So you can't smoke in the building, you can't drink, you can't have affairs at work, all those things.
But they don't have to be LDS, they just have to be, agree to act like LDS, agree to our standards."[467] According to this interviewee, the nature of the productions and the working atmosphere in which this church-affiliated institution is involved is good enough reason for non-Mormons to work there, even though they have to regulate their behavior and might earn more elsewhere.

(3) Self-definition through professional media work: Their emphasis on the advantages of working for the LDS Church or for a church-affiliated institution could have been an attempt by the interviewees to reassure themselves that they had made the right decision about where to work. They also evidently thrived, however, in being able to define their Mormon-being through their work.

> I really believe that there's a dark media landscape and we might be able to make a difference, and so that drives every decision I make. Now is that about being a Mormon?
> I don't know. Maybe it's about being a person who cares about the world, but my version of that is being a Latter-day Saint. So being a Latter-day Saint means this matters to me more than almost anything else. I don't think I would be happier.[468]

The emphasis on doing good and making a difference was, as we have seen, a repeated theme. "Being a person who cares about the world" is not exclusive to Mormons, but for this interviewee it was an idea that fed his understanding of what it is to be a Mormon and was expressed by producing media that enlightened the "dark media landscape."

Several interviewees mentioned the experience of belonging to a minority and of often feeling misunderstood. One of the interviewees explained

---

466 SA5, 15:114.
467 SA5, 15:114.
468 SA5, 4:101.

that he was sometimes given negative accounts of who Mormons are and what they do. This misperception was a strong impetus for telling critics who the Mormons really are.

> And I thought, if people just knew us for who we really are, they wouldn't say such things. They would, it's like anything. You know, you get to know a person, you get a sense of who they are. And then all of a sudden, all of the things that you've heard about them, you can kinda start to separate fact from fiction a little easier. And so that was really at the heart of the decision of what this film should be.[469]

All the media professionals mentioned that they hoped through their media work to change how Mormons are perceived by non-Mormons. Their goal was to change how they are seen from outside by providing a contemporary perspective on the LDS community. According to an independent media professional, they are additionally interested in portraying their own history in a way that did not ignore the past but could be respected by outsiders:

> That's what we've been doing all along, is trying to take a middle of the road between a scholar up here and trying to bring a public to an understanding of what our history is as it's growing and developing and being respected.[470]

The interviewees described their religious convictions being fostered by their work in media production. Media work was seen as a way not only to express their beliefs but also to improve themselves as human beings.[471] "Every time I go out to build a show, I come away a better person because of what I learn from what they [Latter-day Saints] went through and what they did. My work makes me a better person." The media professionals were not interested in telling controversial stories about the church or in relaying criticism of the institution. As faithful people who supported the church with their work, they sought to promote rather than question the church, as was explained during a double interview: "When we started, two things. We were not going to be looking for controversial axes to grind. We're both faithful Latter-day Saints. We believe in the cause. We're trying to help the cause. We're not going to hinder it. You can always tell a controversial story. We're not in the least bit interested. We take criticism.

---

469 SA4, 2.53.
470 SA3, June 22, 2015, Salt Lake City/UT, 5:181.
471 SA3, 5:23.

6. Researching Spaces of Production and Consumption of Latter-day Saints Media

We just don't care."[472] They also explained that they were willing to expose themselves for the sake of the church: "We become poster boys for …", the second interviewee added, "Yeah we just become a target." Then the first resumed: "…for the church."[473] They agreed that "they [non-Mormons] mock the church." SA3 then emphasized the outside perception of Mormons: "They just hate Mormons and they just use us to – an avenue to vent."[474]

While they were intrinsically motivated to tell stories about the LDS Church, the media professionals were not interested in spreading explicit religious messages. Reference was often made to a desire to use entertainment as a vehicle for values of which the audience were not directly aware. One media professional described their communication strategy as follows:

> Yeah, there isn't a secret agenda to preach Mormon doctrine. There is a secret agenda to entertain people so much that they'll think about the things you're talking about, which were, racism, there was a little Asian girl in the community, there's a black FBI, so.[475]

Here entertainment was the primary aim in producing media, with enlightenment a byproduct.

Three dimensions of the relations between religious background and working in the media distinctly illustrate the media professionals' motivation for media work. First, they sought to overcome their alienation from mainstream media, a step they could take by working for the LDS Church or for LDS affiliated institutions, or by supporting the church's cause. They were, secondly, willing accept the smaller income and more limited career that resulted. The sacrifice was deemed worthwhile because, thirdly, they could use their work to define who the Mormons are and specifically who they are as Mormons. This attitude simultaneously reinforced the boundary between Mormons and non-Mormons that is expressed in different communication strategies, as the next aspects demonstrate.

(4) The "Mormonese" language: In light of their occupational background, it is not surprising that the media professionals were sensitive to communication strategies. For example, they divided their audience between Mormons and non-Mormons. The former also need to be educated

---

472 SA3: 5:57.
473 SA2, June 22, 2015, Salt Lake City/UT, SA3, 5:61.
474 SA3, 5:61.
475 SA5, 4:86.

and provided with materials to share. "To some degree, because we're still educating our own people as well, you know, so that's a particularly challenging subject."[476] Media are also deployed to reach out to the non-Mormon world, as the interviewees made clear. Explaining Mormonism to non-Mormons is not the same as explaining Mormonism to Mormons. One interviewee described the difference in light of language. A message cannot be written in "Mormonese" if it is to be heard by non-Mormons:

> Our messages reach everybody but the messages are designed to reach those who are not of our faith and so that helps people that are members to the church who may have a question or be searching or whose faith is struggling. It helps them the same way but if you're around Mormons very much, you'll find out that we have our own language. When Mormons talk to Mormons, they talk in Mormonese. They talk in a way that the average non-member doesn't necessarily understand everything that they say because we have our own way of conversing. It's not a separate language I'm just inventing. Every group has its own vocabulary. We make sure that all of our material from the missionary department is written in non-Mormonese. It's written with the target audience in mind of those who are not of our faith and then if you write it that way, members of the church get it. They're not having any trouble with that but frequently if you write an ad to members of the church, non-members won't understand it.[477]

The media professional gave no further details, but the point was well made: audience dictates not just content but also expression.

The communication styles of the LDS Church departments also vary. The Missionary Department works closely with the Public Affairs Department (I was asked not use the term "public relation department" "because public relations has this sort of connotation of, you know, sort of spin. And, we don't like spin,"[478] as the interviewee explained at the beginning of the interview.). How this lateral communication works was illustrated during one of the interviews on the example of *The Book of Mormon* musical.[479] The church initially saw the music as potentially damaging, as parody that mocked their faith. The musical portrays missionaries and was therefore a particular concern for the Missionary Department. The deci-

---

476 SA6, 2:65.
477 SA1, June 22, 2015, Salt Lake City/UT, 3:31.
478 SA6, 2:16.
479 SA6, 2:32–2:38.

sion was made to deploy a strategy that meant not fighting against the musical but using the attention it was attracting amongst critics and the general public for the church's own purposes. Both LDS Church interviewees seemed proud of how the church had dealt with the challenge, which was evidence of how the Public Affairs Department and Missionary Department can complement one another:

> In some ways, *The Book of Mormon* musical has been a great advertiser for us because most people can't afford to go to that. Places like London, the whole city was about *The Book of Mormon* musical. The ads are on all the buses, all the subway stations, everything, promoting *The Book of Mormon* musical. A lot of people think it's our musical until they go see it.[480]

The church decided to plaster the public transportation near where the musical took place with its own ads, to build a whole campaign around the musical, and even to buy several pages of ad space in the playbill, where slogans like "I've read the book" or "The book is always better" or "Now read the book" were presented along with depictions of likable Mormons.[481]

This example gives an idea of the extent and nuance of the collaboration by those responsible for church communication.[482] The response to the musical was proactive, not defensive. According to the interviewees, the communication strategy applied in New York and London was to be transferred to any other city where the musical was performed, as an "established pattern"[483] used to "teach what the church is really about."[484]

The Public Affairs Department has also applied "non-Mormonese" language in communicating about the temple garment. This underclothing must be worn when visiting the temple, but some Mormons wear it every day.[485] One interviewee noted, "We actually started calling it sacred under-

---

480 SA1, 3:52.
481 Playbill, *The Book of Mormon*, Citi Emerson Colonial Theatre, Boston /MA, September 2015.
482 Similar cooperation between the two departments was applied in the case of the webpage mormonsandgays.com, on the church's attitude towards homosexuality, which was completely revised in 2018.
483 SA6, 2:38.
484 SA6, 2:37.
485 Church Newsroom, *"Mormon Underwear" Is the Temple Garment and Is Sacred to Latter-Day Saints*, accessed May 10, 2019, https://www.youtube.com/watch?v=SkTz_NQqKA8.

235

clothing. And then we realized nobody's going to search for that."[486] The adoption of non-Mormon language was thus designed to facilitate communication with the out-group. This practice is not simply accommodating, for it bolsters a Mormon exclusivity – the new term will be received by existing members of the LDS Church as unfamiliar; it is part of an othering process that distances them from the outside world.[487] "Non-Mormonese" communication fortifies belonging for the community who understand "Mormonese".

(5) Telling who we really are and being authentic: The media professional's description "what the church is really about" was a verbalization often connected with a rhetoric of "being authentic" or "showing who we really are". If non-Mormons are shown who Mormons really were, then, it was hoped, that target audience will want to know more, and will perhaps connect with the church through missionaries. But conversion is not always the first aim, as we see in the case of shows broadcast by the television channel BYUtv, which belongs to Brigham Young University and the LDS Church:

> we'd like to reach out to people who share our values. Not necessarily our faith, our religion, but who share our values all over the world. And entertain them, and enlighten them, and educate them if you can, but mostly entertain and enlighten. And we all know that we can only stand so much education, then want to be entertained. So, BYU broadcasting's goal is to entertain first and then if we do a good job of entertaining, we've earned the right to tell you something that enlightens you and makes you a better person, right?[488]

Again the connection between entertainment and education is vital to the intent behind the media production. This goal was similarly described by an independent Mormon media professional who produced documentary media about the history of the church. He mentioned that non-Mormon media often constructed their own narratives about Mormon history. He and his co-producer saw it as their duty to correct those that are wrong and claim their own perspective.

> People get their story from the media. If nobody is going to speak up and tell what really happened and tell the history as it really happened,

---

486 SA6, 2:37.
487 Sune Qvotrup Jensen, "Othering, Identity Formation and Agency," *Qualitative Studies* 2, no. 2 (October 3, 2011): 63–78.
488 SA5, 4:21.

> then we're going to. The church is starting to tell their story in great detail; their history, controversial subjects. Well we're there too. We are trying to partner and help the cause by telling the story of what really happened so that the people will get correct information. The Joseph Smith papers, our existence, is all for one thing. To remove people's excuses for being ignorant of their history. We're going to tell it and we're going to tell it like it really happened so that people are properly informed.[489]

Telling the story of Mormonism as it "really happened" is not about searching out controversial facts and weaknesses. Media narratives are produced to foster church members and to convince non-Mormons of the positive aspects of Mormonism. Almost in all interviews the terms "authentic" and "real" were used to describe the mode of communication for which the professionals strive in their work, prompted by church leaders.

"Authentic" and "real" express quality. They form a guiding principle, deployed, for example, in reference to *Meet the Mormons*. Both the social actors themselves and the audience had to feel the depictions were authentic. One interviewee explained that anyone who spends two weeks with the social actors who appear in the videos should experience them exactly as they are portrayed. The documentary, the interviewee explained, allows Mormons to feel good about themselves and shows non-Mormons "who we really are, what makes us tick."[490] In defining how they are represented in the media, LDS Church members can influence how Mormons are received in "real life". Media representations and general perceptions are understood to be closely tied together.

The intentions behind the *I'm a Mormon* campaign and its follow-up *Meet the Mormons* were described by one interviewee: [491]

> Let's tell the story of real members, not the story of the institution. Let's tell the story of the members. You know, typically, documentaries in the past about the Church have been, you start with Joseph Smith, and you need to tell the story. And you talk about the doctrine. And you interview church leaders.[492]

Telling the story of "real members" is a communication strategy deployed by the LDS Church to shape a positive image of the LDS institution.

---

489 SA3, 5:148.
490 SA4, 1:159.
491 See for a detailed discussion of this campaign part II, chapter 4.
492 SA6, 2:45.

The producers of both *Meet the Mormons* and the *I'm a Mormon* campaign sought social actors able to talk about their lives in terms of "striving for a better person",[493] a description used by an interviewee who was involved in the production of *Meet the Mormons* to define what it means to be a Mormon. Mormons, the interviewee added, fail and succeed just like anyone else.

Both, church leaders and those making the documentaries sought authenticity: "But we really had, honestly we had quite a bit of autonomy in the making of the film. And again their [the church leaders'], their only guidance was, please, just be authentic."[494] Encouraged to explore how the instruction to be "authentic" was understood, the interviewee continued, "Well it means be honest about who, collectively and individually, does this represent, who we are as a people."[495] The use of "honest" picked up on the idea of being "authentic" and "real". This discussion brings us to the issue of the control exerted by church leaders over the work of the media professionals.

(6) LDS Church control: The media professionals involved with *Meet the Mormons* emphasized the lack of direction from church leaders and that they had felt free to tell the story as they wanted. Church leaders had certainly approached filmmakers about making a new documentary for the visitors' center. But, one interviewee reported,

> That was perhaps the thing that was maybe perhaps most surprising to me is that they continued to say, hey just let us see something when it's done. And so they really didn't, as I mentioned earlier they didn't tell us who, where or what, or when. They said just find –, or even how many stories to do. So they were very open, they said keep us posted. And if there's something that we think you should be concerned about we'll let you know, but I don't know I was going to say that by and large they just said go. And really, the reality is that 100% of the time, they just said, okay.[496]

Church leaders were evidently involved, but somewhat to the surprise of the interviewee they did not intervene. Unlike the interviewed independent producers, as we shall see, the producers of this material highlighted their great freedom in their work. They were, however, required to report

---

493 SA5, 4:1.
494 SA4, 1:141.
495 SA3, 1:142/143.
496 SA4, 1:122.

back to the church, for example, to the Public Affairs Department, supervised by Elder D. Todd Christofferson.

> So because of the way that's structured, we always have a church leader oversight into what we're doing to make sure we stay on the right track. But they don't get into hands-on, day-to-day management. Generally the context and mostly when we call them, maybe some advice or counsel or something. Or maybe there's a particularly big story that's just blown up and we're looking at maybe a response. Most of the times, I would make the decision. But maybe sometimes when I'd like a second opinion and maybe I'm not quite certain about the direction we are going, I might call and say, listen this is what we're thinking about. What do you think? Most of the time they'll say that's fine.[497]

The media professionals were sensitive about when to reach out to their supervisors within the church as decisions were being made. Although they suggested they had significant creative freedom, one interviewee mentioned "bureaucratic red tape", noting that he liked to "cut red tape, so we'll see what we can."[498] The statement suggests the existence of administrative control, but the interviewee described the hurdles it creates good-humoredly.

Two independent Mormon media producers explained that it is better not to ask for financial support from the church because a production funded by the church must go through a complicated and time-consuming process that affects the production schedule. During "correlations" the church leaders consider whether the media content correlates with the image of the church they wish to see broadcast. The independent media professionals emphasized that it is better to have the church's approval, but they termed the process "painful."[499] The church evidently is experienced at controlling production in two ways, depending on the relevant media professionals' relationship with the church. Those involved in projects created within the institutional church reported no church control or mentioned a great degree of freedom; independent media professionals stated, "we have a little more latitude" in relation to their representation of the church,[500] but they then had neither financial or creative support from the

---

497 SA6, 2:21.
498 SA6, 2:48.
499 SA2, 5:93.
500 SA3, 5:94.

church. As we have seen, however, church control is not exercised only in the space of production, for in the space of consumption the Membership Department systematically tracks online comments and responds to them.[501]

(7) Faith and values: During the interviews the media professionals explained their religious worldview and values in a more general way, without relating them explicitly to their occupation. Their comments suggest a conception of religion that is only implicitly shaped by their work experience. Unsurprisingly, the media professionals in this instance were very largely positive about religion.

Faith, as we have repeatedly noted, is understood in terms of agency. Agency is about the self, about a personal coming to faith that is not externally dictated. One media professional explained:

> Because you know one of the main tenants of our faith is not to compel anybody to believe anything. We have this thing called agency, so we want people to – sure we want to help them understand what we believe because it makes us happy, but you can't force something on someone.[502]

All the interviewees said in some way that agency could bring personal challenges, but that they felt rewarded in being able to be active Mormons.

Their statements about their worldviews and religious practices were layered. The interviewees repeated the differences between Mormons and non-Mormons and how difficult it can be for the latter to understand the former. They also talked, however, about strong bonds within the community. Those ties were picked up in the discussion of *Meet the Mormons*, which was well-received amongst members of the LDS Church. In self-identifying as Mormons in the videos, the social actors created a sense of communal togetherness with self-identifying Mormon viewers: "Because we all identify with those members, even though they're different cultures, different countries; we know we all have the same thing in common."[503] The interviewees also emphasized the Christian character of Mormon tradition, not in terms of a single Christian community but rather in light of Christian beliefs. Communicating to non-Mormons that Mormons believe in Jesus Christ was, according to one interviewee, the essential aim of the *I'm a Mormon* campaign:

---

501 SA5, 4:108.
502 SA4, 1:78.
503 SA6, 2:31.

> So all the departments understand that our primary message in the church is that we follow Jesus Christ. Everything centers in that. So when they put their messaging together or when we put our messaging together we've always got this idea of does this help people understand the fundamental Christian nature of the faith? That we're trying to follow him, my following. We're not preaching all the time, but every one of those Mormon, *I'm a Mormon* messages talks about the lifestyle of the person. And we're trying to show the consistency with the way they interpret their faith in their own lives with Christian doctrine, that's the sorta glue that holds us all together.[504]

Adherence to Christian doctrine is presented here as the central reference point for all Mormons and as "the glue that holds us all together." Christian faith is an identity marker for each individual and also for the community, for it bonds an otherwise diverse group.

Interviewees spoke also of the religious community as a strong and supportive network. That network is active when someone involved in a LDS Church campaign leaves the church. The interviewee explained that the leaders of the LDS Church can be informed about "apostates"[505] because members of local congregations are in contact with each other and "Mormons sort of have a network of telling each other what's going on."[506] Within individual congregations members are bonded with each other and in turn congregations are bonded to the church leadership, which provides, the interviewees suggested, strong networks that promote adherence to the church.

The conception of religion expressed by the interviewees was marked by a deep confidence in the religious institution and by "belief in the cause". Media professionals employed directly by the church demonstrated a great commitment to ensuring that their work had value for the LDS Church. The religious dimension was associated with core values that had positive impact on their working life and influenced their decision making.

Financial donors to media productions were deemed by the interviewees to similarly demonstrate their belief in the cause.

> So these donors are people who believe that there's a dark, we call it a dark media landscape. There ought to be some light in there. And they believe in that cause. Just like they believe in, I'm sure the same people

---

504 SA6, 2:28/2:29.
505 SA1, 3:157.
506 SA1, 3:96.

who give us money give money to water for Africa and starving children and hurricane relief and refugees in Syria, and then as part of that gift they give money to us saying, we'd like media to be a little lighter as well.[507]

Again we encounter a possible inconsistency: while interviewees defended religious freedom as an important dimension of their religious self-conception, they understood their own religious worldview in exclusive terms. This tension is expressed in relation to Mormon engagement with the LGBTI community.[508] One interviewee noted that although Mormons will acknowledge different understandings of family, they defend their own conception as a moral issue.

> So there is a time we say well, it's a moral issue but we also defend. We have this, I don't know if you've heard of this, *Articles of Faith* they're called. And one of those says you know we deemed everyone has a right to worship how, where, or what they may. So we really are huge proponents of religious freedom. We don't want everyone to become a Mormon. That's not logical. We just want everyone who wants to have the right to be one or to be a Catholic or to be humanist or to be an atheist or to be whatever.[509]

The interviewee went as far as to state that non-Mormons too can live good lives pleasing to God.

> I think there is plenty of people who go to work and don't think about God at all, and yet they think about being a better person. So that changed my perception. I use to think Mormons might be the only people in heaven, now I am pretty sure that we'll pretty much all be there and we'll all have a role to play.[510]
>
> … all the people that I've met are just wonderful people of all faiths. I can't imagine, I can't believe in a God who doesn't love them as well. I can't believe in a God who doesn't love a great humanist who doesn't even believe in him as long as they're trying to be better people.[511]

---

507 SA4, 4:74.
508 Elizabeth Dias, "Mormon Church to Allow Children of L.G.B.T. Parents to Be Baptized," *The New York Times*, April 5, 2019, sec. U.S., https://www.nytimes.com/2019/04/04/us/lds-church-lgbt.html.
509 SA5,4:4.
510 SA5, 4:104.
511 SA5, 4:11.

This statement parallels a statement by one media professional interviewed that noted that the consumers of LDS Church media productions are not necessarily Latter-day Saints; they need only share LDS Church values. The interviewee used broccoli pizza as a metaphor. Children who do not want to eat healthy broccoli on its own might happily eat broccoli pizza and thus still get the health benefits of the broccoli, even it if comes with less-healthy pizza.[512] A certain "balance" is needed.[513] Such balance is achieved when an audience is entertained, distracted from their own world and brought virtually into another world, and educated about that second world, but without overt reference to religious values that are being inculcated. The interviewees suggested a critical mass of values can be communicated without hindering the production's ability to entertain.

Media professionals and their religious worldview

The seven aspects discussed here together suggest this group of media professionals share markedly similar values and worldviews, which we can usefully summarize.

Aspects 1-3 (Feeling alienated by mainstream media; Working for the LDS Church requires sacrifices; Self-definition through professional media work) highlight a sense of alienation from the mainstream media landscape and of misrepresentation by the media. They are strongly motivated by a need to tell non-Mormons who Mormons really are. They want their work to support the cause of the church. Through their media work, they become, they believe, better people, participate in the production of positive images of the church, and lighten the "dark media landscape".

Aspects 4 and 5 (The "Mormonese" language; Telling who we really are and being authentic) capture how the media productions communicate with their target audience, at the same time drawing boundaries between Mormons and non-Mormons. Cooperation between departments of the church in communicating with non-Mormons is pronounced. All those interviewed appeared to trust that "authentic" and "real" depictions of Mormons would lead to a greater acceptance of the church in the public sphere. The LDS media professionals demonstrated great loyalty to their church and felt responsible for its public image.

---

512   SA5, 4:88.
513   SA5, 4:88; SA4, 1:59, 1:60, 1:81.

Alongside this strong commitment to the church, aspect 6 (LDS Church control) suggests a variety of experience in relation to the control exerted by the religious institution. Interviewees described feeling personal responsibility for their media productions, without restrictions placed by the church leaders; the "authenticity" of the message they convey – a reference to dimension 5 – is, however, adjudicated by church officials.

Dimension 7 (Faith and values) maps Mormon faith as agency, with each individual responsible for their own decisions about the life they should live if they are to become a better person. There is an inherent tension here with the LDS mission goals of finding candidates for baptism and persuading them of the truth of Mormonism. In general, being religious is seen as bringing additional value to media work for the church. Marked commitment to the church institution and to Mormon networks, described as dense and efficient, was evident. For every interviewee religious self-conception and external views of the church focused on claiming an identity as "Christian".

6.3. Persuasion through documentary media

The chapter has applied both quantitative and qualitative methods to examine the production and consumption spaces of documentary media produced by or in association with the LDS Church. The first part focuses on the audience in the space of consumption and how it responds to the values, opinions, and attitudes as revealed by a semio-pragmatic analysis of *Meet the Mormons*; to understand how cultural differences shape the space of consumption the study was conducted in Switzerland and Spain. The second part of the chapter examines the space of production in light of interviews conducted with media and communication professionals who are members of the LDS Church.

As argued, the communication spaces of production and consumption are autonomous. The social actors in these spaces communicate through the space of representation. The media producers encode their message through audio-visual means and the audience decodes the message in the space of consumption. These processes are shaped by the cultural context and hermeneutic horizons of the social actors involved.[514] But what, then, is the benefit of researching two spaces that are entirely distinct? What do a semio-pragmatic analysis and quantitative study and a qualitative study

---

514 See part I, chapter 2.3 and part III chapter 2.

6. Researching Spaces of Production and Consumption of Latter-day Saints Media

add to our knowledge of the interface of documentary media and religion and whether and how they complement or contradict each other?

First, a crucial similarity between the quantitative and qualitative approaches can be located at the level of data: Both studies gathered data, although with different tools. The data presentation takes distinct forms: as statistical tables and as transcribed text. In both cases a hermeneutic process is deployed to draw meaning from the collected material. That meaning is expressed in a coherent narrative communicated to readers to illuminate elements of the interface between religion and documentary.

Second, in both instances the research design focused on participants, on survey-completing spectators of media products and interviewed creators of media products. Their answers are approached with scholarly rigor and evaluated with appropriate methods. We must still be aware that the interviewees' answers provide strictly personal views on a topic, be they from one of 200 college students or one of eight media professionals. According to Ellingson, the partiality of such a research design must be acknowledged:

> Thus, participants' voices should be respected and considered valid accounts of participants' experiences, and researchers should incorporate participants' perspectives into analysis, representing them in ways that honor their perspectives. At the same time, researchers should take great care not to romanticize participants' accounts as objective or somehow authentically true in their efforts to respect participants; all perspectives necessarily are partial, even severely marginalized ones. Releasing the burden of having to produce only Truth that, by definition, must compete with all other proposed truth claims may be quite liberating and affirming for researchers schooled in positivism or immediate-postpositivism.[515]

Research with participants is always momentary, for it takes place in a specific time and at a specific place, and interacts with the researcher's personality and hermeneutic horizons.

Third, returning to the concept of crystallization, the applied quantitative and qualitative approaches are by no means contradictory, not do the current studies intersect, it can often occur through triangulation in mixed studies

---

515 Ellingson, *Engaging Crystallization in Qualitative Research*, 13/14.

245

approaches.⁵¹⁶ The participants in each study, media professionals in one instance and college students in the other, are too different for the data to be consolidated for evaluation. We must be wary of putting the studies in conversation, suggesting potential continuities or parallels. But we can contend that they both contribute to extending our knowledge about the interface between documentary media and religion. They do not overlap but they do have additive impact. Their results illuminate the spaces of production and consumption differently but with methodological parallels.

Fourth, the studies do in fact intersect, not in and of themselves but in the space of representation. In the exploratory audience study the results of the semio-pragmatic analysis of a documentary source were transferred into questionnaires. During the interviews with the media professionals, documentary sources were discussed in detail. Thus, the documentary *Meet the Mormons* was used in the audience study and had been seen by all the interviewed media professionals, four of whom had been involved in its production. On some aspects the media professionals judged the film more positively than did the audience. The mostly US-American LDS media professionals would perhaps still be surprised by the positive attitude of the audiences in Switzerland and Spain towards Mormons and Mormonism in general, a reception that runs counter to the suspicious and negative opinion of Latter-day Saints that they often cited. The audience study suggests that the Latter-day Saints defensive response is less necessary than they might expect.

Finally, the rather positive attitudes towards Mormonism recorded in the audience study could in part reflect an absence of prejudgment. The audience is largely ignorance of the documentary's space of production. Had they known more, they might have been more negative in their assessment. In the US opinions about Mormons and Mormonism are more developed and that public perception is often negatively framed.⁵¹⁷ How are opinions, negative or positive, shaped by knowledge, and specifically by *what* is known and *how much* is known? Which processes nurture or minimize prejudice? Answers to such questions would surely highlight the involvement of media.

---

516 Denzin, "Triangulation 2.0"; Flick, *Triangulation*; John W. Creswell, *Research Design: Qualitative, Quantitative, and Mixed Methods Approaches*, 3rd ed. (Los Angeles: SAGE, 2009), 213/214.

517 "How Americans Feel About Religious Groups | Pew Research Center," July 16, 2014, https://www.pewforum.org/2014/07/16/how-americans-feel-about-religious-groups/.

Part III: The Ethical Space of Documentaries and Religion

7. Sensationalized Mormons

A bundle of bicycles lies in front of a house with a porch (fig. 77). The house is filmed from low down, such that the sky takes up almost half the image and seems endless. A warm soundscape accentuates the uncommon imagery that unfolds over the following seconds. A man in a black suit is superimposed. He stands a little to the right of centre, as if leaving space for someone else. As a result of the perspective, his head is above the roof of the house; his arms hang alongside his body and his smile seems shy (fig. 78). This is Michael. In the voice-over we hear him state: "People may ask, is it possible to love three women all at once?" (00:16:02–00:16:05). As the question is posed, two women are superimposed, taking up their positions on either side of the man (fig. 79) and are then joined by a third woman (fig. 80) while Michael continues: "Yes, I can love more than one woman." Finally, the highly reproductive family, with an impressive 18 children, gathers for the picture, literally made manifest before the camera while Michael Cawley adds: "Genuinely, truly love." The product of what it is to "genuinely, truly love" is obvious, evidence in support of Michael's words. In the last shot the mothers are grouped together with their children, whom they present with pride (fig. 81/82).

Michael's presentation of his family is part of *Meet the Polygamists* (43'), the pilot for the documentary series *Polygamy, USA* (US 2013, six episodes, German title *Polygamie in Gottes Namen*). The narration is styled to introduce not only the Cawleys but also the other families through superimposition, with more members appearing in the picture each time. This method functions to highlight the size of each family. The discussion considers not just what it is like to be part of a huge family but also the legal and emotional difficulties of living polygamously.

Part III: The Ethical Space of Documentaries and Religion

Fig. 77 The house of the Cawley family (Meet the Polygamists, 00:16:01).

Fig. 78 Cawley the husband says: "People may ask, is it possible to love three women all at once? (Meet the Polygamists, 00:16:02–00:16:05)?"

7. *Sensationalized Mormons*

Fig. 79 Two of Cawley's three wives are superimposed (Meet the Polygamists, 00:16:05).

Fig. 80 Michael poses with his three wives: "Yes I can love more than one woman" (Meet the Polygamists, 00:16:10).

Part III: The Ethical Space of Documentaries and Religion

Fig. 81 The whole Cawley family slowly appears together in the picture (Meet the Polygamists, 00:16:11).

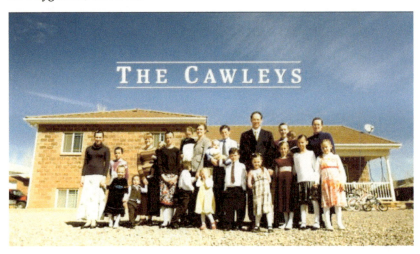

Fig. 82 The family name set against a blue sky appears at the end of the presentation, postcard-like (Meet the Polygamists, 00:16:14).

The narration is focused on polygamous family life, depicting daily routines like preparing and storing food for the numerous family members, cleaning the streets of the community where they live or constructing houses for members of that community. We see family members at their traditional Thanksgiving football game, where married men play against bachelors. The camera enters the family house, where the wives display their kitchens and bedrooms and explain that their husband spends the night in each of his wives' bedrooms in turn. Religion is front and center in the series. The viewer is given information about the community's religious rituals in the context of everyday practices – the saying of prayers before each meal or at the end of community meetings, attendance at church services on Sundays, and fulfillment of missionary duties. Additionally, the first episode depicts a funeral. These practices are presented through a combination of the informative mode and the sensational mode.

After the Cawley family has been introduced in the narrative, we see them prepare to attend Sunday worship. Wives, husband, and children are framed in close-ups. The women brush and braid their hair. Michael Cawley's vocal intonation may be irritating to the audience, for he speaks with a restraint that seems artificially calm. Many children whirl around him, and his quiet attitude therefore appears unnatural. By contrast the statements made by his wives seem authentic and honest. Plural marriage is cited on several occasions as very hard to imagine and many of the women speak of having to deal with feelings of jealousy. When we then see the community at worship, the faces of some of the leaders are blurred, with a commentary explaining that some individuals wished to remain anonymous because of the risk of prosecution.[518] The musical score emphasizes the legal dangers for the community.

Ethical questions in the spaces of communication

The church sequence may draw ethical questions from the viewer. Is it morally justifiable to draw attention to a religious community that lives in seclusion? Should religion be presented sensationally? Further, we might wonder what values are communicated in documentaries about this religious community and how these values are shaped audio-visually. We can tackle such questions by examining the content of the documentaries and

---

518 Bigamy and polygamy are illegal in the United States, although in several states, including Arizona, polygamy is not always strictly prosecuted. The families call their marriages spiritual and refer to the First Amendment, which covers the free exercise of religion. Andrew March, "Is There a Right to Polygamy? Marriage, Equality and Subsidizing Families in Liberal Public Justification," *Journal of Moral Philosophy* 8, no. 2 (January 1, 2011): 251–253.

Part III: The Ethical Space of Documentaries and Religion

in light of the audience's hermeneutic horizons, with their varied implications. Hermeneutic horizons that will be considered in detail further below can be understood as the cultural setting in which the presented values are perceived[519] or in the words of Ralph Potter "the wider context of understanding within which men define and ponder their opinions."[520] Ralph Potter developed four elements of a moral argument of which the wider context is one.

The sequence just recounted, from the episode entitled *Meet the Polygamists*, is produced by Part2 Pictures[521] and was aired on the television channel National Geographic. A dubbed German version of the series was broadcast by the German branch of the National Geographic channel. The six episodes from the docu-series[522] available on Amazon portray several families who are members of the fundamental Mormon polygamist community of Centennial Park, Arizona. The polygamist families continue to practice plural marriage even though The Church of Jesus Christ of the Latter-day Saints (LDS) abandoned this practice in 1890 in order that Utah might join the Union.[523] Each episode contains an autonomous storyline and can therefore be understood as an independent documentary narrative. Through the narration, a viewer unfamiliar with Mormon polygamists will learn significant detail about their lifestyle.

At the end of the first episode an intertitle announces the funeral of Aunt Susie, noting (00:40:50), "Centennial Park has never allowed cameras in for a service of this nature until now." Two women close the door of the church and a second intertitle states (00:40:59): "Several leaders asked that their identity be kept confidential." The narration makes evident to the viewer that witnessing this funeral is sensational – a unique opportunity

---

519 The hermeneutic horizon further entails religious belongings, education and experiences, values, and moral concepts.
520 Potter, "The Logic of Moral Argument," 108.
521 Part2 Pictures is an indie company and aims to produce high-quality documentaries with, in its own words, "a focus on high-end, human-driven storytelling across a range of genres and platforms." "Part 2 Pictures," Part 2 Pictures, accessed October 11, 2018, https://www.part2pictures.com/.
522 Although classified as reality-TV in several databases, the series is taken here as a docu-series because of its dominant narrative style, in which the camera keeps a certain distance from the social actors and the image and the sound design are more elaborated than it is usually the case in reality shows.
523 President of The Church of Jesus Christ of Latter-day Saints (LDS) Wilford Woodruff issued a document that announced that the LDS Church would no longer permit the practice of polygamy. See Shipps, *Mormonism*, 167; Bowman, *The Mormon People*, 2012, 124–151.

and, additionally, the religious community is risking prosecution. The editing, intertitles and camera highlight the privileged access to this religious ritual.

A bird's eye view shows the community in the church. The women are dressed in white; the men wear dark suits and white ties (Fig. 83).

Fig. 83 The church is full as the sermon is given during the funeral service. The coffin and flowers are on the left side of the image (Meet the Polygamists, 00:42:20).

Citing scripture, the sermon praises Aunt Susie (00:41:05–00:41:19): "Who can find a virtuous woman? For her price is far above rubies! The heart of her husband does safely trust in her. She will do him good and not evil all the days of her life. All the days of her life." [524] As we hear the words, crying women are shown wiping their tears or staring into a void. The images are both emotional and intrusive, with close-ups of family members at a very private moment. Whereas the faces of others are blurred. As viewer one feels as intruder into an intimate private circle. The images of the funeral service and of the interment that follows carry both information and emotion. In interviews church members explain what they believe and what death means in their worldview. The emotion-laden sound is engag-

---

524   Proverbs 31:10-12, King James Version.

ing and supports the sentiments of the funeral, but it also bolsters the tensions of the film production at a meta level.

In addition to its documentary mode and to the informational and sensational modes already noted, the film has an entertainment mode. The sequence shows an intimate situation in which the social actors agreed to be filmed. Were they aware of these modes of representation, we might wonder, and how seriously did they evaluate the possible consequences of this observation of their lives and its diffusion worldwide? How might we define a morally acceptable depiction of a religious community? These questions are located in the field of media ethics and form the core of this chapter, which considers the ethics of certain documentaries and TV-reporting.[525]

The documentaries examined are between 35 and 90 minutes in length and shed light on Mormons and Mormonism in multifaceted ways. Two main traits can be readily discerned in terms of the space of production. One group of documentaries is affiliated with the LDS; one group is "independent," in other words not affiliated with any Mormon community. The similarities across the two groups are, however, numerous. Both groups contain documentaries that might be shown on a specific television channel, at a cinema, at a film festival or on a streaming platform. The narrative of the films are communicated in documentary, informational, and sensational modes. With the documentaries' spaces of communication and further reading modes established, we can turn to discuss the films individually and in comparison with other documentaries from the same group. The ethical questions are considered in light of each documentary's spaces of communication and reading modes, with a focus on the production space and how it affects the ethical implications.

The chapter starts with a theoretical perspective that considers ethical questions and their systematization in the context of documentary media and its spaces of communication. In a second step the documentary media are analyzed by category, looking specifically at the hermeneutic horizons of the social actors, the filmmakers, and the audience – for each instance within in the spaces of production, representation, circulation/distribution, and consumption – the allegiances of each party, the gaze of the camera, and the production context.

---

[525] Documentaries and TV-reports differ according to their spaces of distribution and consumption. Whereas documentaries are often shown at festivals and in cinema, TV-reports, as the name indicates, are mostly produced by television companies and aired on television.

8. The Ethics of Entertainment and the Transmission of Information within Spaces of Communication

The example of *Polygamy, USA* shows how documentaries can inform, entertain, and be sensational. They may also tell a story, and the best amongst them may be revelatory and will surely be persuasive. According to film-theorist Bill Nichols, documentaries and lawyers make their cases similarly. Documentaries represent specific interests, interpret the world in certain ways, and "stand for or represent the views of individuals, groups, and institutions. They also convey impressions, make proposals, mount arguments, or offer perspectives of their own, setting out to persuade us to accept their views."[526]

8.1. Values, norms, and moral judgements

This chapter examines the ethics of documentary media, the values they portray and their normative aspects in relation to religion. The approach to media ethics is analytical and descriptive and is situated in the tension between power relations and responsibilities, for the chapter analyses the moral issues at stake in the communication spaces of production, representation, distribution / circulation, and consumption. Focused on media ethics, the approach looks critically at norms in the practice of filmmaking and systems of values applied in the spaces of communication of documentary media. Values and norms are seen as complementary. Thus, norms define how we act, and our actions are based on specific values. As soon as values become generally binding and objectively valid, they have a normative character. In this case each value is connected with a norm that realizes, conserves, and valorizes that value. The reverse also holds: each norm confirms specific values. Thus we can say that people act according to norms and justify their actions with values.[527]

---

526 Nichols, *Introduction to Documentary*, 45.
527 Matthias Kettner, "Werte und Normen – Praktische Geltungsansprüche von Kulturen," in *Handbuch der Kulturwissenschaften*, ed. Friedrich Jaeger (Stuttgart: Metzler, 2011), 220–222.

Spaces of communication are determined by diverse agents that implement media practices in light of moral judgments. Garrett Cullity records, "Moral judgements are judgements about normative relationships between facts and responses – judgements that certain responses *ought* to be made to certain facts."[528] This means that media agents respond to facts in media consumption spaces. They make a myriad of decisions in reference to their understanding of good and bad actions or correct and incorrect behaviour based on certain principles that are deemed universally valid.[529] As social actors perform their actions as media professionals or media consumers, media ethics can be located in the field of applied ethics.[530]

The issue of power relations in the media sphere is central to a perspective coined by a cultural studies approach.[531] Stuart Hall has argued in the context of television that there are always dominant media discourses defined by the power of privileged information brokers.[532] One ethical issue must therefore engage the question of who has the power of representation, an issue that is concerned not only with the space of representation but wholly embraces the spaces of production and distribution, because an audio-visual source needs above all to be available for consumption if it is to wield power. As a result ethical questions arise in the tension between spaces of communication over who has meaning-defining power.

As a result of their role in communication, Michel Foucault has contended, the media are fertile soil for generating and sustaining power relations. Power, he suggests, is effected in the relationship between agents that communicate with each other.[533] For Foucault, "Relationships of communication processes imply finalized activities (even if only the cor-

---

528 Garrett Cullity, "Moral Judgement," in *Routledge Encyclopedia of Philosophy* (London: Routledge, 2016).
529 In the current approach, the universality of moral judgement is understood as contextual and historical, which means that moral judgments can differ according to time and place. See Timothy L. S. Sprigge, "Definition of a Moral Judgment," *Philosophy* 39, no. 150 (1964): 207.
530 Rüdiger Funiok, *Medienethik: Verantwortung in der Mediengesellschaft*, Kon-Texte: Wissenschaften in philosophischer Perspektive (Stuttgart: Kohlhammer, 2011), 51–63.
531 For greater insight into the interface of power, the image, and religion see Fritz et al., *Sichtbare Religion*, 120–152.
532 Stuart Hall, "Media Power: The Double Bind," in *New Challenges for Documentary*, ed. Alan Stuart Rosenthal (Berkeley, CA et al.: University of California Press, 1988), 357–364.
533 Michel Foucault, "The Subject and Power," *Critical Inquiry* 8, no. 4 (1982): 785–788.

8. The Ethics of Entertainment

rect putting into operation of elements of meaning) and, by virtue of modifying the field of information between partners, produce effects of power."[534] Documentaries (or any other media) have an effect on their audience; they "modify the field of information" in Foucault words. "Finalized activities" in the context of documentary media refers to the reading modes, for example their informational, entertaining, or moral character. These modes are related to specific attitudes and responses, which provide information.[535] For example, an affective response to a scene in a film is a "finalized activity." To laugh at the unskilled driver who bumps against a parked car when manoeuvring within a parking space is to exercise power over that driver. The representation allows the spectator to feel superior. The strength of the power effects from finalized activities depends on the response of source and spectator to each other.

This interaction between the spaces of representation and consumption is no less powerful than the interaction of production and representation spaces. According to Hall's encoding and decoding model, each representation permits different readings. There is no obligation to read a source in the dominant-hegemonic way by taking the representation as a given, as truth.[536] An oppositional reading allows a source to be read within an alternative frame of reference. The middle course is then a negotiated reading, which defines its own ground rules. It operates with exceptions, is full of contradictions, has a logic that is unequal to the logics of power, and provides a mixture of adaptive and oppositional elements. Viewers decide which "finalized activity" they select or, in other words, how they address a source and the extent to which they are able and willing to read that source critically. This choice of reading modes relates to responsibility in the space of consumption, another key concept in media ethics.

8.2. Responsibility and power relations

A key concept in the field of ethics, "responsibility" is connected to power relations between and in the spaces of communication. Scholars of French language and film studies Lisa Downing and Libby Saxton understand the ethical as "the *context* in which all filmmaking takes place" and further contend that "[w]henever we negotiate between desire and responsibility,

---

534 Foucault, 787.
535 These modes are distinct to Bill Nichols' modes of representation.
536 Hall, "Encoding/Decoding," 245.

we place ourselves in the arena of ethics."[537] Power relations demand responsible actions that are based on normative principles and can constitute any practice. Rüdiger Funiok, professor of communication and pedagogy, has elaborated the role of responsibility in media ethics.[538] Such responsibility, he proposes, is based on freedom of action and necessary autonomy. Both individual and corporate responsibility are multidimensional. Corporate actions are relevant here because media productions require many different collaborators, who divide up the labour according to their profession and their position in the production-company hierarchy. As each collaborator contributes to the final product, who is responsible for the final product? For Funiok, "Corporate responsibility lives in individual responsibility but cannot be reduced to the sum of each individual responsibility. A system is always more than the sum of its parts."[539] Scholar of multimedia policies Bernard Debatin identifies six aspects of individual and corporate responsibility (table 12).[540]

who (subject of action)	Individual	Corporation
what (action)	single actions	related actions
what for (consequences of actions)	causal consequences of actions	Cumulative and synergetic effects
to whom	person affected by actions and its consequences	
what of (responsibility instance)	conscience, principal, general public	corporate responsibility, general public
because of what (norms and values)	position in the media versus general responsibility	purpose of corporation versus general responsibility

Table 12 Dimensions of individual and corporate responsibility.

Individual responsibility is as important in the context of documentary media and religion as it is in any situation in which decisions are made and actions performed. Power relations are again vital, for the more

---

537 Lisa Downing and Libby Saxton, "Introduction," in *Film and Ethics: Foreclosed Encounters*, ed. Lisa Downing and Libby Saxton (London: Routledge, 2010), 11.
538 Funiok, *Medienethik*, 63–78.
539 Funiok, 71. The German original text reads: "Die korporative Verantwortung ist also lebendig in der individuellen Verantwortung, aber sie reduziert sich nicht summativ auf die Gesamtzahl der Einzelverantwortungen – ein System ist immer mehr als alle seine Einzelteile zusammen." Translated by the author.
540 Bernhard Debatin, "Medienethik als Steuerungsinstrument?," in *Perspektiven der Medienkritik. Die gesellschaftliche Auseinandersetzung mit öffentlicher Kommunikation in der Mediengesellschaft* (Opladen: Westdeutscher Verlag, 1997), 297.

powerful position a person occupies, the more responsibility they have for their actions. This issue is at play in Bill Nichols's question, "What do we do with people when we make a documentary?"[541] The "we" includes the producer who oversees the film production, with its employed professionals, paid film crew and the whole organisation of the production process. The director interacts with the social actors and decides what is to be filmed or left out. The film distributor chooses films to promote for cinema or television. The television program director designs the channel's profile. The social actors decide how much information and insight into their lives they are willing to provide. A spectator may decide to comment on social media about their response to a program. These examples assume the media actors are independent, which is rarely the case. Film production deals with a diversity of restrictions: directors need to respect the budget; the producers wish to sell their product; social actors cannot always say what they really think because of possible repercussions.

The corporate aspect of responsibility is crucial not only in relation to media but also for religion. Religious institutions will often provide guidance, or instruction, on how their members are to deal with the media in the spaces of communication. As we saw in chapter 2, the LDS Church provides guidelines for the use of social media and the Internet.[542] The guidelines distinguish, for example, between appropriate and inappropriate uses of online resources. Fundamentally, a member who wishes to launch a blog or any other form of digital communication must first request permission, and in doing so the applicant releases all rights to the Intellectual Reserve, Inc. (IRI), its related entities, and their respective employees, agents, and representatives.[543] IRI is based in Salt Lake City and operated by the president of The LDS Church. The cooperation watches over the church's intellectual property and owns 88 church-related trademarks.[544] In this case the institutional LDS church controls and also coordinates the communication spaces from production to consumption. The

---

541 Nichols, *Introduction to Documentary*, 45.
542 "Social Media Helps for Members," accessed September 28, 2017, https://www.lds.org/pages/social-media-helps?lang=eng; "Use of Online Resources in Church Callings," accessed September 28, 2017, https://www.lds.org/pages/online-resources-for-church-callings?lang=eng.
543 "Permission Form Example," n.d., https://www.lds.org/bc/content/shared/content/english/pdf/create/participant-release.pdf.
544 "Apply for a Trademark. Search a Trademark," trademarkia.com, accessed January 4, 2018, https://www.trademarkia.com/company-intellectual-reserve-inc-613675-page-1-2.

Part III: The Ethical Space of Documentaries and Religion

responsibility determined by its guidelines is not intended for a wider general public, for their principal audience comprises LDS members, who require permission for their presence on websites, in blogs and in other digital spaces. The norms and values they express will then explicitly represent the interests of the corporation, in this instance the LDS. When the space of communication is not controlled by a religious institution, the media can apply their own entertaining or informative modes, as we shall see.

8.3. Ethical spaces of documentaries

Documentary media pursue different goals. Their communication of values is part of the moral reading mode. The maker's authority and credibility are required for the consumers to accept the narrative, a process that produces values of truth.[545] Persuasive narratives can only be realized in cooperation with the audience. A documentary that is not entertaining or informative per se can still entertain and inform its audience. Again, the semio-pragmatic approach to documentary media and religion understands the ethical field in light of the interaction of practices from the spaces of production and representation or representation and consumption or production and circulation/distribution.

Entertaining, informative and moral modes are expressed by different film styles. Patricia Aufderheide's subgenre categories for documentaries help us understand how these modes can be characterized. One distinction she makes is between public affairs[546] and advocacy[547] documentaries. Public affairs documentaries

> typically undertake an investigative or problem-oriented approach, feature sober exposition with narration and sometimes a host, make liberal use of background footage or b-roll, and focus on representative individuals as they exemplify or illustrate the problem. They promise an authoritative, often social-scientific view of an issue, speaking as professional journalists on behalf of a public affected by the problem.[548]

A public-affairs documentary would therefore provide a balanced picture of religion and mainly function in the informative and moral modes. De-

---

545 See section "The Semio-Pragmatics of Documentary Media" in chapter 2.3.
546 Aufderheide, *Documentary Film*, 56–64.
547 Aufderheide, 77–90.
548 Aufderheide, 56/57.

8. The Ethics of Entertainment

pending on the narrative's subject, a problem's cause might be identified or a problem's perpetrators accused. The investigative dimension, in which a problem is summarized, described, and scrutinized, is then crucial. Such documentaries have close parallels with broadcast TV in being a significant and informative source on religion, as a seasoned, thoughtful, and substantial form of news.

Advocacy documentaries, by contrast, are produced for political ends and are persuasive in intent. They

> are tools of an organization's mobilization for action on specific issues or causes. Advocacy films are usually highly focused and designed to motivate viewers to a particular action. Like government propaganda films, they may be made in good faith by people who profoundly agree with an organization's agenda. They, like propaganda films, deserve attention from anyone who wants to understand the techniques of persuasion—and nothing persuades like reality.[549]

The institutional dimension of the production is essential to this subgenre. Often the filmmaker's agenda converges with the agenda of the institution behind the production, with the persuasive purpose then dominant. The entertaining mode is also engaged, for documentaries seek to entertain, to generate active audience responses such as laughter, shock, or surprise. Dry media communication that neither interests the audience nor keeps their attention will hardly be successful. Such physical responses benefit the communication process in which a message is perceived. Entertainment and bodily engagement are part of persuasion.

In this review of the ethical issues of documentaries, structural considerations allow us to identify where moral reasoning is located. The current chapter looks specifically at interactions between the spaces of production, representation and consumption that have distinct ethical implications. One of the first systematic approaches to the ethics of the documentary was formulated by film theorist Vivian Sobchack.[550] In her groundbreaking paper "Inscribing Ethical Space: Ten Propositions on Death, Representation and Documentary" Sobchack constructed an ethics of documentaries through an analysis of death, whose representation, she proposes, violates a visual taboo. Its justification is therefore necessary and is achieved

---

549 Aufderheide, 78.
550 Vivian Sobchack, "Inscribing Ethical Space: Ten Propositions on Death, Representation, and Documentary," *Quarterly Review of Film Studies* 9, no. 4 (September 1, 1984): 283–300.

in the responses generated by camera and filmmaker.[551] The latter "physically mediates his or her own confrontation with death, the way s/he ethically inhabits a social world, visually behaves in it and charges it with a moral meaning visible to others."[552] Sobchack includes the recipients in the ethical space: "[T]he viewer's very act of looking is ethically charged and is, itself, the object of ethical judgement when it is responsible viewed: The viewer is held ethically responsible for his or her visible response."[553] The institutional aspect of responsibility we have noted is less significant. Sobchack's focus lies rather on the individual, be it the cinematographer, the filmmaker, or the spectator. The essence of Sobchack's position here was extended to areas other than death by documentary theorist Bill Nichols in his *Representing Reality. Issues and Concepts in Documentary*.[554] Nichols identifies the ethical space of the documentary with the term *axiograhics*, which embraces the interaction between filmmaker, camera, and the "historical world" that appears before the camera:

> Documentaries, then, offer aural and visual likenesses or representations of some part of the historical world. They stand for or represent the views of individuals, groups, and institutions. They also convey impressions, make proposals, mount arguments, or offer perspectives of their own, setting out to persuade us to accept their views.[555]

Persuasive arguments in documentaries are also formulated within the historical world, of which they become part through the reception process. Thus Nichols's focus on individuals, groups, and institutions can be transferred to religious communities in documentaries, where religious actors represent themselves, their lifestyles, and their attitudes. However, the space in front of the camera is not as readily conveyed as Nichols's wording could suggest, for the "historical world" is shaped by cinematic devices such as the camera frame, sound, and editing and in particular by the interaction of filmmaker and the social actors who appear before the camera. They together shape the historical world. This interaction, the "axiographics", is constitutive of documentary media. Nichols writes, "Axiographics would address the question of how values, particularly an ethics of repre-

---

551 Sobchack, 291.
552 Sobchack, 292.
553 Sobchack, 292.
554 Bill Nichols, *Representing Reality: Issues and Concepts in Documentary* (Bloomington: Indiana University Press, 1991), 76–103.
555 Nichols, 45.

sentation, comes to be known and experienced in relation to space."[556] This relationship exists in the interaction of the spaces of production and representation and influences how a film is received in the space of consumption. The gaze of the camera, which characterizes the ethical space in a documentary, is controlled by the filmmaker's choices and interaction with the social actors. Sobchack and Nichols discern a variety of gazes that includes, for example, the *accidental gaze*, where the camera catches an event by accident. The *helpless gaze* shows the inability of the camera to influence events. The *endangered gaze* comes from a filmmaker who encounters danger during filming. The filmmaker's *interventional gaze* on the historical world might take the form of a voice claiming something about the social actors or a deliberate active presence in front of the camera.[557] "Such moments are rare," Nichols acknowledges, "but they indicate what stakes exist when the filmmaker chooses to act in history alongside those filmed rather than operate from the paradoxically 'safe place' of authoring agent, a place that can never be made fully secure in documentary."[558] The *clinical or professional gaze* of reporters and journalists is located at the boundaries of the ethical because it is "marked by ethical ambiguity, by technical and machine-like competence in the face of an event which seems to call for further human response."[559] As Nichols notes, journalists tend not to intervene even when the precarious situation in the historical world requires engagement.

The ethical space can be extended by a further interaction particularly important for religion. The filmmaker behind the camera is not alone in looking at the social historical world, for the social actors in front of the camera might look back too, depending on the situation and on how comfortable they feel. The interaction of and relationship between the media professionals and the social actors in front of the camera are essential to the ethical space. The religious affiliation of social actors and filmmaker has an additional dynamic that influences the camera's gaze. The figure below maps possible interactions between religious agents in the ethical space of documentaries (fig. 84).

---

556 Nichols, 77.
557 Vivian Sobchack, "Inscribing Ethical Space: Ten Propositions on Death, Representation, and Documentary," *Quarterly Review of Film Studies* 9, no. 4 (September 1, 1984): 295–298.
558 Nichols, *Representing Reality*, 85.
559 Sobchack, "Inscribing Ethical Space: Ten Propositions on Death, Representation, and Documentary," 298.

Part III: The Ethical Space of Documentaries and Religion

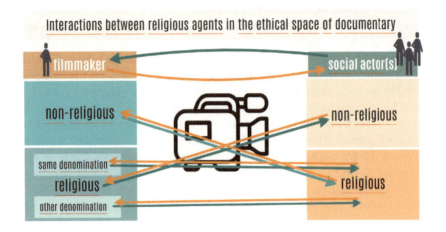

Fig. 84 Possible interactions between religious and non-religious actors.

The interactions depicted here allow for diverse combinations, for example for a non-religious filmmaker to be working with religious social actors or a religious filmmaker to be filming with non-religious actors. Filmmaker and religious social actors may both be religious but belong to different denominations. As this simple model shows, the chain that runs filmmaker – camera gaze – social actor has several variations and can also run vice versa, so social actor – camera gaze – filmmaker. When social actor and filmmaker belong to the same religious group a *solidary gaze* or *promoting gaze* or even a *noncritical/idealizing gaze* comes into play. Living in the same social/historical world might result in a shared ethical space. If a Mormon filmmaker makes a documentary about a Mormon community, the filmmaker's engagement with the community is in all likelihood much smoother than for an outsider, whatever personal difference may exist. At the same time critical distance could be lacking.

8.4. Loyalties and hermeneutic horizons of the social actors

How can we analyse the filmmaker – camera gaze – social actor relationship and its ethical implications in particular? How can that relationship be systematized? We note, for example, three forms of presence that can help define the ethical space. The filmmaker may appear in the scene in front of the camera or only the filmmaker's voice may be audible, for example in an interview or as commentary. The gaze of the camera, as discussed in detail by Sobchack and Nichols, can be a third form of presence. The hermeneutic-analytical consideration of our documentary sources that follows is particularly concerned with the religious background of the filmmaker and the social actors, as shown in figure 84.

For the ethical space of documentaries, the space of representation is relevant, with its combination of plot and specific aesthetics subsumed under the term narration.[560] In this space moral reasoning is expressed for, in Nichols' words, "Style attests not only to 'vision' or to a perspective on the world but also to the ethical quality of that perspective and the argument behind it."[561] But how might we explore the "ethical argument" of a documentary? Ralph B. Potter, emeritus professor of social ethics at Harvard Divinity School, designed a systematics of moral reasoning in his essay "The Logic of a Moral Argument".[562] Widely known in the field of media and communication, Potter's four-step method is known as the *Potter Box* (fig. 85).[563] The model aids in ethical decision-making, asks about empirical facts, and identifies the hermeneutic horizons of the parties involved as a possible source of conflict. The loyalties of the disputants are relevant to the positions they adopt. Finally, the model asks about ethical principles or modes of reasoning that lead to a greater good.[564] The steps are repeated until they no longer conflict and an ethical decision can be made.

The model seeks to find a solution through moral reasoning that can be logically reproduced. Potter notes: "Hence, the ethicists will try to reinforce respect for the conventions of an argument that demand that reason be given in support of moral judgements and that principles appealed to be capable of being universalized."[565] The "conventions of an argument" thus count in the ethical space of documentaries but without aspirations to universality. At this point the Potter box diverges from the documentary model as the empirical facts of the historical world as represented in the narration cannot be altered. The representations can, however, still affect the future and induce change. Our aim here is to interpretatively systematize the ethical space by considering interactions in the production space

---

560 David Bordwell, Kristin Thompson, and Jeff Smith, *Film Art: An Introduction*, 11th ed. (New York: McGraw-Hill Education, 2017).
561 Nichols, *Representing Reality*, 80.
562 Potter, "The Logic of Moral Argument."
563 Clifford G. Christians, *Media Ethics: Cases and Moral Reasoning* (New York: Routledge, Taylor & Francis Group, 2017), Kindle location 329.
564 Potter, "The Logic of Moral Argument," 108/109. Further discussed in Clifford G. Christians, *Media Ethics*, Kindle Location 329.
565 Potter, "The Logic of Moral Argument," 106/107.

Part III: The Ethical Space of Documentaries and Religion

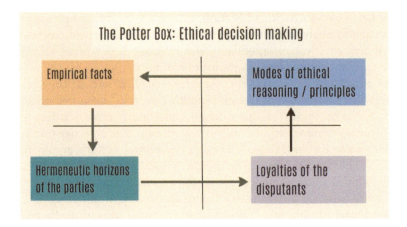

Fig. 85 The Potter box of moral reasoning.

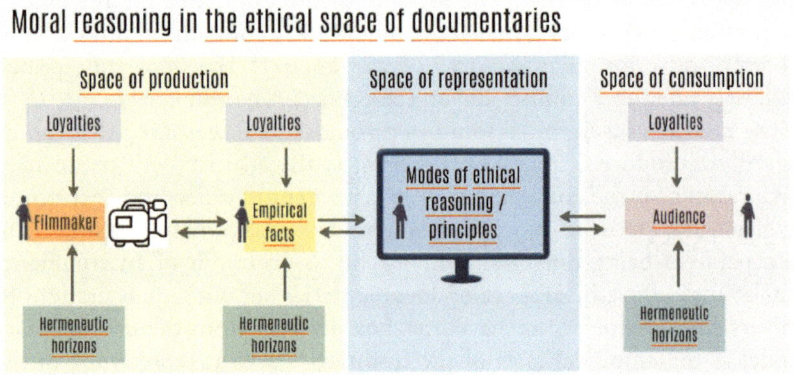

Fig. 86 Moral reasoning in spaces of communication.

between the filmmaker and the social actors in front of the camera, as discussed previously. Additionally, we should consider the mediation of empirical facts, which expresses moral reasoning based on ethical principles. The audio-visual narration makes visible a moral reasoning that the audience then decodes in light of its hermeneutic horizons and affiliations. The scheme below systematizes the interactions between social actors that are involved in moral reasoning in the ethical space of the documentary (fig. 86).

8. The Ethics of Entertainment

Affiliations and hermeneutic horizons[566] influence the actions of the filmmakers and the social actors in the space of production, while the audience in the space of consumption provide their own interpretation within their hermeneutic horizons and in light of their affiliations, which here include their religious belonging. The loyalties expressed by the spectators are informed by their religious belonging, education and experiences, values, and moral concepts.

The spectrum of documentaries about Mormons is very broad. In the following, films by filmmakers affiliated with Mormonism, mostly with the LDS, will be discussed in chapter 9 "The Spectrum of Mormon Documentaries". Films produced by private or public television channels or independent filmmakers are then also addressed in chapter 10, "Telling about Mormons". The aim is to show how religion functions within the ethical space of documentary media by focusing on modes of interactions between the filmmaker and the social actors and by considering possible responses by diverse audiences.

---

566 Hans-Georg Gadamer, *Hermeneutik I: Wahrheit und Methode: Grundzüge einer philosophischen Hermeneutik*, vol. 1, Gesammelte Werke / Hans-Georg Gadamer (Tübingen: Mohr Siebeck, 2010), 442–494; Anselm Haverkamp and Paul Ricoeur, eds., "Die Metapher und das Hauptproblem der Hermeneutik," in *Theorie der Metapher*, (Darmstadt: Wissenschaftliche Buchgesellschaft, 1996), 370–372.

9. The Spectrum of Mormon Documentaries

Our discussion of six documentaries starts with a short synopsis and an overview of the empirical facts, the hermeneutic horizons and affiliations of the social actors involved. As fig. 84 highlights, the analysis focuses on Mormon filmmakers' involvement in the narrative, whether as visible in the image, audible in the sound score, or present in the gaze of the camera. We are particularly concerned to establish how the Mormon filmmaker interacts with the world that he or she frames with the camera and in which reading mode the argument of moral reasoning is expressed in the space of representation.

9.1. Mormons and the race debate

The first documentary, *Sisterz in Zion* (US 2006, 61') by Melissa Puente, tells a successful integration story. The film portrays young and recently converted LDS women from New York City who come from low-income and immigrant families. They travel to a camp called *Especially for Youth*, held at Brigham Young University, in Provo/UT, and organized by the LDS. The film accompanies the five women from New York City to Provo/UT, observes them during the camp, and then stays with them as they return home. The narration relates the camp's activities, with a focus on the experiences of these particular women. Although these women mention that they feel like outsiders because they are the only non-Caucasian women, the film depicts their experience as generally positive. The narrative shows Mormon faith expressed in songs and prayer practices overcoming cultural differences.

The production *Sisterz in Zion* has close ties to the LDS Church. It was produced by Brigham Young University and the production company American Fork (Utah) is partner of the LDS affiliated company Covenant Communications. The documentary was first shown on Brigham Young University television (BYUtv), which is connected to the LDS Church and owned by Brigham Young University. The filmmaker Melissa Puente is a former Brigham Young University student[567] and at the time of the production was an LDS Church youth leader. Puente was president of the Young Women Organization, the LDS organisation for young women, in Manhattan.and graduated from the film school at Brigham Young University.[568] Puente's hermeneutic horizons provides her with insider knowledge of her topic and, additionally, her affiliation enables her access to the institution she is depicting. Her loyalties are to the church's teachings, which she knows well. The hermeneutic horizons of the social actors take two forms. The women from New York City came originally from the Caribbean, South America and Asia; they are all converts and stem from low-income families. The young Caucasian LDS women have their roots mainly in the Midwest and come from a more prosperous background, as their expensive leisure time activities such as skiing and watersports indicate. The teenagers from NYC explicitly note that they have never experienced such activities. We can assume that social actors from both sides wish their contribution to satisfy the director and other LDS officials, with further opportunities within the church organization in mind. They are in a way dependent on Melissa Puente if they are to make a positive impression that will be appreciated by the church. The LDS converts from New York City, especially the Latina women, tend to stick together, as they mention in the interviews. Their sense of being different became more acute during the camp and is expressed through cultural activities such as listening to hip-hop music, but also in speaking English with a Spanish accent and vocabulary (Spanglish); their clothing and behavior are also different.

The camera provides a *solidary gaze*, close to the social actors as it observes the young women and has them tell their own stories, for example when they introduce themselves. At the same time the documentary promotes LDS diversity by using the young women to prove that the church is open to people from different backgrounds. In a scene portraying a meeting at the camp in Provo (24 minutes into the film) a "love circle" is depicted, in which individuals hug their neighbors and say, "I love you." This

---

567 Cody Clark, "Teens from Different Worlds Become One: In Spirit in New LDS Documentary," *Daily Herald*, October 13, 2006, http://www.heraldextra.com/lifestyles/teens-from-different-worlds-become-one-in-spirit-in-new/article_d877d125-65cb-5c42-af75-702205054fce.html.
568 John M. Murphy and Leslee Thorne-Murphy, "Sisterz in Zion, Directed by Melissa Puente," *BYU Studies* 45, no. 4 (2006): 4.

practice is used to foster bonds between the participants. The camera is placed within the circle, as if itself a participant (Fig. 87–89).

Fig. 87 The camera participates in the circle of love. The protagonists seem uncomfortable with the intimacy of the situation (Sisterz in Zion, 00:22:24).

Fig. 88/ Fig. 89 The participants are more relaxed as they watch friends from NYC or the Caucasian teenagers hugging (Sisterz in Zion, 00:22:29/ 00:24:50).

In another situation the camera gaze is noted and commented upon by one of the social actors. The NYC teenagers are rehearsing the Latino dance Merengue, to be performed at the contest. They are very engaged, loud and excited, but at the same time they seem nervous, unsure if the jury will approve of their performance. Sereda is suddenly aware of the camera and signals her dislike of the situation and of the camera's recording the scene (Fig. 90–92).

Part III: The Ethical Space of Documentaries and Religion

Fig. 90/ Fig. 91/ Fig. 92 Sereda realizes that the camera is observing, shakes her head to signal her disapproval, laughs and waves in order to say: "Stop filming!" (Sisterz in Zion, 00:33:04/ 00:33:05/ 00:33:06).

The camera is acquainted with the social actors but they are not as one. The filmmaker is in a privileged position, allowed to observe this compromising situation in which a single social actor demonstrates discomfort. The NYC teenagers are depicted as the other, as different from their Caucasian friends.

On the surface the narration's ethical mode of reasoning defends the principle of equality. When the NYC teenagers are depicted as other, however, boundaries are drawn, with some excluded and some included.[569] This mode of othering raises a challenging question: for the LDS Church everyone is the same, but how can that be realized? The film aims to show how differences might be resolved. Additionally, the story is told from the perspective of an integrated and experienced LDS member who seeks to present the church's efforts at creating equality between Caucasians and non-Caucasians against the ambivalent and challenging history of how the church has dealt with racism.[570] Some LDS Mormons have an immigrant background, while others do not; their origins may shape their interpretative framework. Particular focus is directed here, however, on people from the Caribbean and South America and on young adults who are members of the church or interested in church activities.

---

[569] Wimmer, "The Making and Unmaking of Ethnic Boundaries: A Multilevel Process Theory"; Mark A. Pachucki, Sabrina Pendergrass, and Michèle Lamont, "Boundary Processes: Recent Theoretical Developments and New Contributions," *Poetics*, Culture lines: Emerging research on boundaries, 35, no. 6 (December 1, 2007): 331–51; Lamont and Molnár, "The Study of Boundaries in the Social Sciences."

[570] See more on this topic in Margaret Blair Young and Darius Aidan Gray, "Mormons and Race," in *The Oxford Handbook of Mormonism*, ed. Terry L. Givens (New York: Oxford University Press, 2015), 363–385.

Also dealing with the challenging topic of race in the LDS Church, *Nobody Knows. The Untold Story of Black Mormons* (Darius A. Gray and Margeret B. Young, US 2008, 73') adopts a historical perspective. In a partially apologetic mode and partially informative mode, the film reconstructs the contested issue in LDS Church history of discrimination against black Mormons between the founding of the church and the granting of equal access to the priesthood; until 1978 only Caucasian men could become priests.[571] This documentary also provides a success story. The film's narrative is largely reproduced in a chapter in an introduction to Mormonism written by the directors.[572] The chapter provides an instructive historical and theological overview of the role of race in Mormonism. The opening credits announce that this is an independent project, highlighting that the film does not necessarily represent the official position of the LDS Church. The filmmakers, Gray (Fig. 93) and Blair Young (Fig. 94), appear several times in front of the camera. Gray additionally represents two perspectives within the narration, for he both interviews and is interviewed. He recounts his own experiences as a member of the church, introducing himself at the start with "I'm a proud black man." Yet he is not explicitly identified in the opening titles as one of the documentary's directors; that information is reserved for the closing credits, leaving the audience establish this fact for themselves at the moment. Presented as a successful and integrated black Mormon role model, Darius Gray is also interviewed in the documentary *Meet the Mormons* (Blair Treu, US 2014, 78'), which will be discussed later in this chapter.

The gaze in *Nobody Knows* is largely academic, with interviews of university scholars such as well-known professor of sociology and religious studies Armand L. Mauss (Fig. 95) and professor Newell Bringhurst (Fig. 96).

Filmed as talking heads, these experts are left to address the audience interrupted. Other social actors, mainly African Americans appear as oral witnesses to the history of the LDS Church and people of color and to recount how black people now feel towards the LDS Church (fig. 97/98).

Most of the numerous black people interviewed are LDS members. Sometimes the speaker's name fades in. In other instances the speaker is anonymous, as is the case for the woman who tells the story of black Mormon woman Jane Manning James bringing flour to a starving (white) Mormon mother (fig. 99), a story that is partly reenacted.

---

571 Blair Young and Gray.
572 Blair Young and Gray.

Part III: The Ethical Space of Documentaries and Religion

Fig. 93/ Fig. 94 Directors Darius A. Gray and Blair Young stage themselves and look at each other (Nobody Knows, 00:02:03 / 00:06:51).

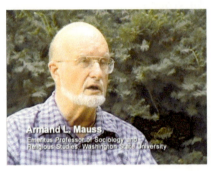 

Fig. 95/ Fig. 96 Armand L. Mauss and Newell Bringhurst provide their professional and authoritative view of LDS Church history in relation to black people (Nobody Knows, 00:12:10/ 00:31:52).

Some apologetic voices are heard. Caucasian author and LDS member Gregory Prince tells the story of an LDS apostle in the 1950s who traveled to Hawaii, where he met an extraordinary male LDS member with African ancestors (fig. 100). The apostle asked the president if an exception could be made in this instance that would allow this man to enter the priesthood. According to Prince the president denied the request but in his response made clear that the exclusion of black men from the priesthood was policy and not doctrine. Prince's central message is that the attitude toward black Mormons was not theologically driven. Their exclusion and subsequent inclusion reflected church rules only and is evidence of the LDS Church's ability to adapt to shifting circumstances.

9. The Spectrum of Mormon Documentaries

Fig. 97/ Fig. 98 Although he is not a Mormon, Pastor Cecil provides a very moderate view of the LDS Church's racial history. His opinion is similar to that of attorney and LDS Relief Society president Marguerite Driessen (Nobody Knows, 00:17:51/ 00:47:13).

Fig. 99 Sitting at the memorial to Jane Manning James, this woman tells the story of the venerated black Mormon (Nobody Knows, 00:10:08).

Fig. 100 Gregory Prince, author and LDS member, provides a refreshingly critical view of LDS history (Nobody Knows, 00:23:32).

Other interviewees speak out on how the church should acknowledge historical discrimination. Marvin Perkins, for example, proposes that church leaders should explain its erroneous practice (fig. 101): "We spoke with a limited understanding and without the light knowledge that is now commented to the world." Others speak with perhaps surprising openness about their experiences of discrimination. Thus Tamu Smith states (fig. 102): "First time when I was called a nigger I was in the Salt Lake temple."

Like the directors, most of the social actors are loyal to the LDS Church, even as they might criticize it. The film provides a diversity of well-chosen

Part III: The Ethical Space of Documentaries and Religion

Fig. 101 Marvin Perkins is introduced as an entrepreneur and lecturer (Nobody Knows, 00:47:43).

Fig. 102 Tamu Smith is an author and actress (Nobody Knows, 00:49:30).

Fig. 103 The director interviews the jazz musician Paul Gill in the intimate setting of a church (Nobody Knows, 00:16:15).

contemporary voices on the LDS Church's history of engagement with race. The final scene, in which the director Gray resumes the conversation with Paul Gill, a Jazz musician, condenses the broader aim of the narrative into a single sequence. Gill is the only social actor to be shown together with Gray in a two shot. Gray appears to place himself within the same ideological space as his interviewee, as the following analysis will show (fig. 103).

At the beginning of the sequence Gray listens to Paul Gill's music performance (fig 104). The camera zooms in to Gray to show his emotions and he is evidently moved (fig. 105).

9. The Spectrum of Mormon Documentaries

Fig. 104 / Fig. 105 Director Gray becomes focus of the narration. It is also his story that has been told (Nobody Knows, 01:08:54/ 01:09:07).

Fig. 106 / Fig. 107 The film ends with feelings of sadness and empathy being expressed as the director Gray hugs the emotional jazz musician Gill (Nobody Knows, 01:10:05/ 01:10:40).

Gray asks Gill: "If you have the power to do the one change what would that be? Gill answers: "... To convince others that the Gospel is true... to let them understand how I feel and why I feel ... to have that ability." Gill becomes emotional and starts to cry (fig. 106). The camera's gaze is now fixed on Gill as before it was fixed on Gray. After giving Gill a tissue to wipe away his tears, Gray hugs him (fig. 107).

It seems that the director has found his alter ego in Paul Gill, for the musician expresses exactly how Gray feels. The closeness is made visible in the two-shot and close-ups of the director and the social actor. Even though Gill's experience as an African American was often humiliating, he still feels loyal to the church. His identification as a Latter-day Saint is not to be questioned. But he needs to find a way to synchronize his experience of discrimination with his loyalties to the church and his religious identity.

Gray and Gill share an affiliation with the church that needs to come to terms with the church's history of racial discrimination. Gray defends his continued membership of the LDS Church through *Nobody Knows*, which vocalizes problem aspects of the church but has as its final message that, as Gill says, the most important goal must be "to convince others that the Gospel is true." The documentary ends with a "higher truth" that prevails over the challenging and not fully rehabilitated history of the church. Gray has forgiven the church its wrongdoing. The audience have to choose whether to follow Gray's path to forgiveness. To do so might be an option for loyal black LDS members and for a broader membership who no longer have to be ashamed of belonging to a formerly racist church. But to do so might be far harder for former LDS members who left the church because of discrimination and are unable or do not want to overcome their disappointment and anger. From this perspective the documentary's take on a problematic chapter of LDS history might seem too simplistic. The documentary's self-proclaimed mode of moral reasoning, stated on the DVD cover, is "the right to know," to which might be added, "and to forgive", as the narration's moral reasoning. Gray has forgiven the church its error and in turn now seeks forgiveness from the black Mormons in the narrative and in the audience and also of all others who are troubled by the LDS Church's racial history and policy. In this sense *Nobody Knows. The Untold Story of Black Mormons* and *Sisterz in Zion* are similar, for they both present the LDS Church in a positive light by distinguishing between us and them. "Them", the others, are those who do not accept that the church's racialized policy has changed and that racism now belongs to the LDS past.

9.2. Who are the Mormons?

We turn now to two documentaries that function in an entertaining mode that is reinforced by humor based on the limited knowledge of Mormons in the United States and Europe. The directors, producers, and hosts Daryn Tufts and Jed Knudsen turn the tables on their ignorant subjects in the low-budget production *American Mormon* (US 2005, 35') and its sequel, *American Mormon in Europe* (US 2006, 50'), which was made with a more substantial budget and is twenty minutes longer. The narrative concerns two Mormon directors from Salt Lake City, UT, who want to establish what people think about Mormons, about who they are and what they believe. They mostly reveal their identity only at the end of each conversation. Commentary is given on the often error-filled answers by way of inserted graphics and goofy sounds, which ridicule the misinterpretations of Mormonism. The opening title of *American Mormon* announces the theme of the documentary: "What you are about to see is real. Real people." "Real people" fades and a superimposition follows: "Real answers." Finally, a new title appears: "Really" (00:02:23–00:02:31).

The opening titles and their cartoon style can be understood as helping the audience understand the two Mormon protagonists as comic figures (fig. 108): they travel the United States in their white car accompanied by a peppy music score with a dominant electric rock guitar.

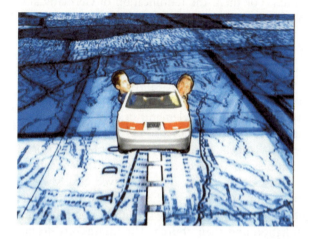

Fig. 108 The music accompanying the opening credits announces the documentary mode as funny and light-hearted (American Mormon, 00:01:28).

Tufts and Knudsen seek to demonstrate through humor the lack of accurate knowledge of what Mormonism is. *American Mormon in Europe* follows the same strategy, but this time Tufts and Knudsen travel to Europe, as the title suggests. They continue to ask people in the streets about Mormonism but in this sequel they also research recent history at the Berlin mission and visit the first mission in Europe, founded in Herefordshire, in the United Kingdom, by Wilford Woodruff. Tufts and Knudsen are Mormons and also former LDS missionaries. We would expect their hermeneutic horizons to be profoundly shaped by these experiences. They evidently know how to approach and engage people on the street, with

Part III: The Ethical Space of Documentaries and Religion

Tufts particularly self-confident in front of the camera. In *American Mormon* Knudsen is behind the camera and Tufts in front, but in the sequel Knudsen also conducts interviews. They talk with Mormons and non-Mormons, including Amish people, in the United States, and with Americans and a diversity of Europeans from Italy, France, Germany, and England among other countries. The European social actors know little about Mormons and many have never previously met a Mormon.

The filmmakers are specifically interested in German Mormons. In *American Mormon in Europe* an extended digression documents the Mormon community in Berlin. Knudsen talks with German Mormons in Berlin about the fall of the Berlin Wall in 1989 and the reunification of Germany the following year. The German Mormons they interview identify strongly with the church. For them the reunification of Germany also meant the reunification of the Berlin stake, which had been divided for almost four decades.[573]

The loyalties of the filmmakers are explicitly expressed in the film style. For example, they feel an obvious familiarity with two future missionaries whom they encounter in the streets of Las Vegas in *American Mormon* and are eager to present them in a positive light, unlike the occasions when wrong answers met with ridiculing sound elements or titles. With the exception of the two future Mormon missionaries in Las Vegas, the loyalties of the other social actors who appear in this first documentary are not in line with narration's affinities. In the sequel, however, Mormons from wards in England, Italy and Germany who are interviewed clearly are in sympathy with the filmmakers. While all of the Mormon social actors know that Knudsen and Tufts are from their own church; non-Mormons are ignorant of their affiliation and their church. The filmmakers do not compromise their own group, but they do expose non-Mormons for that ignorance. The privileging and validating gaze of the two filmmakers is introduced at the beginning of both productions: in *American Mormon* Tufts and Knudsen talk to the camera, revealing their identity as Mormons and providing information about Mormons with references to, for example, "thousands and thousands of missionaries around the world" or Mormon celebrities (Fig. 109).

---

573 A "stake" is a unit used in the LDS Church for a community; each community consists of several "wards."

9. The Spectrum of Mormon Documentaries

Fig. 109 Knudsen and Tufts bow toward the camera and talk to the audience. They want to draw the audience onto their side (American Mormon, 00:00:03).

Fig. 110 Beside the well-chosen shirts Knudsen and Tufts repeat an introduction to the narration that is similar to that in American Mormon (American Mormon in Europe, 00:00:02).

Referring to a headline in the *Times* magazine the directors note that Mormonism is the fastest growing religion in the world. They appear to be selling Mormonism as a successful and widely practiced religion. This information also suggests to the audience that people who know so little about Mormonism must be very ignorant. In the opening sequence of the second, Europe-focused documentary, Tufts and Knudsen talk again into the camera, inviting the audience to join them on their journey (fig. 110).

Film clips in which Mormons are obviously misrepresented or ridiculed are inserted to show "pretty interesting" ideas, as Tufts ironically describes these concepts. Additional factual information is presented, such as that since 1995 there have been more Mormons outside than inside the United States; the explanation is that "This church had gone global" (00:01:45). They then reveal the two questions they will ask non-Mormons (1) and Mormons (2) they encounter in Europe (00:01:55):
1) What do people think about the Mormons around the world?
2) What is it like being a Latter-day Saint outside America, the country where the religion was founded?

Using animated images the opening credits show where they will travel: Rome, Berlin, Paris, London, the Vatican and famous sites like the Eiffel Tower, the Pantheon, Stonehenge, and the Arc de Triomphe. The title of the second part then repeats elements from the first: "once again, what you're about to see is real." After a while "Really" is added to the sentence, which then fades out so that only "Really" remains.

Part III: The Ethical Space of Documentaries and Religion

We can explore a number of scenes from *American Mormon* to establish how the camera is employed to comment on the social actors' answers. For example, when Tufts asks two women – probably mother and daughter – what they know about Mormons, the elder women describes them as "backward". Tufts asks, "Do Mormons use microphones?" The woman answers, "I think they are still churning butter." Tufts comments on this answer by grimacing into the camera such that the social actors cannot see his response (fig. 111).

Fig. 111 Tufts reacts with a grimace as commentary on the social actor's answer that "Mormons are still churning butter" (American Mormon, 00:08:12).

Fig. 112 The young man challenges Tuft's patience as he refuses to answer his question and instead invents an adventurous story (American Mormon, 00:05:27).

On another occasion, rather than answer Tuft's question as to who Mormons are directly, a young man at Venice Beach in Santa Monica invents his own story. Tufts initially listens but soon signals with his hand that the story is taking too long. A ticking clock, advancing the time after each cut, is imposed to highlight that the young man's exhaustive story is boring (fig. 112).

Sometimes people questions in turn, with Tufts expected to respond. He often fails to react to such queries. When a woman asks: "Did you – did you see *The Passion* by the way? Wasn't it … [the woman hesitates to go deeper, she seems surprised by her bravery] *of the Christ*? Tufts in turn hesitates, conveying the impression that he is unsure whether he should admit he has seen the movie. After a short pause he says as he gazes into the camera (fig. 113): "I did see *The Passion*. I rented it from a place called *Cleanflix*, actually."

Fig. 113 Tufts again talks with the camera, behind which his colleague Knudsen is standing (American Mormon, 00:12:40).

Fig. 114 Tufts stands with the musicians and it seems that his loyalties are fully with them (American Mormon, 00:23:44).

Cleanflix is a streaming platform, its name alluding to the more popular *Netflix*. With this reference Tufts tells the audience and the couple that he is aware of the negative judgments about *The Passion of the Christ* (Gibson, US 2006), specifically from the LDS Church. He also knows that representatives of his church might learn of his response.[574] The scene shows that the filmmaker's gaze is more interested in the filmmaker's own standing and performance than in the views of the social actors. The hosts' behavior changes when they meet the two Mormon street musicians who will soon serve as missionaries (fig. 114).

As the titles suggest, the filmmakers are on the search for other Mormons. Tufts' gaze on the two Mormon street performers in Las Vegas is unlike that used in previous scenes and he reveals early on that he is also Mormon. It seems that he does not want to compromise the two young Mormons. On learning that the two young street musicians are from Salt Lake City, Tufts immediately changes his attitude. Rather than mock them, he expresses hearty familiarity and exuberant sympathy. His loyalties are immediately clear. He stands at the same distance from the camera as the two men and stages the two social actors in a very positive light. Although Tufts and Knudsen encounter these colored T-shirt wearing Mormons on the Las Vegas strip, but this misleading and compromising situation will soon be rectified. In the credits of *American Mormon* a photograph

---

[574] The film is explicit in its depiction of violence and use of language, which is against LDS film policy.

of the two men is inserted in which they are neatly and tidily dressed in the suits of missionaries (fig. 115/116).

Fig. 115/ Fig. 116 In the end credits the two street musicians encountered in Las Vegas are presented as neatly dressed young men ready to serve their mission and as still having fun (American Mormon in Europe, 00:33:35/ 00.33.40).

The titles tell where they will serve – one in Oregon and one in the Philippines. *American Mormon* ends with Tuft's voice: "To both of you and to all you other missionaries out there. We wanna wish you the very best as you go out and really talk to people about the Mormons." These closing words from the host summarize the intent behind the documentary. As former missionaries, Tufts and Knudsen seek to show why it is important for Mormons to talk to non-Mormons about Mormonism. They want the world to know who Mormons really are. The film is designed in part to motivate future missionaries, by showing the lack of knowledge about Mormonism in the United States and the humor that can emerge in tackling ignorance. There was evident potential for a sequel, with Europeans perhaps even less well informed than the people they encountered in the United States.

American Mormon in Europe adds another story line, combining it with the existing pattern of asking questions with the interviewee very unsure of the answer. Tufts provides further information that again seems to be intended for his audience rather than for the social actors. The first question, presented in a title, is: "What do they know about Utah?" The passers-by indicate that the answer is "very little." Their wrong answers are used as an opening sequence and are compared with those that would be given by Mormons responding to the same question.

For example, when Tufts meets a group of young women who don't know where Utah is, he draws a map in the air to instruct them (fig. 117).

Fig. 117 That Tufts is the center of attention is expressed by his proximity to the camera. He even covers some of the social actors (American Mormon in Europe, 00:04:23).

Fig. 118 Tufts even pushes people aside so that they don't stand in the way of the camera. His behavior says that the space in front of the camera does not belong to the social actor; it is Tuft's space (American Mormon in Europe, 00:29:03).

The host is the center of attention, with the interviewees listening and seemingly amused. He sits in front of one social actor and obscures her from our sight. Later Tufts turns so that the interviewees do not block the camera's view of him (fig. 118).

On another occasion a social actor returns his question by asking, "Do you know the shape of Israel?" Tufts tries to draw Israel but gives up, admitting that he doesn't know its form. Then he states about religion: "There is a religion that is headquartered in Utah." One social actor guesses: "It must be Catholic?" Tufts replies, (fig.119) : "uuu ... good guess. The Catholic church is – their headquarters are in Rome."

Even though his answer is only partly right – namely the headquarters of the Roman Catholic Church are in the Vatican City, he allies with the audience, who probably know full well that Utah is not associated with the Roman Catholic Church, by looking again into the camera.

Often the host is very close to the social actors. Tufts is of above-average height, which intensifies the impression of too great closeness, as in the case of the two Frenchmen in front of the Eiffel Tower (fig 120).

The editing combines all the answers into a continuous flow in which a lack of knowledge about Mormonism is exposed. Some of the social actors overtly claim to know certain Mormons as soon as Tufts mentions them; for others the names mean nothing. Knudsen also conducts interviews in Europe, but unlike Tufts he interviews only Mormons and he asks them

Part III: The Ethical Space of Documentaries and Religion

Fig. 119 The social actor responds seriously to the questions in a strong German accent, from Saxony. He seems ignorant for although the host does not speak his language, he outclasses the young German man with greater knowledge of Mormonism (American Mormon in Europe, 00:06:47).

Fig. 120 The two French men in front of the Eiffel Tower have to look up to the host. Had the host taken a short step to the side, the unfavorable position of the interviewees could have been avoided (American Mormon in Europe, 00:07:12).

Fig. 121 The Mormon German woman looks into the camera while Knudsen is focused upon her (American Mormon in Europe, 00:09:05).

Fig. 122 Relaxed, Knudsen listens to a French Mormon who praises Utah and the number of people who speak French (American Mormon in Europe, 00:09:54).

what they know about Utah. His style as a host is different, with almost no comments and leaving more space for the social actors, so that they sometimes even dare to look at the camera (fig. 121).

Knudsen intervenes less and seems to listen without judging. He often turns slightly away from the camera and in doing so allows the social actors to be frontally visible (fig. 122/fig. 123).

Fig. 123 The Italian Mormon in Rome faces straight on to the camera whereas Knudsen is turned away. Again the host's reactions and interventions are limited and very reluctant (American Mormon in Europe, 00:35:19).

Fig. 124 Knudsen shows great patience and respect for the social actors. Here a German woman starts to cry when she talks about her memories of visiting the temple with her family (American Mormon in Europe, 00:18:17).

This interviewer's evident attachment to his interviewees seems to be based on their shared religious affiliation and also appears to be a product of a less dominant and more tentative personality. This attitude generates closeness and intimacy during conversations, as is the case with a Mormon woman in Germany who starts to cry when she tells of a particular experience in going to the temple with her family (fig. 124). Knudsen listens attentively to this personal and precious memory. Elegiac music intensifies the emotional charge. Knudsen's respectful presence leaves space for the social actors.

The narration repeatedly highlights how little non-Mormons know about Mormonism and Mormons. In a repetitive pattern, passers-by are asked how many Mormons live in their country. Their guesses are contrasted with the actual numbers, which are superimposed (fig. 125).

Part III: The Ethical Space of Documentaries and Religion

Fig. 125 Asked if there are many Mormons in England, two English women respond in the negative. The correct information is superimposed for the audience: 138,441 Mormons currently live in England (American Mormon in Europe, 00:20:19).

Fig. 126 The social actors claim the space in front of the camera. Knudsen conducts a serious conversation based on genuine attention and authentic interest (American Mormon in Europe, 00:45:48).

The narration goes even further. If a guess is very far from the correct number, an intertitle "huh?" appears as commentary. This is also the case when an interviewee has no English or cannot comprehend what Tufts is asking.

After almost 45 minutes a new topic is introduced – the Mormon ward in Berlin, with discussion of how a member's life was before the Wall came down and how it changed subsequently. The tone of the documentary becomes more serious. Knudsen listens with empathy and interest to the stories the Berlin Mormons tell him (fig. 126).

As the Berlin Mormons recall their history, their emotions often fill the space before the camera. The host's gaze again is intimate and suggests his respect for the people and their stories.

In the closing sequence of the film, the moments at the end of each conversation when Tufts reveals he is a Mormon are connected together by editing. When the hidden camera is revealed, the passers-by who have been interviewed feel they have been caught out, a pattern known from other similarly staged television shows (fig. 127).

Finally, both Mormons and non-Mormons are asked for advice for Mormons in Utah. In general the answers are positive and encouraging: "Stay strong!" (00:47:57). "Find out for yourself!" (00:48:05). "Search a lot for the right friends!" (00:48:17). "Fulfill your callings!" (00:48:21). "My testimony is – für Gott ist nichts unmöglich" (00:50:07). As a woman says these last

9. The Spectrum of Mormon Documentaries

Fig. 127 When Tufts explains that they are Mormons, people respond with surprise and sometimes with embarrassment at their own previous comments (American Mormon in Europe, 00:47:24).

words, she starts to cry. Tufts again interrupts and comments and Knudsen listens.

We turn now to the moral reasoning applied in the narration of *American Mormon* and *American Mormon in Europe*. On one hand, the filmmakers are telling the documentary's audience that they should not take the non-Mormon world too seriously, that non-Mormons are simply ignorant. On the other hand, Tufts and Knudsen promote the Mormon faith by letting audience and non-Mormon social actors know that they have a sense of humor. There is a tit-for-tat approach here: as long as they are making fun of us, we are allowed to make fun of them and their ignorance. The mode of moral reasoning can therefore be described as adjusting for equality. This approach embraces the experience of many Mormons in being the other or "peculiar people".[575] The film's narration is based in reciprocity and refers to the Mormon experience of being different.

What audience do the makers have in mind? Spectators who know little about Mormons might be less interested in the narration because the humor mostly works when the viewers' frame of reference includes a degree of knowledge about Mormonism, at least more than the average non-Mormon social actor possesses. We can assume that Mormons find the documentaries particularly funny. The documentaries may have an additional relevance for future missionaries: at the end of *American Mormon* the hosts

---

575 Fluhman, *A Peculiar People*; Decker and Austin, *Peculiar Portrayals*.

Part III: The Ethical Space of Documentaries and Religion

explicitly state that "Mormons should go and talk to people about the Mormons and Mormonism," which can be understood as a call to mission.

9.3. The LDS Church and Mormon truth, historical and global

Whereas the documentaries discussed up to this point have mainly been generated on the initiative of producers and filmmakers, the last two films we shall analyze were produced by two leading Mormon institutions. The LDS Church is responsible for *Meet the Mormons* (Blair Treu, US 2014, 78') and Brigham Young University for *Journey of Faith* (Peter Johnson, US 2006, 86'). The first film was a surprise success, making $6,047,363 at the US box office.[576] It was made to replace an older introductory film on Mormonism that was shown at the church visitor centers, but the test audiences were so positive about *Meet the Mormons* that the producers decided it should first be screened in public theaters. The second documentary, *Journey of Faith*, is a more educational and historical film. The end credits acknowledge the Foundation for Ancient Research and Mormon Studies at Brigham Young University and Timpanogos Entertainment. Most of the experts who are interviewed teach at Brigham Young University, which is affiliated with the LDS Church. The sequel, *Journey of Faith: The New World*, was produced one year later, again directed by Peter Johnson, and continues the story of how Lehi and his descendants arrived and settled in Central America.

Meet the Mormons is a corporate video in the form of a documentary that promotes the Mormon faith by depicting outstanding Mormon social actors with above average capabilities who are embedded in impressive landscapes and filmed by an empathic and supportive camera. The representation of Mormonism is entirely controlled by the LDS. Neither film includes critical voices. *Meet the Mormons* shows contemporary places and people, whereas in *Journey of Faith* the people and places are historical. The latter tells the story of an Israelite tribe that Mormons understand as their ancestors. The tribe fled Israel out of fear of persecution. As a historical event, the story poses a different challenge for the documentary mode, although the documentaries share the aim of presenting Mormonism and the LDS Church at their best. The discussion that follows will consider how this goal is achieved and what kind of moral reasoning is applied.

---

576 "Meet the Mormons (2014) – Box Office Mojo."

Meet the Mormons provides portraits of six Mormons. They live or work(ed) in different countries and talk about their successful lives, what they have achieved, and how their Mormon faith influences their lives. The protagonists are introduced with intertitles: *The Bishop* Jermaine Sullivan works as an academic counselor and is now stake president in Atlanta, GA; *The Coach* Ken Niumatalolo is a head college football coach in the US; *The Fighter* Carolina Muñoz Marin is a mixed martial arts fighter from Costa Rica; *The Humanitarian* Bishnu Adhikari is an engineer born in Nepal who now lives in the US; *The Candy Bomber* Gail Halvorsen, a pilot during the Berlin Airlift, lives in the US; *The Missionary Mom* Dawn Armstrong resides in the US. The social actors represent the church as a global institution for they include individuals from countries other than the US and Americans who live and work in foreign countries.

The analysis here will focus on *The Humanitarian*. The sequence depicts and explains how the Mormon faith can be lived by someone who does not come from a Mormon or American cultural and religious background. The message is that the LDS Church family accepts members of various cultural origins. The clip also emphasizes that Mormons are Christians. Although it does not address religious practices and rituals directly, the protagonist and his wife explain in some detail their relationship to Jesus Christ. At another point a picture of the protagonist's baptism is inserted to illustrate his conversion to the LDS Church. *Meet the Mormons* is professionally and conventionally told, which is in keeping with the director's professional background. An experienced director, Blair Treu has worked for the Disney Channel and is himself a Mormon. He graduated from Brigham Young University and works now for the official Mormon TV BYUtv, located in Provo, UT.

Two cultures influence the hermeneutic horizons of the protagonist Bishnu Adhikari, *The Humanitarian*, an attribution explained by the narration. Adhikari was partly educated in the US and lived with his wife and three children in Kathmandu. From the start the narration connects Bishnu Adhikari strongly with his Hindu and Nepalese heritage; only toward the end of this section do we see the LDS Church meetinghouse, after the protagonist has spoken of experiencing the presence of God on the "summit of Mount Everest." A traveling shot of the impressive Nepalese mountain landscape from a bird's eye view introduces this new topic. Adhikari met Mormon missionaries in Russia, where he was also baptized; we see the image of his baptism while hearing Adhikari speak repeatedly of how happy he is about his decision to be baptized. The protagonist's Hindu background is called "cultural practices and family tradition"; his current

Part III: The Ethical Space of Documentaries and Religion

affiliation with the LDS Church is called "faith". Adhikari claims: "Becoming a Christian doesn't mean to abandon your culture." His wife, who shares her husband's religious affiliation, is also involved in church activities and directs the choir at the LDS Church meetinghouse.

Meet the Mormons is a commissioned film, and the filmmaker's loyalty is to the commissioning the LDS Church. At the time he made this documentary, Blair was already involved in the *I'm a Mormon* campaign, and the stylistic and narrative similarities are conspicuous. To some extent the documentary is an extended version of that campaign's videos.[577] The social actors endorse the church, a loyalty echoed by supporting parties who are largely family members and co-workers. Succinctly put: this is a Mormon narrative about Mormons, who represent themselves through their activities and visually. This strategy is fostered by moderator Jenna Kim Jones, an entertainer who is a Mormon. She opens the documentary by asking people at Times Square in New York City what they know about Mormons. She acts as guide throughout the narration of *Meet the Mormons* and introduces the protagonists in voice-overs. Jones also appears in one of the shorts from the *I'm a Mormon* campaign. The narrative of *Meet the Mormons* is focussed largely on social actors from the United States, with one protagonist from South America and, in the "extras", one woman from Italy who lives in the United States. Those responsible for the production and those who appear within the documentary are all affiliated with the LDS Church; the diversity within the documentary comes from the latter's cultural backgrounds. As we shall see, the camera gaze in the section entitled *The Humanitarian* (00:47:44-00:58:40) portrays this loyalty to the church along with a particular cultural diversity.

The sequence starts with several bird's eye shots of Hindu temples in Kathmandu and mountains. A woman is dancing a traditional Hindu dance, and images of the lively town of Kathmandu at night are accompanied by rhythmic music of Hindi pop. In the first shot Bishnu Adhikari is sitting on a chair speaking to the camera (00:49:12): "I love my country Nepal." The setting changes, and the protagonist is now with his family in the kitchen of his home. The camera is in the middle of the kitchen like a guest (fig. 128). Bishnu Adhikari introduces his wife and each of his children by name (Fig. 129–132).

---

577 See chapter 4 in this book.

9. The Spectrum of Mormon Documentaries

Fig. 128 The camera is invited to stay close to the Adhikari family (Meet the Mormons, 00:49:15).

Fig. 129 "My wife, Mangala" (Meet the Mormons, 00:49:17).

Fig. 130 "Our first daughter, Smina" (Meet the Mormons, 00:49:19).

Fig. 131 "Second daughter, Rebecca" (Meet the Mormons, 00:49:21).

Fig. 132 "And then our son Jeewarshav" (Meet the Mormons, 00:49:23).

Fig. 133 The protagonist introduces us to the place where he was raised (Meet the Mormons, 00:49:32).

Then the camera follows Bishnu Adhikari as he visits the village where he was raised (fig. 133). Jenna Kim Jones states in the voice-over: "Bishnu and his ten siblings grew up in this remote village of Lamjung, nestled deep within the foothills of Himalayan mountain range."

295

Part III: The Ethical Space of Documentaries and Religion

Fig. 134/ Fig. 135/ Fig. 136/ Fig. 137/ Fig. 138/ Fig. 139/ Fig. 140 Bishnu Adikari guides the camera through his world and provides access to private spaces that otherwise would be difficult to visit. His gaze becomes the camera's gaze (Meet the Mormons, 00:50:20/ 00:50:27/ 00:50:35/ 00:51:15/ 00:51:16/ 00:51:36/ 00:51:37).

As the protagonist tells his conversion story, the camera frames him in a close shot (fig. 134). The shot changes and Bishnu is shown alone in the landscape (fig. 135), suggesting a respectful distance is required at this important moment. Then the camera follows the dynamic protagonist (fig.

9. The Spectrum of Mormon Documentaries

136) and becomes a passenger on board a plane (fig. 137), catching a view of the hills around Katmandu from above (fig. 138). The protagonist defines the camera gaze, showing where it should be directed, for example toward a mother and her two children when he greets them (fig 139). The protagonist opens his world to the camera, which is able to enter unobtrusively. As a local, Adhikari enables the audience to access these private spaces. On occasion the camera adopts a beneficial distance, helping localize the plot spatially (fig. 140).

Fig. 141/ Fig. 142/ Fig. 143/ Fig. 144/ Fig. 145/ Fig. 146 The camera gaze follows a pattern whereby it is close and in the middle of the action and also provides the "bigger" picture, often of scenic surroundings (Meet the Mormons, 00:51:51/ 00:52:00/ 00:52:18/ 00:52:36 /00:52:09/ 00:52:40).

Bishnu Adikhari meets contractors (fig. 141), visits the inhabitants of a small village (fig. 142), is invited to the opening of a school he has funded (fig. 143). Sometimes the camera seems almost invisible and it is always

Part III: The Ethical Space of Documentaries and Religion

discrete (fig. 144). Some activities are explained by the protagonist's commentary – he argues, for example, that education is key to escaping poverty. By inserting longshots that explain his actions, the camera integrates Adhikari within the context in which he works and acts (fig. 145/146).

The cinematographer and the director are not present; although the protagonist speaks to them a few times, as in a scene when Adhikari explains technical aspects of water resources to the filmmaker, no reaction is given. The space behind the camera remains mute (fig. 147/148).

Fig. 147 Bishnu Adhikari now talks to the cinematographer but there is no reaction (Meet the Mormons, 00:53:02).

Fig. 148 The protagonist turns around and looks to the left of the camera toward someone. He is explaining how he will bring water to the valley (Meet the Mormons, 00:53:10).

The only permitted interaction is between the protagonist and his social entourage. When school children line the path, the camera looks on with Adhikari's gaze (fig. 149). He comments that he feels uncomfortable when people give him extra emphasis. The line with the school children is very long. The camera again reveals Adhikari's extraordinary context (fig. 150/151), at the same time staying very close in this shot (fig. 152). During the adulation of this LDS Church member, he himself comments in the voice-over: "As a son of our Heavenly Father, they and myself in His eyes are equal." On one occasion a local man addresses the director, but the director does not respond. He strictly observes only, with his presence expressed exclusively through the camera lens, and does not engage personally with the social actors.

9. The Spectrum of Mormon Documentaries

Fig. 149/ Fig. 150/ Fig. 151/ Fig. 152 The camera is very present, but the director hides behind it. Questions from social actors remain unanswered (Meet the Mormons, 00:53:27/ 00:53:46/ 00:54:00/ 00:54:05).

The protagonist is presented not only undertaking his professional duties but also dancing at a private party. The scene tells the audience that Mormons can relax and have fun. Within the LDS Church meetinghouse they evince greater seriousness. The humanitarian's life is presented as manifold, vivid, and accountable.

The closing scene brings the narration back to the village where it started. The protagonist affirms his Mormon belonging and the joy it brings with his comment (00:56:19) "I am so very happy that I made that decision." Finally, he visits his father, greeting him by touching his forehead to his father's feet (fig. 153). The gesture is filmed in slow motion, adding an emotional layer. The gesture indicates the highest respect, his daughter explains. Adhikari's father comments in the voice-over and then as a talking head (fig. 154): "I feel very blessed to be respected like that. I feel really blessed to be respected by my son."[578] The narration connects Bishnu Adhikari's more recent affiliation with the LDS Church to his family heritage, showing how they can be combined.

After more than 10 minutes in which a successful man is presented at his best – engaged in his community, supporting the less privileged and

---

[578] Original language is Nepalese. The dialogue is taken from the subtitles of the DVD.

299

Part III: The Ethical Space of Documentaries and Religion

Fig. 153/ Fig. 154 At the end of section entitled The Humanitarian, the protagonist returns to his village, where he meets his father (Meet the Mormons, 00:57:38/ 00:57:48).

with seemingly boundless energy – a summary of the message of this section is provided, as the very decent protagonist recounts (00:48:41): "I'm not close to the perfection but I'm perfect in one thing – I'm perfect in trying." Not just his behavior but also his self-assessment is humble.

The modes of moral reasoning in *Meet the Mormons* adopt a variety of strategies. Generally, the narrative defends the Mormon worldview and its people: Mormon faith is Christian and global, tolerant and open to other cultures. Mormons are exceptional and successful. Their faith enables them to achieve. The only voices heard in the documentary are affirming of the church. No experts appear anywhere in this documentary – normal Mormons are inherently sufficient to prove the worth of Mormonism.

The film is likely to be of particular interest to Mormons, for whom it can provide self-affirmation. The response of the audience will depend very much on their experiences with Mormons. Past negative experiences may result in a refusal to cooperate with the message, a sense that here again Mormons are telling only half-truths. Non-Mormons with little knowledge of Mormonism and Mormons themselves will likely be impressed by the diversity of the church membership, by their success and positivity, with the documentary thus fostering mission and enhancing the image of the church. The educational aspect is certainly less significant, with little new factual information communicated. The ethical space in *Meet the Mormons* matches the LDS Church's worldview, with its wish to promote the integrity of its members and their success. The documentary does not tackle Mormon dogmatic teachings or exclusivity.

An educational purpose is central to our last example of a Mormon documentary. *Journey of Faith* is intended as validation of *The Book of Mormon*. As we will see, a good number of experts address Lehi's journey from Jerusalem to America and propose how he and his flock survived in the desert.[579] The opening title of *Journey of Faith* highlights the scholarly nature of the narrative (00:00:11): "This documentary is based on current research into the epic journey of Lehi and his family through the Arabian Peninsula to the Americas. These are the Middle Eastern locations where Lehi likely traveled." The account begins in Jerusalem and tells how Lehi refused to adapt to the adulterous lifestyle of his contemporaries, who were "not living the spirit of the law [of Moses] that was given to them" (00:07:17). Under serious threat from his opponents, Lehi is told by God to leave Jerusalem with his tribe.

Experts from a wide range of fields – archeology, history, ancient scripture, law, and classical antiquity, philosophy, Islamic studies, Arabic, political science, botany, plant ecology, and Middle Eastern history – use their authority to bolster the narrative of *The Book of Mormon*. The case is made with repeated examples, presented largely within a repeated structure. First an event from *The Book of Mormon* is described or read. By adding further evidence, an expert located at the relevant site or in a studio reassures the audience that the events that have been described did indeed happen. The expert explains why the excerpt from the text seems valid from the perspective of that expert's field of study. Additionally, the narrative argues that while *The Book of Mormon* is consistent with recent scientific findings, Joseph Smith could not have known that evidence – Joseph Smith was a genuine prophet, with his translation of the golden plates from "reformed Egyptian"[580] to English a product of divine revelation.[581] The various claims made through the documentary are never contradictory and complement the argument perfectly. The whole narration functions as a unified and harmonized defense of the validity of *The Book of Mormon*.

LDS-affiliated institutions, which the end credits reference, form the production context. Most of the experts who appear in the narration teach at Brigham Young University, which is affiliated with the LDS Church. Their university affiliation is not stated in the narration, which could suggest a desire to conceal that relationship. The sequel, *Journey of Faith: The New world*, recounts in similar style how Lehi and his descendants arrived in Central America and the events that followed.

---

579 According to *The Book of Mormon*, Lehi was a prophet in Jerusalem (approximately 600 BC) who guided his tribe to the Americas and is understood by Mormons as their forefather.
580 Joseph Smith and Laurie F. Maffly-Kipp, *The Book of Mormon*, trans. Joseph Smith (New York et al.: Penguin Classics, 2008), 548.
581 "..., I make a record in the language of my father, which consists of the learning of the Jews and the language of the Egyptians." See Smith and Maffly-Kipp, 3.

Part III: The Ethical Space of Documentaries and Religion

The hermeneutic horizons and loyalties of filmmaker and producer Peter Johnson are a product of his LDS Church membership. Johnson first worked in the Hollywood film industry and later produced and directed for Brigham Young Motion Pictures.[582] Johnson has a personal commitment to convincing the audience that Joseph Smith's story is authentic. The hermeneutic horizons of the specialists in the film are similarly influenced by their Mormon affiliations, specifically to Brigham Young University. Their contributions make evident their believe in *The Book of Mormon*. Their testimony seeks to provide evidence in support of their worldview, for example by proving that the town of Nahem existed. An emotional mode is also activated, as, for example, when the subject of the role of women in ancient times is broached.

The social actors' loyalties intersect with their hermeneutic horizons, with the majority of those who contribute LDS members who are defending their own church's position. Through their specialized knowledge they are able to furnish the argument with credibility. Through their appearance and statements they also prove their loyalty to their religious institution and its teachings. As in *Meet the Mormons*, the social actors gain from their participation by voicing religious and institutional self-affirmation.

As noted, two strategies for the argument are applied. We see both factual and emotional modes operating in a sequence about Sariah, Lehi's wife, launched by kitschy shots of sunsets over the sea and mountains. The director is neither visible nor audible. Our analysis will reveal that *Journey of Faith* seeks to be objective, concealing the relativity of the historical narrative.

The sequence starts with Virginia H. Pearce, introduced as an educator and author (fig. 155). "It's impossible not to love this story!" she enthuses, smiling empathically and happily.

She explains admiringly how Nephi prioritizes his family, suggesting that even today for a man to do so is extraordinary. A drawing depicting Sariah, Lehi's wife, is inserted (fig. 156).

The second expert in the sequence addresses ancient texts. Ann N. Madsen explains the role of women during Lehi's time (fig. 157): "Men had power and the women had influence."

Madsen's point is that in ancient times while women were not vocal in public, their husbands listened to their opinions in private. A male expert describes the challenges of managing domestic tasks during the journey

---

582 "Films by Latter-Day Saints: Directors, Producers," accessed February 24, 2018, http://www.ldsfilm.com/dir.html#Pro.

9. The Spectrum of Mormon Documentaries

Fig. 155 Virginia H. Pearce opens the sequence, addressing the role of women during Lehi's journey to America while smiling warmly and empathetically (Journey of Faith, 00:18:44).

Fig. 156 The drawing shows Lehi's wife during a rest on the journey. Sariah is preparing food. In light of the challenges of preparing food for so many people, experts deem her contribution outstanding (Journey of Faith, 00:19:03).

Fig. 157 Ann N. Madsen explains that in these times men paid attention to their wives only in private (Journey of Faith, 00:19:03).

Fig. 158 The drawing puts Sariah behind Lehi and shows the moment when Lehi tells Sariah that he has been told by God to leave Jerusalem (Journey of Faith, 00:20:50).

and an additional female expert then illustrates in detail how bread could be made at that time, describing each step. Pearce then highlights the important constellation of the family in *The Book of Mormon*. It's a "real family" with problems and tensions, as another male academic mentions in a serious tone. Talking about pressures and rivalries within a family, Pearce becomes more emotional (00:20:35): "We see sibling rivalries, we see tension, and we can imagine what that does to a mother."

Shortly afterward Pearce shows empathy with Sariah, with a slight tremor in her voice: (00:20:50): "I imagine that the moment Lehi told her about what the Lord had instructed him to do, she anticipated what this

Part III: The Ethical Space of Documentaries and Religion

would do to her family." Another drawing is inserted, to illustrate Pearce's comment (fig. 158).

Then two male experts explain that Lehi's sons, Laman and Lemuel, belonged to the ruling class in Judea and viewed their father as a "class traitor" (00:21:13). In Lehi's family and its conflicts the experts see Judea in microcosm. Even though the two sons do not want to join the journey, they are loyal to their father, the experts repeat and emphasize. We should note that as soon as the topic changes to the relationship between father and sons, all the expert commentary is by men. These experts conclude that Laman and Lemuel transferred their anger with their father to their brother Nephi. Then Pearce brings an emotional component into the story with the comment (00:23:10): "The thing that is heartbreaking for me, women I know who have children like Laman and Lemuel often take great comfort, great comfort, if they still have a loving relationship with family members. They will say they have left the faith, but we still love one another, and we still have a good time together. And there is great comfort in that for the women. But Sariah never ever had that. And that breaks my heart for her."

This short sequence makes evident how the relationship between women and men should function, with specific and distinct roles within the family. The historical account is used to draw a picture of the ideal Mormon family structure, in which the husband and father is the leader, the sons are loyal to their father, the wife follows her husband in whatever he does, is responsible for the preparation of food and further domestic duties, and will love her children even if they don't behave. The narration uses *The Book of Mormon* as evidence in support of contemporary family values.

Another strand to the argument in this documentary is to show that *The Book of Mormon* contains accurate information that could not have been known to Joseph Smith – its narrative therefore was not invented. Thus, for example, a map showing the travels of Lehi and his tribe includes a place named "Nahom", where Nephi's father-in-law was supposedly buried (Fig. 159):

9. The Spectrum of Mormon Documentaries

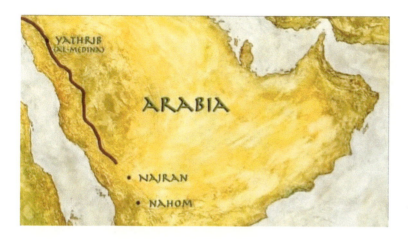

Fig. 159 A map with a red line that moves across the Arabian Peninsula is inserted to show Lehi's journey (Journey of Faith, 00:33:26).

William J. Hamblin, whose subject is Middle Eastern history, comments (00:37:31): "The chances of finding that exact name from that time in that exact place by random chance are just astronomical." The town of Nahom is mentioned in *The Book of Mormon*, yet it was unknown in the time of Joseph Smith. LDS Church archeologists believe that they have now located Nahom. The film shows ruins and the pillars of a temple on which the name "Nahom" is inscribed with the three letters *NHM*, from which Joseph Smith deduced the name *Nahom* (fig. 160).

The documentary claims that three further temples are also inscribed with the name *Nahom*. Thus the narrative provides visual evidence and oral claims that the place existed (fig. 161). Most of the experts here are male and they support each other's positions.

Scholar of law and antiquity John W. Welch brings home this point (00:39:05): "The witnesses tell us that Joseph didn't even know that the city of Jerusalem had walls around it. But if he didn't know that there was a wall around Jerusalem, he certainly didn't know that there was a city or a site out in Yemen called Nahom." A female expert comments (00:39:33): "One has to ask the question how could Joseph Smith possibly have known Nahom?", highlighting Joseph Smith's miraculous knowledge as indirect proof of the authenticity of *The Book of Mormon*.

The moral reasoning in this historical documentary combines three reading modes: personal belief, emotional involvement, and scholarly rhetoric. The last of these is adopted to propose that *The Book of Mormon* has historic pedigree and that its contents will be empirically proven. Mor-

Part III: The Ethical Space of Documentaries and Religion

Fig. 160 The letters NHM are inscribed on this pillar. Joseph Smith could not have known of the city, which was not discovered until the 20th century, yet it appears in The Book of Mormon (Journey of Faith, 00:38:42).

Fig. 161: The narration explains that three temples have been found on an archeologic site on which NHM is inscribed. The longshot of the archeological excavation should prove the existence of Nahom (Journey of Faith, 00:38:59).

mon theology is a separate matter, but, the film suggests, archeological evidence supports the story of Lehi and therefore also *The Book of Mormon*. The evidence for Lehi's journey from Jerusalem to the sea is apparently overwhelming – no opposing voices are heard. The narrative appears both strong and authentic and suggests that the facts and belief are in accord. At the meta level, the documentary intertwines the interpretation of historical sources and the educational, cultural and religious background of the interpreting scholar. The lack of transparency about the experts' hermeneutic horizons casts some doubt on the credibility of their views.

The mode of moral reasoning distinguishes between male and female voices. The mostly male experts provide cognitive and intellectual support for the argument that is presented. The female specialists, Pearce and Madsen, show how *The Book of Mormon* and its wisdom touch its reader emotionally. They have empathy for the characters in the story, whose views and experiences they seek to convey. This combination of factual evidence and emotion is presented as supporting the veracity of *The Book of Mormon*. The rational mode of the argument is enhanced by an emotional mode, which supports the LDS Church's insistence on an individually experienced faith. In the moral mode *Journey of Faith* combines right living with the evidence of historical fact.

The documentary reinforces Mormon beliefs and loyalties. The moral reasoning provides reassurance against doubt. While some knowledge of *The Book of Mormon* will help the viewer access the narration's purpose, those who know little of *The Book of Mormon* are also addressed. The documentary's rational mode, in its presentation of historical fact, will probably be attractive to those in the latter category, who will then learn of Mormon history and Mormon values as they are inscribed in Lehi's story and explained by experts.

9.4. Participants' loyalties and their impact

These Mormon documentaries are intended for both Mormon and non-Mormon audiences, even though their affinities and frames of reference are quite different. The documentaries tell stories that can both convince the non-believer and fortify the believer. They do not engage contrary views, although doing so could add credibility for a non-Mormon audience.

The filmmakers' loyalties are to the LDS Church as an institution. They are advocates of their faith, an attitude that, as we have seen, is inscribed in the gaze of the camera. Their hermeneutic horizons are often determined by a broad familiarity with Mormon history, as in the case of the experts and director of *Journey of Faith*, or with contemporary Mormonism, as in the case of Tufts and Knudsen in *American Mormon* and *American Mormon in Europe*. The documentaries may even exclude non-Mormons who lack

Part III: The Ethical Space of Documentaries and Religion

specific knowledge of Mormonism or do not share the loyalties of church members. All these documentaries make a strong case for the truth of Mormonism, but they draw on values that are not necessarily shared with a non-Mormon audience, and in so doing risk becoming a focus for further criticism of Mormonism. Their moral reasoning would not then correspond with the goal they pursue. The closeness of the camera, of the director's gaze, to the social actors could fortify that negative estimation.

Other than the expert scholars, the Mormons who appear here before the camera openly recount their lives and personal experiences. They are instrumental for the documentaries' credibility. Despite all their variety, the Mormon social actors in these documentaries represent the dominant view of the LDS Church. This unity may help convince the audience. What do they gain by participating? Their involvement in the production, both their presence and their words, may strengthen their ties to the institutional church. Is so, both parties benefit. But what if the social actor's opinion changes and no longer corresponds with the original message of the documentary? The film still exists and may well be available to view in various contexts, particularly online. In this instance neither party – participant nor institution – would benefit as previously; indeed, both may now be disadvantaged. Whether the documentary should still be distributed becomes an ethical concern. The moral dimension of a longer-term perspective on distribution applies not only to Mormon documentaries but also to documentaries produced in non-Mormon contexts, as the following chapter will show.

10. Telling about Mormons

Documentaries produced by non-Mormons often have a purpose different from that of documentaries produced by Mormons. We focus here on the role played by Mormonism, its presentation and the ethical implications. Perhaps not unexpectedly, a more critical view of Mormonism is prevalent. The outlook of the filmmakers is usually not in accord with the Mormon worldview; the production has no ties to or dependency on Mormon networks. To understand how their critical argument is formulated and what moral reasoning is at work, here too, in the case of non-Mormon sponsored productions, we will explore the hermeneutic horizons of the filmmakers and social actors and their affinities. The camera gaze is again revelatory as we ask how moral reasoning shapes the narration and thus the depiction of the represented world.

The discussion addresses four presentations, all of which are considered documentaries although their formats differ according to production and distribution contexts. *Tabloid* (Errol Morris, US 2010), and *Sons of Perdition* (Tyler Measom and Jennilyn Merten, US 2010) are typical Indie productions intended for film festivals; *Polygamy, USA* and *Meet the Mormons* (Lynn Alleway, series *Real Stories*, UK, 2015) are intended primarily for television viewing and streaming platforms.

10.1. Getting close to Mormons

As we saw at the start of this chapter, the moral reasoning of the docu-series *Polygamy, USA* combines two modes, the sensational and the informative. Both are referenced at the very beginning of each episode (except in the first episode) when white letters appear on a black background, channeling the spectator's attention toward the words "The following program reveals the lives of practicing polygamists. Due to the sensitive nature of their beliefs, some individuals have requested that their names be changed" (*Meet the Polygamists, Polygamy USA*, 00:00:13).[583] The narration promises to shed light on a phenomenon that has not been seen publicly

---

[583] The title of the episode is not to be confused with the already discussed documentary *Meet the Mormons* (Blair Treu, US 2014).

Part III: The Ethical Space of Documentaries and Religion

before. The announcement raises expectations and curiosity, but also feeds a craving for sensation, for something new. In indicating that the community opened itself up to being filmed, the narrative seeks to assure the audience that those who chose to participate are not being exploited. Some faces, mostly of male leaders, are blurred and names are changed. While intrusive, the filming is thus apparently sensitive and founded on mutual consent. That mutual consent flourishes at the start of the production; whether all participants are in agreement with the final product is a separate consideration. The social actors become part of the narrative argument and are used to entertain and inform the audience. As part of that audience, the social actors may find they do not agree with the presentation of their words, appearance, and absence, as we will see in the example of *Tabloid*.

Tabloid reconstructs the story of a young American woman, Joyce McKenney, and her relationship with Mormon missionary Kirk Anderson in the late 1970s. McKenney was accused in the United Kingdom of having kidnapped and raped Anderson. The film covers the different views of the events and shows how tabloid newspapers, mainly the *Daily Mirror* and the *Daily Express*, competed to provide the most sensational coverage of the incident. The director, Errol Morris, produced extensive interviews with a number of the protagonists to present their personal viewpoints. The narration weaves the conflicting versions into a single story, without claiming to have established the truth or resolving contradictory evidence. The film is indicative of Morris's directorial strategy, which seeks to question documentaries' ability to represent objective truth. In the words of film scholar David Resha: "His [Morris's] films challenge the idea that there exists a reality to which documentary has privileged access."[584] The film style is very evident in the *Tabloid*, and it highlights the relation between the presentation of pure facts and their construction. This narrative strategy denies the documentary film's ability to show reality. At the end the audience does not know what "really" happened, for what actually happened may not be what they have been told over the previous 87 minutes had happened. We should note that Mormonism is widely discussed, and the audience is fed with information about Mormon theology and practices, as we will see, although no church member speaks directly on those topics.

By the time *Tabloid* was produced, Morris was already a successful filmmaker. It was his ninth documentary: alongside those other documentaries

---

584 David Resha, *The Cinema of Errol Morris* (Middletown, CT: Wesleyan University Press, 2015), 6.

he had also made mini-documentaries, further mini-docu-series, short-documentaries, and documentaries for television. He also directed television commercials, which helped finance his documentary productions. *Tabloid* was shot quickly: the interviews were filmed over three days and the film was edited over the course of just three months. The film premiered at the Telluride Festival in 2010 and many other festivals followed. It played for eleven weeks at 37 theaters in the US and took $700,000 dollars at the box office.[585] Its success was a surprise, as were the mostly positive reviews by critics. The LDS Church did not react to the depiction of Mormonism, but non-Mormon protagonist Joyce McKinney sued Morris for, along with other accusations, misrepresenting her as "engaging in S&M for money"[586] and because she had been "tricked into giving an interview."[587]

An acclaimed documentary filmmaker, Errol Morris has a unique documentary style. He never attended film school and left two universities (Princeton and UC Berkeley) without graduating.[588] One of his most successful films is *The Thin Blue Line* (US 1988), in which through interviews he reconstructed events surrounding the crime for which Randall Dale Adams had been sentence to death. The film proved Adams' innocence and brought about his release from prison.[589]

Morris had no direct ties to Mormonism or to this specific incident, which came to be known as the case of the "Manacled Mormon" as it was known in the public. His interest was in the tabloid-told story, namely in how the events were reported and recounted from different perspectives. He did not have particular loyalties, therefore, to a specific party. The filmmaker plays with the different views and profits from the social actors' interest in defending their unique versions, using their statements as raw material for his own story. In this sense his loyalty is to his story and, we might say, to the audience who are to be entertained with the story of the tabloid coverage. He chose to interview McKinney and not to interview

---

585 "Tabloid (2011) – Box Office Mojo," accessed November 1, 2018, https://www.boxofficemojo.com/movies/?id=tabloid.htm.
586 Michael Hann, "Joyce McKinney Sues Errol Morris over Tabloid," *The Guardian*, November 8, 2011, sec. Film, https://www.theguardian.com/film/2011/nov/08/joyce-mckinney-sues-errol-morris-tabloid.
587 Roy Greenslade, "Judge Finds for Filmmaker in 'manacled Mormon' Case," *The Guardian*, October 17, 2013, sec. Media, https://www.theguardian.com/media/greenslade/2013/oct/17/joyce-mckinney-california.
588 Resha, *The Cinema of Errol Morris*, 13.
589 Linda Williams, "Mirrors without Memories: Truth, History, and the New Documentary," *Film Quarterly* 46, no. 3 (1993): 12–14.

others. Anderson, and also others involved in the original events, did not wish to participate.

When we approach the documentary in light of what it tells its audience about Mormonism, Ex-Mormon Troy Williams is a central figure, alongside the female protagonist Joyce McKinney. Those interviewed are eager to defend their own truth as effectively as possible, as in the case of Williams, who seeks to defend his decision to leave the church. While his hermeneutic horizons are those of a member of the church, his loyalties are no longer to the church, a combination we see repeated in non-Mormon documentaries. Both Joyce McKinney and Troy Williams wish to speak of LDS Church practices and beliefs, and with no one in the documentary to contradict them, their opinion of Mormons and Mormonism is dominant in the narration. McKinney and Williams support each other's arguments and pursue the same goal, namely to denounce the church for suppressing and brainwashing its members. They use their appearance in the documentary to communicate what "really" happens in the church, a view that goes uncontradicted.

All social actors are interviewed with the Interrotron technique, invented by Morris and first used in *Mr. Death: The Rise and Fall of Fred A. Leuchter, Jr* (US 1999).[590] The technique has been copied by other filmmakers, most recently by Wim Wenders in his *Papst Franziskus – Ein Mann seines Wortes* (US 2017). The camera acts as Morris' gaze onto his social actors, and is the only perspective provided. No observational scenes are included. As noted, Anderson was central to the events but refused to be interviewed for the film; Mormonism is therefore explained through the eyes of McKenney and Williams, accessed by Morris' Interrotron technique. This method is based on the principle of the teleprompter. In place of the teleprompter text, which is attached to a camera, an image of the interviewer appears before the interviewee, with the interviewee's image in turn transmitted to a teleprompter to which the interviewer has access. During the conversation the interviewee is therefore looking directly into the camera and at the interviewer's face on a monitor, while the interviewer sees the interviewee's face. Although filmmaker and social actor see each other as if in a mirror and talk to that mirror image, each party can perceive the immediate responses and gestures of the conversation partner. With no diversion available in the surroundings in this artificial setting, the focus is intensely on the interview itself. Framed in a medium close-up, the social actor sits relatively close to the camera and almost trapped by its

---

590 Resha, *The Cinema of Errol Morris*, 115.

Fig. 162/ Fig. 163/ Fig. 164/ Fig. 165 Morris uses a graphic style that references tabloid newspapers. (Tabloid, 00:05:02/ 00:05:03/ 00:05:04/ 00:05:05).

gaze. In a review that appeared in the *New York Times* and commented on the effect of keeping the camera on the social actor until the whole story has been told, Morris was described as a "collector of souls."[591]

Modes of moral reasoning in relation to religion are steered by this interview style. All the social actors are filmed against the same greyish background and the interviews are edited by inserting blacks that punctuate their statements. Jump cuts between the statements add further dynamics to the interviews. Morris allows his social actors to explain their thoughts and views, which may be obviously mistaken or inconsistent. This is the case when the absent Anderson is introduced by Joyce McKinney and Peter Tory, a *Daily Mirror* journalist who reported on the case.

McKinney first explains "When I met my Kirk…," then a black-and-white portrait of Anderson is inserted (Fig. 162) and for three seconds at a time graphic statements by McKinney about Anderson are superimposed below his name: "beautiful blue eyes" (fig. 163), "the cleanest skin" (fig. 164) and "dedicated Mormon" (fig. 165).

---

591 A. O. Scott, "'Tabloid,' Errol Morris's Take on 'Manacled Mormon' - Review," *The New York Times*, July 14, 2011.

Part III: The Ethical Space of Documentaries and Religion

Fig. 166 Kirk Anderson is not a typical "object of desire." He looks like the perfect Mormon missionary rather than like someone who might evoke such feelings (Tabloid, 00:05:10).

Fig. 167 Joyce McKinney describes her first meeting with Kirk Anderson as like a romantic tale where a couple's eyes meet and love at first sight is inevitable (Tabloid, 00:05:14).

The orchestrated introduction of Anderson ends with McKinney's voice saying: "… it was like in the movies." Finally the image remains static and the words spell out "Kirk Anderson" and, on a new line, "object of desire" (fig. 166).

The interview with McKinney continues as she explains (fig. 167): "When the girl comes down the stairs, and their eyes meet. When Juliet looks at Romeo, and it's …phew! That's how it was. He had the most beautiful blue eyes and the sexiest smile, …" Her vivid narrative sounds very authentic, with the audience following her feelings in this moment and imagining the blue eyes and the sexy smile.

As McKinney continues, "…and he always had the cleanest skin," the 16 mm footage in home-movie style that follows, apparently of Anderson, (fig. 168) gives the viewer reason to question her description.

The slow-motion footage suggests Anderson is rather introverted, clumsy, and definitely less attractive than McKinney describes. The editing allows the audience to speculate that this "object of desire" is a projection by McKinney. Tory's voice in the following stylistically similar sequence confirms this suspicion (00:05:45–00:05:48): "Kirk Anderson was a very big, rather flabby, 300-pound, 6 foot 3, …." Tory appears, filmed by the Interrotron technique, as his voice continues,

10. Telling about Mormons

Fig. 168 Kirk Anderson gets out of a car and walks toward a building. McKinney is enthusiastic about Anderson's personality and the impression he made; another social actor will later be less positive (Tabloid, 00:05:45).

> ...not athletic or attractive-looking man in the accepted sense of the word, who had a very shuffley kind of walk, the last person in the world that you would think would be the object of a kind of strange sexual passion.
> [cut to black]
> He had known Joyce McKinney in Salt Lake City. And she had fallen in love with him. Fallen in love with him... become **obsessed** (highlighted by a fading title) by him, because another thing about Joyce is obsession. I mean, she just obsesses about things.
> [cut]
> I don't know what the details of their relationship was in Salt Lake City, but they obvious had some kind of romance or love affair, if one's to believe Joyce at all, he had promised her a family and children.[592]

Tory tells the story from the opposite angle, so that it collides with McKinney's version. Although their descriptions of Anderson do not coincide,

---

592 *Tabloid*, 00:05:45–00:06:32.

Part III: The Ethical Space of Documentaries and Religion

Fig. 169 Goofy sound accompanies Kirk's lollypop-like rotating spiral eyes (Tabloid, 00:18:46).

Tory at least agrees that Anderson and McKinney "had some kind of a romance or love affair." This moment in the narration clearly marks that different versions of the same story exist. According to Resha, "Morris shifts through these breakthroughs and errors, prompting the viewer to raise larger questions about the workings and limits of human knowledge."[593] On a meta level the filming certainly raises larger questions, concerning, for example, how reality is reconstructed in documentaries. The protagonists are each given space to relate the events in accord with their individual experiences and imaginations. The speechless Mormon Anderson plays a central role in the multidimensional reasoning as an empty canvas for not only McKinney's but also all the other social actors' projections.

The audience is presented with a particular picture of Mormons and Mormonism and it seems likely that most of that audience will not be in a position to counter that picture with other evidence. All the various stories converge on the silent Anderson. Such narratives are sometimes expressed in fanciful terms (fig. 169), as when McKinney distinguishes between Kirk number one, the beloved Kirk, and "cult Kirk", the number two Kirk.

---

593 Resha, *The Cinema of Errol Morris*, 7.

10. Telling about Mormons

In a digression, the mission duty that falls to each young male Mormon is explained by an Ex-Mormon missionary after McKinney has recounted the only problem she and Anderson had (00:06:32–00_08:16): "I was wanting to get married in the Christian church, and he was getting pressure from the other side, and so one day, he vanished into thin air. I don't mean he left me. I don't mean he abandoned me. I don't mean he left me for another woman. I mean he evaporated into thin air." As a result, she moved to Los Angeles, worked hard to hire a private investigator and traveled to England, where the private investigator found him. "The Mormons had him." McKinney's last sentence introduces another testimony in Morris's tabloid story, that of Ex-Mormon Tory Williams, who is also introduced with tabloid-style graphics, described as "radio talk show host", "gay activist" in mirror writing, and "gay rights activist", ending with his name, "Troy Williams, former missionary" (fig. 170). Williams explains: "All young men in the church from the time when they are young boys were indoctrinated to prepare to go on mission. We sing songs like 'I hope they call me on a mission'" (00:08:38–00:08:51).

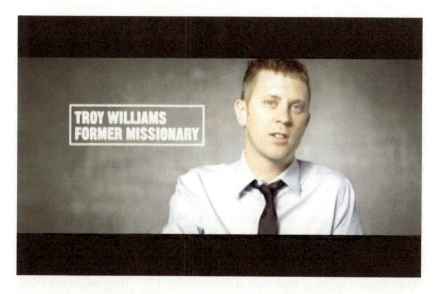

Fig. 170 Troy Williams explains trenchantly what being a missionary means (Tabloid, 00:08:43).

This song is played within the music score and again 16 mm footage shows a happy and light-hearted Anderson shortly before he disappeared, the nar-

Part III: The Ethical Space of Documentaries and Religion

rative suggests. The closeness to Anderson appears a way to a better understanding of who he is (fig. 171/172).

Throughout this footage the LDS Church missionary song is sung by a child's voice. The sequence creates a romanticized and naïve atmosphere that is associated with the Mormon missionary duty. Williams returns, finishing his version of the narrative, which is illustrated with footage from the cartoon *The God Makers* (Ed Decker and Steve Hunt, Jeremiah Films, US 1984): "You leave as a boy you come back as a man. For Kirk when he reaches the age of 19, [insert portrait of Joyce McKinney] he doesn't get whisked away from Joyce. [A still from *The God Makers* is inserted, showing a blond young man dressed in white with other young people in the background.] He is fulfilling his religious-spiritual responsibilities (00:08:57–00:09:13)." Another still from *The God Makers* shows a priest between two columns surmounted with fire. The imagery refers to the spiritual preparation undertaken by missionaries. The sequence ends with a black and tells in pragmatic terms that Anderson had to leave for his mission service and that he was not abducted by the Mormons as McKinney's versions suggest. The two versions of the same events are consistent in content but not in interpretation – one speaks of love and forced separation (McKinney), the other of standard Mormon practice (Williams).

In addition to mission service, Mormon theology and other practices are also addressed by the documentary. McKinney explains at the beginning and again as illustrated by the cartoon *The God Makers* what Mormonism is all about. A white hand energetically knocks at a door. McKinney introduces Mormonism in the voice-over: "They were Mormons." A woman opens the door and looks at the person who was knocking. "They didn't tell me what Mormonism is all about. He didn't say we are a group that believes ..." An elderly man with a white beard who stands in front of the door is filmed in a close-up frame and subjective shot. He looks at the audience/the women behind the half-open door. McKinney continues: "...that Jesus was a polygamist and was married to Magdalene (fig. 173). He didn't say that God lives on a star named Kolob (fig. 174). He didn't say that black people were cursed with the mark of Cain (fig. 175)." Accompanied by dramatic music the white Mormons change to black ones (fig. 176). "They made me think they were a church (fig. 177). They made me think that they were family oriented" (fig. 178).

McKinney presents herself as a victim who found something good in Mormonism, but the audience is introduced to Mormonism as problematic. They receive an image of Mormonism when African Americans had not yet been accepted by the church, as was the case in 1977, when McKinney

10. Telling about Mormons

Fig. 171 Kirk Anderson speaks with two other men, who, the voice-over suggests, are Mormon missionaries (Tabloid, 00:08:51).

Fig. 172 The camera, probably as a result of image manipulation during editing, zooms closer to the still light-hearted Kirk Anderson (Tabloid, 00:08:51).

Part III: The Ethical Space of Documentaries and Religion

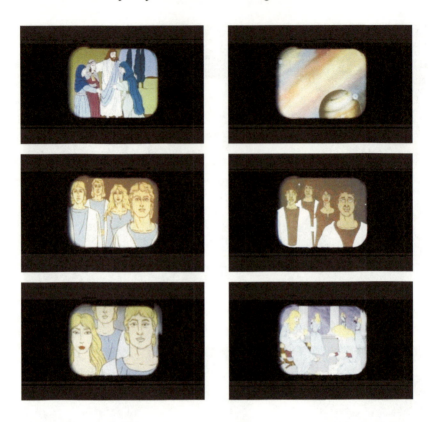

Fig. 173/ Fig. 174/ Fig. 175/ Fig. 176/ Fig. 177/ Fig. 178 The footage of The God Makers is rather simple and the audience might be surprised that Joyce McKinney, with a self-declared IQ of 168, believes everything Mormons say about themselves (Tabloid, 00:03:14/ 00:03:21/ 00:03:22/ 00:03:27/ 00:03:30/ 00:03:32).

met Anderson. No mention is made of the change to this policy in 1978. By 2010 this characterization of the institutional church was anachronistic, but McKinney's statement about what was hidden from her remains valid. Mormon dress is a further topic addressed here. McKinney explains that while she and Anderson were in the rented cottage she wanted to massage his back but was unable to do so because of the garment covering Anderson's body. "How am I supposed to give a back rub with this Mormon thing on it (00:21:58–00:22:01)?" She decided to rip the garment off and burn it in the fire place "…because they smelled, you know, and they had those, … occultic symbols…(fig. 179)."

10. Telling about Mormons

Fig. 179 Some random "occultic symbols" are faded in (Tabloid, 00:22:06).

Fig. 180 The tabloid shows how the McKinney case led to Mormonism becoming a matter of public interest. With the reconstruction of the story, these "secrets" are again brought to life (Tabloid, 00:22:40).

Accompanied by explanations given by Williams, extracts from the English tabloid *Sunday People* are shown in rapid succession, ending as a gong resounds as the title "Chastity suit revealed" (fig. 180) appears. The editing alludes not only to the printing of the newspaper but also to the sensational effects provoked by the *Sunday People*.

Williams explains that people continue to wear the garments even though they no longer attend the Mormon church. His gestures are intended to suggest the underwear is absurd.

The next religious lesson concerns sexuality, with Williams again the expert and his explanations again illustrated with the Mormon cartoon *God Makers*, in which a blond young man becomes Lucifer to the sound of thunder claps. The transformation into the devil is contrasted with a couple who marry in white, walk into heaven, and fly into space. In a voice-over during the cartoon Williams explains the temple ritual of the Melchizedek priesthood during which the members receive the "sacred underwear" and a secret knowledge of the key to heaven. During this ritual of endowment they are told "in a menacing tone" (00:32:43) that those who do not abide by the covenants into which they have entered – for example, in remaining chaste – they will end up under the control of Lucifer. Chastity is understood as meaning that intercourse happens only with a legally married partner. During this temple ritual an actor plays the part of Lucifer. The sequence is accompanied by a mystical music score.

During the interview Morris asks Williams: "'Manacled Mormon Sex Slave' wrecks that?" referring back to the tabloid headlines recently displayed. Williams answers: "Completely wrecks that. If Kirk Anderson was a willing 'Manacled Mormon', he will have violated his temple covenants,

Part III: The Ethical Space of Documentaries and Religion

violated the law of chastity, violated his temple covenants." "Manacled Mormon" is inserted as soon as Williams repeats the title. "What he risks is excommunication from the church and ... [cut] ... greater than that [cut] ... unless he repents, he won't be able to ultimately become a God ... and have his own planet. That is Mormon theology. That's what they are working towards." As Williams names the law requiring chastity a black-and-white photo of McKinney posing with a snake and an apple is inserted. Red markings signal that the photo was the work of a professional photographer (fig. 181).

Fig. 181 The insert of the photograph show McKinney referencing Eva and the garden of Eden motive with an apple and a snake (Tabloid, 00:33:29).

The lesson about Mormon theology is steered by the director's question, which quotes a tabloid headline. The sensationalism of the digression comes from the use of tabloid styling. While the facts about Mormonism are correct, the narrative shapes their presentation in an entertaining mode.

Most of the information about Mormonism provided by this documentary comes in the first third of the film, through the gazes of ex-missionary Williams, McKinney and Morris. The moral reasoning mode involves the combination of an intimate mode, achieved through the interview recording technique, and a sensational mode. Although all the social actors agreed to be interviewed, the interviews are a central artistic means of posing ethical questions. And what of the responsibility of the director? The camera gaze shows that the protagonists seem to enjoy receiving Morris's attention during the interviews. The focus on the church's suppressive tactics and brainwashing and on sex sensationalizes and entertains. The figure of the mute Mormon and the story of three days of S&M experience are especially sensational when set against the Mormon ideal of chastity.

The complex narrative structure makes it difficult to determine the possible loyalties of the viewer. The film might offend Mormons, for Kirk Anderson is presented as strange and inapproachable; neither are they likely to identify with Joyce McKinney, who loves the man but rejects his religious affiliations. Non-Mormons receive a one-sided and only partly accurate picture of Mormonism, as the narrative does pursue neither neutrality nor advocacy; indeed, its presentation of the information is distinctly skewed. The mode of moral reasoning can be described as involving the impossibility of access to absolute information or as relaying that life events exist in multiple versions, dependent on the perspective from which they are told and how they are experienced.

The account of Mormonism given in the documentary is not current. The narration refers to Mormonism in 1977, when, for example, black people were not given equal rights by the church. So what are the hermeneutic horizons of the film in relation to Mormonism? Knowledge of McKinney's story and the "Manacled Mormon" of 1977 is now limited and largely a product of a vague memory of the tabloid version of the incident. A cinephile audience, film scholars for example, will situate *Tabloid* in the context of Morris's oeuvre. Mormons are not the intended audience. Ex-Mormon Williams reinforces the exclusion of Mormons from the story as his specialist knowledge is critical and negative. His account of the church's teachings is often condescending, and his rhetoric is enhanced by the style of the narration. *Tabloid* does not provide a balanced representation of Mormonism, which is instead used in an argument about the ambiguities of the representation of reality. Religion is an obvious and effective realm in which to situate that argument, for its interpretative nature allows for different perspectives. Inadvertently, through his silence the "manacled Mormon" Anderson supports the version of Mormonism delivered by Errol Morris, Joyce McKinney and Troy Williams, whose criticism is recounted via tabloid sensationalism. The next two documentaries discussed here adopt a different strategy for convincing their audiences of the case they seek to make, for their filmic style is less complex and at the same time very close to their social actors.

Part III: The Ethical Space of Documentaries and Religion

10.2. Revealing abuses in the FLDS Church

The documentary *Sons of Perdition* (Tyler Measom and Jennilyn Merten, US 2010, 85') deals with the Fundamentalist Church of Jesus Christ of Latter-Day Saints (FLDS) and sheds light on abuses in the community through the eyes of four teenagers who are no longer members. The title *Sons of Perdition* references a term used in Mormonism for followers of Satan who will not live in a Kingdom of Glory. The boys who are the subject of the documentary were under enormous pressure to please the leader in order to be allowed to marry. Marriages were arranged by Warren Jeffs, the prophet and leader of the polygamy-practicing FLDS, who decides how worthy a man is on the basis of that man's submissiveness to his own directions. Women are chosen for marriage by the leader and assigned to a man, who may be far older than his wives. If a man is obedient to the system and regarded as worthy by the leader, he may be rewarded with several wives. The details of this polygamist marriage practice are specific to the FLDS and are not shared by all polygamist groupings. With one man marrying more than one woman, not all men can marry. Male teenagers and young men who decide to leave the group are called "sons of perdition" – they have left the sacred space of the religious community and are living in what FLDS members believe to be the "sinful world outside."

The film shows the difficulties faced by teenagers who no longer live according to the strict rules of the polygamist lifestyle controlled by Warren Jeffs and have left their families. Some of the teenagers portrayed in the documentary are guests in a couple's home for a while; others go to a shelter for teenagers from polygamist families. The film follows the social actors organizing their lives from scratch: some work on constructions sites, others prepare to go to high school as soon as they have the fixed address needed for enrollment. One important narrative thread is filmed with a hidden camera and is both thrilling and sensational. The film team accompanies Joe (17), who was beaten by his father, as he tries to get his mother and siblings out of the community; after two unsuccessful attempts his mother and siblings finally arrive with him.

Sons of Perdition premiered at the Tribeca Film Festival in New York City and was also presented at other festivals, where it received several prizes. At the Salt Lake City Film Festival it won the *Best of Fest Award*, which is not surprising as its critical view of polygamy is in line with the stance of the LDS Church.⁵⁹⁴ It was also screened in several theaters in the US, usually for no longer than a week. The film was produced by Left Turn Films, of which both directors are partners. The film was coproduced and distributed by the OWN documentary club, owned by media personality Oprah Winfrey. Winfrey praised the film when it was aired on her network on 2 June 2011 and also appears on the DVD. The end credits start with a reference to Holding Out Help, an organization that supports those who leave polygamous groups, with a mission to help people "to transition from isolation to independence."⁵⁹⁵ The reference to this organization is indicative of a central aim of the documentary in seeking to inform its audience about the situation facing outcasts from polygamous groups and the repressive lifestyle of these groups.

Directors Tyler Meason and Jennilyn Merten are both ex-LDS members, which determines their hermeneutic horizons and loyalties.⁵⁹⁶ Meason served as a missionary but left the church because of its support for Proposition 8, created by opponents of same-sex marriage. Both directors know Mormonism as insiders and share their opinions publicly.⁵⁹⁷ Meason took part in the counter campaign *I Am an Ex Mormon* with the video *I'm a searcher, I'm a wanderer, I'm a filmmaker* (US 2011) and he was the field producer of *Believer* (US 2018), a documentary about the front man of the rock band *Imagine Dragons*, a former LDS Mormon.⁵⁹⁸ Their loyalties are clearly with the teenagers and all Ex-Mormons. Their interest in informing audiences about abuses in the FLDS community intersects with the LDS Church leaders' opinion, who have very clearly distanced themselves from polygamy. The LDS Church is not the filmmakers' focus, although some Ex-FLDS members reach out to become members of the LDS Church. The documentary's critical take on how polygamy is experienced is in line with

---

594 "Sons of Perdition Screenings," accessed November 13, 2018, http://www.sonsofperditionthemovie.com/Sons_of_Perdition_Screenings.html.
595 "Holding Out Help – Helping, Encouraging, & Loving Polygamists," accessed November 12, 2018, http://holdingouthelp.org/.
596 Measom appears as interview host on the blog "Mormon Stories," where Ex-Mormons talk about their experiences after leaving the church. See "900–902: Tyler Measom – Documentary Filmmaker," *Mormon Stories* (blog), accessed November 9, 2018, https://www.mormonstories.org/podcast/tyler-measom/.
597 "Reason.Tv: The Sons of Perdition Filmmakers on Warren Jeffs' Polygamist Church – Hit & Run," Reason.com, July 29, 2010, accessed November 9, 2018, https://reason.com/blog/2010/07/29/reasontv-the-sons-of-perdition.
598 "'I'm a Searcher, I'm a Wanderer, I'm a Filmmaker.' | I Am an Ex Mormon," accessed November 13, 2018, http://www.iamanexmormon.com/2011/08/im-a-searcher-im-a-wanderer-im-a-filmmaker/.

Part III: The Ethical Space of Documentaries and Religion

the LDS Church's interest in rejecting its polygamous past, which is not the case for other shows, such as *Sister Wives (TLC, US 2010–2020)*, *Three Wives, and One Husband (Netflix, US 2017, six episodes)* or the documentary series *Polygamy, USA*, which present a more positive view of polygamy.

Unlike the filmmaker, the social actors have had limited experience of the world beyond the FLDS. The narrative makes this ingenuousness clear to its audience as, for example, when Joe is shown confusing Hitler with Bill Clinton. The scene could have been cut to protect the social actor, but the directors appear to have been concerned to show the young people's lack of education. Joe explains to Merten, who is not in the picture, the nature of the history he was taught (01:00:11–01:00:36). Warren Jeffs, he recounts, talked only of the prophets' lives. Mertens asks about the subject of the previous night's discussion. Joe answers that it was "Pretty cool. We talked about World War I and II and Bill Clinton about how he fried all the little kids." Merten responds with surprise: "Bill Clinton? Not about Bill Clinton." Joe asks: "What's his name?" Mertens: "You mean Hitler?" Joe confirms: "Hitler. Who is Bill Clinton?" Joe is left sitting with this question, for the director does not respond, and his ignorance has been exposed to the audience. During the three seconds the camera rests on Joe in a medium shot, it makes evident that he does not know what he is talking about and feels uncomfortable (fig. 182).

Fig. 182 The camera's gaze rests on Joe's irritated face when he confuses Hitler and Bill Clinton and does not know who Bill Clinton is (Sons of Perdition, 01:00:36).

Only a few experts participate on camera. A number of Ex-FLDS adults who handled the transition successfully tell about their experiences. Author Jon Krakauer, whose non-fiction book *Under the Banner of Heaven*

10. Telling about Mormons

Fig. 183 Children and mothers in prairie dresses are picnicking in a park. One woman is evidently pregnant. They are filmed from a car window (Sons of Perdition, 00:03:17).

(2003) is set in an FLDS milieu, appears in a short interview.[599] Most of the social actors share a background in the FLDS, which they have fled recently or some time ago. They have traumatic experiences in common and most have lost contact with their families. They share the sympathies of the filmmakers. Loyalty to the FLDS runs counter to the thrust of the documentary's moral reasoning and is represented only rarely and mostly without prior agreement, filmed with a hidden camera and with faces obscured.

The hidden camera and other approaches to the social actors are revealing of modes of moral reasoning at play in this documentary. In the opening sequence, for example, several long shots from a car window show in blurred slow motion the landscape where members of the FLDS Church live. Men are working in the fields and women in colored prairie dresses are looking after the playing children. Warren Jeffs preaches in the voice-over, accompanied by harmonic and slow banjo riffs. The inserted title says: "Voice of the prophet Warren Jeff": "All young people, eternity is within your reach, if you will just live faithful so the prophet can place you properly in marriage. I want you to believe these stories. There are no monogamous in heaven (fig. 183). Men have many wives. And that is the way men become gods and wives become heavenly mothers. I want to tell you young people, it's a sin to even talk about boyfriends and girlfriends because you know the right way. But what happens to people who turn away from it? The revelation says they will be destroyed."

---

[599] Krakauer, *Under the Banner of Heaven*.

Part III: The Ethical Space of Documentaries and Religion

After this panoramic introduction to the place where the teenagers have been raised with Warren Jeff in the voice-over, 17-year-old Sam is introduced. He is sitting in a car and looking out of the window. The editing suggests that the audience follows the young man's gaze and listens to his inner voice, where he is remembering Jeff's prophetic sermon. The director then asks Sam if he gets nervous when he returns to his home place. The camera frames his face in an extreme close-up from the side. Sam does not appear comfortable, with the question seeming already to describe Sam's current emotional state. He quickly rejects the thought because "they can't do anything to me... I'm getting nervous when I see my Dad though" (00:04:22–00:04:00).

The close camera on the protagonist's face combined with the view out of the window immediately establish that the gaze of this documentary is on the young former member of the FLDS Church. It also tells the audience that the narration is seeking to be as close as possible to the social actors. The camera wants to grasp the fear and insecurity the teenager feels before he meets his parents. Another moment of intimacy and exposure is even closer, when the teenagers are dancing at the home of Don and Suzanne, a couple who host teenagers who have left (01:05:45–01:08:31). Some of the young people are obviously drunk (fig. 184). Sabrina and her friend dance exuberantly to the rhythm of loud stomping disco music. They seem no longer aware of the camera.

Fig. 184 Sabrina and her friend are dancing exuberantly, filmed by a camera that takes part in the action without being noticed (Sons of Perdition, 01:05:41).

In a conversation cut in between the dancing scenes, Hillary recounts that she knew nothing of sex when she got married aged 17. At the time of the documentary she is 24. Her four children still live in the FLDS community. After the interview Sabrina is again shown drunk and dancing, now on another occasion (she is wearing different clothes). Exhausted from the dancing, she finally falls down on the floor. The other young people try to help her to get up, give her some water to drink, and ask her if she needs assistance. Sabrina gets up, walks into the kitchen and accidentally smashes a glass on a counter. Her brother moves her away from the pieces of broken glass. Sabrina cries, stumbles back into the living room and again falls on the floor (fig. 185/186).

 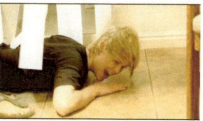

Fig. 185/ Fig. 186 The camera is extremely close, exposing Sabrina's misery. When she cries, the camera zooms out and the social actor is permitted some more intimate space, but the focus is still painfully close (Sons of Perdition, 01:07:59/ 01:08:08).

After a while Sabrina starts to cry hysterically. Joe comments: "When she is drunk all the memories from the Crick come out." The sequence ends with a sad and speechless Joe filmed in a medium shot. What is the function of this intimate mode in the narration? Should the camera film such moments when the social actors are not in control of the situation or of themselves? Are the filmmakers still loyal to their protagonists or are they more interested in filming intimacy or even sensation? The scene suggests that the social actors enjoy their freedom but are not yet in control of their lives. Their behavior is not at all in accord with the moral standards by which they lived in the FLDS community. The intimate mode has become sensational and the audience has become voyeuristic, an experience neither required nor necessary.

We have noted the sensational mode that is a product of the use of a hidden camera. This mode is adopted when some of the social actors have not agreed to be filmed, which is ethically problematic. We see such an example when Joe's father drives to the house where his wife is staying with their children after leaving the family home (fig. 187). The husband asks about his wife and wants her to come out to talk to him in person. Joe's host appears to be talking to the husband and then hands him a cell phone so that he can talk to his wife. The husband rejects this suggestion and insists (00:37:32): "I'm not answering to you. I want to hear her say no."

Fig. 187 The hidden camera films the dialogue between the rejected husband and the person hosting his family, who tries to negotiate (Sons of Perdition, 00:37:39).

The scene is filmed through the window of a car parked on the street opposite the house. Although the dialogue is fairly audible, subtitles transcribe it. The host calls the police, and the teenagers standing close to the car seem nervous. Suspense-generating music indicates the dangers of the situation. The same camera and editing style are repeated in other situations, too, when the teenagers meet members of the FLDS Church who would similarly not have agreed to be filmed.

The mode of moral reasoning is used here to reveal inequality, to show how a religious system suppresses these teenagers, and to call for an end to such exploitation. The lives of the teenagers are at the center of the narration. The oppression they have experienced is represented by images taken from a car as it is driven through the community. These images are in a way stolen, as we can assume that this filming took place without permission. Additionally, the underage teenagers are open and allow the camera to be present in intimate situations. Even though the filmmakers are loyal to their subject, we wonder if they will benefit from appearing in the documentary, with its intimate depictions, in the long term. Further we might consider the extent to which the filmmaking has steered the story and events. For example, when Joe goes to his family's home to persuade his mother to leave the community, the presence of the camera supports his plans and encourages him. The camera provides the social actor with some protection because everything is being filmed; it can claim to be part of the teenager's emancipation, with the final credits depicting the three main characters in their new lives and suggesting their achievements (01:24:05–01:24:30). Joe is employed at a prestigious resort in Park City, Utah. Sam, who poses with his brother Wayne, works full time and looks after his younger brother, who was forced to leave Colorado City, AZ. Bruce is married and "the proudest father you'll ever meet" according to the title. He is shown with his wife and baby. Hillary, Joe's sister, and his other siblings go to school; Jorjina is writing a cookbook "that should sell like hot cakes." At the very end a picture of Warrens Jeff is inserted with the caption: "In August 2011, Warren Jeffs was sentenced to life by the Texas Prison System. He still maintains control over Colorado City." Jeff may be controlling Colorado City but he is no longer controlling Joe, Wayne, Bruce, Hillary and Jorjina, a new situation to which the film has contributed.

We would expect the loyalties of the audience to lie with the teenagers; only members of the FLDS community might feel differently and with all forms of media consumption strictly forbidden, they are unlike to watch the documentary. The film uses an advocacy mode[600] to convince the audience of a cause, but it also applies sensational and intimate modes. The film's purpose is to attract the audience's attention and to cause them to side with the Ex-FLDS teenagers and young adults. Some scenes show footage of Warren Jeff being arrested, in court or in prison. His weak voice becomes menacing when heard in the context of the teenagers' stories. The audience are encouraged by the narration to form a specific picture of the FLDS Church. They are provided with information – for example television footage is used to inform the audience about the history of the FLDS Church after Warren Jeff's father handed its leadership to his son – in a form that presents it as a strange, repressive, secluded, and abusive religious group. The narrative excludes positive or even neutral statements about the FLDS Church. While no member of the FLDS community may have been willing to talk to the filmmakers, it seems also possible that they were omitted on purpose. The documentary is not intended to provide a balanced depiction of the FLDS and its former members. *Sons of Perdition* informs its audience about sexual and mental assaults within a religious community that were inflicted on social actors who are willing to be open about their experience. This balance of exposure and information is also an issue in the next documentary we shall consider.

---

600 Aufderheide, *Documentary Film*, 77–90.

Part III: The Ethical Space of Documentaries and Religion

10.3. The LDS Church as supervising shadow

Meet the Mormons (UK 2015, 46') was produced by Channel 4 in the series *True Stories* and distributed by the streaming platform *Real Stories*, which specializes in documentaries.[601] The platform has a section entitled "Religious Documentaries," which contains films that are mostly critical of religious institutions. The section includes titles such as *Forced Marriage Cops* (Channel 4, UK 2015) and *Scientology: Mysterious Death* (NTV, DE 2014). *Meet the Mormons* (which should not be confused with the documentary of the same name that is produced by the LDS Church and was discussed earlier in this chapter) tells about the hardships and sacrifices of becoming and being a young missionary. Unlike the narratives produced directly or indirectly by the LDS Church, this narrative takes an outsider perspective. The filmmaker, Lynn Alleway, follows 20-year-old Josh Field as he becomes a missionary. While staying with a Mormon couple, Field spends seven months at the missionary center in Lancaster, United Kingdom, where he is taught about proselytizing, *The Book of Mormon*, and the daily routine of a missionary. He is also taught about the people he may encounter: they may be struggling in their marriages, with health problems or financial issues, the instructor at the mission center explains to the newly arrived. Such individuals may in turn be looking for help, friends, and comfort in the gospel. Through the "setting-apart" ritual, Field is finally incorporated into the community of the LDS Church mission, separated from his family and sent out as a missionary in Leeds, United Kingdom. The film focusses on Field's emotional struggles, particularly as he misses his family; while other missionaries are also homesick, they seem better able to live with their unhappiness. During the filming, the director comes to care for the main social actor and feels for him in his misery. Elder Field, his official missionary title, continues in his mission even though he is fighting homesickness and sadness or even suffering depressive episodes.

The filmmaker's hermeneutic horizons are influenced by her professional experience as a journalist. Currently Lynn Alleway is a producer and director of documentaries for *Modern Times*, a BBC Two documentary series.[602] During the production of a film Alleway will often spend a great deal of time with the social actors. *Meet the Mormons* was filmed over six

---

601 Again the title of the episode is not to be confused with the already discussed documentary *Meet the Mormons* (Blair Treu, US 2014).
602 "Lynn Alleway – About," accessed December 4, 2018, http://www.lynnalleway.com/about/.

months, during which the director met Field several times. She was never able to speak to him alone, as a church representative was always also present, listening and observing their conversation. Repeated reference to this situation is made by means of cutaways. Cutaways usually present a secondary activity parallel to the main scene. They provide the context for an activity, for the camera can show only what is in front of it and not what is happening simultaneously to the left, right or behind it. Alleway's loyalties are evidently with Field. She is the only person that Josh Field meets outside the church. All the social actors are Mormons who know what it means to be a missionary. They differ from Field only in their positive relation to the mission. That positive relationship can be combined with the sadness of mothers who weep as their sons leave for the missionary field.

The director's interactions with the main social actor and the camera gaze that tries to encounter him in a private space are key to the film's efforts to ensure the audience sympathizes with Field. The film uses different narrative styles. Discussions involving filmmaker and social actors alternate with information about Mormonism and specifically about missionary work. The nature of life as a Mormon is commented in voice-over by the filmmaker and represented visually with, for example, images of Mormon temples from inside and outside, references to Mormon underwear, and observation of missionaries during training or going about their daily routines.

At the very beginning of the documentary, the filmmaker explains that she was allowed to enter a temple and that the church wanted her to make a positive film about the LDS faith. She explains what baptism of the dead is, and images of fountains with twelve oxen are shown, signifying the twelve tribes of Israel. Alleway remarks (00:01:48–00:02:19): "I soon realized that this was a church anxious about its public image." After this introduction to the issue of image control, Alleway meets the main social actor at a parking lot and accompanies him to a Mormon dance evening. Des, a representative of the LDS Church is introduced, with the director explaining that he will be consistently present (00:03:13–00:03:26): "He is going to be present for all of the filming, listening to everything that I say to Josh and everything Josh says back to me. It was strange not be able to talk to Josh on my own."

Control and observation by church officials during filming are treated in detail in a scene in which the filmmaker visits Field at the Leeds home of his hosts, both church members, where he is preparing for the mission. The sequence introduces Richard as LDS Church supervisor and an un-

333

Part III: The Ethical Space of Documentaries and Religion

wanted presence during filming. Alleway complains in the voice-over that she was unable to ask the questions she wanted to, for example on the subject of celibacy (00:09:46–00:11:06): "Questions about being celibate had already got me into trouble. But I hadn't yet asked Josh about how he coped with the rules governing sex and masturbation. We should be joined by church official Richard. He'd been told to listen to all the conversations in the home including in twenty-year-old Josh's bedroom."

In general, the presence of LDS Church representatives within the narrative skews the director's intent. They define who will appear on the screen and deprive the filmmaker of the ability to select her own subjects. Often the church officials emerge from the background to intrude into the space of representation. The LDS Church representatives reverses roles: rather than have the camera enter into private lives, the LDS Church takes up an unwelcomed place in front of the camera (fig.188).

Fig. 188 Richard is reading in a corner, trying not to attract attention (Meet the Mormons, 00:09:39).

Fig. 189 Richard is leaving his hiding-place after his hosts have requested that he says hello (Meet the Mormons, 00:09:47).

The question of who decides what happens and what is shown becomes a power game played by filmmaker and LDS Church. The camera is the filmmaker's personal weapon. It records places and situations that are evidence of hierarchy amongst the social actors and demonstrates that Josh is low on the ladder.

The first time Alleway mentions the mute guest hidden behind the camera, she jokes: "He made himself so scarce that we can't find him." She invites Richard to speak (fig. 189): "Come say hello, Richard," and explains to the audience, "The church's representative today is Richard."

Richard's task is to stay close enough to hear everything that is said but at the same time to keep out of the picture. He emerges to say: "Good evening, I just sit." Then Josh asks Richard if he would like something to

10. Telling about Mormons

drink. It seems odd that Richard is hidden in a corner, invisible to the camera, with so much attention upon him. Alleway doesn't surrender. She films Richard sitting in the corner and drinking his glass of milk (fig. 190).

Fig. 190 The church official inconspicuously drinks his glass of milk. His intended discreetness is penetrated by the camera gaze (Meet the Mormons, 00:10:08).

Fig. 191 Richard is no longer amused and seems to feel hassled by the camera (Meet the Mormons, 00:10:14).

Richard finally agrees to being questioned and the filmmaker asks what he is doing here. At this point the camera is close to the social actor and frames Richard from a high angle (fig. 191).

Richard can evade neither the gaze of the camera nor her question: "What instructions has the church given you?" Richards starts stammering: "I think it's – it's – it's just really to facilitate – to reassure – ." "Reassure what?" asks the filmmaker. The camera shows Field looking out the window. The shot highlights that there is nothing here to facilitate or about which to reassure. From off-screen Richard continues: "…just the fact that everything is ok. And there is someone there who, who, who, not just is responsible but who, who is there to – um – that everything is above board."

As the living room does not provide privacy, the filmmaker asks Field if they can talk in his bedroom. She is obviously looking for a private space where she can talk to Field alone. Field asks almost impatiently: "Why do you want me?" but the filmmaker seems more concerned about Richard: "Where is Richard going?" Field: "Richards sits down at the door" (00:11:06–00:11:17). Again, the camera shows Field's perspective on Richard, who is sitting around the corner (fig. 192). As soon as Field mentions "the law of chastity", Richard lifts his head and listens attentively.

335

Part III: The Ethical Space of Documentaries and Religion

Fig. 192 Again, Richard sits around the corner, attentively listening to the conversation between the filmmaker and Josh when the keyword "chastity" is used (Meet the Mormons, 00:11:16).

Fig. 193 For the first time Josh is framed in a close-up and is able to answer the filmmaker's questions (Meet the Mormons, 00:11:27).

Eventually the camera frames Josh in a close-up and it seems that for the first time the filmmaker is able to approach Josh without interference from a church official (fig. 193). During the conversation with Josh, cutaways to Richard let the audience know that the discussion is being supervised.

The conversation between Josh and Alleway centers on sexuality and its regulation for unmarried LDS Church members. At first Josh seems to provide personal insights into the topic, but the footage from an LDS Church educational film explaining the meaning of virtue proves otherwise, for Josh's statement exactly corresponds with the church's official opinion about sexuality. The editing makes evident that Field's thoughts have been memorized from the church's official teachings.

During the course of the narrative the filmmaker expresses sympathy for Field's situation. She is critical of church officials, confronting the missionary president as the following sequence shows (00:22:01–00:26:33). The filmmaker comments that Elder Field was crying and asks him why. Ashamed, Field answers that he misses his family. The camera is directed at an LDS Church official who is sitting around the corner and listening to the conversation. Field explains that he has realized that he will not see his family for two years. "This makes me sad" (00:22:30-00:22:32). He sniffs and tries to suppress his tears (fig. 194). The filmmaker exposes Josh's emotional condition and at the same time becomes his friend.

10. Telling about Mormons

Fig. 194 The filmmaker approaches Josh who is struggling because he misses his family so badly. Pitilessly, a close-up reveals his emotional condition (Meet the Mormons, 00:22:34).

Fig. 195 The camera frames Josh in a close-up and waits until he is able to talk (Meet the Mormons, 00:24:05).

Finally, the filmmaker confronts the mission president with Elder Field's sadness: "Couldn't he be a good missionary and still talk to his mum?" she asks. The president laughs: "Contact could actually be worse," he explains, continuing that this is a period of adjustment and that he is a counselor and therapist with experience in dealing with such emotional conditions. He gives Field some mind-quieting techniques. In a parallel editing with the interview, Field is shown sitting in classes at the mission center with his colleagues. The filmmaker's relationship with Josh is now more exclusive. By this point she is the only person outside the missionary center with whom Josh is in contact. In the voice-over Alleway explains that Josh has become completely isolated. She asks Josh if he wants to talk. Josh cries, unable to control his emotional low (00:24:22–00:24:24). "Just sad," he says. The filmmaker responds: "I would like to give you a hug, but I'm not allowed to." Josh holds on to the positive aspects of being on mission (00:24:32–00:24:51): "I have to say I'm so happy to be here but it's just at the same time it is hard because you are giving up the ones you love. It's just difficult. That's just a part of it." Elder Field is under visible stress caused by his homesickness (fig. 195).

In the voice-over the filmmaker relates that it is hard to understand why Field does not return home to his family when he feels so unhappy. She immediately provides a response to her own question. Young people are expected to stay as a matter of faith, she states, with sorrowful music accompanying her comment. The narrative returns to the classes, showing other missionaries listening to the instructors. The first part of the narrative finishes with a final shot portraying the fairly depressive atmosphere at the missionary center. Elder Field is ready for his mission in Leeds.

Part III: The Ethical Space of Documentaries and Religion

Fig. 196 The Swiss missionary Baumann, Elder Field's companion, seems sure that he has the right to listen to the conversation between Alleway and Field. The low-angle shot emphasizes his intrusion (Meet the Mormons, 00:36:14).

Fig. 197 The camera catches people listening in to the conversation, like this man around the corner, who is probably Richard (Meet the Mormons, 00:36:22).

The filmmaker is increasingly concerned about Field's condition. During her visits to his apartment, Richard, the church official, is again present. The film observes the missionaries in their daily routines, such as starting their studies with a song followed by prayer. The filmmaker explains in the commentary that the missionaries must remain with their companions all the time.

> They must always stay in the same room together and the only time when they can be apart is when they go to the bathroom. This way they can keep an eye on each other in case they are tempted to stray. They always sleep in the same room and get up and go to bed at exactly the same time as each other because they must never even try to be alone,[603]

referencing her inability to film Field in private. Field's bleak situation is illustrated with cutaways of passers-by in Leeds, many of them with religious markers such as headscarves or turbans. The sky and streets in Leeds seem to be always grey, a harshness emphasized by intense classical piano music.

On another occasion, as the filmmaker tries to speak to Elder Field she hears a sound in the adjacent room. She asks if his companion Elder Baumann is there, because she heard his cellphone beeping (00:36:13-00:36:15). Baumann explains that "we usually stay within sight and sound of each other" (fig. 196).

---

603 *Meet the Mormons*, 00:34:15–00:34:40.

Elder Baumann seems to complete the control team, alongside Richard. He is instantly revealed in a cutaway shot of his hand holding the door frame (fig. 197). Other ears are evidently listening to the conversation.

Finally, Alleway asks how Elder Field is feeling (00:36:33–00:37:29): "I'm tired [smiles] but I feel ok. It's just difficult getting used to this [makes a gesture towards the bedroom]. It's just hard at the moment. But yeah, you get better." A long shot of Leeds is shown, with brown houses and brown trees, while Field continues: "I'm a bit down but it's a grieving process. It takes a while to adjust to missing people." Field tries almost apologetically not to admit that he is still depressed. And finally, the filmmaker asks: "If you were on your own you don't have someone here, a few feet away I mean, do you think you still be here?" Josh replies: "I would say, I cannot do it, I cannot do it." He sighs and looks at the filmmaker with a sad smile. In the voice-over she explains the duties of Mormon missionaries and the conditions in which they live (00:37:35–00:38:02): "Mormon missionaries have to work 356 days a year. So, for two years they never get a whole day off. Their set goals: In the first year the target is to recruit four new converts. To become a Mormon you are expected to pay 10% of your income to the church. And as full members you will also be expected to wear special underwear." The numbers are intended as evidence of the efforts and personal investment the church asks of its missionaries. With long shots of Bauman and Field on mission on the streets of Leeds, Alleway highlights again how demanding missionary work is.

The Elders' proselytizing efforts on mission are evidently not bearing fruit. They ask those they meet if they can talk about *The Book of Mormon*, but their offer is consistently rejected. Alleway comments (00:39:16–00:41:02): "For the last 18 days Elder Field has been constantly in his companion's presence. He hasn't been allowed to speak with any of his friends or family. He is forbidden from reading books or newspapers, listening to the radio, watching television, going on the Internet, going to the cinema, theater and nearly any other cultural activity."

Light and melodious guitar music accompanied by singing helps generate empathy for those experiencing the emotionally cold and disciplined daily life of mission. The two Elders are back in their room. Another morning begins. At sunrise they wake, kneel on the floor with their elbows on the bed, and pray. The shadow of a guardian, perhaps Richard, is shown in a cutaway (Fig. 198).

Part III: The Ethical Space of Documentaries and Religion

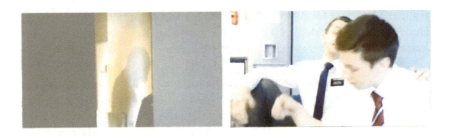

*Fig. 198 The missionaries' disciplined life is emphasized by the cutaway showing the shadow of the LDS Church official (*Meet the Mormons*, 00:41:02).*

*Fig. 199 Elder Baumann symbolizes with his hand on Elder Field's shoulder that Elder Field belongs to him and is under his control (*Meet the Mormons*, 00:44:20).*

A last unsuccessful attempt by Alleway to talk to Field takes place at the end of the documentary. The filmmaker's voice seems almost desperate during her visit (00:41:04–00:41:10): "I was concerned how Elder Field was coping. I wanted a moment with him to check if he is ok." The filmmaker tries to talk alone with Field, who explains that Elder Bauman will be present. Baumann stresses that he does not speak for Field but that "they stick together." Field mentions that on the previous occasion he was uncomfortable about being alone with her. The filmmaker asks (00:43:05–00:43:11): "How is it the two of you? I mean you have no privacy now." Elder Baumann repeats that he and Elder Field are friends, that they stick together. His comments seem almost intrusive, as is his physical presence: on several occasions he cups his hand on Josh's shoulder (fig. 199) and is often standing or sitting very close to him. In claiming that closeness to Field, Baumann is competing with the filmmaker.

Field supports Baumann's remarks and explains how great it is to do everything with a friend. He believes that God will reward him in life and in the afterlife for his sacrifice in going on mission. The filmmaker appears to doubt him and seeks, unsuccessfully, to dig deeper. The film ends with a longshot of Elder Bauman and Elder Field undertaking missionary work on the street; they ask passersby if they are interested in *The Book of Mormon*, but nobody is.

In *Meet the Mormons* the camera is used as a tool to reveal the harshness of the missionaries' daily life. The filmmaker Lynn Alleway is concerned about Fields' emotional state. The documentary shows how difficult it is to adapt to mission and how much these young men have to invest of themselves. The filmmaker's comments provide factual information about what is required of the missionaries. She equips the audience with knowledge about missionary work undertaken by members of the LDS Church. While the documentary proposes that circumstances experienced by the missionaries are unfair, even abusive, it also exposes the missionaries by asking questions they find embarrassing. Alleyway shows how that missionary life is controlled and allows no privacy, with the missionary expected to be submissive.

Through the cinematic mean of cutaways, the omnipresence of the church is referenced and revealed. With Elder Baumann the narrative presents an example how the institution successfully moulds young people according to its moral standards. The mode of moral reasoning presents the mission as demanding, with exaggerated requirements for the young people. The film shows how they are constantly observed and convinced to follow the church's ideals without question. The one-sided narrative allows for few divergent audience perspectives on the topic. The narrative unambiguously laments the suffering of Josh Field. The empathic attitude of the director facilitates the audience's sympathies for the young missionary and argues against the attitude of church officials.

But the reception of the documentary will still depend on the audience's hermeneutic horizons. Convinced Mormons loyal to the institution's mission practice might see Field's experience as an isolated case in which a weak young man is unable to adapt to the requirements of the mission. For Mormon missionaries with similar experiences, the film may be a relief and acknowledgement of their suffering. Non-Mormons would find it hard not to sympathize with Field and his homesickness, as reviews of the television show confirm. Reviews also highlight the filmmaker's unprecedented access to the LDS Church mission experience,[604] and the uncommon relationship between Alleway and Field: "Perhaps this breaks some conventions of documentary making, but the film is all the more touching and human for it."[605] One critic notes the lack of answers from "blank faced Elder Field. [...] These reminders of his inscrutability only made our frustration more acute."[606] Another review complains about the general unwillingness of the

---

[604] "Meet the Mormons, TV Review: Very Few Revelations on Mission," The Independent, June 27, 2014, http://www.independent.co.uk/arts-entertainment/tv/reviews/meet-the-mormons-tv-review-very-few-revelations-on-mission-to-uncover-mormonism-9566619.html.

[605] Sam Wollaston, "Meet the Mormons – TV Review," *The Guardian*, June 27, 2014, sec. Television & radio, https://www.theguardian.com/tv-and-radio/2014/jun/27/meet-the-mormons-tv-review.

[606] "Meet the Mormons, TV Review."

church's representative to talk about topics such as underclothing, sex, and the mission rules.⁶⁰⁷ That lack of information is key to the narrative of the documentary, which shows how young men are taught to obey without questioning. Alleway reveals the mechanisms of the missionary strategy with a journalistic gaze, applying an interventionalist mode that generates information about the emotional state of one of the missionaries. The director is sympathetic to Field, but she also has a responsibility for the wellbeing of the social actors. Her interventions are interrupted in turn by church members who want to be in control of the situation and intervene as they deem necessary in Alleway's relationship with Field.

One ethical question concerns whether the film improved Field's situation. We might wonder if he profited from his emotional openness or if the gains were reaped only by the documentary audience and the filmmaker. The journalistic gaze and interventional mode may have positive future outcomes but at the cost of the social actors. Field did not leave the mission and the filming may have reinforced his misery. But might the church itself or future missionaries be given pause for thought by *Meet the Mormons*? And perhaps the film will arouse sympathy or even compassion for young people who are on the street eager to talk to strangers about *The Book of Mormon*.

10.4. Telling about strange and perverted Mormon practices

Closing the circle of this sub-chapter entitled "Telling about Mormons," I pick up again the discussion of the episode *Meet the Polygamists* from the docu-series *Polygamy USA*. We end with a number of general observations and consider, for example, how the mode of moral reasoning of this documentary series is to be understood and where power lies in the images of religion given by the documentaries. As we have noted, the narrative of *Meet the Polygamists* combined sensational and informative modes. At the end of the first episode a title informs the audience that other than some leaders who feared legal persecution – their faces are blurred – most of the community agreed to be filmed. Some members express doubts about having allowed the cameras into their community at the end of the last season,

---

607 "Meet the Mormons, Channel 4, Review: 'awkward but Revealing' - Telegraph," accessed December 5, 2018, https://www.telegraph.co.uk/culture/tvandradio/tv-and-radio-reviews/10928747/Meet-the-Mormons-Channel-4-review-awkward-but-revealing.html.

but they hope for greater acceptance of their religion and polygamous family constellations. The mode of moral reasoning in this documentary is based on tolerance – the non-FLDS audience is asked to tolerate a community that wants to live its particular lifestyle in peace and seeks to convince the audience that it is harmless.

Meet the Polygamists includes images of children, with the permission of their parents. But when they are adults, how will these children feel about their having been filmed? This issue of permission-granting on behalf of minors is central to the ethical dimensions of the film. Another ethical aspect concerns the patriarchal nature of the community. Young women receive revelation about who they are to marry and the man chosen will surely agree, as one bachelor notes – polygamy means fewer women are available for first marriages. Both husbands and wives promote the filming of their community, but the men in polygamous marriages are at greater legal risk: they have multiple wives; their wives have only one husband. Wives still risk, however, the dissolution of their primary social unit. Are all parties fully conscious of the potential risks of being filmed? Many of the social actors know little of the world beyond Centennial Park, with their hermeneutic horizons limited to their family and community life. In 2013, when the docu-series was produced, they may have been ignorant of what it could mean to be filmed.

As we explore the ethical implications, we should also note that the filmed interactions between filmmaker and Mormon social actors in this production are less explicit and conspicuous than in other productions discussed in this work. The National Geographic documentary style defines the camera's gaze and the narrative style, which is informative and entertaining. Thus, during the interviews the filmmaker(s) is (are) never in the image and their voice is audible in the off only on a few occasions. The episodes are aesthetically developed but still essentially conventional, and on the whole the social actors are carefully and respectfully filmed. The results is a distance between the social actors of Centennial Park and the camera. The camera is seldom very close to its subject and it does not enter private or intimate spaces, unlike, again, in other documentaries discussed here. The production is not highly critical of the lifestyle of the community's members – indeed the image is of 1,500 people living a life of love and community spirit. National Geographic Ltd seems uninterested in revealing problems that might disturb the audience; their goal is to entertain that audience, not to challenge them with morally ambivalent issues that demand reflection. As their target audience includes families, the narration must be appropriate for minors. The audience is left to focus simply on the Centennial Park community and its

Part III: The Ethical Space of Documentaries and Religion

sympathetic residents without distraction. The hermeneutic horizons of the audience will influence their reception of the documentary. If they know little of Mormonism, then they may normalize this depiction, accepting it as a regular Mormon lifestyle, yet LDS Church Mormons reject both polygamy and its depiction, sensitive to being tarred with that brush. The documentary's reception by Ex-FLDS members who formerly practiced polygamy will surely be influenced by their negative experiences in this setting, while those who are open-minded about polygamy might watch the series with curiosity or even satisfaction. How, we might wonder, would the children of *Sons of Perdition* or of the inhabitants of Centennial Park respond to the documentary?

Having discerned the different loyalties and hermeneutic horizons in the communication spaces of the documentaries, we now must ask who has the power of meaning making in the space of production? The interaction between the camera and the social actors is crucial to defining the ethical space of a documentary. All the productions in this chapter depended on their social actors agreeing to be filmed. All who did agree shared some form of interest in having their story told. Some of them may have been comfortable with the camera; others, like Mormon Kirk Anderson in the *Tabloid*, did not want to participate; some, like the leaders of the Centennial Park community, wished to remain anonymous. Most of the wives and other women in *Meet the Polygamists* appear shy and were reluctant to talk with the director; at the end of the docu-series one wife mentions that they had not felt comfortable with the camera around them. Elder Field in *Meet the Mormons* (Lynn Alleway) was evidently not always at ease with the camera. Others, however, were self-confident and sometimes joyful in their interactions with the camera, as was the case for Joyce KcKinney, former Mormon Troy Williams, and *Daily Mirror* journalist Peter Tory in *Tabloid*, who avidly shared their versions of the story. In *Sons of Perdition* the camera seems almost like a friend to the teenagers, with the directors their allies in their difficult separation process from their religious community. The examples show the power of the camera and of the images that functions independently of the interests of the social actors. The latter might decide what they are willing to reveal about themselves, but how those revelations are filmed is not ultimately in their control. For the way a scene is filmed, how close the camera is and how the raw material is edited leave much space for the directors to steer a particular finalized reading mode, to use Foucault's term. This process empowers the filmmakers to define meaning and leaves the social actors who appear in front of the camera in a potentially weaker position. The camera is a tool deployed to wield power.

11. Religion as Sensation and Infotainment

The focus in the current chapter has been on the camera gaze and how it frames the events in front of the camera to analyze their ethical impact. Actions take place not only in front of the camera but also behind it, in the space of consumption where the audience is involved in the events by watching the documentaries. The examples show that religion is never depicted "objectively" or "neutrally". The representation of religion has meaning that is produced in the tension between the filmmaker, the camera and the social actors. The filmic meaning shapes the gaze on the social actors, the representation of religion, and the production's moral modes.

The modes used to represent religion and its related values communicate different moral reasonings. But where are these values located, what kind of values are they, and how do these values come to life? Documentaries always frame and value the facts of their subject from a specific perspective. These represented values are reproduced in the relationship between the spaces of representation and consumption. They are effective as soon as they are perceived and valorized by the audience. Each film and its moral reasoning therefore needs an audience, which is involved in the reception process.

Documentaries that address religion may not distinguish between facts and fiction, for example between historical facts and religious narratives, in their moral reasoning. The result can be an instrumentalization of religious narratives which are then presented as either true and good or ridiculous and dangerous with nothing in between. An observational mode is often missing, with the gaze on religion polarizing and sensational. Religion may appear as a hidden force for which people are only partly accountable – something extraordinary is happening to them and what they do is not theirs to decide.

Associated with a sensationalist intent are depictions of religion that are designed to be highly entertaining. Religion's role in a narrative may be to provide an OMG (Oh my God) moment, a term used to describe an emotional response involving surprise, disgust and fascination. The goal then is not an accurate representation of religion but rather engagement of the audience. This entertaining mode is one of the two main moral reading modes that define the gaze of the camera and it stirs an active audience response – laughter, shock, disgust, for example. It is also closely connected with the sensational mode, which may tell the audience that what they are seeing is extraordinary and therefore worth observing, and also filming. Sensationalism may be concerned to discover something new about religion that steers the audience's emotions and it may be deployed when the social actors have not agreed to be filmed. The emotional mode is similar, but the responses it raises involve a stronger connection, positive or negative, to the subject, for example in the form of empathy or animosity. An intimate mode reaches in close to the social actors. It crosses the public space and enters the private sphere, potentially at the cost of the social actor's privacy. And the final mode with entertaining qualities is the interventional mode. It may involve a journalistic gaze that tries to uncover problems and induce change that in the best case will have positive results for the social actors in future.

The second main moral reading mode is the informative mode, which aims to persuade the audience of a cause. It is closely connected to three other modes. The observational mode, which as we have noted is rarely applied in this selection of documentaries, is concerned not with audience response but instead shows its subject evolve in front of the camera, which is in turn always aware that its presence can change what it is filming. The advocacy mode always has informational qualities, but it seeks to convince its audience of a cause and elicit an active response. And, finally, the rational mode, the least common, is applied through moral reasoning based on a sound argument. The mode neither take sides nor manipulates the audience by steering its emotional responses.

These modes of moral reasoning are based on certain ethical principles. While the various documentaries discussed here are based on different principles, each pursues a distinct goal in its moral reasoning. Here we can usually consider those goals in terms of the group of films produced by Mormons and that produced by non-Mormons. On the surface, in *Sisterz in Zion* the mode of moral reasoning embraces the principle of equality. Its communication is not entirely successful as boundaries are still drawn between participants from different backgrounds, but this distinction is not the product of a conscious decision. The moral reasoning of the narration is guided by the ethical principle of equality within the LDS Church. A different principle guides *Nobody Knows. The Untold Story of Black Mormons*, in which Darius Gray has evidently forgiven the church its error. The ethical principle of forgiveness is therefore seen as a viable means of dealing with the racist past of the LDS Church. *American Mormon in Europe* and *American Mormon* apply a blunt moral reasoning, insisting or almost warning that non-Mormons must be well informed before they start to judge LDS Church members. The ethical principle here concerns avoiding judging without really knowing. In *Journey of Faith* the principle of moral reasoning has three features: scientific rhetoric is combined with emotional involvement and personal belief. The academic experts are personally invested in the cause of proving that *The Book of Mormon* is true. According to the film, both scientific accuracy and religious belief are needed to access the ethical principle of truth. The last production in institutional Mormonism-related films is *The Humanitarian*, discussed as pars pro toto of *Meet the Mormons*, which depicts LDS Church member Bishnu Adhikari, who is more successful than many in all that he turns his hand to. The film's moral reasoning defends the Mormon worldview by including only insider opinions and telling the audience not to underestimate Mormons. It connects the Mormon people's success with their religious affiliation and worldview. The ethical principle is based on the injunction: "Be a good Mormon and you will find success, for Mormonism is the best way of life." The productions in this section differ fundamentally from the other documentaries that are more critical of Mormonism, its teachings, practices, and worldview.

In *Tabloid* Errol Morris shows with a combination of the intimate and sensational modes that the truth cannot be accessed. He deconstructs any possibly credible story and lets the audience know that truth cannot be represented. Specifically, no truth is contained in religious worldviews. As an acclaimed documentary filmmaker Errol Morris has his own authority. Incredible events become credible because of the filmmaker's background. The moral reasoning is based on the principle that what really happened, the truth, can never be revealed. *Sons of perdition* applies a different moral reasoning, for as Ex-Mormons the filmmakers are personally involved. Their message is related to the principle of uncovering inequality, with a summons to stop the exploitation evident in the suppression of teenagers carried out within the religious system they depict. We might wonder if *Sons of Perdition* took the interests of the protagonists to heart, a question we might also ask of Lynn Alleway's *Meet the Mormons*. We would need to understand what those interests were, the subject for another documentary in its own right. The moral reasoning of Alleway's film is based on the ethical principle of accusation, presenting the LDS Church mission as demanding, with exaggerated requirements made on young people, and accusing the church of abusive practices. As we have seen, the filmmaker was intrusive and persistent in trying to keep up contact with the main social actor, Josh Field. Finally *Meet the Polygamists (Polygamy, USA)* is based on the ethical principle of tolerance, which asks outsiders to be open and accepting of the polygamist lifestyle. The narration shows the modest and morally correct interactions of the community and calls on its audience to be curious rather than judgmental.

Finally, we can consider the idea of responsibility. Is the entertaining mode, with its intimate, sensational, emotional, and interventionalist character, morally justified, and if so, under what circumstances? How shall we respond when people are filmed and exposed in situations of which they are not in control? Do we always have a right to know what is/has been going on in religious communities? Public interest arguments might give grounds for the boundaries of the private sphere to be crossed, even in an entertaining mode, but at the same time the gaze in the entertaining mode exposes victims and may be unhelpful or even harmful, a reality often rejected or at least left unexplored. Documentary narratives enter the private sphere of religious actors and communities because the lives of people who are different are fascinating. If the gaze is respectful and a distance is maintained, the audience might enter a foreign world and enlarge their horizons, but as we have seen, such is not always the case, for all parties defend their own interests, follow their own agendas, and made their own demands of the audience. The filmmakers are in a privileged position, with a power to show, and thus make permanently public, the private sphere of religious actors. Responsibility does not end with the production's distribution: the audience is the final link in a chain of production and consumption and must decide whether a depiction is morally justified or harmful for those involved – including the audience itself.

Part IV: Approaching Religion and Ethics in the
 Communication Spaces of Documentary Media

12. Concluding Thoughts

Each study, this one included, aims to redeem its promise to answer questions posed at the outset. In this final chapter the principal findings of this project are assembled into a single picture composed of details from each chapter. In particular, the discussion here will highlight the consequences of adopting different perspectives on the spaces of communication of religion in documentary media. Its goal is not to be comprehensive. Rather, just as light that has passed through a crystal fractures to reveal the range of the color spectrum, here the questions posed of our subject produce a visible spectrum comprising its component parts. It is those colors we turn to now.

How effectively has this study heightened our knowledge of communication of religion? For, in the words of Roger Odin:

> The tools proposed by the semio-pragmatic model don't claim any psychological or cognitive existence. Even if the starting point is phenomenological (one has to start somewhere), as soon as the tools are inscribed in the theory, they become purely heuristic. They are evaluated by demonstrating their efficacy in throwing light on communication processes.[608]

The theoretical basis of this study involved developing the semio-pragmatic model of communication spaces to systematize the interface of documentary media and religion and to understand how religion is reconstructed by documentary media. At the same time the research explored the role of documentary media in the communication and perception of religion in the public and private spheres.

The structure of this final chapter is as follows: first, we revisit the preceding chapters through an overview of the results of the research; then, by evaluating the reading modes worked out in the individual chapters, we

---

608 Odin, *Les espaces de communication*, 142. "Toutefois, les outils proposés dans le modèle sémio-pragmatique ne revendiquent pas une existence psychologique ou cognitive quelconque. Même s'ils ont un point de départ phénoménologique (il faut bien partir de quelque chose), une fois inscrit dans la théorie, ils prennent un statut purement *heuristique*. Leur évaluation se fera en fonction de leur efficacité à éclairer les processus communicationnels." Translation mine.

Part IV: Approaching Religion and Ethics in the Communication Spaces

consider how religion and Mormonism are engaged by the sources examined in the study; and, finally, we look again at the concept of religion encountered in this study.

12.1. *The interface of documentary media and religion*

The first part of the study presents the semio-pragmatic approach to documentary media in the spaces of communication, so in the spaces of production, representation, circulation/distribution, and consumption. Fundamentally, the approach locates the process of meaning making in the tensions between the space of consumption and the space of representation and as also shaped by the spaces of production and circulation/distribution. In this study the space of representation includes documentaries, television reports, advertisements, corporate films, and reality television shows, all of which are subsumed under the term "documentary media."

Documentary media offer different reading modes. The most salient is the documentary reading mode, in reference to a real enunciator that communicates a "reality" to which, in an ideal reception situation, reference is made by all the social actors in the spaces of communication. In such a case all those involved are located on the same "axis of relevance". Another reading mode closely related to the documentary reading mode is the moral mode, which produces values. The audience for documentary media will always ask if what they are seeing is true. Truth in the form of the authentic representation of events is understood as a positive and constitutive value of documentary media. Only if the documentary is credible will it persuade its audience of its moral reasoning.

The social actors in the spaces of communication are central to a semio-pragmatic understanding of documentary media and its connected practices. Religion is therefore approached through its social actors and their meaning-making practices, with religion itself understood as a form of communication. The reading modes in the space of consumption determine how religion is communicated – encoded and decoded by the social actors involved – in the various media practices.

12.2. *Spaces of communication under scrutiny*

The second part of the study, chapters 4–6, draws on varied sources and methods to explore the four spaces of communication. The discussion in

12. Concluding Thoughts

chapter 4 shows that although *I'm a Mormon* (LDS, 2010–2015) and *I Am an Ex Mormon* (US 2010–2015) differ in their spaces of communication, the two video campaigns also intersect. The analysis of the communication spaces reveals how the video series are in conversation with each other.

Thus, for example, for both video series displaying the happiness of the social actors is key. In the The Church of Jesus Christ of the Latter-day Saints (LDS Church) campaign the social actors are happy because they are members of the LDS Church; in the counter-campaign the social actors are happy because they no longer are members of the LDS Church. Similarly, the LDS Church has not made it possible for comments to be made on the campaign's webpage, whereas the *I Am an Ex Mormon* webpage facilitates such online discussions. Comment on the LDS Church videos is possible on YouTube. The church has tried to control access to the videos as it seeks to adopt a new face for the institution by avoiding the name "Mormon". The prominence and success of the *I'm a Mormon* campaign, which has left a strong mark in the public sphere, is a complication for this endeavor. The two video series demonstrate that the space of documentary media, and specifically the space of circulation in the Internet, cannot be controlled completely. The *I Am an Ex Mormon* videos are a response to the LDS Church campaign and as a result participate in the LDS Church space of communication. The discussion of the two campaigns in this study has highlighted how religious worldviews are reinterpreted and reconstructed in the documentary spaces of communication that influence, transform, and redefine the practices of religious communities.

Chapter 5 considers reality shows (RTV) that depict Mormons and Mormonism and asks about the relation between the binary categories of the private and the public and about how they influence the communication processes of religion. The comparison between the two RTV shows *The District* (LDS Church, US 2006/2012) and *Sister Wives* (TLC, US 2010–2020) demonstrates that both shows apply instructional and entertaining reading modes, if in different forms.

The District places the LDS Church institution at the center of the documentary narrative and provides detailed information about its mission activities and the rite of baptism. At the same time, however, the young missionaries' proselytizing experiences also contain entertaining qualities. In contrast, *Sister Wives* keeps the religious institution to which the polygamous family belongs in the background and entertains the audience with the vibrant everyday lives of the four wives, their husband, and their numerous children. The polygamous family uses the show, however, to pro-

Part IV: Approaching Religion and Ethics in the Communication Spaces

vide information about its problematic legal status and advocates in the public space created by the show for the legalization of polygamy.

In both cases, the show's success is measured by viewer numbers. In the case of *The District*, the producers hope that viewers will be open to contact the church, perhaps through missionaries like those depicted, and ideally might eventually present themselves for baptism, as also depicted in the show. In the case of *Sister Wives*, the producers hope that high viewer figures will help sell the advertising space available before, after and during the broadcast of the show. In both cases the social actors are a vital link in a business strategy and religion is part of commodification.

Chapter 6 examines religion in the communication spaces of documentary media with approaches developed in social science. The results of the semio-pragmatic analysis of a sequence from *Meet the Mormons* (Blair Treu, US 2015) were used to produce questionnaires about perceived values, opinions, and attitudes. The study confirmed the effectiveness of the semio-pragmatic tool for scrutinizing the reading modes of a documentary. It also revealed, however, cultural differences between participants in Spain and participants in Switzerland: the former were generally less critical of the depiction of Mormons and Mormonism, but the later expressed greater interest in knowing more about Mormonism. These differences might be explained by the extent of existing knowledge of Mormonism, including prejudices toward the church, or a more positive attitude toward documentary media or religion. The study also disclosed how effectively documentaries can promote a positive attitude toward Mormonism, and thus potentially toward other religious institutions and religion more broadly.

The second part of chapter 6 looks at a series of interviews with LDS Church media professionals that addressed how their religious background interacts with their media work. The evaluation of these qualitative interviews focuses on seven aspects that emerged in these conversations. Firstly, the media professionals note feeling alienated from much mainstream media production and suggest that they are motivated to work in the media as a means of bringing light to this "dark media landscape." Second, they mention their willingness to forego career and money in order to work for the LDS Church, finding their reward instead in being able to contribute to productions in line with their worldview. Third, their professional media work allows them to define Mormonism for themselves and for the audience. Fourth, they produce media for the non-Mormon world but also for Mormons, which included the use or nonuse of an emic communication style that one interviewee called "Mormonese". Fifth, media productions for non-Mormons are an opportunity to show who the Mormons "really" are by representing "authentic" Mormons. Sixth, media professionals appointed by the church do not feel their professional contributions are controlled by church leaders, but independent LDS Church media professionals value the greater freedom of productions not dependent on the financial backing of the church. Seven, the LDS Church media professionals talked about their faith, highlighting individual agency in determining the truth of *The Book of Mormon* and whether to become a member of the LDS Church, a concept that could be in conflict with the proselytizing efforts of LDS Church missionaries.

Together the audience study and the interviews show how the communication spaces of consumption and production meet in the space of representation. Both studies refer to the documentary *Meet the Mormons*, but in different ways. Notably, the media professionals were sensitive to negative perceptions of Mormonism by non-Mormons, and yet the audience study demonstrated a more positive attitude than their concerns suggest, although the different geographical locations for the two approaches may have contributed to that disjuncture. Broadly, however, the two studies show how documentary media influence opinions about and attitudes towards religion and that greater knowledge does not necessarily mean greater approval. The media can mold the image of a religious group and religion both positively and negatively. This capability is related to issues of responsibility and power relations in the ethical space of documentaries, which are considered in part III of the study.

12.3. The ethical space of documentaries about religion

The descriptive-analytical approach to the ethical space of documentaries considers the values and norms that constitute the moral reading mode. As noted at the beginning of the study, the moral reading mode is closely related to the documentary reading mode and influences moral judgements in the spaces of communication. The analysis centers on the interaction between the social actors behind, aka the filmmakers, and in front, aka the protagonists, the camera. This relation is expressed in the space of representation: some filmmakers appear on camera and interact with protagonists; some filmmakers are aurally present only but communicate with the social actors in front of the camera; some filmmakers are completely absent from the narration. The interactions between these social actors are defined by power relations that influence responsible actions, which are based in turn on specific moral judgements. Power relations and responsibility together define the documentary's mode of moral reasoning. By including the social actors' hermeneutic horizons and the production context, the analysis can scrutinize the ethical principles on which the moral judgements of the social actors involved are based.

The analysis looks in particular at two groups of documentaries: the first comprises six films by Mormon filmmakers who are dependent on the LDS Church and the second comprises four films by independent filmmakers. The modes of moral reasoning in each group are based on different principles. The documentaries produced in the LDS Church context each highlight particular principles: *Sisterz in Zion* (Melissa Puente, US 2006) defends diversity and equality in the LDS Church. *Nobody Knows. The Untold Story of Black Mormons* (Darius A. Gray, Margeret B. Young, US 2008) addresses forgiveness and tackles the issue of how to deal with the racist history of the church. *American Mormon* (US 2005) and *American Mormon in Europe* (US 2006) claim impartiality and that people should know Mormonism before they judge it. *Meet the Mormons* (Blair Treu, US 2014) presents Mormonism as an ethical code in and of itself that generates tolerance, happiness and success. *Journey of Faith* (Peter Johnson, US 2006) champions the ethical principle of historical truth, arguing that (historical) knowledge ought to include religious belief.

The independent documentaries are similarly ethically framed. *Tabloid* (Errol Morris, US 2010) deconstructs truth claims by defending the plurality of perspectives on past events. *Sons of Perdition* (Tyler Meason and Jennilyn Merten, US 2010) speaks out for the vulnerable, advocating on behalf of the weak. *Meet the Mormons* (Lynn Alleway, series *Real Stories*, UK, 2015) is accusatory as it displays Alleway's moral mode of reasoning. The docu-serie *Polygamy, USA* (National Geographic, US 2013) explores openness toward different lifestyles.

Documentaries frame historical facts and events with filmic means; their depiction is not simply what in fact happened, nor is the evidence conveyed plain fact. The audio-visual narrative makes no explicit distinction between fiction, non-fiction, and religious narratives on a stylistic level. Instead, the moral reasoning of the documentary narrative marks the depictions as true and real by linking them with certain values. The modes of ethical reasoning define religion, which is never objectively depicted. As a result, the documentaries largely depict religion in binary categories: good versus bad; true versus ridiculous. A more differentiated middle course is often absent; neutrality is not the aim. This polarization can result in religion's exploitative representation as a hidden and uncontrollable power.

Our depictions are also entertaining, leaving audiences surprised, attracted or disgusted, for example. They are also informative, drawing their audience to accept the moral reasoning of their narrative. Observational, defensive, and rational reading modes provide the audience in different ways with information.

As the analysis shows, the ethical principles of these various documentaries engage the issue of responsibility. The filmmakers are in a privileged position as they control the production process to a great extent. They need to consider their goals and whether the depictions of religion and social actors that they pursue to those ends are justified. The protagonists' reasons for participation may not be evident. Respectful handling of the social actors' private sphere in front of the camera is the responsibility of the filmmaker, even if the loyalties of the two parties do not intersect. The filmmaker may also have a responsibility to provide the audience with an even-handed depiction of their subject, while the audience themselves must make moral judgements about the presentation of religion if they are to be responsible consumers.

12.4. Reading modes of Mormonism in the spaces of communication

The semio-pragmatic analysis of the diverse sources establishes and works through various reading modes of religion. These modes allow for comparison of the aims and effects of the sources, but they also determine how religion and religious lifestyles are positioned within the communication spaces of documentary media. The discussion here now presents these reading modes with reference to the sources analyzed in parts II and III.

The *documentary mode*, introduced at the beginning of the study, is constitutive for documentary media. It has close ties to the *moral reading mode*, considered in detail in the ethical space of documentary media. The two modes reference "real" events in different ways. The documentary mode communicates by means of internal and external reading instructions stories about "real" events and "real" people. The moral mode then combines these narratives about real people and events with credibility and authenticity. The social actors have to be credibly and authentically represented if the audience is to be convinced of the veracity of the events depicted. In the case of documentaries that address religion, such credibility and authenticity cannot be achieved if religion is challenged or even presented as false. The credible presentation of religion is connoted with positive values, whereas a depiction of religion that seems implausible is connected with negative values that deconstruct religion as false and unauthentic. Further reading modes are applied in the communication spaces of documentary media in support of such goals.

The *performative reading mode* invites audiences to perform specific actions, be it to get in contact with the LDS Church or to resign from the LDS Church. This mode often includes religious social actors in the space of representation. They perform their values, worldviews, and lifestyles in self-portraits and ask the audience to become like them. The *advocacy mode* involves convincing the audience of the film's cause and asking for ideological support, and sometimes financial support, as in the case of *Sons of Perdition*, where the end credits refer to Holding Out Help, an organization that supports people who have left polygamous groups. The LDS Church also applies the advocacy mode when its logo appears at the end of each *I'm a Mormon* video, signing off on its message. The *interventional mode* in which the filmmaker takes concrete action is rare but can be very effective. The filmmaker Lynn Alleway applies it when she asks to see miserable young missionary Josh Field in *Meet the Mormons*. She feels responsible and seems worried when she has not heard from him for some time. Her aim, the audience is told, is not simply that this documentary should be made, for she also feels a personal need to respond to Field's condition. The interventional mode is heightened when she meets one of the church officials and asks if Elder Field may be allowed to call his mother. The audience is invited to participate all three modes, performative, advocacy, and interventional.

The *emotional mode* engages the audience's emotions to draw them into a cause or strengthen the argument. While, as we have seen, reality shows are particularly liable to apply this reading mode, we readily find it in other sources too. Emotionality is often involved in the depiction of family and children. It may provoke a physical response from the viewer.

The *advertising mode* is embraced when the producers want to sell a product, in this case usually Mormonism is presented as an outstanding lifestyle. We have seen this mode in particular in the context of the *I'm a Mormon* campaign produced by the LDS Church. The campaign's aim was to shape the church's image. The social actors in front of the camera are remarkable individuals who are willing to step forward for the sake of an institution to which they are deeply loyal. For the advertising mode to be effective, the religious actors must appear sincere. The advertising mode achieves increased recognition for its product by means of film style, for although stylistic strategy risks reducing the credibility of the representation, it can be vital to the effectiveness of the advertising mode.

The *identity mode* divides the audience into in-groups and out-groups, which in this study means Mormons and non-Mormons. Media produced by the LDS Church often distinguish between these two groups by constructing boundaries between "us" and the rest of the world. This insider perspective differs from an outsider perspective on Mormonism and Mormons that may be more critical toward Mormonism but addresses both Mormons and non-Mormons. Critical representations of Mormonism do not specifically exclude Mormons from their audience, but many Mormons might feel alienated by such accounts of their church, as the audience survey and analysis of online discussions showed. The identity mode requires the audience to take sides in order to be included in the narrative.

The *informational, instructional* and *factual modes* convey background knowledge about Mormonism and the Mormon/non-Mormon social actors who are part of the narrative. With their references to facts and figures, these modes are effective tools for generating credibility and authenticity. The information they provide may in fact not be accurate, but it is framed in these modes to be believable. The informational mode provides background knowledge indirectly. For example, when Kody Brown's first three weddings are discussed in the RTV show *Sister Wives*, pictures from each event are inserted, conveying information about the dresses his wives wore and the nature of their wedding receptions. In the voice-over each wife describes how her marriage was celebrated. The sequence provides information about the biographies of the three wives, about fundamental Mormonism, and about reasons for living this religious lifestyle. The instructional mode is applied during the baptism scene in *The District*, which is depicted in detail that involves even underwater shots. It provides instructions, with future candidates and missionaries in mind, about how a Mormon baptism is performed. The commentary in the voice-over explains the meaning of baptism to the virtual audience. The factual mode refers to figures and facts and is a basic ingredient of historical documentaries.

In documentaries, the *entertaining mode* is often combined with the informational and instructional modes and serves to keep the audience watching. It is related to the fictional mode in recounting a consistent and closed story that is not necessary part of the real events recorded by the camera. The entertaining mode aims to distract from concerns about the veracity of the events displayed. We hear it, for example, in the extradiegetic music that echoes the editing rhythm in the opening sequence of *The District*. We see it in *Tabloid* and *American Mormon in Europe* when graphic signs are inserted as humorous commentary on statements made by participants. These filmic means do not add anything to the credibility and authenticity of the social actors but as diversions they bring momentary pleasure as sheer entertainment.

The entertaining mode is intensified by the *sensational mode* or *spectacular mode*. In the examples in this project, these two reading modes entertain the audience by conveying the extraordinary or dramatic in the depiction of religion and religious individuals. The reading modes of such portrayals can be at the expense of a social actor, who might be unaware of the effect or consequences of such filmic means. For example, *Sons of Perdition* uses a hidden camera: the social actors probably did not know they were being filmed and would likely not have agreed to being filmed, so secret filming is ethically problematic. The boundary between an ethically justified representation of religion and an unjustified representation of a social actor is easily crossed in this reading mode.

A similarly thin line defines the *intimate reading mode*, during which the camera shows highly personal moments. Film makers may develop a close relationship with their subjects during the production process, but they retain a responsibility that is heightened by their position of power. Using the intimate mode for entertaining purposes can exploit social actors who share their stories with the person behind the camera. This mode is applied in Lynn Alleway's *Meet the Mormons*, where the young missionary struggles with home sickness. Alleway is the only person with whom the missionary is in contact beside his mission colleagues and church officials. The filmmaker's engagement in the intimate mode seems honest and careful. Her aural presence in the narration also supports the moral and documentary modes because it increases the narrative's credibility and authenticity.

As demonstrated the reading modes of documentaries engage their audiences in discourses about Mormons, Mormonism, religion and religious lifestyles. The viewers do not simply passively consume these audio-visual depictions, for they are active participants in the process of consumption in light of their insider and/or outsider perspectives and their hermeneutic horizons.

12.5. Religion through the lens of documentary media

Approaching religion, religious lifestyles, and a religious community through the lens of documentary media and its spaces of communication provides access to a realm where religion takes place in manifold ways. The media not only report, distribute, and mediate religion but also produce, shape, influence, and transform it. Some of the documentary media sources explored for this project hold up positive depictions of Mormonism, while others aim to show a harmful side to Mormon communities. Both approaches construct stories and formulate arguments whose veracity is dependent on the plausibility of their narration and the quality of the information they present. Religion provides a rich fundus of stories that characterize a religious lifestyle and are communicated, and thus shaped, by the media. Yet not only is the communication of religion determined by the media, but the media in turn is defined by the religiously colored message.

Documentary media reference the factual world of religious beliefs, religious actors, religious lifestyles, and religious communities in various modes that aim at credibility, authenticity, and the communication of values. Most of the sources present a coherent image of religion and religious ideals within their narrative. Conspicuous differences exist, however, across the sources and their understanding of religion. The value coherence of the religious lifestyle (a concept discussed in the introduction, chapter 1.1 Religious lifestyles in the media) presented by each narrative is shaped by the filmmakers' and social actors' ideas of religion. The religious worldviews of traditional institutions are expressed in such productions. Documentary narratives thus provide source material that expresses a diversity of religious lifestyles. This argument can be taken further: the manifold religious lifestyles presented in the media provide value coherence that is in competition with traditional religious values.

Value coherence in documentary media therefore forms on two levels: It plays an elementary role in the credible depiction of religion and religious lifestyles, and it is also central to the media's search for credibility and authenticity. Religion becomes a tool used to achieve a narrative worthy of being believed. The relation between, on the one hand, the interactions of the director and social actors in front of the camera and, on the other, how the narrative is shaped by the filmic means (as extensively discussed in part III) is at the core of the effective documentary narrative. On that score, documentary media can be deployed to influence the meaning and function of religion, which is a heterogeneous formation. Documentary media and their makers present various ideas of what religion and Mormonism are, and the spectators add their own understandings. Religion is thus a versatile concept for the semio-pragmatic endeavor that is this study: Within the tension between, on one hand, the spaces of production, distribution, and representation and, on the other, the audience, the approach tak-

Part IV: Approaching Religion and Ethics in the Communication Spaces

en by this study situates religion as scientific concept with a variety of reading modes.

In the world constructed by the spaces of communication, the boundaries between religious traditions, religious institutions, religious groupings, and religious individuals are blurred. Each film focuses on a narration that it seeks to convey as sincere, no matter the aspect of religion it addresses. The depiction of religious facts or fiction, religious social realities, or religious narratives is not distinct. No filmic aesthetic convention dictates some single correct way in which to depict religion. The social actors, who may include scholars of religion, convey their own knowledge, ideas, and agendas. The audience will variously appreciate the reading modes depending on the extent of their critical engagement with the sources. Extra effort has to be invested if the reading mode of a documentary is to be challenged, and knowledge of religion can certainly help in resisting an intended effect.

This semio-pragmatic study demonstrates the complex processes of religious communication, where inside and outside perspectives cannot be clearly discerned and no perspective is necessarily unbiased. The only way to decode the diversity of reading modes of religion is to put the source's spaces of communication and the social actors involved under the microscope. People, communities, and institutions engage in the mediatization of religion. They construct religion. Here the reading modes are just as diverse as the representations of religion. The scholar of religion is one of those social actors within the space of consumption and oscillates between reading modes to establish meaning and effect.

Bibliography

"900–902: Tyler Measom – Documentary Filmmaker." Accessed November 9, 2018. https://www.mormonstories.org/podcast/tyler-measom/.

"Apply for a Trademark. Search a Trademark." Accessed January 4, 2018. https://www.trademarkia.com/company-intellectual-reserve-inc-613675-page-1-2.

Arens, Edmund. "Religion as Communication." In *The Social Psychology of Communication*, edited by Derek Hook, Bradley Franks, and Martin W. Bauer, 249–65. London: Palgrave Macmillan UK, 2011.

Askar, Jamshid Ghazi. "LDS Missionaries Are Stars of New Reality TV Series." DeseretNews.com, October 12, 2012. https://www.deseretnews.com/article/865564309/LDS-missionaries-are-stars-of-new-reality-TV-series.html.

Aufderheide, Patricia. *Documentary Film: A Very Short Introduction*. Very Short Introductions. New York: Oxford University Press, 2007.

Baffelli, Erica, Ian Reader, and Birgit Staemmler, eds. *Japanese Religions on the Internet: Innovation, Representation, and Authority*. Vol. 2. Routledge Studies in Religion, Media, and Culture. New York: Routledge, 2011.

Baker, Sherry Pack. "Mormon Media History Timeline, 1827–2007." *Brigham Young University Studies* 47, no. 4 (2008): 117–23.

Baker, Sherry, and Daniel Stout. "Mormons and the Media, 1898–2003: A Selected, Annotated, and Indexed Bibliography (with Suggestions for Future Research)." *All Faculty Publications*, January 1, 2003. http://scholarsarchive.byu.edu/facpub/1045.

Bal, Mieke. "Visual Essentialism and the Object of Visual Culture." *Journal of Visual Culture* 2, no. 1 (April 1, 2003): 5–32.

———. "Working with Concepts." *European Journal of English Studies* 13, no. 1 (April 1, 2009): 13–23.

Baur, Nina, Jörg Blasius, and Cornelia Helfferich, eds. "Leitfaden- und Experteninterviews." In *Handbuch Methoden der empirischen Sozialforschung*, 559–557. Handbuch. Wiesbaden: Springer, 2014.

"Be in a Video! | I Am an Ex Mormon." Accessed November 6, 2017. http://www.iamanexmormon.com/join-us/.

"Becoming Children of Christ." Accessed June 15, 2019. https://www.churchofjesuschrist.org/media-library/video/2007-01-0003-becoming-children-of-christ.

Bennion, Janet. "History, Culture, and Variability of Mormon Schismatic Groups." In *Modern Polygamy in the United States: Historical, Cultural, and Legal Issues*, edited by Cardell Jacobson and Lara Burton, 101–124. Oxford, New York: Oxford University Press, 2011.

———. *Polygamy in Primetime: Media, Gender, and Politics in Mormon Fundamentalism*. Brandeis Series on Gender, Culture, Religion, and Law. Waltham, Massachusetts: Brandeis University Press, 2011.

———. "Progressive Polygamy in Western United States." In *Beyond Same-Sex Marriage: Perspectives on Marital Possibilities*, edited by Ronald C. Den Otter, 25–37. Lanham: Lexington Books, 2016.

———. *Women of Principle: Female Networking in Contemporary Mormon Polygyny*. New York, N.Y.: Oxford University Press, 1998.

"Bible Videos – The Life of Jesus Christ – Watch Scenes from the Bible." Accessed June 14, 2019. https://www.churchofjesuschrist.org/bible-videos?lang=eng&_r=1.

Biressi, Anita, and Heather Nunn. *Reality TV: Realism and Revelation*. London, New York: Wallflower, 2005.

———. *Reality TV: Realism and Revelation*. Wallflower Press, 2012.

Blair Young, Margaret, and Darius Aidan Gray. "Mormons and Race." In *The Oxford Handbook of Mormonism*, edited by Terryl Givens, 363–385. New York: Oxford University Press, 2015.

Boehm, Andreas. "Grounded Theory – wie aus Texten Modelle und Theorien gemacht werden." edited by Andreas Boehm, Andreas Mengel, and Thomas Muhr, 121–40. Schriften zur Informationswissenschaft 14. Konstanz: UVK Univ.-Verl. Konstanz, 1994.

Böhm, Nadine Christina. "Sakrales Sehen: Strategien der Sakralisierung im Kino der Jahrtausendwende." Transcript, 2009.

Bordwell, David, and Kristin Marie Thompson. *Film Art: An Introduction*. 10th ed. New York: McGraw-Hill, 2013.

Bordwell, David, Kristin Thompson, and Jeff Smith. *Film Art: An Introduction*. 11th ed. New York: McGraw-Hill Education, 2017.

Bowman, Matthew. *The Mormon People: The Making of an American Faith*. New York: Random House, 2012.

Branigan, Edward. *Narrative Comprehension and Film*. Sightlines. London: Routledge, 1992.

Buckland, Warren. *The Cognitive Semiotics of Film*. Cambridge: Cambridge University Press, 2000.

Bushman, Richard Lyman. *Joseph Smith: Rough Stone Rolling*. Reprint. New York: Vintage, 2007.

Campbell, Heidi. *Exploring Religious Community Online: We Are One in the Network*. Vol. 24. Digital Formations. New York: P. Lang, 2005.

———. "How Religious Communities Negotiate New Media Religiously." In *Digital Religion, Social Media, and Culture: Perspectives, Practices, and Futures*, edited by Pauline Hope Cheong, 81–96. Digital Formations. New York: Peter Lang, 2012.

———. *When Religion Meets New Media*. Media, Religion and Culture Series. Abingdon: Routledge, 2010.

Casanova, José. "Eurozentristischer Säkularismus und die Herausforderung der Globalisierung." In *Politik, Religion, Markt: die Rückkehr der Religion als Anfrage an den politisch-philosophischen Diskurs der Moderne*, edited by Wilhelm Guggenberger, Dietmar Regensberger, and Kristina Stöckl, 4:19–40. Innsbruck: Innsbruck University Press, 2009.

"Chapter 8: Crossing the Sea." Accessed June 15, 2019. https://www.churchofjesuschrist.org/media-library/video/2010-12-08-chapter-8-crossing-the-sea.

Chen, Chiung Hwang. "Diverse Yet Hegemonic: Expressions of Motherhood in 'I'm a Mormon' Ads." *Journal of Media and Religion* 13, no. 1 (January 2, 2014): 31–47.

———. "Marketing Religion Online: The LDS Church's SEO Efforts." *Journal of Media and Religion* 10, no. 4 (November 18, 2011): 185–205.

"Church History Library." Accessed June 19, 2019. https://history.churchofjesuschrist.org/section/library?lang=eng.

Church Newsroom. *"Mormon Underwear" Is the Temple Garment and Is Sacred to Latter-Day Saints*. Accessed May 10, 2019. https://www.youtube.com/watch?v=SkTz_NQqKA8.

Clark, Cody. "Teens from Different Worlds Become One: In Spirit in New LDS Documentary." *Daily Herald*, October 13, 2006. http://www.heraldextra.com/lifestyles/teens-from-different-worlds-become-one-in-spirit-in-new/article_d877d125-65cb-5c42-af75-702205054fce.html.

Clark, Lynn Schofield. *Religion, Media, and the Marketplace*. Piscataway/NJ: Rutgers University Press, 2007.

Claudia L. Bushman, and Richard L. Bushman. *Building the Kingdom: A History of Mormons in America*. New York: Oxford University Press, 2001.

Clifford G. Christians. *Media Ethics: Cases and Moral Reasoning*. New York: Routledge, Taylor & Francis Group, 2017.

Connolly, Kate. "Bavarians Wary of New Law Requiring Crosses in All Public Buildings." *The Guardian*, May 31, 2018, sec. World news. https://www.theguardian.com/world/2018/may/31/bavarians-wary-of-new-law-requiring-crosses-in-all-public-buildings.

Cullity, Garrett. "Moral Judgement." In *Routledge Encyclopedia of Philosophy*. London: Routledge, 2016.

LDS Daily. "Daughter of Famous Polygamist Family Denied Baptism," October 14, 2015. http://www.ldsdaily.com/world/daughter-of-famous-polygamist-family-denied-baptism/.

Davies, Douglas James. *An Introduction to Mormonism*. Cambridge: Cambridge University Press, 2003.

Debatin, Bernhard. "Medienethik als Steuerungsinstrument?" In *Perspektiven der Medienkritik. Die gesellschaftliche Auseinandersetzung mit öffentlicher Kommunikation in der Mediengesellschaft*, 287–303. Opladen: Westdeutscher Verlag, 1997.

Decker, Mark T., and Michael Austin. *Peculiar Portrayals: Mormons on the Page, Stage and Screen*. Utah State University Press, 2010.

Deery, June. "Reality TV as Advertainment." *Popular Communication* 2, no. 1 (March 2004): 1–20.

Denzin, Norman K. "Moments, Mixed Methods, and Paradigm Dialogs." *Qualitative Inquiry* 16, no. 6 (2010): 419–27.

———. "Reading Film - Filme und Videos als sozialwissenschaftliches Erfahrungsmaterial." In *Qualitative Forschung: ein Handbuch*, edited by Uwe Flick, Ernst von Kardorff, and Ines Steinke, 416–428. Rororo. Reinbek: Rowohlt Taschenbuch Verlag, 2015.

———. "Triangulation 2.0." *Journal of Mixed Methods Research* 6, no. 2 (2012): 80–88.

Dias, Elizabeth. "Mormon Church to Allow Children of L.G.B.T. Parents to Be Baptized." *The New York Times*, April 5, 2019, sec. U.S. https://www.nytimes.com/2019/04/04/us/lds-church-lgbt.html.

Dijk-Groeneboer, Monique C. H. van. "Religious Education in the Secularised Netherlands." *International Studies in Catholic Education* 9, no. 1 (January 2, 2017): 17–28.

"Discover What's inside | ComeUntoChrist.Org." Accessed May 20, 2019. https://www.comeuntochrist.org/beliefs/book-of-mormon/discover.

Downing, Lisa, and Libby Saxton. "Introduction." In *Film and Ethics: Foreclosed Encounters*, edited by Lisa Downing and Libby Saxton, 1–15. London: Routledge, 2010.

Einstein, Mara. *Brands of Faith: Marketing Religion in a Commercial Age*. Religion, Media, and Culture Series. London: Routledge, 2008.

Ellingson, Laura L. *Engaging Crystallization in Qualitative Research: An Introduction*. Los Angeles: SAGE, 2009.

tlc.de. "FAQ." Accessed March 21, 2019. https://www.tlc.de/info/faqs.

"Filming in Utah – More Videos in June! | I Am an Ex Mormon." Accessed December 4, 2017. http://www.iamanexmormon.com/2011/05/filming-in-utah-more-videos-in-june/.

"Films by Latter-Day Saints: Directors, Producers." Accessed February 24, 2018. http://www.ldsfilm.com/dir.html#Pro.

Flick, Uwe. *Qualitative Sozialforschung: eine Einführung*. Rororo. Reinbek bei Hamburg: Rowohlt Taschenbuch Verlag, 2016.

———. *Triangulation. Eine Einführung*. Qualitative Sozialforschung. Wiesbaden: VS Verlag, 2011.

———. "Zur Verwendung von Dokumenten." In *Qualitative Sozialforschung: eine Einführung*, 321–332. Rororo. Reinbek bei Hamburg: Rowohlt Taschenbuch Verlag, 2016.

Flick, Uwe, Ernst von Kardorff, and Ines Steinke, eds. "Theoretisches Kodieren: Textanalyse in der Grounded Theory." In *Qualitative Forschung: ein Handbuch*, 475–485. Rororo. Reinbek: Rowohlt Taschenbuch Verlag, 2015.

Fluhman, J. Spencer. *A Peculiar People: Anti-Mormonism and the Making of Religion in Nineteenth-Century America*. Chapel Hill: University of North Carolina Press, 2012.

Foucault, Michel. *Sexualität und Wahrheit*. [Versch. Aufl.]. Suhrkamp-Taschenbuch Wissenschaft. Frankfurt am Main: Suhrkamp, 1977.

———. "The Subject and Power." *Critical Inquiry* 8, no. 4 (1982): 777–95.

Franzmann, Andreas. "Entstehungskontexte und Entwicklungsphasen der Objektiven Hermeneutik als einer Methodenschule." In *Die Methodenschule der Objektiven Hermeneutik: Eine Bestandsaufnahme*, edited by Roland Becker-Lenz, Andreas Franzmann, Axel Jansen, and Matthias Jung, 1–42. Wiesbaden: Springer Fachmedien Wiesbaden, 2016.

Fritz, Natalie. "Von Rabenvätern und Übermüttern: das religionshistorische Motiv der heiligen Familie im Spannungsfeld zwischen Religion, Kunst und Film." Schüren, 2018.

Fritz, Natalie, Anna-Katharina Höpflinger, Stefanie Knauß, Marie-Therese Mäder, and Daria Pezzoli-Olgiati. *Sichtbare Religion: eine Einführung in die Religionswissenschaft*. De Gruyter Studium. Berlin: De Gruyter, 2018.

Funiok, Rüdiger. *Medienethik: Verantwortung in der Mediengesellschaft*. Kon-Texte: Wissenschaften in philosophischer Perspektive. Stuttgart: Kohlhammer, 2011.

"Gabe Reid – Former NFL Player, Polynesian Father, Mormon." Accessed December 5, 2017. https://www.mormonchannel.org/watch/series/im-a-mormon/gabe-reid-former-nfl-player-polynesian-father-mormon.

Gadamer, Hans-Georg. *Hermeneutik I: Wahrheit und Methode : Grundzüge einer philosophischen Hermeneutik*. 7. Aufl. (durchges.). Vol. 1. Gesammelte Werke / Hans-Georg Gadamer. Tübingen: Mohr Siebeck, 2010.

Genette, Gérard, and Marie Maclean. "Introduction to the Paratext." *New Literary History* 22, no. 2 (1991): 261–72.

Germany, Süddeutsche de GmbH, Munich. "Papst Franziskus als Friedensmahner." Süddeutsche.de. Accessed October 19, 2017. http://www.sueddeutsche.de/news/panorama/kirche-papst-franziskus-als-friedensmahner-dpa.urn-newsml-dpa-com-20090101-170910-99-991119.

Givens, Terryl. *The Oxford Handbook of Mormonism*. New York: Oxford University Press, 2015.

Givens, Terryl L. *People of Paradox: A History of Mormon Culture*. Oxford University Press, 2007.

Goodstein, Laurie. "Mormon Ad Campaign Seeks to Improve Perceptions." *The New York Times*, November 17, 2011, sec. U.S. https://www.nytimes.com/2011/11/18/us/mormon-ad-campaign-seeks-to-improve-perceptions.html.

Greenslade, Roy. "Judge Finds for Filmmaker in 'manacled Mormon' Case." *The Guardian*, October 17, 2013, sec. Media. https://www.theguardian.com/media/greenslade/2013/oct/17/joyce-mckinney-california.

Habermas, Jürgen. "Religion in der Öffentlichkeit der 'postsäkularen' Gesellschaft." In *Nachmetaphysisches Denken II. Aufsätze und Repliken*, 2:308–328. Berlin: Suhrkamp, 2012.

Bibliography

Hall, Stuart. "Encoding/Decoding." In *Documentary Research*, edited by John Scott, 1:233–246. Sage Benchmarks in Social Research Methods. London: SAGE, 2006.

———. "Introduction." In *Representation: Cultural Representation and Signifying Practices*, edited by Stuart Hall, Jessica Evans, and Sean Nixon, 2nd ed., xvii–xxvi. Los Angeles, CA: SAGE, 2013.

———. "Media Power: The Double Bind." In *New Challenges for Documentary*, edited by Alan Stuart Rosenthal, 357–364. Berkeley, CA et al.: University of California Press, 1988.

———. *Representation: Cultural Representation and Signifying Practices*. Culture, Media and Identities. London: SAGE in association with The Open University, 1997.

Hammarberg, Melvyn. *The Mormon Quest for Glory: The Religious World of the Latter-Day Saints*. New York: Oxford University Press, 2013.

Hann, Michael. "Joyce McKinney Sues Errol Morris over Tabloid." *The Guardian*, November 8, 2011, sec. Film. https://www.theguardian.com/film/2011/nov/08/joyce-mckinney-sues-errol-morris-tabloid.

Hansen, Klaus J. "Mormonism." In *Encyclopedia of Religion*, edited by Lindsay Jones, 2nd ed., 9:6192–95. Detroit: Macmillan Reference USA, 2005.

Haverkamp, Anselm, and Paul Ricoeur, eds. "Die Metapher und das Hauptproblem der Hermeneutik." In *Theorie der Metapher*, 2nd ed., 356–375. Darmstadt: Wissenschaftliche Buchgesellschaft, 1996.

Haws, J. B. *The Mormon Image in the American Mind: Fifty Years of Public Perception*. Oxford University Press, 2013.

"He Is Risen." Accessed June 15, 2019. https://churchofjesuschrist.org/media-library/video/2011-10-025-he-is-risen.

Hendershot, Heather. *Shaking the World for Jesus: Media and Conservative Evangelical Culture*. Chicago: University of Chicago Press, 2004.

———. *What's Fair on the Air?: Cold War Right-Wing Broadcasting and the Public Interest*. University of Chicago Press, 2011.

Hepp, Andreas, and Veronika Krönert. *Medien, Event, Religion: die Mediatisierung des Religiösen*. Medien – Kultur – Kommunikation. Wiesbaden: VS Verlag für Sozialwissenschaften, 2009.

"History of the Saints | Product Categories Downloads." Accessed October 13, 2017. http://historyofthesaints.org/product-category/history_of_the_saints_products/downloads/.

"History of the Saints – Television Documentary Series." Accessed June 15, 2019. https://historyofthesaints.org/.

Hjarvard, Stig. "The Mediatisation of Religion: Theorising Religion, Media and Social Change." *Culture and Religion*, 2011, 119–35.

———. "The Mediatization of Religion: A Theory of the Media as Agents of Religious Change." *Northern Lights: Film & Media Studies Yearbook* 6, no. 1 (2008): 9–26.

———. "Three Forms of Mediatized Religion. Changing the Public Face of Religion." In *Mediatization and Religion: Nordic Perspectives*, 21–44. Göteborg: Nordicom, 2012.

Hofstee, Wim, and Arje Van der Koij. "Introduction." In *Religion beyond Its Private Role in Modern Society*, edited by Wim Hofstee and Arje Van der Koij, 20:1–14. Leiden: Brill, 2013.

"Holding Out Help – Helping, Encouraging, & Loving Polygamists." Accessed November 12, 2018. http://holdingouthelp.org/.

Hölscher, Barbara. *Lebensstile durch Werbung?: zur Soziologie der Life-Style-Werbung*. Opladen: Westdeutscher Verlag, 1998.

"Home – Www.Miekebal.Org." Accessed June 16, 2019. http://www.miekebal.org/.

Hoover, Stewart M. "Concluding Thought: Imagining the Religious in and through the Digital." In *Digital Religion: Understanding Religious Practice in New Media Worlds*, edited by Heidi Campbell, 266–268. Abingdon: Routledge, 2013.

———. "Media and Religion." In *Encyclopedia of Religion*, edited by Lindsay Jones, 5805–5810. Detroit: Macmillan Reference USA, 2005.

———. "Media and the Imagination of Religion in Contemporary Global Culture." *European Journal of Cultural Studies* 14, no. 6 (2011): 610–25.

———. "The Culturalist Turn in Scholarship on Media and Religion." *Journal of Media and Religion* 1, no. 1 (February 1, 2002): 25–36.

Hopf, Christel. "Qualitative Interviews – ein Überblick." In *Qualitative Sozialforschung: eine Einführung*, edited by Uwe Flick, Ernst von Kardorff, and Ines Steinke, 349–360. Rororo. Reinbek bei Hamburg: Rowohlt Taschenbuch Verlag, 2016.

Höpflinger, Anna-Katharina. *Religiöse Codes in der Populärkultur. Kleidung der Blackmetal-Szene*. Baden Baden: Nomos Verlag, 2020.

"How Americans Feel About Religious Groups | Pew Research Center," July 16, 2014. https://www.pewforum.org/2014/07/16/how-americans-feel-about-religious-groups/.

Howard, Robert Glenn. *Digital Jesus: The Making of a New Christian Fundamentalist Community on the Internet*. The New and Alternative Religions Series. New York: New York University Press, 2011.

Hudson, Valerie M. "Mormon Doctrine on Gender." In *The Oxford Handbook of Mormonism*, edited by Terryl L. Givens, 349–362. New York: Oxford University Press, 2015.

iamanexmormon. *I'm Happier than I've Ever Been in My Entire Life and I'm an Ex Mormon*. Accessed November 24, 2017. https://www.youtube.com/watch?v=vWp9l0qTFC0.

"I'm a Mormon." Accessed May 19, 2019. https://www.mormonchannel.org/watch/series/im-a-mormon/sort:latest/page:6.

"I'm a Mormon." Accessed November 6, 2017. https://www.mormonchannel.org/watch/series/im-a-mormon.

Bibliography

"'I'm a Mormon' Campaign Provide Glimpse into Lives of Latter-Day Saints." Accessed May 21, 2019. http://www.mormonnewsroom.org/article/-i-m-a-mormon-campaign.

"'I'm a Searcher, I'm a Wanderer, I'm a Filmmaker.' | I Am an Ex Mormon." Accessed November 13, 2018. http://www.iamanexmormon.com/2011/08/im-a-searcher-im-a-wanderer-im-a-filmmaker/.

Jacobson, Cardell K., and Lara Burton. "Prologue: The Incident at Eldorado, Texas Cardell K. Jacobson and Lara Burton." In *Modern Polygamy in the United States: Historical, Cultural, and Legal Issues*, edited by Cardell K. Jacobson and Lara Burton, xvii–xxvi. Oxford, New York: Oxford University Press, 2011.

Jecker, Constanze. *Religionen im Fernsehen: Analysen und Perspektiven.* Kommunikationswissenschaft. Konstanz: UVK, 2011.

Jensen, Sune Qvotrup. "Othering, Identity Formation and Agency." *Qualitative Studies* 2, no. 2 (October 3, 2011): 63–78.

John, Mark D. "Voting 'Present': Religious Organizational Groups on Facebook." In *Digital Religion, Social Media, and Culture: Perspectives, Practices, and Futures*, edited by Pauline Hope Cheong, 151–168. Digital Formations. New York: Peter Lang, 2012.

John W. Creswell. *Research Design: Qualitative, Quantitative, and Mixed Methods Approaches.* 3rd ed. Los Angeles: SAGE, 2009.

Jorgenson, Derek A. "Media and Polygamy: A Critical Analysis of Sister Wives." *Communication Studies* 65, no. 1 (January 2014): 24–38.

Joseph M. Reagle. *Reading the Comments: Likers, Haters, and Manipulators at the Bottom of the Web.* First MIT Press paperback edition. Cambridge, MA: The MIT Press, 2016.

The Interpreter Foundation. "Journal." Accessed July 26, 2017. http://www.mormoninterpreter.com/journal/.

Kessler, Frank. "Historische Pragmatik." *montage a/v, Zeitschrift für Theorie und Geschichte audiovisueller Kommunikation* 11, no. 2 (2002): 104–112.

Kettner, Matthias. "Werte und Normen – Praktische Geltungsansprüche von Kulturen." In *Handbuch der Kulturwissenschaften*, edited by Friedrich Jaeger, 219–231. Stuttgart: Metzler, 2011.

Kirby, Danielle, and Carole M. Cusack, eds. *Religion and Media. Critical Concept in Religious Studies.* Critical Concepts in Religious Studies. London: Routledge, 2017.

Knoblauch, Hubert. "Benedict in Berlin: The Mediatization of Religion." In *Mediatized Worlds: Culture and Society in a Media Age*, edited by Andreas Hepp and Friedrich Krotz, 143–58. London: Palgrave Macmillan UK, 2014.

———. *Populäre Religion: auf dem Weg in eine spirituelle Gesellschaft.* Frankfurt am Main: Campus-Verlag, 2009.

———. "Populäre Religion. Markt, Medien Und Die Popularisierung Der Religion." *Zeitschrift Für Religionswissenschaft* 8, no. 2 (2000): 143–162.

Knott, Kim, Elizabeth Poole, and Teemu Taira. *Media Portrayals of Religion and the Secular Sacred: Representation and Change.* Burlington: Ashgate, 2013.

Kozloff, Sarah. *Invisible Storytellers: Voice-over Narration in American Fiction Film*. Berkeley: University of California Press, 1988.

Krakauer, Jon. *Under the Banner of Heaven: A Story of Violent Faith*. New York: Anchor Books, 2003.

Krech, Volkhard. "Religion als Kommunikation." In *Religionswissenschaft*, edited by Michael Stausberg, 49–64. Berlin: De Gruyter, 2012.

Kreis, Bridget. "'The District': Where Are They Now?" *Third Hour* (blog), March 16, 2015. https://thirdhour.org/blog/hasten/district-now/.

Krotz, Friedrich. "Die Veränderung von Privatheit und Öffentlichkeit in der heutigen Gesellschaft." *Merz: Medien + Erziehung. Zeitschrift für Medienpädagogik* 8/09, no. 53 (2009): 12–21.

———, ed. "Medienkommunikation als Modifikation von Kommunikation, Typen von Kommunikation und der Bedeutungswandel mediatisierter Kommunikation." In *Mediatisierung: Fallstudien zum Wandel von Kommunikation*, 85–116. Wiesbaden: VS Verlag für Sozialwissenschaften, 2007.

Krüger, Oliver. *Die mediale Religion: Probleme und Perspektiven der religionswissenschaftlichen und wissenssoziologischen Medienforschung*. Band 1. Religion und Medien. Bielefeld: Transcript, 2012.

———. "Exkurs: Die Präsenz von Religionen im deutschen Fernsehen." In *Religionen im Fernsehen: Analysen und Perspektiven*, edited by Constanze Jecker, 161–184. Kommunikationswissenschaft. Konstanz: UVK, 2011.

Kurt, Ronald, and Regine Herbrik. "Sozialwissenschaftliche Hermeneutik und hermeneutische Wissenssoziologie." In *Handbuch Methoden der empirischen Sozialforschung*, edited by Nina Baur and Jörg Blasius, 473–91. Wiesbaden: Springer Verlag, 2014.

Labuschagne, Bart C., Wim Hofstee, and Arje Van der Koij. "Religion and Politics in Post-Secular Society: Beyond the Public / Private Divide." In *Religion beyond Its Private Role in Modern Society*, 13–28. Leiden, Boston: Brill, 2013.

Lamont, Michèle, and Virág Molnár. "The Study of Boundaries in the Social Sciences." *Annual Review of Sociology* 28, no. 1 (August 1, 2002): 167–95.

Larcher, Gerhard. *Zeit, Geschichte und Gedächtnis: Theo Angelopoulos im Gespräch mit der Theologie*. Vol. Band 5. Marburg: Schüren, 2003.

"LDS Media Library - Art, Videos, Pictures, and Audio Downloads." Accessed September 28, 2017. https://www.lds.org/media-library?lang=eng&_r=1.

"LDS Seminary Is a Global, Four-Year Religious Educational Program for Youth," April 12, 2013. http://www.mormonnewsroom.org/topic/seminary.

"LDS Statistics and Church Facts | Total Church Membership." Accessed January 29, 2019. http://www.mormonnewsroom.org/facts-and-statistics.

"LDS Videos - Largest Collection of Official Mormon Videos Online." Accessed May 5, 2020. https://www.churchofjesuschrist.org/media-library/video?lang=eng.

Linderman, Alf G. "Approaches to the Study of Religion in the Media." In *Rethinking Media, Religion, and Culture*, edited by Stewart M. Hoover, 305–315. Thousand Oaks, CA: Sage Publications, 1997.

Lingenberg, Swantje. "Öffentlich(keit) und Privat(heit)." In *Handbuch Cultural Studies und Medienanalyse*, edited by Andreas Hepp, Friedrich Krotz, Swantje Lingenberg, and Jeffrey Wimmer, 169–79. Wiesbaden: Springer Verlag, 2015.

Lizzie's Heritage Inn. "Lizzie's Heritage Inn." Accessed March 20, 2019. https://lizziesheritageinn.com/.

Louis D. Giannetti. *Understanding Movies*. 13th ed. Boston: Pearson, 2014.

Lövheim, Mia. "Introduction: Gender – a Blind Spot in Media, Religion and Culture?" In *Media, Religion and Gender: Key Issues and New Challenges*, edited by Mia Lövheim, 1–15. Media, Religion and Culture. London: Routledge, 2013.

———. *Media, Religion, and Gender: Key Issues and New Challenges*. London; New York: Routledge, 2013.

Lundby, Knut. "Theoretical Framework for Approaching Religion and New Media,." In *Digital Religion: Understanding Religious Practice in New Media Worlds*, edited by Heidi Campbell, 225–237. Abingdon: Routledge, 2013.

Lyden, John. *Film as Religion: Myths, Morals, and Rituals*. New York: New York University Press, 2003.

"Lynn Alleway - About." Accessed December 4, 2018. http://www.lynnalleway.com/about/.

Mäder, Marie-Therese. "A Cultural Studies Approach to Film and Religion, Context and Film Analysis of YES (Potter, GB / USA 2004)." In *Approaches to the Visual in Religion*, edited by Daria Pezzoli-Olgiati and Christopher Rowland, 10:101–118. Research in Contemporary Religion. Göttingen: Vandenhoeck und Ruprecht, 2011.

———. "Auf den Spuren eines Stummfilms. Zwei Filme eine Geschichte." In *Leid-Bilder. Eine interdisziplinäre Perspektive auf die Passionsgeschichte in der Kultur*, edited by Natalie Fritz, Marie-Therese Mäder, Daria Pezzoli-Olgiati, and Baldassare Scolari, 51–69. Marburg: Schüren, 2018.

———. *Die Reise als Suche nach Orientierung: eine Annäherung an das Verhältnis zwischen Film und Religion*. Marburg: Schüren, 2012.

———. "Documentary Media and Religious Communities." *Journal for Religion, Film and Media (JRFM)* 1, no. 1 (2015): 31–36.

———. "Film und Religion am Beispiel von EXISTENZ (David Cronenberg, USA 1998)." In *Outer Space: Reisen in Gegenwelten*, edited by Charles Martig and Daria Pezzoli-Olgiati, 13:256–282. Marburg: Schüren, 2009.

———. "Film und Religion: ein multidisziplinäres Forschungsfeld." In *Religiöse Blicke - Blicke auf das Religiöse: Visualität und Religion*, edited by Bärbel Beinhauer-Köhler, Daria Pezzoli-Olgiati, and Joachim Valentin, 325–348. Zürich: TVZ, 2010.

———. "The Mormon Quest for Glory: The Religious World of the Latter-Day Saints by Melvyn Hammarberg." *Religion* 45, no. 1 (January 2, 2015): 128–31.

Mäder, Marie-Therese, and María T. Soto-Sanfiel. "'We Are Open-Minded, Tolerant, and Care for Other People': Comparing Audience Responses to Religion in Documentaries." *Journal of Media and Religion* 18, no. 3 (July 3, 2019): 98–114.

March, Andrew. "Is There a Right to Polygamy? Marriage, Equality and Subsidizing Families in Liberal Public Justification." *Journal of Moral Philosophy* 8, no. 2 (January 1, 2011): 246–72.

Martig, Charles. *Kino der Irritation: Lars von Triers theologische und ästhetische Herausforderung.* Marburg: Schüren, 2008.

Matthias J. Fritsch, Martin Lindwedel, and Thomas Schärtl. *Wo nie zuvor ein Mensch gewesen ist: Science-Fiction-Filme: angewandte Philosophie und Theologie.* Regensburg: Pustet, 2003.

McDannell, Colleen. *Catholics in the Movies*. New York: Oxford University Press, 2008.

"Meet the Mormons (2014) – Box Office Mojo." Accessed January 22, 2018. http://www.boxofficemojo.com/movies/?id=meetthemormons.htm.

"Meet the Mormons, Channel 4, Review: 'awkward but Revealing' - Telegraph." Accessed December 5, 2018. https://www.telegraph.co.uk/culture/tvandradio/tv-and-radio-reviews/10928747/Meet-the-Mormons-Channel-4-review-awkward-but-revealing.html.

"Meet the Mormons, TV Review: Very Few Revelations on Mission," June 27, 2014. http://www.independent.co.uk/arts-entertainment/tv/reviews/meet-the-mormons-tv-review-very-few-revelations-on-mission-to-uncover-mormonism-9566619.html.

Melton, J. Gordon. *Melton's Encyclopedia of American Religions*. 8th ed. Detroit: Gale, Cengage Learning, 2009.

———, ed. "Polygamy-Practicing." In *Melton's Encyclopedia of American Religions*, 8th ed., 646–51. Detroit, MI: Gale, 2009.

Miles, Margaret R. *Seeing and Believing: Religion and Values in the Movies*. Boston, Massachusetts: Beacon Press, 1996.

Misoch, Sabina. "Qualitative Sozialforschung." In *Qualitative Interviews*, 1–23. Berlin, Boston: De Gruyter Oldenbourg, 2015.

Mohn, Jürgen. "Die Religion im Diskurs und die Diskurse der Religion(en). Überlegungen zu Religionsdiskurstheorien und zur religionsaisthetischen Grundlegung des Diskursfeldes Religion." In *Religion – Wirtschaft – Politik: Forschungszugänge zu einem aktuellen transdisziplinären Feld*, edited by Antonius Liedhegener, Andreas Tunger-Zanetti, and Stephan Wirz, 1st ed., 84–111. Baden-Baden: Nomos, 2011.

Mohr, Hubert. "Auf der Suche nach der Religionsmedienwissenschaft oder: Wie die audiovisuellen Medien unser heutiges Bild von Religion verändern." In *Aspekte der Religionswissenschaft*, edited by Richard Faber, 159–182. Würzburg: Königshausen & Neumann, 2009.

Morgan, David. "Religion and Media: A Critical Review of Recent Developments." *Critical Research on Religion* 1, no. 3 (November 15, 2013): 347–56.

———. "Religion, Media, Culture: The Shape of the Field." In *Key Words in Religion, Media, and Culture*, edited by David Morgan, 1–19. New York: Routledge, 2008.

———. *The Sacred Gaze: Religious Visual Culture in Theory and Practice*. Berkeley: University of California Press, 2005.

Mormon Channel. *Bullying - Stop It*. Accessed September 28, 2017. https://www.youtube.com/watch?v=FYVvE4tr2BI.

"Mormon Channel's Top 10 YouTube Videos of 2014." Accessed September 28, 2017. https://www.mormonchannel.org/blog/post/mormon-channels-top-10-youtube-videos-of-2014.

www.mormonnewsroom.org. "Mormon.Org 'I'm a Mormon' Effort Launches in New York City," June 16, 2011. http://www.mormonnewsroom.org/article/mormon-ads-new-york-city.

Muñiz, José, Paula Elosua, and Ronald K. Hambleton. "Directrices Para La Traducción y Adaptación de Los Tests: Segunda Edición." *Psicothema* 25, no. 2 (2013): 151–57.

Murphy, John M., and Leslee Thorne-Murphy. "Sisterz in Zion, Directed by Melissa Puente." *BYU Studies* 45, no. 4 (2006): 151–155.

Murray, Susan, and Laurie Ouellette. *Reality TV: Remaking Television Culture*. 2nd ed. New York: New York University Press, 2009.

"My Name Is Heather and I'm an Ex Mormon | I Am an Ex Mormon." Accessed November 26, 2017. http://www.iamanexmormon.com/2011/07/my-name-is-heather-and-im-an-ex-mormon/.

My Sisterwife's Closet. "My Sister Wife's Closet." Accessed March 19, 2019. https://mysisterwifescloset.com/.

Nichols, Bill. *Introduction to Documentary*. 2nd ed. Bloomington: Indiana University Press, 2010.

———. *Representing Reality: Issues and Concepts in Documentary*. Bloomington: Indiana University Press, 1991.

Norwegian National Ethics Committees. "Ethical Guidelines for Internet Research," December 2014. https://www.etikkom.no/globalassets/documents/english-publications/ethical-guidelines-for-internet-research.pdf.

O'Dea, Thomas Francis. *The Mormons*. 8th ed. Chicago: University of Chicago Press, 1975.

Odin, Roger. *De la fiction*. Bruxelles: De Boeck, 2000.

———. *Les Espaces de communication: Introduction à la sémio-pragmatique*. Grenoble: Presses universitaires de Grenoble, 2011.

———. "Spectator, Film and the Mobile Phone." In *Audiences: Defining and Researching Screen Entertainment Reception*, edited by Ian Christie. Amsterdam: Amsterdam University Press, 2012.

———. "The Home Movie and Space of Communication." In *Amateur Filmmaking: The Home Movie, the Archive, the Web*, edited by Laura Rascaroli, Gwenda Young, and Barry Monahan, 15–27. Bloomsbury Publishing USA, 2014.

———. "Wirkungsbedingungen des Dokumentarfilms. Zur Semio-Pragmatik am Beispiel 'Notre planète la terre' (1947)." In *Perspektiven des Dokumentarfilms*, edited by Manfred Hattendorf, Band 7:85–96. Diskurs Film. München: Diskurs-Film-Verlag Schaudig & Ledig, 1995.

www.mormonnewsroom.org. "'On Faith' Blog: The Real Mormons Behind TV Advertising," October 31, 2011. http://www.mormonnewsroom.org/article/on-faith-blog-real-mormons-behind-tv-advertising.

Orth, Stefan, Joachim Valentin, and Reinhold Zwick. *Göttliche Komödien: religiöse Dimensionen des Komischen im Kino*. Köln: KIM, 2001.

Ouellette, Laurie. *Lifestyle TV*. Routledge Television Guidebooks. New York et al.: Routledge, 2016.

Pachucki, Mark A., Sabrina Pendergrass, and Michèle Lamont. "Boundary Processes: Recent Theoretical Developments and New Contributions." *Poetics*, Culture lines: Emerging research on boundaries, 35, no. 6 (December 1, 2007): 331–51.

Pack Baker, Sherry. "Mormonism." In *Encyclopedia of Religion, Communication, and Media*, edited by Daniel A. Stout, 261–266. Routledge Encyclopedias of Religion and Society. New York: Routledge, 2006.

Parents Guide. Accessed October 13, 2017. http://www.imdb.com/title/tt0421030/parentalguide.

Part 2 Pictures. "Part 2 Pictures." Accessed October 11, 2018. https://www.part2pictures.com/.

Penley, Constance. *The Future of an Illusion: Film, Feminism, and Psychoanalysis*. Vol. 2. Media and Society Series. Minneapolis: University of Minnesota Press, 1989.

"Permission Form Example," n.d. https://www.lds.org/bc/content/shared/content/english/pdf/create/participant-release.pdf.

Peterson, Daniel C. "'Let a Hundred Flowers Blossom': Some Observations on Mormon Studies." *Mormon Studies Review*, no. 1 (June 2014): 80–88.

Pezzoli-Olgiati, Daria. "Eine illustrierte Annäherung an das Verhältnis von Medien und Religion." In *Religiöse Blicke – Blicke auf das Religiöse: Visualität und Religion*, edited by Bärbel Beinhauer-Köhler, Daria Pezzoli-Olgiati, and Joachim Valentin, 245–266. Zürich: TVZ, 2010.

———. "Film und Religion: Blick auf Kommunikationssysteme und ihre vielfältigen Wechselwirkungen." In *Religious turns – turning religions: veränderte kulturelle Diskurse – neue religiöse Wissensformen*, edited by Andreas Nehring and Regina Ammicht Quinn, 46–66. Stuttgart: Kohlhammer, 2008.

———. "Religion in Cultural Imaginary. Setting the Scene." In *Religion in Cultural Imaginary: Explorations in Visual Und Material Practices*, edited by Daria Pezzoli-Olgiati, 13:9–38. Religion – Wirtschaft – Politik. Zürich, Baden-Baden: Pano Verlag Nomos, 2015.

———. "Religion und Visualität." In *Religionswissenschaft*, edited by Michael Stausberg, 343–364. Berlin, Boston: de Gruyter, 2012.

———. "Vom Ende der Welt zur hoffnungsvollen Vision: Apokalypse im Film." In *Handbuch Theologie und populärer Film*, edited by Thomas Bohrmann, 255–275. Paderborn: Schöningh, 2007.

Plate, Brent S. "Filmmaking and World Making. Re-Creating Time and Space in Myth and Film." In *Teaching Religion and Film*, edited by Gregory J. Watkins. Teaching Religious Studies Series. Oxford: Oxford University Press, 2008.

Plate, S. Brent. *Religion and Film: Cinema and the Re-Creation of the World*. Vol. 43. Short Cuts. London: Wallflower, 2008.

———. *Representing Religion in World Cinema: Filmmaking, Mythmaking, Culture Making*. New York: Palgrave Macmillan, 2003.

Pollack, Detlef, and Gergely Rosta. *Religion in der Moderne: ein internationaler Vergleich*. Schriftenreihe "Religion und Moderne." Frankfurt am Main: Campus-Verlag, 2015.

Potter, Ralph B. "The Logic of Moral Argument." In *Toward a Discipline of Social Ethics: Essays in Honor of Walter George Muelder*, edited by Paul Deats, 93–114. Boston: Boston University Press, 1972.

Pratt, Orson, and Church of Jesus Christ of Latter-day Saints. *The Doctrine and Covenants of The Church of Jesus Christ of Latter-Day Saints*. LaVergne/TN: Kessinger, 2009.

Radde-Antweiler, Kerstin. "Religion as Communicative Figurations – Analyzing Religion in Times of Deep Mediatizations." In *Mediatized Religion in Asia: Studies on Digital Media and Religion*, edited by Kerstin Radde-Antweiler and Xenia Zeiler, 11–24. Routledge Research in Digital Media and Culture in Asia. New York: Routledge, 2019.

Reason.com. "Reason.Tv: The Sons of Perdition Filmmakers on Warren Jeffs' Polygamist Church - Hit & Run," July 29, 2010. https://reason.com/blog/2010/07/29/reasontv-the-sons-of-perdition.

Rees, Myev. "Sister Wives. The Protestantization of Mormon Polygamy." In *Religion and Reality TV: Faith in Late Capitalism*, edited by Mara Einstein, Diane Winston, and Katherine Madden, 107–120. Milton: Routledge, 2018.

Reichertz, Jo. "Objektive Hermeneutik und hermeneutische Wissenssoziologie." In *Qualitative Forschung: ein Handbuch*, edited by Uwe Flick, Ernst von Kardorff, and Ines Steinke, 514–524. Reinbek: Rowohlt Taschenbuch Verlag, 2015.

Resha, David. *The Cinema of Errol Morris*. Middletown, CT: Wesleyan University Press, 2015.

Justia Law. "Reynolds v. United States, 98 U.S. 145 (1878)." Accessed May 31, 2019. https://supreme.justia.com/cases/federal/us/98/145/.

Richard S. Van Wagoner. *Mormon Polygamy: A History*. Salt Lake City, Utah: Signature Books, 1986.

Richards, Tom, and Lyn Richards. "Using Hierarchical Categories in Qualitative Data Analysis." In *Computer-Aided Qualitative Data Analysis: Theory, Methods and Practice*, edited by Udo Kelle, Gerald Prein, and Katherine Bird, 80–95. London: Sage, 1998.

Riesebrodt, Martin. *Cultus und Heilsversprechen: eine Theorie der Religionen.* München: Beck, 2007.

Robinson, Stephen E. *Are Mormons Christians?* Deseret Book, 2010.

Rüegg, Michael. "Warum wir in Europa Religion brauchen." NZZ am Sonntag. Accessed October 19, 2017. https://nzzas.nzz.ch/meinungen/warum-wir-in-europa-die-religion-dringend-brauchen-ld.1314055.

Rüpke, Jörg. "Religion medial." In *Religion und Medien: vom Kultbild zum Internetritual*, edited by Jamal Malik, 4:19–28. Vorlesungen des Interdisziplinären Forums Religion der Universität Erfurt. Münster: Aschendorff, 2007.

Şahin, Reyhan. "Symbol of Isalm, of Emancipation, or of Oppression? Various meanings of Muslim Head Coverings in Germany." *Journal jüdisches Museum Berlin*, no. 16 (2017): 47–54.

Saints, The Church of Jesus Christ of Latter Day. "Are Mormons Christian?" Accessed November 12, 2017. /topics/christians.

Sanghani, Radhika. "Burka Bans: The Countries Where Muslim Women Can't Wear Veils." *The Telegraph*, July 8, 2016. https://www.telegraph.co.uk/women/life/burka-bans-the-countries-where-muslim-women-cant-wear-veils/.

Schade, Sigrid, and Silke Wenk. *Studien zur visuellen Kultur: Einführung in ein transdisziplinäres Forschungsfeld.* Vol. 8. Studien zur visuellen Kultur. Bielefeld: Transcript, 2011.

Schofield Clark, Lynn. "Introduction: Identity, Belonging, and Religious Lifestyle Branding (Fashion Bibles, Bhangra Parties, and Muslim Pop)." In *Religion, Media, and the Marketplace*, 1–36. Piscatawa/NJ: Rutgers University Press, 2007.

Schrader, Paul. *Transcendental Style in Film: Ozu, Bresson, Dreyer.* New York, N.Y: Da Capo Press, 1972.

Scott, A. O. "'Tabloid,' Errol Morris's Take on 'Manacled Mormon' - Review." *The New York Times*, July 14, 2011.

"Seeking Participants | I Am an Ex Mormon." Accessed December 5, 2017. http://www.iamanexmormon.com/2011/04/seeking-participants/.

"Share Goodness." Accessed June 14, 2019. https://www.churchofjesuschrist.org/church/share/goodness?lang=eng.

Shipps, Jan. *Mormonism: The Story of a New Religious Tradition.* Urbana, Chicago: University of Illinois Press, 1987.

———. *Sojourner in the Promised Land: Forty Years among the Mormons.* Urbana: University of Illinois Press, 2000.

Smith, Joseph, and Laurie F. Maffly-Kipp. *The Book of Mormon.* Translated by Joseph Smith. New York et al.: Penguin Classics, 2008.

Sobchack, Vivian. "Inscribing Ethical Space: Ten Propositions on Death, Representation, and Documentary." *Quarterly Review of Film Studies* 9, no. 4 (September 1, 1984): 283–300.

"Social Media Helps for Members." Accessed September 28, 2017. https://www.lds.org/pages/social-media-helps?lang=eng.

"Social Media Index Page - LDS Media Library." Accessed June 14, 2019. https://www.churchofjesuschrist.org/media-library/social?lang=eng.

"Sons of Perdition Screenings." Accessed November 13, 2018. http://www.sonsofperditionthemovie.com/Sons_of_Perdition_Screenings.html.

Soto-Sanfiel, María T., and Marie-Therese Mäder. "Identifying with a Religious Character." *Journal of Religion in Europe*, 2020, 1–31, doi:10.1163/18748929-20201471.

Sprigge, Timothy L. S. "Definition of a Moral Judgment." *Philosophy* 39, no. 150 (1964): 301–22.

Stacey, Jackie. "Desperately Seeking Difference: Jackie Stacey Considers Desire Between Women in Narrative Cinema." In *Reading Images*, edited by Julia Thomas, 109–22. London: Macmillan Education UK, 2001.

Stark, Rodney. "The Rise of a New World Faith." *Review of Religious Research* 26, no. 1 (1984): 18–27.

———. *The Rise of Mormonism*. Edited by Reid Larkin Neilson. New York: Columbia University Press, 2005.

Starks, Helene, and Susan Brown Trinidad. "Choose Your Method: A Comparison of Phenomenology, Discourse Analysis, and Grounded Theory." *Qualitative Health Research* 17, no. 10 (December 1, 2007): 1372–80.

"Statistics and Church Facts | Total Church Membership." Accessed June 16, 2019. http://newsroom.churchofjesuschrist.org/facts-and-statistics.

Stewart M. Hoover. *Religion in the Media Age*. Religion, Media and Culture. London: Routledge, 2006.

Stolz, Fritz. "Religiöse Symbole in religionswissenschaftlicher Rekonstruktion." In *Religion und Rekonstruktion: ausgewählte Aufsätze*, edited by Daria Pezzoli-Olgiati, 62–83. Göttingen: Vandenhoeck & Ruprecht, 2004.

Stolz, Jörg, Judith Könemann, Mallory Schneuwly Purdie, Thomas Englberger, and Michael Krüggeler. *Religion und Spiritualität in der Ich-Gesellschaft: vier Gestalten des (Un-)Glaubens*. Vol. 16. Beiträge zur Pastoralsoziologie. Zürich: Theologischer Verlag Zürich, 2014.

Stout, Daniel A. *Media and Religion: Foundations of an Emerging Field*. New York: Routledge, 2012.

Stout, Daniel A., and Judith Mitchell Buddenbaum. *Religion and Mass Media: Audiences and Adaptations*. Thousand Oaks, CA: Sage Publications, 1996.

Strassberg, Maura. "Scrutinizing Polygamy: Utah's Brown v. British Columbia's Reference Re: Section 293." In *Beyond Same-Sex Marriage: Perspectives on Marital Possibilities*, edited by Ronald C. Den Otter, 167–203. Lanham: Lexington Books, 2016.

Strübing, Jörg. "Grounded Theory und Theoretical Sampling." In *Handbuch Methoden der empirischen Sozialforschung*, edited by Nina Baur and Jörg Blasius, 457–72. Wiesbaden: Springer Verlag, 2014.

"Style Guide — The Name of the Church," April 9, 2010. http://www.mormonnewsroom.org/style-guide?lang=eng.

Sullivan, John L. *Media Audiences: Effects, Users, Institutions, and Power*. Thousand Oaks, CA: SAGE, 2013.

"Swiss Parliament Will Not Enforce Handshakes in School." Accessed February 8, 2019. https://www.swissinfo.ch/eng/business/religion-in-the-classroom_swiss-parliament-will-not-enforce-handshakes-in-school/43549838.

"Tabernacle to Temple: Provo's Legacy of Worship." Accessed October 20, 2017. https://history.lds.org/exhibit/historic-sites/utah/provo/provo-city-center-temple?lang=eng.

"Tabloid (2011) - Box Office Mojo." Accessed November 1, 2018. https://www.boxofficemojo.com/movies/?id=tabloid.htm.

Taylor, Charles. "Why We Need a Radical Redefinition of Secularism." In *The Power of Religion in the Public Sphere*, edited by Eduardo Mendieta and Jonathan Vanantwerpen, 43–59. Columbia University Press, 2011.

Teddlie, Charles, and Abbas Tashakkori. "Overview of Contemporary Issues in Mixed Methods Research." In *SAGE Handbook of Mixed Methods in Social & Behavioral Research*, edited by Abbas Tashakkori, 2nd ed., 1–44. Thousand Oaks, CA: SAGE, 2010.

"The Correct Name of the Church." Accessed June 11, 2019. https://www.churchofjesuschrist.org/study/general-conference/2018/10/the-correct-name-of-the-church?lang=eng.

"The District." Accessed February 8, 2019. https://www.mormonchannel.org/watch/collection/the-district.

"The Mission of Brigham Young University | Mission & Aims." Accessed March 30, 2017. http://aims.byu.edu/.

Thomas, David R. "A General Inductive Approach for Analyzing Qualitative Evaluation Data." *American Journal of Evaluation* 27, no. 2 (June 1, 2006): 237–46.

Thompson, Wayne Luther. "Religion and the Media." In *Encyclopedia of International Media and Communications*, edited by Donald H. Johnston, 81–90. New York: Elsevier, 2003.

Comcast Spotlight. "TLC," January 26, 2010. https://comcastspotlight.com/content/tlc.

"TLC Rings in Records Ratings for 2018; A Top Three Cable Network for Women – Discovery, Inc." Accessed June 13, 2019. https://corporate.discovery.com/discovery-newsroom/tlc-rings-in-record-ratings-for-2018-a-top-three-cable-network-for-women/.

"Use of Online Resources in Church Callings." Accessed June 14, 2019. https://www.churchofjesuschrist.org/pages/online-resources-for-church-callings?lang=eng.

"Use of Online Resources in Church Callings." Accessed September 28, 2017. https://www.lds.org/pages/online-resources-for-church-callings?lang=eng.

Van Dyke, Blair G. "The Mormon University on the Mount of Olives: A Case Study in LDS Public Relations." *Journal of Media and Religion* 12, no. 4 (October 1, 2013): 181–95.

Warneke, Lothar. *Transzendenz im populären Film*. Vol. 59. Beiträge zur Film- und Fernsehwissenschaft. Berlin: Vistas, 2001.

Weber, Brenda R. *Latter-Day Screens: Gender, Sexuality, and Mediated Mormonism*. Durham: Duke University Press, 2019.

———, ed. *Reality Gendervision: Sexuality & Gender on Transatlantic Reality Television*. Durham and London: Duke University Press, 2014.

———. "Trash Talk: Gender as an Analytic on Reality Television." In *Reality Gendervision: Sexuality & Gender on Transatlantic Reality Television*, edited by Brenda R. Weber, 1–34. Durham and London: Duke University Press, 2014.

Weber, Max. *Max Weber, Schriften, 1894–1922*. Edited by Dirk Käsler. Kröners Taschenausgabe. Stuttgart: Kröner, 2002.

———. *The Protestant Ethic and the Spirit of Capitalism*. London: Routledge, 2005.

Weber, Max, and Anthony Giddens. *The Protestant Ethic and the Spirit of Capitalism*. Translated by Talcott Parsons. London, New York: Routledge, 2001.

Wernet, Andreas. *Einführung in die Interpretationstechnik der objektiven Hermeneutik*. Qualitative Sozialforschung. Wiesbaden: VS Verlag für Sozialwissenschaften, 2009.

BYUtv Giving. "What We Do." Accessed March 25, 2019. http://www.supportbyutv.org/what-we-do.

White, Kelly O. "The Sister Wives: Has Incest and Sexual Assault Become the New Reality? The United States District Court for the District of Utah Grants Polygamists the Holy Grail." *Creighton Law Review* 48, no. 3 (June 2015): 681–708.

White, O. Kendall, and Daryl White. "Polygamy and Mormon Identity." *Journal of American Culture* 28, no. 2 (June 2005): 165–77.

Whittaker, David J. "Mormon Studies as an Academic Discipline." In *Oxford Handbook of Mormonism*, edited by Terryl L. Givens and Philip L. Barlow, 92–105. New York: Oxford University Press, 2015.

Williams, Linda. "Mirrors without Memories: Truth, History, and the New Documentary." *Film Quarterly* 46, no. 3 (1993): 9–21.

Wimmer, Andreas. "The Making and Unmaking of Ethnic Boundaries: A Multilevel Process Theory." *American Journal of Sociology* 113, no. 4 (2008): 970–1022.

Winter, Rainer, and Sebastian Nestler. "'Doing Cinema': Filmanalyse als Kulturanalyse in der Tradition der Culltural Studies." In *Film – Kino – Zuschauer, Filmrezeption = Film – cinema – spectator, film reception*, edited by Irmbert Schenk, 99–115. Marburg: Schüren, 2010.

Wolff, Stephan. "Dokumenten- und Aktenanalyse." In *Qualitative Forschung: ein Handbuch*, edited by Uwe Flick, Ernst von Kardorff, and Ines Steinke. Rororo. Reinbek: Rowohlt Taschenbuch Verlag, 2015.

Wollaston, Sam. "Meet the Mormons – TV Review." *The Guardian*, June 27, 2014, sec. Television & radio. https://www.theguardian.com/tv-and-radio/2014/jun/27/meet-the-mormons-tv-review.

Woodhead, Linda. "Five Concepts of Religion." *International Review of Sociology* 21, no. 1 (March 1, 2011): 121–43.
———. "New Forms of Public Religion: Spirituality in Global Civil Society." In *Religion beyond Its Private Role in Modern Society*, 29–52. Leiden: Brill, 2013.
Wright, Melanie Jane. *Religion and Film: An Introduction*. London: Tauris, 2006.
Yelle, Robert A. *Semiotics of Religion: Signs of the Sacred in History*. Bloomsbury Advances in Semiotics. London: Bloomsbury, 2012.
Zablocki, Benjamin D., and Rosabeth Moss Kanter. "The Differentiation of Life-Styles." *Annual Review of Sociology* 2, no. 1 (1976): 269–98.

Film Index

Chapter 1

The Politics of Religion (Marie-Therese Mäder, CH/US 2013)

Chapter 2

8: The Mormon Proposition (Reed Cowan and Steven Greenstreet, US 2010)
American Mormon (Daryn Tufts and Jed Knudsen, US 2005)
American Mormon in Europe (Daryn Tufts and Jed Knudsen, US 2006)
Big Love (US 2006–11, HBO)
Dawn Porter unter Polygamisten (ZDF neo, 2007)
Der Kampf ums Weisse Haus (ARTE, 2012)
Die größten Mormonenmythen (ProSieben, 2014)
History of the Saints (US 2010–present, five seasons)
I Am an Ex Mormon (US 2010–2015, video series)
Inside Polygamy: Life In Bountiful (Olivia Ahneman, US 2009)
I'm a Mormon (LDS Church, US 2010–16, video series)
Inside Bountiful, Polygamy Investigation (GlobalNEWS, CN 2012)
Life After Polygamy: The Daughters & Wives of A Polygamist Cult Reclaim their Hometown (HBO, US 2016)
Mitt (Greg Whiteley, US 2016)
Nobody Knows. The Untold Story of Black Mormons (Darius A. Gray and Margeret B. Young, US 2008)
Polygamie in Gottes Namen – Willkommen bei den Polygamisten (DokuTV, 2013)
Secrets of Mormon Cult, Breaking Polygamy (ABC, US 2012)
Tabloid (Errol Morris, US 2010)
The Culture Show – The Mormons Are Here (BBC, GB 2013)
The District (LDS Church, US 2007–2013)

Chapter 3

Big Love (HBO, US 2006–11)
God's Army (Richard Dutcher, US 2000)
Homefront (LDS Church, US 1972–2009)
The Best Two Years (Scott S. Anderson, US 2003)

Film Index

Chapter 4

I Am an Ex Mormon (US 2010–2015, video series)
I'm a Mormon, Polynesian Father, and Former NFL Player (*I'm a Mormon*, LDS Church, US 2015)
I'm a Mormon (LDS Church, US 2010-2016, video series)
I'm a Mormon and Mother to 79 Orphaned Children (*I'm a Mormon*, LDS Church, US 2012, video series)
I'm a Mormon Wedding Dress Maker and Patron of Beauty (*I'm a Mormon*, LDS Church, US 2015, video series)
I'm a Mormon, Mother, and Caretaker of Bulgarian Orphans (*I'm a Mormon*, LDS Church, US 2012, video series)
I'm a Mormon, Parisian, and Mother of 7 (*I'm a Mormon*, LDS Church, US 2012, video series)
I'm a Mormon, Viennese Violinmaker, and Fantastic Aunt (*I'm a Mormon*, LDS Church, US 2011, video series)
Maria and Henning Schnurr – We are German Ex Mormons (*I Am an Ex Mormon*, US 2011, video series)
My Name is Heather and I'm an Ex Mormon (*I Am an Ex Mormon*, US 2012, video series)
Our Marriage Has Survived a Crisis of Faith (*I Am an Ex Mormon*, US 2011, video series)
Seeking participants (*I Am an Ex Mormon*, US 2011)
We are the Leavitt Family (*I Am an Ex Mormon*, US 2011)

Chapter 5

#Seekingsisterwife (TLC, 2018)
All about Christine (*Sister Wives*, season 9, episodes 6, US 2015)
All about Janelle (*Sister Wives*, season 9, episodes 4, US 2015)
Big Love (HBO, 2006–2011)
Four Wives and counting (*Sister Wives*, season 1, episode 7, US 2010)
Meri Behind the Scenes (*Sister Wives*, season 8, special episodes, US 2015)
My 5 Wives (TLC, US 2013–2016)
Polygamy, USA (National Geographic, US 2013)
Robyn Behind the Scenes (*Sister Wives*, season 8, special episodes, US 2015)
Sister Wives (TLC, US 2010–19)
Sisters' Special Delivery (Sister Wives, season 3, episode 12, US 2011)
The District 1 (LDS Church, US 2007)
The District 2, 8 Stories (LDS Church, US 2012/13)
Turning Point (*The District 2, 8 Stories*, episode 2, US 2012/13)

Film Index

Chapter 6

Meet the Mormons (Blair Treu, US 2014)

Chapters 7–11

American Mormon (Daryn Tufts and Jed Knudsen, US 2005)
American Mormon in Europe (Daryn Tufts and Jed Knudsen, US 2006)
Believer (Don Argott, US 2018)
Forced Marriage Cops (Channel 4, UK 2015)
I'm a searcher, I'm a wanderer, I'm a filmmaker (*I'm a Mormon*, US 2011)
Journey of Faith (Peter Johnson, US 2006)
Meet the Mormons (Blair Treu, US 2014)
Meet The Mormons (Lynn Alleway, Channel 4, UK 2015)
Meet the Polygamists (*Polygamy, USA*, episode 1, US 2013)
Mr. Death: The Rise and Fall of Fred A. Leuchter, Jr (Errol Morris, US 1999)
Nobody Knows. The Untold Story of Black Mormons (Darius A. Gray and Margeret B. Young, US 2008)
Papst Franziskus – Ein Mann seines Wortes (Wim Wenders, US 2017)
Polygamy, USA (National Geographic, US 2013)
Scientology: Mysterious Death (NTV, DE 2014)
Sister Wives (TLC, US 2010–2020)
Sisterz in Zion (Melissa Puente, US 2006)
Sons of Perdition (Tyler Meason and Jennilyn Merten, US 2010)
Tabloid (Errol Morris, US 2010)
The Thin blue Line (Errol Morris, US 1988)
Three Wives, and One Husband (Netflix, US 2017)

Chapter 12

American Mormon (Daryn Tufts and Jed Knudsen, US 2005)
American Mormon in Europe (Daryn Tufts and Jed Knudsen, US 2006)
Journey of Faith (Peter Johnson, US 2006)
Meet the Mormons (Blair Treu, US 2014)
Meet the Mormons (Lynn Alleway, Channel 4, UK 2015)
Nobody Knows. The Untold Story of Black Mormons (Darius A. Gray and Margeret B. Young, US 2008)
Sister Wives (TLC, US 2010–2020)
Sisterz in Zion (Melissa Puente, US 2006)
Sons of Perdition (Tyler Meason and Jennilyn Merten, US 2010)
Tabloid (Errol Morris, US 2010)
The District (LDS Church, US 2006/2012)